# READING RHETORICAL TEXTS
## AN INTRODUCTION TO CRITICISM

**James R. Andrews**
*Indiana University*

**Michael C. Leff**
*Northwestern University*

**Robert Terrill**
*Indiana University*



Houghton Mifflin Company    Boston    New York

*Sponsoring Editor:* George Hoffman
*Senior Project Editor:* Fred Burns
*Production/Design Coordinator:* Deb Frydman
*Manufacturing Manager:* Florence Cadran
*Marketing Manager:* Pamela Laskey

Cover design: Diana Coe
Cover image: WA Rogers. *Mayor Jones Speaking at the County Fair, Westerville.* Culver Pictures.

Part openers: WA Rogers. *Mayor Jones Speaking at the County Fair, Westerville.* Culver Pictures.

Acknowledgments are on page 424.



Printed in the U.S.A.

Library of Congress Catalog Card Number: 97-72438

ISBN: 0-395-73156-9

1 2 3 4 5 6 7 8 9 – QF –01 00 99 98 97

# Contents

# Preface

George Campbell wrote in his introduction to *The Philosophy of Rhetoric* that without "eloquence, or the art of speaking . . . the greatest talents, even wisdom itself, lose much of their luster, and still more of their usefulness." A person's "own conduct may be well regulated" by wisdom, Campbell observed, but the art of speaking "is absolutely necessary for diffusing valuable knowledge, and enforcing right rules of action upon others."*

For centuries past, as in our own time, men and women have communicated with each other in order to transmit what they have learned and to influence each other's actions. This communication has taken many forms, but undoubtedly much of it has been through public discourse. Campbell's *Philosophy of Rhetoric* was published in London in 1776, a time when some of the greatest orators of the English language—Edmund Burke, William Pitt, Charles James Fox—debated the great questions of empire, and when Americans like James Otis, Patrick Henry, and Samuel Adams brought their persuasive powers to bear on the creation of a new nation. Throughout history, and certainly in the present day, issues of great moment have been and are argued publicly. Living as we do in a rhetorical world, heirs as we are to a rhetorical tradition, it is essential that we understand the operations of public persuasion.

This book is designed to orient the beginning student to the nature and function of rhetorical criticism, to acquaint the student with those elements in the rhetorical situation that warrant serious attention, and to teach the student a useful strategy with which to begin to practice criticism.

Scholars and teachers will see that the focus of this book is clearly on public speeches. We recommend careful critical attention be paid to those aspects of the rhetorical act that have long been recognized as comprising the fundamental ingredients of public persuasion. This work is not, however, a call to return to some past critical age. The authors' assumption is that the beginning student should start first with a discreet object for critical scrutiny and with a practical way of examining that object. There should be no ideological or philosophical restraints on the critical imagination other than those of sound schol-

*George Campbell, *The Philosophy of Rhetoric,* ed. Lloyd Bitzer (Carbondale, IL: Southern Illinois University Press, 1963), xlix.

arship, and this book does not seek to impose any. But there must be some place to begin. As the painter first learns to draw the human figure, to suggest perspective, to appreciate the uses of color, and the like, so the rhetorical critic begins by studying the basic factors in persuasion, and by practicing the technique of explicating the ways in which those factors interact.

This, then, is not a handbook to guide or direct all critical inquiry. It is meant to launch a critical voyage and not to chart its eventual course: for the rest of her or his life the serious critic, through the study of discourse, of theory, and of the critical works of others, and through the practice of the critical art, will continue to develop abilities, to refine judgment, and to create more perceptive methods and approaches. This book, it is hoped, is a beginning.

Along with mastering basic concepts, the beginning critic will also be given the opportunity, through the study of examples and essays suggesting a variety of critical approaches, to begin grappling with fundamental and enduring critical issues. For the student whose formal experience will be limited to this one course, this book is designed also as a starting point, a means to equip that student with the basic knowledge and skill to confront rhetoric critically and to understand the usefulness of such a confrontation to him or her as a consumer and producer of communication.

We have included in this book texts and examples of how critics have studied those texts. In Part II we offer two historical texts along with our own critical readings of those texts. We have attempted to guide the student with appropriate commentary through our essays, pointing out the critical moves we made as we examined the text. We hope these studies will serve as examples of what critics might do and how they might do it, as well as examples to stimulate discussion.

Part III presents two texts and illustrations of the various critical responses to these texts. The first, Richard Nixon's "Address on the Vietnam War," is followed by an exchange between two of the critics, Forbes Hill and Karlyn Kohrs Campbell, that highlights important issues for critics and provides insight into the basic assumptions and methods of practicing critics. In this section, we include Jesse Jackson's "Common Ground and Common Sense" along with two critical studies of that speech. Finally, in Part IV, several examples of critical readings by rhetorical scholars illustrate different ways to approach texts.

In all cases, we have included the texts under examination. Students may read these texts, form their own impressions, and offer their own analysis and interpretations that they can compare and contrast with those of seasoned critics. We expect that such a process will lead to lively and informative discussion and debate in the classroom.

In a work of this kind it is impossible to name all those who have contributed to it—either directly or indirectly—since it is the result of what we have learned over the years as students ourselves, as practicing critics, and as teachers. Certainly our work has been informed by the critical work of many others and by both formal and informal interactions with colleagues and students. In particular we would like to express our appreciation for the contributions of the following individuals: Stephen H. Browne, Penn State University; Bruce E. Gronbeck, University of Iowa; David Henry, California Polytechnic State University; Martin J. Medhurst, Texas A&M University; Stephen O'Leary, University of Southern California; and Martha Solomon Watson, University of Maryland at College Park. While we acknowledge all the help and encouragement we have received, we also acknowledge that whatever shortcomings this work might have are our responsibility.

James R. Andrews
Michael C. Leff
Robert Terrill

# READING RHETORICAL TEXTS

## AN INTRODUCTION TO CRITICISM

# PART I • CRITICAL FOUNDATIONS

# 1

# The Nature of Criticism: An Overview

## Defining Criticism

Everyone reacts to things produced by others, but is everyone a critic? The student who responds to a question about a political speech with "It was boring"; the ten-year-old who pronounces the latest *Die Hard* sequel "great"; the parent who comments that the music that his or her child enjoys is "too loud"; the visitor to an art gallery who observes that a new painting "doesn't look like anything" — all are reacting to products of human talent and imagination in a personal and idiosyncratic way. In our common, everyday use of the word, some of these comments might be labeled "critical."

In common parlance, criticism has become associated with carping, with tearing down, with the pointed, negative comment. We tend to label someone "too critical" when we mean that the person appears to be harping on insignificant details, or objecting for the sake of objecting, or looking for something that is wrong. In this sense, the "critic" is the builder of roadblocks, the troublemaker, or the cynic.

But such popular notions of criticism are certainly not the basis for defining the activity of serious critics. John Dewey, a critic and philosopher, observed that "criticism . . . is not fault-finding. It is not pointing out evils to be reformed. It is judgment engaged in discriminating among values. It is taking thought as to what is better and worse in any field at any time, with some consciousness of *why* the worse is worse."[1] One way to define criticism succinctly would be as *the systematic process of illuminating and evaluating products of human activity.*

As a *process* of illumination and evaluation, criticism does not result solely in ultimate pronouncements. Rather than attempting to have "the final say," such criticism presents and supports one possible interpretation and judgment. This interpretation, in turn, may become the basis for other interpretations and judgments. Thus, the critical impulse is not one that leads toward a summary dismissal of some product of human endeavor; the goal is not some statement that defines the object of criticism for all time, effectively preventing all further discussion of it. Instead, the critical impulse is to build understanding. The serious study of criticism should be free of the misleading conceptions of "destructive" criticism and "constructive" criticism. Criticism in the sense that the term is used here can never be destructive, and to say that it is constructive is redundant. At its best, criticism leads us to a fuller and richer understanding of a particular work as it exists within the context of human endeavor.

*The critic of rhetoric focuses his or her attention on human efforts to influence human thought and action.* Students of the art of rhetoric have not achieved universal agreement on what the critic of rhetoric should be studying. Nevertheless, both common sense and the evidence presented by what critics actually study suggest that persuasive public discourse is an obvious and sensible object for critical examination. Whereas mature scholars and critics may argue that a variety of phenomena may be studied rhetorically, certainly the best place to begin to deal with the problems of rhetorical criticism is with persuasive public discourse.

One reason that this is the best place to start is that the vocabulary and concepts most useful to rhetorical critics developed at a time when the spoken word was the chief medium of public communication. Rhetoric was established as a field of study in the ancient Greek democracies of the fifth century B.C., where citizens were expected to participate in political debate and represent themselves in courts of law. There was a need for instruction in the skills needed to discern the elements of an effective speech, and teachers of rhetoric, referred to as "sophists," were among the first to fill this need.[2] The study of rhetorical texts, then, has flourished for over two thousand years, but mostly during a time when spoken and written words were the primary means of public influence. Certainly in the twentieth century these terms and concepts can be applied productively toward understanding the persuasive characteristics of a wide variety of cultural artifacts and social relations. But the beginning critic, like generations of rhetorical critics, can exploit productively the symbiotic relationship between speech texts and the vocabulary of rhetorical analysis.

Another reason that the study of speech texts is important is that speech remains a significant medium for self-expression and public influence. While film, radio, television, and now perhaps the Internet have challenged the primacy of oral speech as the most pervasive rhetorical medium of our culture, speeches retain their central position in our democracy. As only one example, consider the fact that after Bill Clinton won reelection to a second term as president in 1996, the two most eagerly awaited events of the beginning of his second term were his inaugural address and his State of the Union address. Both were considered important enough to preempt the regularly scheduled programs on all the major radio and television networks, because both were seen as opportunities for the president to establish his — and, thus, to a large extent, our nation's — agenda for the next four years. The words uttered by President Clinton on those occasions had the potential to affect people all over the world, and a great many hours of air time and inches of newspaper column space were devoted to their analysis and critique. We discuss in the next section of this chapter the fact that, because the tools of the rhetorical critic are especially well suited to the analysis of speeches, skill in their use can help students of contemporary events become more discerning consumers of the public discourse that defines those events.

Finally, and perhaps most importantly, the analysis of speech texts is important today for the same reason it was important in ancient Greece. As many of those first teachers of rhetoric understood, rhetoric resides not in handbooks or textbooks but in rhetorical texts themselves. That is, rhetorical texts can be thought of as storehouses of rhetorical possibilities, as places where people have employed a variety of techniques and strategies to address or change situations through the skillful use of language. Therefore, the study of speech texts offers the opportunity to observe principles and theories animated by their engagement with particular situations. It is not only more interesting to study persuasive strategies as they are used and modified by real people trying to accomplish real tasks, but it is also more useful to study them in this way: it is within speech texts that rhetorical theory is given life, achieves form, and gains coherence. Even within a highly technological culture such as the one we inhabit, the spoken and written word is still the means of persuasion used by most of the people most of the time. To apply the vocabulary of rhetorical criticism toward understanding how others have used words to achieve their ends is to make their discourse available as what Kenneth Burke has called "equipment for living."

## Responding Critically: Consumers of Rhetoric

It is necessary early on to distinguish between responding critically and being a critic. Learning to respond critically is one of the possible, and very important, outcomes of the study of criticism. Persuasion invites response, and the nature of the responses to any given message can vary widely. Responses can be personal, impressionistic, or global. Many times the response tells more about the person responding than about the message. For example, in a group of people listening to an address by the president of the United States, a listener might respond favorably because the listener happened to be of the same political party as the president, or because the listener found certain of his or her own frustrations echoed in the speech, or because the president sounded so sincere, or because the listener found himself or herself agreeing with what the president said. Or a listener might respond negatively to the speech because he or she never did trust the president, or because the speech sounded slow and monotonous, or because the listener found nothing in the speech with which he or she could directly identify, or even because the speech preempted the latest episode of a favorite TV show.

To respond critically to a message, however, is to be able to distinguish between what is relevant and what is irrelevant in the message. It is to try to discern what the speaker was aiming to do, what the speaker said, and what the speaker meant. It is to make some sense out of the speech by comparing the problem as it is addressed by the speaker with the problem as it is seen by the listener and by others who have experienced the problem, by comparing the solution offered by the speaker with other solutions, and by matching the solution with the dimensions and subtleties of the problem as the listener evaluates them. The listener, responding critically, can ask many questions, such as: Who is the speaker and what does he or she have to gain by giving this speech? What are the circumstances that gave rise to the speech? Did the speaker articulate some purpose or goal in giving the speech? What were the speaker's major points? How did he or she support these points? The listener who responds critically is the listener who tries to decide what the speech is all about, what it means, and what there is in the speech that should lead the listener to make some kind of decision or take some kind of action. The critical listener will realize that ideas and not gray hair denote wisdom; that clear thinking is not dependent on a youthful, handsome profile; that being smooth and glib is not an indication of sound reasoning.

Learning to respond critically is, in part, learning to apply the perspective and the methods of a critic. Some students who read this book will become rhetorical critics, serious and continuing students of rhetoric and of the way rhetoric influences and is influenced by human events. Other students, however, will seek to make intelligent responses to public discourse by adopting a critical stance toward communication. They will *do* criticism not because they hope to become professional critics, but because they hope to acquire the point of view and the skills that will help them to respond critically.

In the final analysis, developing the ability to respond critically will be extremely useful on a personal level. The critical listener will be able to make more informed judgments that will improve the quality of his or her response to public messages. Just as one who studies music can respond to certain musical works with more pleasure and appreciation, and just as one who studies poetry can read words of poetry with a deeper sense of personal satisfaction and identification, one who learns to respond critically to public communication can develop a fuller and more complex appreciation and understanding of the communication.

## Improving Communication Skills: Producers of Rhetoric

Approaching communication critically involves learning how and why communication is effective. As students begin to understand the basic factors that underlie rhetorical messages, they increase their own chances of shaping those factors advantageously. Specifically, in the following areas a knowledge of the operation of rhetoric can help to make students of criticism better communicators.

*Awareness of the impact of the context on a message* directs a speaker's attention to the influences operating both outside of and within the immediate speaking situation. Such an awareness should help speakers focus their purposes more sharply and highlight the historical, political, and cultural factors that will impinge on the accomplishment of those purposes.

*Understanding the nature of audiences* will also contribute to the development of the speaker's purpose by helping the speaker understand what can and cannot reasonably be accomplished. The critic's ability to discern the factors that can influence an audience — their knowledge of the topic, the groups with whom they identify, their receptivity to the message — can be carried over when the critic becomes a speaker. Such a speaker can tailor his or her message to fit audience needs and perspectives.

*Appreciating the role of ethos, or speaker image,* should lead speakers to discover ways in which they can deal with perceptions that audiences have of them. Because ethos can change as the audience forms a new image of the speaker while she or he is speaking, understanding the impact of image can also move speakers to find ways to use the situation, the message itself, and the delivery of the message to enhance their own credibility.

*Analyzing the argument* will enhance a speaker's ability to construct and employ rhetorical structures that use evidence effectively through persuasive reasoning. Attention to the function of language in promoting argument can help speakers make stylistic choices that best fit their purposes and audience expectations.

*Interpreting and judging rhetorical acts* will heighten the speaker's awareness of the ways in which rhetoric interacts with the values and cultural standards of society. The same intellectual discipline needed by the critic to unearth strategic relationships will help speakers understand the ways in which their own rhetorical efforts fit into the larger rhetorical pattern. Further, such a critical process will aid speakers in forming and adopting not only their own standards of effective communication, but their own standards of ethical communication as well.

So far, we have been discussing the ways in which the study of criticism can influence listening and speaking behaviors. Now, let us consider criticism as the activity of specialists in the study of rhetoric.

## Characteristics of a Critic

A critic is a specialist who must be able to communicate to others the results of his or her critical observation and inquiry. A critic combines knowledge with a systematic way of using that knowledge and constantly seeks to refine his or her practice of criticism.

In the most fundamental sense the critic is an educator. He or she confronts a message. His or her reaction to that message is not the same as the reaction of the casual or even the critical listener. The critic seeks to understand what is going on in order to interpret more fully the rhetorical dynamics involved in the production and reception of the message and to make certain judgments about the quality of the message. Finally, the critic must report his or her findings in a readable and reasoned manner, contributing to an understanding of the message he or she has interpreted.

All critics do not go about their work in the same way, nor do all critics reach the same conclusion about a particular message. The critical impulse — the impulse to illuminate and evaluate — may be similar in all critics; the demands for system and rigor likewise obtain for all criticism; and whereas all critics seek to ask significant questions and go about answering those questions in a methodical fashion, the questions themselves and the means of answering them are not the same for all critics.[3]

For the beginning critic two considerations are primary. First, it is necessary to understand the kinds of questions that appropriately can be raised about a rhetorical message, and, second, it is crucial to develop a methodical way of answering those questions. The remainder of this chapter is devoted to a discussion of the possible function of rhetorical criticism as a way of pointing out the major questions that a critic may address. The remainder of the book presents a framework within which the critic may go about answering these questions systematically.

## Critical Functions: Searching for Effect

In what was probably the most influential essay on rhetorical criticism written in this century, Herbert Wichelns observed that rhetorical criticism "is not concerned with permanence nor yet with beauty. It is concerned with effect. It regards a speech as a communication to a specific audience, and holds its business to be the analysis and appreciation of the orator's method of imparting his ideas to his hearers."[4] Certainly the purpose of any rhetorical message is to persuade, to influence human feelings or beliefs or actions in some way. When any speaker faces an audience, he or she wants members of that audience to *do* something. We think of an "effective" speaker as one who is able to accomplish his or her rhetorical purposes. It is logical and eminently understandable that one possible function of rhetorical criticism is to assess rhetorical effect.

At first glance this function may seem a somewhat simple one, a matter of determining what the auditors did after a speech was given. But just to count the votes at the end of a debate or the number of orders at the end of a sales pitch, or even to consult national polls hardly illuminates a rhetorical message. Nor does it tell us in reality very much about the causal relationship between the message and the actions that followed the message.

In trying to understand effect, the basic question that the critic needs to raise is more complex than simply, What was the effect of the speech? The crucial question focuses the attention of the critic on the interaction between the speaker, the message, and the total context. This question might be stated, What potential did the message have to influence what audience or audiences in what ways? or, perhaps, In what ways did the text invite what audience or audiences to act in what ways? Answering such a question involves careful analysis, interpretation, and evaluation — processes that are discussed in more detail in the following chapters of this book. At this point, however, it is appropriate to consider the most relevant factors that engage a critic's attention.

To understand rhetorical effect, it is crucial to understand the dimensions of purpose and possibility. A speech functions within a larger context and happens because of things that are happening in the world. A speaker may wish to rally public opinion behind a proposal, create goodwill for an organization or a group in society or a country, or induce members of the audience to take some specified action such as giving money or signing a petition or buying a product. Great oratory often grows out of a series of events that precipitate a crisis which calls for immediate action, or it delineates a serious problem which demands a solution. Whatever the circumstances, a rhetorical message is a purposive message; its aim is to get a response from an audience. The critic who would search for effect must try to discern the ways that the text is crafted so as to invite a particular response from the audience. The first step in this search is to attempt to discern, to the extent possible, what effect is desired by the speaker. In discovering this purpose the critic will need to know what events brought the speech about, what was or is in the speaker's present position or background that caused him or her to speak at this time, what the speaker actually says in the speech that explicitly defines the purpose, and what there is in the speech that may reveal an unstated purpose.

A speaker's purposes are not always apparent or easy to determine. The speaker may have an underlying purpose that is more pressing and important than the apparent one. It has been argued, for example, that during a political campaign a speaker's real purpose is to "ingratiate" himself or herself with an audience.[5] Whereas the topic of a speech might be foreign policy and the speaker's purpose may seem to be to convince the audience that the NATO alliance should be strengthened, the speaker's "real" purpose might be to convince the audience that he or she is a well-informed and capable leader.

Once the critic has put together the best possible reconstruction of the speaker's rhetorical purpose, she or he will consider the possibilities for effecting that purpose. Here the critic must understand the constraints that are likely to affect the outcome of a speech. For example, political, personal, and social realities may shape or limit the achievement of rhetorical goals. A member of Congress might listen to a particularly well crafted speech — clear, well organized, amply documented, and supported — but still vote against the speaker's proposal because of his or her own party's commitment to an opposing point of view. A listener may hear a speech given by someone he or she distrusts and dislikes, and even though the speaker's ideas may match those of the listener, the listener may respond negatively because of his or her overpowering personal antipathy to the speaker. A speaker favoring a Constitutional amendment that would prohibit abortion would be unlikely to devise any speech that would win support from an audience of members of the National Organization for Women because the social viewpoints of the speaker and listeners are separated by a deep, unbridgeable chasm. This does not mean, of course, that the speaker and the listener must always be in perfect agreement. If that were the case, there would be no such concept as persuasion; there would be no change and no need for change. But it does mean that *persuasion must take place within the limits of the possible,* and one of the critic's tasks is to try to determine what those limits are and the extent to which the speaker has recognized the limits and operated within them.

After having discerned to the extent possible these elements of the purpose of the speaker and the context of the speech, the critic will look to the text of the speech itself to discover clues as to the speaker's identification of an appropriate audience or audiences and the ways in which the speaker has sought to move those audiences. Through a careful textual analysis, the critic attempts to understand the ways in which persuasive potential has been exploited.

The critic's search for effect, then, involves him or her in the examination of both external and internal factors. The study of context sheds light on the nature of the issues being addressed, the speaker's relationship to those issues, and the speaker's personal potential to exert influence, as well as the audience's relationship to the issues and its potential to influence change in the direction urged by the speaker. An examination of the internal factors — that is, those elements that the critic discerns within the message itself — should provide insights into how the speaker crafted the speech to appeal to the audiences he or she was attempting to reach, and how the speaker attempted to persuade them to act in the ways he or she wanted them to.

Forbes Hill, a professor and rhetorical critic, maintains that Aristotle's rhetoric provides a "comprehensive inventory" of the means whereby a speaker can persuade audiences. He asserts that the end of criticism "is to discover whether the speaker makes the best choices from the inventory to get a favorable decision from a specified group of auditors in a specific situation. It does not, of course, aim to discover whether or not the speaker actually gets his favorable decision. . . ."[6] The critic does not make the absolutely causal assessment embodied in the judgment "The speech was effective." In other words, the critic is not trying to find out how many people responded in what ways to the message. Rather, rhetorical investigation leads the critic to a conclusion concerning the *probable* effectiveness of the message.

Data of various kinds are available to a critic concerning actions taken or statements made following a speech. But the critic must be extremely cautious in dealing with such data. It would be simplistic and misleading, for example, to say that a political candidate won an election as the direct result of a speech or even a series of speeches.

In a relatively limited number of cases, students of contemporary speaking have some poll data. These polls usually are conducted only after what are considered by members of the press to be extremely important speeches. While they may be "accurate" according to some statistical formula, they are of relatively little use to the rhetorical critic. Polls may register impressions of certain audiences at a particular time, but they will never tell the critic that the speaker's use of certain kinds of evidence changed auditors' minds, or that the organizational pattern of the speech functioned persuasively — indeed, such data cannot establish any direct relationship between specific rhetorical behaviors and specific outcomes. So, these polls do little to provide answers to the sorts of questions that rhetorical critics ask.

Critics also are able to find a variety of personal reactions to speeches; some listeners record their responses in their diaries or in letters to friends or even in public statements. But all such manifestations of behavior that occur after a speech are vague and can be extremely unrepresentative, and therefore constitute unsound bases upon which to argue direct effect. As noted earlier in this chapter, people may respond to a persuasive message in a particular way for any number of reasons.

The critic should not ignore these types of data, but he or she needs to use them with care and to put recorded reactions to speeches into proper perspective. As Wayne Minnick, a professor and rhetorical critic, has observed, "Contemporary testimony and post-speech behaviors best serve the critic if he [or she] treats them as establishing hypotheses to be supported rather than as conclusive evidence of effect itself." For the rhetorical critic who would attempt to assess effect, Professor Minnick's conclusion is a sound one: "A hypothetical effect based on testimony and/or post-speech behavior is supported with evidence that the speaker reached an appropriate audience and employed rhetorical methods which, on the face of it, seemed adequate to produce the effect." Furthermore, the probability that the alleged effect actually took place is increased when the critic can demonstrate that "the speaker presented a broadly distributed, rhetorically adequate case in a context which allows the negation of extra-speech events as major causal factors."[7]

Determining effect, in short, is not just finding out what happened after a speech was given; it is a careful examination of the interrelationships between speaker, message, and context in order to offer the most reasonable explanation for the probable result of any given message.

## Critical Functions: Illuminating Events, Context, and Speakers

At various times in human history, public discussion and debate of important issues has been a crucial mode of solving or contributing to the solution of the problems faced by human societies. In democratic countries in modern times public discourse has accompanied political and social change. Public argument is a part of the Anglo-American tradition.

By turning its attention to such public argument, rhetorical criticism may function to illuminate specific historical events and the social/cultural context in which these events occur. However, a rhetorical critic offers a perspective that differs significantly from that of a historian. A careful historical investigation of any set of events or period may well reveal hidden forces at work, or at least reveal submerged forces of which the participants in events might be only dimly aware. Examining historical data by looking back on events may lead the historian to discover patterns of behavior and motivations for behavior of which the participants in those events were not fully cognizant. Historical perspective might lead one in a sense to describe what "really" happened.

Careful attention to the rhetorical dynamics of the public communication that defines and affects historical events can complement the historical perspective. A prime function of rhetoric is to interpret and make meaningful what is in the process of happening. The reality of one's world at any given moment is the reality as it is perceived. Speeches afford concrete evidence of how people living through history perceive what is going on and how they try to shape the perceptions of others. A speaker may judge events imperfectly or incorrectly or may even interpret events deceptively, but what he or she says is an effort to make sense out of events and to project courses of action consistent with that sense.

The critic does not study speeches carefully only to learn what conclusions the speaker reaches or what positions the speaker holds. Also of essential interest to the rhetorical critic is the way in which the speaker attempts to make issues salient and ideas persuasive. Very often, it is within speech texts that issues and ideas are defined and refined at the time of their importance. The critic should be able to discover the implicit and explicit points of clash between differing views. Much rhetorical activity is devoted to the struggle for control of the issues. A careful reading of speeches that focuses not only on the ideational content but also on rhetorical method will uncover the ways in which issues emerge, the ways in which they jostle each other for supremacy, the ways in which they assume hierarchical values, and the ways that their interactions change their shape.

Since the rhetorical critic is concerned with rhetorical method, he or she is compelled to come to grips with the totality of a speaker's argument. A full examination of argument can generate insights into the nature of the society in which that argument flourishes. For example, the critic searches for the uncontested premises of an argument. He or she attempts to uncover the fundamental premises that the speaker perceives as being so basic that they do not need elaboration or justification. These uncontested premises may be among those generally held by the culture in which the speaker is operating, or at least by the perceived audience.

These premises provide clues to a culture's value structure. This basic structure can be filled in as the critic begins to look at other rhetorical factors. The critic can find much that is instructive in the forms of evidence used by a speaker to determine what that speaker considers to be compelling. But the critic does more than simply identify forms of support. If, for example, testimony is a predominant form of evidence, it could be enlightening to know the source of *authoritative* testimony. One might, for example, construct the outlines of the social history of the United States by uncovering the time in our own history in which religious leaders, or the founding fathers, or business leaders, or scientists were considered the ultimate voices of authority. Certainly there are critics practicing today who try to understand power relationships among groups by understanding the language strategies consciously or unconsciously employed.

To be persuasive, a speaker must involve his or her audience in the message itself; the speaker must make that message meaningful or salient to those who listen and must appeal to what the speaker conceives to be the most motivating of audience needs. As the critic examines the rhetorical methods of achieving salience and determines what hierarchical patterns of audience appeals exist, the critic begins to fit into place some of the tiny pieces that make up the mosaic of a culture. *A legitimate function of rhetorical criticism, then, is to try to determine how people argue as a means of describing who those people are.*

Within the general context of culture, rhetorical criticism can also provide specific illumination of individuals through the study of their rhetorical practices. Not only does an examination of the various parts of a discourse shed light on the society in which that discourse flourishes, it can also tell the investigator much about the ways in which the particular speaker thinks and the way the speaker sees his or her world. Rhetorical criticism can thus contribute much to biographical study since it uncovers the rhetor's ideas in action as he or she seeks to persuade or otherwise exert influence over an audience.

## Critical Functions: Social Criticism

If criticism can illuminate historical and cultural contexts, it surely must be able to contribute to the understanding of contemporary events as they are occurring. The rhetorical criticism of contemporary messages may perform what Karlyn Kohrs Campbell describes as a "social function." According to Professor Campbell, "this function requires that critics appraise both the techniques used and the ends advocated in rhetorical acts, in addition to the immediate and long-range effects of both." Campbell goes on to define social criticism as "criticism that evaluates the ways in which issues are formulated and policies justified, and the effects of both on society at a particular historical moment."[8] What Campbell implies is that critics enter the fray of public discussion, using their critical abilities and perspective to become active *participants* in the solution of problems by their careful investigation of rhetoric and its consequences.

The social function of rhetorical criticism is a matter of some controversy. An argument against such criticism might go something like this: The criticism of rhetoric involves the evaluation of *rhetorical* choices. If the function of rhetoric is to persuade, then the critic of rhetoric has as his or her task the discovery of the ways in which, and the extent to which, a message was persuasive. When one begins to make judgments about whether the aims of persuasion are good or bad for our society, or judgments about whether the policies advocated are practical and useful solutions to problems, one ceases to be a *rhetorical* critic and ventures into the realm of other disciplines. This is not to say that the rhetorical critic cannot comment on contemporary affairs; he or she does so, however, as an intelligent, educated observer might do, not as a *rhetorical critic.*

On the other hand, there is a compelling argument that such a view limits too severely the possible functions of rhetorical criticism. When public discussion takes place, *how* the participants in that discussion argue is as important as the conclusions they reach. If rhetoric does, indeed, shape perceptions, then the critic of rhetoric should be able to make evaluative statements concerning the accuracy and the implications of those perceptions as the speaker would have them.

There would be little disagreement that a rhetorical critic may, for example, legitimately focus his or her attention on arguments. The critic can make descriptive statements about the structure of an argument, but the investigation does not end there; an assessment of the quality of an argument is surely within the realm of rhetorical criticism. Quality may be judged upon a variety of standards. The potential effectiveness of the argument is certainly a standard that can be applied, but it is not the *only* standard. Consider the quantity and quality of evidence used to support argumentative conclusions. Is the critic's legitimate standard a measurement of how convincing an audience might find the evidence? An argument, after all, is a structure that must be utilitarian as well as pleasing. A house may be well designed, beautiful, and functional; it may sell at a high price and return a substantial profit to the builder, but the firmness of the foundation and the quality of the support beams, which are not readily discernible to the untrained consumer, may be such that the building collapses on the new occupants during the first storm. Building codes are designed to provide some protection for the consumer by demanding expert certification of soundness. Should not the expert in argument be prepared to expose the shaky premises or the tenuous supporting evidence that underpins a conclusion advocating actions that affect our lives?

Such critical response is not as simple as pointing out a deliberate prevarication on the part of the speaker. It is more subtle than that; it may entail raising the question of whether a speaker has adequately "proved" a point. For the critic who is concerned only with effect, "adequate" is defined as what an audience accepts, but for the social critic "adequate" can be defined as convincing enough to establish the probable truth of a claim for the discerning, informed, skeptical observer. In establishing probable "truth," the critic becomes a *participant* in the rhetorical process. The critic who is trained in rhetoric knows what *is* persuasive. When that critic enters into a controversy, it is to argue the question of what *should be* persuasive. The rhetorical critic can argue, for example, that the speaker's selective choice of supporting material ignores relevant data and thus distorts perceptions of events, or that the speaker's argument hinges on acceptance of a premise that conflicts with widely held values, or that there is an incongruity between the problem as the speaker outlines it and the solutions to that problem which he or she proposes.

Critics, like other human beings, have a perspective that shapes their perceptions. When they enter into a controversy, they bring with them their own biases and experiences. Complete objectivity in any critical activity is a quixotic goal. Certainly in the realm of social criticism the nature of the critic's subjectivity has the potential to distort his or her judgment. Some critics argue that such bias is not only inevitable but a positive good. They would have all critics champion causes, entering into the fray as partisans. While few would question the notion that, as citizens, all of us should work for an improved society, many would maintain that the best forum for such advocacy is not in the realm of scholarship. Activism expressed through academic journals is not likely to effect significant change. It may even be a comfortable way of excusing oneself from engagement in the rough-and-tumble — and potentially dangerous — world of political action.

Whatever position one takes, it seems sensible for critics to remind themselves that they have one prime obligation to those whom they address — and that is to apply the same rigorous standards to *all* rhetorical efforts they seek to judge. A good critic scrutinizes the position with which she or he agrees just as carefully as opinions that conflict with the critic's own position. Political judgments are inevitably formed in part on the basis of rhetorical messages; what the critic seeks to avoid is making a judgment of rhetorical soundness on the basis of political conviction.

## Critical Functions: Development and Refinement of Theory

Another primary function of criticism, in a sense, subsumes all others: The criticism of rhetoric contributes to the development and refinement of rhetorical theory. Theory, like criticism and rhetoric, is a term that has a variety of specialized and popular meanings. Contrasted with *applied* or *practical, theoretical* connotes for some people a kind of idle speculation on the ideal. However, that is not what is meant by the term when we talk of rhetorical theory. On one level, theory can mean, essentially, *explanation,* a way of helping us understand how various factors came together to work in a particular way in a particular case, what has been called a "theory of the particular case."[9] On another level, theory may be conceived as a body of plausible generalizations or principles that explain a complex set of facts or phenomena. A theory looks at a series of related events and tries to tell us why things happen as they do, and if the explanation of why things happen is accurate, then that explanation may be able to tell us what will happen in a similar set of circumstances. Rhetorical theory, then, can be visualized, in the words of Samuel Becker, as an "explanatory-predictive mosaic."[10]

The mosaic image is a very useful one in discussing the relationship between theory and criticism. Pieced together with tiny bits of glass or stone that form patterns, the completed mosaic is a total picture in which the smaller patterns merge into a complete whole. Looked at in this way, all criticism is implicitly theoretical; the more we learn about what happened in one particular situation — that is, the more information bits that can be adduced — the better able we will be to generalize a pattern of rhetorical behavior. As these patterns are formed, and compared and contrasted with other patterns, a basis for predicting what will happen in similar cases is established.

To say, however, that every critical study is implicitly theoretical is not to say that every study must be explicitly theoretical. Our word "theory" comes from a Greek word that has to do with sight; a "theory" is a way of seeing. That is, a theoretical understanding can help a critic see a particular rhetorical event in some particular way. But, of course, a theory is also a way of *not* seeing. Think again about Forbes Hill's reference to Aristotle's "comprehensive inventory" of the available means of persuasion. If a critic were to use Aristotle's theoretical understanding of the ways in which a speaker might be persuasive as a "lens" through which to view some particular speech, there is indeed a very large number of persuasive techniques that this "lens" would allow the critic to see. But, there is also an infinite number of persuasive tactics and strategies that the critic might miss because they are not discussed by Aristotle. Just as the theory might help the critic to see some elements of the speech, it hides from the critic other elements that are equally, or perhaps more, important for interpreting and understanding the text. To limit your critical perspective explicitly and rigidly to a theoretical construct, then, is a sure way to miss seeing the wide variety of bits and patterns that make up the mosaic. Indeed, to demand that all critical studies make an explicit connection with and contribution to some specific theory would be to devalue a rhetorical analysis that helps us to understand what is unique in any given situation — a "theory of the case" would be rejected by such a demand. Critical insights that further our understanding of a particular historical event or person are valid and important contributions to knowledge. The critic need not attempt in every case to strain for theoretical implications as predictable or overarching generalizations inherent in that case.

Most students of speech communication have had experience in dealing with theory even though they might not be fully aware of it. Take, for example, the study of public speaking. Any good textbook on public speaking is really an embodiment of theory, no matter how "practical" it is alleged to be or perceived to be. When the author of a textbook advises the student on how to prepare for a speech, for example, that author is really laying down certain principles. The author may recommend rules to be observed when organizing a speech, present the characteristics of a good introduction to a speech, explain the ways in which to test the validity of an argument, or suggest the basis upon which evidence ought to be judged, and so forth. What the author of the textbook is really saying is that if a student organizes well, develops a valid argument with good supporting materials, and follows a whole range of suggestions in the text, then the student is likely to be successful in achieving his or her purpose in speaking. That is, the author implicitly asserts that certain patterns of rhetorical behavior will lead to certain results; from the theory (what we know about public speaking) certain procedures are recommended (the practice of public speaking) that should lead to predictable results (getting the desired audience response).

Criticism plays a vital role in this chain of rhetorical events. The critic focuses intensely on the practice of public discourse, and his or her findings may strengthen or weaken the predictive or explanatory power of any theory or may generate hypotheses upon which new theories can ultimately be built.

## Critical Functions: Pedagogical Criticism

Every critic is, in some sense, an educator. Rhetorical criticism teaches all of us something about the nature and operations of the persuasive process. In the classroom, however, the teacher-critic is most clearly concerned with applying his or her critical powers to the task of modifying behavior.

It is hoped that all criticism will have some impact on the way people produce and react to messages. But the critical functions we have been examining thus far do not aim at producing such effects immediately or directly. In the educational setting, criticism functions to improve the quality of messages and to increase audiences' awareness of the ways in which they respond to messages.

The critic's first task as a teacher is to identify and explain the criteria for judgments as to how poorly or how well a student is communicating. A textbook certainly helps the teacher by presenting, in an organized fashion, basic principles that serve as a guide to behavior. The teacher's job is to see that students understand that these principles are just that: they are generalizations to be used by the student when planning and executing his or her message. The teacher-critic should never lose sight of the principles. The student must not be allowed to form the impression that there are a raft of techniques, a series of unrelated "helpful hints" to remember when giving or listening to a speech. The critic, rather, points to standards of excellence and illustrates the ways in which and the extent to which these standards are being met in actual student performance.

It is in the pedagogical role that the critic has the opportunity to discuss most fully not only what was happening but what should be happening. The issue is not so much one of raising standards as of helping the student learn what the standards are and how to apply them in creating and delivering a message or responding to a message.

The critic in this situation clearly and explicitly matches standards to performance when making a judgment. The specificity of the matching process is crucial. It simply will not do for a critic to tell a student, "Your ideas were not clear." There are standards relating to organizational patterns, development of argument, use of evidence, and language choice, all of which can impinge on the clarity of ideas. The critic, in his or her pedagogical role, must specify these standards and point directly and explicitly to the ways in which their violation contributed to a lack of clarity.

The teacher-critic then takes the next step: suggesting to the student possible strategies for putting these principles into operation. Strategies will grow out of a careful examination of the principles and what went wrong in previous efforts to implement them. Beginning critics, if they are not consciously attuned to the need for careful analysis and the communication of the results of that analysis to the student, are tempted to respond as casual observers rather than as trained professionals. Instead of relating experience to principles and shaping future behavior by helping the student use these principles in devising strategies, the teacher may end up being "critical" in the popular sense and not in the sense we have been using that term. This teacher will respond to the student with the useless observation: "You weren't clear; be clearer when you give your next speech." The true critic, on the other hand, will relate judgments to standards and will communicate specifically the ways in which standards can be made operational in future communication efforts.

## Summary

In this chapter, we have said that the rhetorical critic is one who is engaged in the systematic process of illuminating and evaluating rhetorical messages. As the critic functions, he or she may be searching for the potential effects of messages, investigating messages to discover the light they shed on events that have occurred or the society that gave rise to the messages, evaluating the social utility or worth of messages, relating the practice of persuasion exemplified in particular messages to theoretical constructs, or seeking to modify the behavior of persuaders and their audiences.

As should be apparent, these functions are not mutually exclusive. The search for effect, for example, may lead to modifications in, or implications for, rhetorical theory. Theoretical conceptions may serve as a starting point for the critic who would study persuasive discourse in order to illuminate the underlying values of a society. Certainly one of the best ways to understand the functions of criticism is to see how critics really work. This volume provides the beginning student the opportunity to study the ways in which mature critics have approached this process and to understand the variety of ways in which they have put the functions discussed into critical practice.

Whatever function, or functions, apply in any given critical work, the practicing critic needs to pursue them systematically. What follows in the remaining chapters is an attempt to construct a system. That is to say, the constituents of the rhetorical act that are invariably present are examined in order to explain what is essential for the beginning critic to know about them in order to move to analysis and judgment. Then, the specific elements to be subjected to analysis and a procedure for carrying out the analysis are presented. What the critic must know in using the results of the analysis in making interpretations and judgments is discussed, and, finally, varieties of ways are suggested in which critics can pattern the results of their investigations in order to illuminate and evaluate different aspects of the total rhetorical process.

## *Notes*

1. Cited by Marie Hochmuth, ed., *A History and Criticism of American Public Address*, vol. 3 (New York: Longmans, Green, 1955), p. 4.
2. See George A. Kennedy, *A New History of Classical Rhetoric* (Princeton: Princeton University Press, 1994), pp. 3–10; and John Poulakos, *Sophistical Rhetoric in Classical Greece* (Columbia: University of South Carolina Press).
3. The case studies in criticism that appear later in this book illustrate this point. The other critical studies cited in the bibliography afford a wide range of examples of different critical approaches.
4. Herbert Wichelns, "The Literary Criticism of Oratory," reprinted in William A. Linsley, ed., *Speech Criticism: Methods and Materials* (Dubuque, Iowa: Wm. C. Brown, 1968), p. 32.
5. Michael C. Leff and G. P. Mohrmann, "Lincoln at Cooper Union: A Rhetorical Analysis of the Text," *Quarterly Journal of Speech*, 60 (1974), 346–358.
6. Forbes Hill, "Conventional Wisdom — Traditional Forms: The President's Message of November 3, 1969," *Quarterly Journal of Speech*, 58 (1972), 374.
7. Wayne C. Minnick, "A Case Study in Persuasive Effect: Lyman Beecher on Duelling," *Speech Monographs*, 38 (1971), 275–276.
8. Karlyn Kohrs Campbell, "Criticism: Ephemeral and Enduring," *Speech Teacher*, 23 (1974), 10–11.
9. See Michael Leff, "Textual Criticism: The Legacy of G. P. Mohrmann," *Quarterly Journal of Speech*, 72 (1986), 378; and David Zarefsky, "The State of the Art in Public Address Scholarship," *Texts in Context*, ed. Michael C. Leff and Fred Kauffeld (Davis, CA: Hermagoras Press, 1989), p. 22.
10. Samuel L. Becker, "Rhetorical Studies for the Contemporary World," *The Prospect of Rhetoric* (Englewood Cliffs, NJ: Prentice-Hall, 1971), p. 41.

# 2

# Constituents of the Rhetorical Act: Context and Audience

## Beginning the Critical Process

One of the rhetorical critic's first problems is deciding where to begin. If one is going to undertake to explicate and interpret the rhetorical dimensions of a particular message, be it a speech, a pamphlet, an editorial, or a proclamation, it makes obvious and good sense to begin with the message itself. The problem arises when it is realized that all the constituents of the rhetorical act are exerting mutual influence on each other even as the act occurs. What the critic must do, in effect, is freeze an ongoing process, sort out its various elements, and examine sequentially matters that occur simultaneously.

In a speaking situation, for example, there is always a speaker, a message produced by that speaker, an audience responding to that message, and a complex context made up of a multiplicity of factors ranging from prevailing ethical standards and the importance of the issues involved to the size and temperature of the room and the speaker's energy level. The critic has to deal in some way with all these constituents one by one.

Of course, no critic approaches any rhetorical activity from a completely naive point of view: To be a critic in any discipline presupposes some prior knowledge and background. One would hardly be ready to become a literary critic after reading his or her first novel, nor could one decide to be a music critic and then listen for the first time to a symphony. No student could reasonably expect to become a rhetorical critic after reading one text.

But the student who would master the critical craft must make a beginning. The nature of that beginning partly depends on the background and knowledge which the student brings to the situation. Whereas the text of the speech is a logical place to start, the student who knows something about the historical, political, and social factors that surround a particular speech obviously will understand better what the speaker is saying and what the speaker is trying to do. It is always advisable for the beginning rhetorical critic to start by reading, carefully and thoughtfully, the text of the message to be studied. The close analysis of that text may come later in the critical process, but initial study of the text must precede a systematic investigation of all the constituents. Following the careful reading of the text, the critic who is not already fully versed in the subtle and complex background to, and events surrounding, any communication event, will need to move backward, as it were, in order to understand what gave rise to the speech, how the issues involved emerged over time, what their relevance and importance was, and to whom they were significant. Since messages are designed to influence the way people think and act, the critic must come as close as he or she can to a full comprehension of what those who actually experienced the message thought and felt and believed.

## Rhetorical Imperatives: Historical and Political Factors

One of the first factors to be considered by the rhetorical critic is the events that made it possible or necessary for a speaker to address an audience at all. People speak in order to solve problems, to gain adherents, to rouse interest and sympathy, or to compel action because there is something going on in the world around them that is in *need* of modification or is threatened and must be defended. In other words, rhetoric grows out of events that a speaker wants us to see as important. Historical and political events and trends can force certain issues into our consciousness; the situation can make it *imperative* that we somehow come to grips with issues. Let us consider some brief examples of such rhetorical imperatives and how they take on special importance for the critic.[1]

In the 1960s African-Americans began a concerted and determined effort to gain for themselves the rights that were guaranteed to them by the Constitution and to reverse the economic and social effects of years of discrimination. Laws in several states barred them from eating in restaurants, sleeping in motels, and even drinking from water fountains reserved for "whites only." Requirements for registering to vote were so stated and interpreted by white registrars as to effectively disenfranchise large numbers of African-Americans. While exercising their rights to petition and protest, African-Americans were often assaulted by police or set upon by dogs. Unemployment among blacks far exceeded that of whites, and the road to improvement through special job training and increased education was blocked to many African-Americans. Some groups, particularly the NAACP, attempted to work through the courts to redress wrongs, and had secured a landmark Supreme Court decision, in *Brown v. Board of Education,* that separate schools for African-Americans were inherently unequal and thus unconstitutional. Black leaders had lobbied for legislation that would improve the lot of their people, and prior to 1963, several Civil Rights Acts had passed Congress. But, in spite of these efforts, the plight of most African-Americans in the United States was still seen as desperate. The tactics of sit-ins, demonstrations, and civil disobedience were employed to dramatize the problems of African-Americans, to make clear the extent and depth of black feeling, and to clearly set forth black demands.

In response to this surge of black protest, white leaders reacted in a variety of ways. Labor leaders like Walter Reuther, religious leaders like Eugene Carson Blake, and political leaders like Hubert Humphrey pressed for congressional action. Others, like Governor George Wallace of Alabama, tried to assert the right of the states to determine the nature of black-white relationships, particularly arguing for the right of the state to control such matters as education and voting rights. Many whites became alarmed at the potential for violence and frightened by the frustrated outbursts that erupted in major cities.

In 1963, at a massive rally, with major civil rights legislation pending in Congress, Martin Luther King, Jr., gave his most famous speech, "I Have a Dream." A critic would need to know details of the factors that brought forth and surrounded the speech before he or she could begin to appreciate such matters as King's purpose in giving the speech, his major premise concerning the American dream and the argument derived from it, the hopes and fears of the various audiences who heard the speech as they stood massed on the Mall in front of the Lincoln Memorial or watched their television sets at home, and the ways in which King's message might succeed. One would need to know about the challenge to King's leadership from militant African-Americans who were increasingly embittered by brutal treatment and were growing more impatient with the results of what King called "creative suffering." One would also need to know the key provisions of the civil rights bill and what efforts were being made to weaken and strengthen it.

## Rhetorical Imperatives: Social and Cultural Values

In reconstructing rhetorical imperatives, historical and political events obviously must be considered. Social and cultural values and traditions also must be understood as they pertain to a speaking situation. In the civil rights movement, to continue the previous example, consider the paternalistic myth of the "happy Negro." It was often alleged that African-Americans were happy with their lot; they didn't want contact with white society; they were content to move in the circles prescribed for them and in accordance with the traditions of white supremacy; the role of whites was to "take care of" African-Americans; and African-Americans, when they were not interfered with by "outside agitators," were docile and satisfied. When one recognizes the existence of such a cultural misconception, one begins to see the need for speakers like King to shatter it. And along with the deep-seated racial prejudices and stereotypes embedded in the culture were conflicting American values that held that all Americans should be treated equally under the law, that ours was a land of equal opportunity, that basic to all religious convictions was the brotherhood of man — values that were available to King and others who sought to awaken the conscience of white Americans. For the critic to understand the rhetorical problems that King had to face, the rhetorical opportunities that were open to him, and the constraints that were placed on him by events in the past and his role in those events and by prevailing attitudes and beliefs, one would have to reconstruct the imperatives that brought about King's speech.[2]

What we are discussing here is much more than a painted backdrop against which the principal scene is played; we are talking about matters that have an active and direct impact on the very nature of the message itself. The speaker cannot control what is going on in an audience's mind; that is determined by what the listeners have experienced, what they know, and what they believe. The speaker cannot ignore what is important or salient to an audience or assume that what he or she thinks is important will be recognized as such by his or her listeners. So the critic who would assess what the speaker *has* done, working within the limitations imposed by events and by the social and cultural milieu, must know the significant contextual factors that have the potential to influence the message. How could a future critic, for example, hope to render any kind of explanation or judgment about a political speech dealing with the direction of American foreign policy in 1995 who did not know in detail the impact of the Persian Gulf War, or rescue efforts in Somalia, or UN efforts in the Balkans? Who could hope to shed any light on the rhetorical strategies of Democratic liberals in the 1990s seeking to reverse the Republican electoral surge who did not appreciate the facts and feelings associated with growing social conservatism and pervasive disillusion with politicians?

The rhetorical critic faces certain problems that are somewhat different from those encountered by the historian, although both are engaged in a reconstruction of the past. Whereas traditional historians may search for an accurate account of what happened, they may not be as vitally concerned with *perceptions* of what happened. The historian, for example, may take up the issue of English "tyranny" at the time of the American Revolution and question whether British actions and policy were, indeed, "tyrannical" in regard to political or economic restrictions. The rhetorical scholar is likely to be more interested in how speakers and audiences of the time *interpreted* British actions so that they might be seen and understood as tyrannical. Historians looking back at the Clinton-Bush presidential race in 1992 might be able to discover what was "really" happening to the American economy, whether policies advocated by politicians would have or could have had real impact on the deficit. The rhetorical critic will focus attention more directly on attitudes and beliefs — whether mistaken or not — that people held toward economic matters. He or she may seek to uncover the cultural forces at work in shaping communication. In short, the "imperatives" we are discussing are those that are imperative to speakers and audience at the time discourse is being produced and not unseen forces at work in human affairs. "Nationalism," for example, may be a rising tide, but for the rhetorical critic the ways in which speakers and listeners translate such a conception into concrete reality becomes of primary importance; attempts to stem nationalism or a willingness to be engulfed by it can only be assessed and understood within the context of some public *consciousness* of it. The critic's historical task, then, is the reconstruction of such a consciousness.

## Discerning Issues

Once the critic can master the swirl of events and perceptions of events and can discern some pattern of conflicting and complementary forces — the rhetorical imperatives — that bring matters to a rhetorical head, then the critic needs to turn his or her attention to the emerging issues as they are molded, shaped, distorted, or sharpened in public debate. What really *is* at issue is a matter of serious concern in any controversy. In the civil rights struggle, for example, was the issue legal, social, and educational equality of opportunity for African-Americans? Or was it the constitutional right of the states to govern themselves in matters beyond the legal right of the federal government to intervene? Was it civil rights or states' rights? Was the issue whether citizens had the right to peaceful protest with the expectation that the forces of the government would protect them in carrying out this right? Or was it whether an orderly society could tolerate protest capable of, or even designed to, provoke violence or to disrupt the normal functioning of those who were unsympathetic to or disinterested in the movement? Was it civil rights or civil wrongs?

To take another example, one might ask what was at issue in the debate in the United States Senate over the confirmation of President Bush's nominee, John Tower, for secretary of defense. Tower, formerly a powerful conservative Republican senator from Texas, had impressive credentials but also was plagued by personal scandals. So the issue at stake revolved around how one might answer contradictory sets of questions. *Was the issue a constitutional one* involving such questions as: Should the President have the right to name whomever he chooses to his Cabinet? What is the proper role of the Senate in advising and consenting to presidential nominations? *Was the issue a moral one*: Did John Tower's personal conduct render him unfit to hold a high office? *Was the issue a practical one*: Did John Tower's use of alcohol disqualify him from holding a sensitive governmental position in which he could be called upon at any time to make important decisions affecting the lives of millions of people? Would his past association with defense contractors make him biased in their favor? *Was the issue a personal one*: Did John Tower's sometimes strained relations with other senators when he was chairman of the Armed Services Committee contribute to a personal dislike on the part of some senators so intense that they wished to deny him the office he so clearly wanted? Various sectors of public opinion tended to coalesce around what each believed to be the "real" issue, and much of the debate centered on what the debate itself was about.

The rhetorical critic must discern in the context the nature of the issues as various parties see them. Consider the following historical example for its relevance to perception of issues. During the American Civil War, both the Union and the Confederate States gave much diplomatic attention to the question of the recognition of the Confederate States by the government of Great Britain. Recognition by England would have greatly benefited the South; the federal blockade could be weakened, the shipbuilding activities of the Confederates in England would have been made easier, the North would likely have become embroiled in a war with Britain, and so forth. In England, the ongoing debate over the government's stance toward the warring sides touched on a variety of issues: Was it in Britain's best economic interests to encourage the permanent separation of a country that was fast becoming a major trade rival? Should the arrogant, uncouth Yankee industrialists be allowed to bully the more courtly, civilized southerners? And, most pertinently, should the federal blockade of the South be allowed to ruin Britain's important textile industry by creating a "cotton famine" in England? Such formulations of the issues certainly tilted toward the South. But those who were sympathetic to the North put the war in a perspective that was ultimately more captivating to most Englishmen when they described the war as one to eliminate slavery. For Great Britain — a nation that had almost singlehandedly eliminated the African slave trade and had abolished slavery in its own West Indian dominions; a nation whose rising working classes exhibited a strong antipathy to slavery even when the cotton famine brought personal hardship — the issue of slavery was an overriding moral consideration. The promulgation of the Emancipation Proclamation by President Lincoln in 1863 helped define the issue for the English clearly as one that rested on the slavery question and thus tilted the balance in favor of the pro-Union faction in England. Once the central issue of the debate was defined, the outcome was no longer in doubt.

## An Argumentational History

As the rhetorical critic studies the context, he or she must construct what might be called an argumentational history of issues along with his or her reconstruction of events. As events unfold, people interpret their meaning, argue about their significance, and deliberate on their ultimate effect. Any message occurs at some point in this process that goes on until the issues are resolved, or supplanted by other issues, or until they diminish in perceived relevance. For a critic to make sense out of the context in which a speech took place, he or she must know what the issues were and were perceived to be at that point.

An argumentational history goes further than the definition of the issues. Surely the critic approaching a speech would need to know how others had argued the question in the past, since the speaker and the audiences would be likely to have such information or at least have been exposed to it. By studying the ways in which particular matters have been argued, the critic can come to understand what kinds of evidence, what appeals to traditional values, what relationships between ideas have been offered in the past and the extent to which such things persist or fade away. How much better an assessment can be made of a rhetorical event when we know whether the arguments and the support for those arguments are original, or whether they have been used so frequently in the past (and gone unchallenged or only ineffectively combated) as to be conceded as "truths," or whether they have been discarded or discredited long ago.

Take, for example, the debate over the teaching of evolution, an issue that some thought had been laid to rest. In the current controversy, those who oppose on religious grounds what they understand to be evolutionary theory no longer argue the question of whether the Genesis story is "true"; rather, they focus on the concept of "theory." The appeal to the ultimate truth of the literal interpretation of the Bible as opposed to "Godless" science has faded as an appeal to general audiences. The argument now asserts that there are opposing "theories," and, in the interests of academic freedom and fair play, both "theories" ought to be taught in the public schools. As a part of the attack on what is called "secular humanism," this argument relies less on proof derived from scriptural quotation and more on the implied opposition of God and Christian principles to secular and human interpretations of events. The critic who would understand how such arguments have evolved must understand the social and cultural context and the way the arguments have developed to reflect that context.

## Rhetorical Conventions

Another factor to be considered is one of unique importance to the rhetorical critic. In any given time and place there are rhetorical conventions that apply and communication styles that prevail. Sometimes these are the function of a historical period. In England in the eighteenth and nineteenth centuries, for example, it was not uncommon for a speaker to address the House of Commons in a speech lasting several hours, a practice that few would tolerate in twentieth-century America. The change in the length of speeches is an obvious example of a rhetorical convention that operates within a specific context. These conventions, or common practices, are rooted in audience expectations. A Puritan divine in colonial New England could sermonize for three hours because his audience expected such a lengthy talk; a modern preacher whose sermons consistently ran more than twenty or thirty minutes would probably find his congregations melting away. Modern traditional churchgoers expect that church services will not greatly exceed an hour or so.

Beginning rhetorical critics, when studying texts of speeches that were given in the past, are often struck not only by their length but also by what they perceive as the complexity of their style. The matter of prevailing historical styles is a complicated one. Much of what a critic knows about the style of a time comes from his or her immersion in the rhetoric of the period. In the present state of the art of rhetorical scholarship, we have little solid, normative data on stylistic practice. What the critic has, largely, is his or her own impressionistic perceptions of the way in which language was used by speakers in a particular period. (This fact should reinforce the notion that the would-be critic must read widely and extensively in the period in which he or she intends to work.)

The matter of audience expectations goes much deeper than conventions concerning such matters as length and style; we consider these issues further in the discussion of audiences. But it is essential for the critic who embarks on the study of historical rhetoric to bear in mind that what sounds right to the contemporary ear or reads right to the contemporary eye is not what appeared right to the eighteenth- or nineteenth-century listener and reader; indeed, many audience expectations have changed from the 1960s to the 1990s.

## Ethics and Context

Perhaps one of the most difficult elements contributing to a full understanding of context is the ethical one. If we take the ethics of any group to be a set of behaviors that are judged to be acceptable when measured against some prevailing code of conduct, we can see that what is essential is an understanding of the prevailing code, which, however, is not always spelled out in a specific, concrete fashion. There are, to be sure, "codes of ethics" that professional groups adopt and that are supposed to guide the conduct of their members. The National Communication Association, the National Association of Broadcasters, the American Psychological Association, the American Medical Association, and others all have written statements of what they, as a group, consider ethical behavior by members of their profession.

Along with various professional codes are religious codes — the most notable one in the Judeo-Christian tradition being the Ten Commandments — that are designed to prescribe and circumscribe ethical behavior. But anyone who has studied arguments based on religious principles knows that the precise meaning and the application of these codes are subject to wide varieties of interpretation and emphasis. "Thou shalt not kill," for example, seems to be a straightforward injunction, but pacifists have never been able to convince large numbers of people that this commandment applies in all cases and in *all* situations. There are also laws that define acceptable behavior. "Conflict of interest" laws, for example, attempt to set out procedures governing the behavior of public officials, particularly in regard to financial matters. These laws are based on the precept that those who are elected to public office should not profit economically through the use of the power derived from holding office. But laws alone do not determine ethical behavior; who has not heard the phrase, often employed by those whose actions generate public suspicion or outrage, "It may be unethical, but it's not illegal."

Of utmost importance to the rhetorical critic is what might be called the ethical tenor of the times, the feelings that most people have concerning what is right or wrong behavior, whether or not such behavior is specifically articulated in any written code. For example, take a speaker who attacks a political leader for giving to friends and relatives public offices with no real duties assigned; these friends and relatives are thereby paid from the public treasury for doing nothing. Surely, such a charge, if proven, would do serious damage to a modern American politician's career. Those precise charges were leveled against leading political figures in England in the early nineteenth century by radical speakers, and they were most decidedly true. Yet the practice of giving political supporters and family members honorary jobs that entailed no duties ("sinecures," as they were called) was common at the time, and it engendered few denunciations on ethical grounds from the governing classes of England.

Determining the ethical climate of a period is never easy. Major problems confound any attempts that one might make to discern the ethical climate. In any society, competing ethical standards seem to be held simultaneously; subgroups within a society may hold conflicting standards or emphasize different standards. Societies, like individuals, may seem to profess standards that do not, in fact, guide their actions.

In contemporary American society, for example, we are repeatedly faced with choices for which there may be conflicting ethical precepts.[3] One of the most persistent strains to which Americans have been subjected is that of dealing with the demands placed on them by professed ethical imperatives while, at the same time, experiencing the decided urge to succeed. We are often considered a people with a strong sense of what is expedient. In the past, we have been proud of our lack of doctrinaire politics. As Erik H. Erikson reminds us, "American politics is not, as is that of Europe, 'a prelude to civil war'; it cannot become either entirely irresponsible or entirely dogmatic; and it must not try to be logical. It is a rocking sea of checks and balances in which uncompromising absolutes must drown."[4] In the past, American politicians have avoided the rigid adherence to principle at all costs and have seen the virtue of our pragmatism contrasted with the factious, splintered politics of Europe. In the 1990s, however, partisanship seems to grow ever more intense in America, and deeper ideological fissures seem to be appearing in the political landscape.

In politics and in life, success has been our touchstone. Some students of American culture have observed that the will to get ahead, the need to compete successfully with our fellows, may be bred into us.[5] In this connection, the legendary Alabama coach "Bear" Bryant's aphorism that "football is life" may be a most apt metaphor. Facing the forces that would hold them back, Americans combine physical stamina, strategy, determination, and occasionally bursts of enthusiastic drive to reach their goal. To score, to win is essential, and in this process the American may feel compelled, at times, to gouge, kick, and cheat.

For some, this contradiction has been disquieting. In *Young Radicals*, Kenneth Keniston reported on an interview in which a young man described his family: "It seems to have a lot of tensions in terms of its orientation — what your aspirations are, what they should be or shouldn't be. 'It isn't important that you make money, it's important that you be godly. But why don't you go out and make some money?' A whole series of contradictions. In terms of what I should do, what my life should be like."[6]

On the whole, however, Americans have learned to live with contradiction. As Gabriel A. Almond observed: "Under normal circumstances this conflict does not appear to have a seriously laming effect. It tends to be disposed of by adding a moral coloration to actions which are really motivated by expediency, and an expediential coloration to actions which are motivated by moral and humanitarian values."[7]

An excellent example of this attempt to render these contradictory values compatible appears in John F. Kennedy's inaugural address. Why should we help the world's poor who are "struggling to break the bonds of mass misery"? In the words of Kennedy, "not because the Communists may be doing it, not because we seek their votes, but because it is right." The moral coloration is given to what is, after all, expedient policy (the Communists, with whom we were in competition, *are* doing it; we do want votes in the sense that we want international support to check and contain our perceived rival and enemy, the Soviet Union). Yet the most interesting thing about this excerpt is that the sentence that immediately follows the one just quoted gives expedient coloration to what has been stated as a moral stance. There can be no doubt of the implication in "If a free society cannot help the many who are poor, it cannot save the few who are rich." The rich, in this teeming world of the poor, are obviously the

Americans, and we are invited to attend to the realization that, although we may be acting out of principle, when the principle operates in such a way as to help save a few — and the few are us — the moral purpose is given a recognizable practical cast.[8]

A critic's examination of the context will also help him or her understand when a debate is perceived as being over moral issues. In such cases, a tolerant examination of opposing arguments is difficult, for certainly virtue cannot tolerate vice; nothing is sacred in such a confrontation. "We make no secret of our determination to tread the law and the Constitution under our feet," Wendell Phillips asserted at an abolitionist meeting, at a time when practical political questions were beginning to become overwhelmed and overshadowed by the moral question of slavery.[9] Phillips's fiery colleague, William Lloyd Garrison, in asserting the primacy of the moral issue, epitomized the rejection of moderation. "I will be as harsh as truth, and as uncompromising as justice," Garrison told his readers in the January 1, 1831, issue of *The Liberator*. "On this subject, I do not wish to think, or speak, or write, with moderation. No! no! Tell a man whose house is on fire to give a moderate alarm; tell him to moderately rescue his wife from the hands of the ravisher; tell the mother to gradually extricate her babe from the fire into which it has fallen; but urge me not to use moderation in a cause like the present."[10] When a speaker for a cause envisions a kind of Armageddon, his or her rhetoric reflects the moralist's impatience with expediency. As Barry Goldwater reminded the triumphant, cheering right-wing delegates to the Republican National Convention in 1964, "Extremism in the defense of liberty is no vice. And . . . moderation in the pursuit of justice is no virtue."[11]

The conflict between competitive goals and professed moral values seems to be firmly rooted in our American culture, and the rhetorical critic must be aware of it. The value placed on success in a competitive society has within it the seeds of another conflict. The need to succeed implies a kind of individualistic drive to best others in competition. Yet when a child is reared and judged against the actions of his or her peers, when what constitutes success (particularly in its material dimension) is generally agreed upon, when the methods of attaining success are to some degree prescribed, and when the constraints of the society necessitate teamwork and cooperation, individuality itself is tempered by conformity.

These two elements — individuality and conformity — have existed in a state of tension, pulling at us, shaping, in part, our character. Alexis de Tocqueville worried about the conformity induced by the tyranny of the majority, and Frederick Jackson Turner hypothesized that the great American frontier bred the independent qualities of self-reliance. We extolled "rugged individualism" on the one hand and developed the "organization man" on the other.

Any student of the American character would agree that we are more than a sum of separate traits and characteristics; the whole is extremely complex. The qualities of American culture such as those that help to shape the rhetorical behavior alluded to here are uncovered through careful historical research and analysis, and they might be helpful in understanding what is going on in a given period of American rhetoric. It is important that the critic uncover, to the extent possible, the prevailing ethical standards that govern the culture within which a specific example of public communication was designed to function.

As is evident, understanding the prevailing ethical code of any given time is a complex matter. In the final analysis, the most gaping pitfall to be avoided by the rhetorical critic is the assumption that the ethical standards of his or her time or group or culture can be imposed on the subject of investigation. The critic who believes in the absolute immutability of ethical standards will have difficulty with the conception that ethical standards are relative to the context in which they flourish. But there can be little argument that the ethical climate that permeates a rhetorical situation will vary from setting to setting, if only with the interpretation and manner of putting ethical conceptions into effect in practical affairs. Certainly the critic is at liberty to apply to discourse any ethical standards he or she wishes, to argue that evils are evils no matter where or when they occur. But to act as if others besides the critic, similarly removed in time and place from the original rhetorical situation, necessarily would make similar assumptions, would blind the critic to the ways in which rhetoric actually functions in a particular situation. The critic may be shocked or repelled by ethical practices or norms, but no sound rhetorical judgments can be made about discourse if the critic fails to understand the prevailing codes.

## The Setting for a Speech

We have discussed the larger context in which rhetorical activities take place. Any message occurring in this broad context also takes place within a more particularized setting. The speech is not only occasioned by past and immediate events, by elements that make rhetoric imperative, but it happens at a given moment in time, in certain surroundings, on a discrete occasion. A speech is an event, and the event has the potential for impact on the message and its reception.

First, there is the *public nature* of the occasion, which can shape the expectations that the audience will have and which speakers will feel constrained to meet. An audience will have a sense of what is fitting to be said in the circumstances, which will relate both to the substance and the manner of the speech. Some occasions are ceremonial. They tend to be formal, to have persuasive ends of stimulating feelings of unity, heightening common emotions, or extolling shared values; they tend to concentrate on general or abstract principles. Certain occasions are more frankly issue-oriented, calling for arguments that attempt to move audiences to action or to shape their beliefs. Still other occasions demand that persuasion be muted while the dissemination of information takes precedence.

Contrast, for example, the acceptance speech of a candidate for the presidency given to the nominating convention with the inaugural address of a newly elected president. When the candidate appears before partisan supporters, addressing them and, at the same time, the nation, clearly a "political" speech is expected. This is the right occasion for the speaker to laud the virtues of one's own party and to point to the failings of the opposition. Audiences, both those in the convention hall and those in front of their television sets, know that such an occasion does not call for a careful weighing of all the alternative solutions to problems; it does not call for a modest appraisal of one's own political shortcomings. The clarion sounded in such a speech on such an occasion is a call for a political army to unify, to gird itself to fight for American ideals and against the political enemy who would undermine or fail to live up to those ideals. Most listeners who would readily accept such partisanship in an acceptance speech would be shocked by the same sentiments, expressed in the same way, in an inaugural address. Typically, an inaugural address is an effort to rise above the recently ended political battle and instill a sense of national unity and concerted purpose. For example, John F. Kennedy, in his inaugural address, aptly described the inauguration as a "celebration of freedom," and not a victory of party. The ceremonial occasion of the inaugural, then, raises expectations that are different from the frankly political acceptance speech.

The setting of a speech also has a concrete, specific physical surrounding. It can be indoors or outdoors, in a large auditorium or a small meeting room; it can be given before a small group or large masses of people; it can be amplified by a public address system or heard only by those within earshot of the speaker's voice. The audience may be jammed together, elbow to elbow, or spread thinly throughout the room. The physical surroundings can have a real impact on the way a message is constructed and how it is delivered, again, because of what an audience expects in any given setting.

Everyone has experienced the effects of the setting of a speech on listeners or speakers. One might sit in a dormitory room or in a friend's living room and talk about what's going to happen if tuition costs are to continue to rise; the same person might give a speech in a public speaking class about tuition costs; and the same person might speak on behalf of students at a meeting of the university's board of trustees. Some of the differences in the messages will be determined by audience factors, which are discussed later, but the physical factors of the setting will affect the formality/informality of the discourse, including such matters as language choice, whether the speaker speaks extemporaneously or uses a manuscript, and the nature of audience response and participation. The prescribed behavior of the classroom, for example, rarely leads audience members to cheer or to heckle a speaker. In such a setting the audience does not expect a speaker to exceed a certain level of loudness and would be made uncomfortable or embarrassed by a speaker whom they perceived as "shouting" at them, whereas increased volume may be necessary and deemed quite appropriate at an open-air rally. A political candidate who was asked to state his or her position on the issues at a neighborhood gathering in a supporter's home would not be expected to produce a manuscript and read it to that group, but, called upon to speak at a press club luncheon on the same topic, the candidate may be expected to deliver a manuscript speech.

A critic must understand and appreciate the potential significance of a specific setting, which, like the broader context, will be reflected in a variety of ways in the message. The setting can influence the speaker's delivery and style, as well as the emotional and intellectual responses of his or her listeners. For example, students are often concerned about large lecture classes as opposed to small, less formal classes. Many students believe that the opportunity to respond in a smaller class, the feeling of more direct contact with the instructor, and the fact that in smaller classes students know each other and are better known by the instructor, all contribute to their ability to respond better intellectually. Consider also Martin Luther King, Jr.'s "I Have a Dream" speech, for which the setting clearly contributed to the heightened emotional response of the audience. Thousands of people gathered in a large crowd on the Mall and faced the statue of Abraham Lincoln as King spoke. One of the authors of this book was in the audience for that speech. At the point in King's speech when he stressed the need for blacks and whites to work together, an African-American man standing next to Andrews, who is white, put an arm around his shoulder and said, "We're in this together, brother." This natural, spontaneous emotional act of response to the speaker was prompted not only by the content of the speech but by the physical surroundings; it would not have been likely to occur in an auditorium. And the presence of such feelings in an audience, along with the opportunity to display them, had an influence on King's speech itself that a perceptive critic understands as he or she analyzes and evaluates the message.

The circumstances of Dr. King's speech suggest another important consideration for the critic in studying the impact of setting. While thousands listened to the speech in Washington, millions watched the speech on television throughout the country. The television viewers may or may not have sensed the emotional environment that surrounded the speech, but they certainly could not experience it in precisely the same way as those who were there. The *medium* through which listeners receive a speech is an aspect of the setting that can profoundly affect the listener's reactions. There are situations, such as King's speech or an inaugural address, in which viewers are looking in on an event. Their unseen presence will certainly influence what is going on, but their expectations are colored by the total event. This situation differs somewhat from a speech given, for example, by the president of the United States directly to the American people via television. Nevertheless, whichever case obtains, television itself presents a unique setting for a speech.

For one thing, television viewers tend to be in smaller groups and less subject to the moods, attitudes, and actions of those around them, and are likely to be more passive than a live audience. The speaker will receive no stimulation from a television audience, whereas various types of feedback from a live audience might encourage him or her to become more excited or to "tone down" his or her material, or might suggest to a speaker that she or he combat restlessness by moving rapidly to a new point. The medium itself, because it brings the speaker into the living room, encourages a muted presentation that is more conversational in tone. It also provides a more concentrated focus on the speaker, so that other factors of the *speaker's* setting are either eliminated (there are no other people to look at or outside noises to contend with) or highlighted (the American flag may be unobtrusively, but nonetheless obviously, displayed in the background). Audience attention may be directed toward visual materials, and subtle nuances of delivery, such as facial expression, may be more pointedly brought to listeners' attention. On the other hand, the television audience is far less captive than a live one. A viewer can switch to another channel, begin to read a newspaper, or even get up and leave.

Perhaps the most important, and obvious, aspect of the television medium is its highly visual nature, which tends to emphasize what is *seen* at the possible expense of what is *said*. Audiences can form judgments about the speaker's competence, compassion, and intelligence based on what the speaker looks and sounds like close up, and not only on what he or she says. It has often been observed, for example, that the outcome of the first televised presidential debate — between Richard Nixon and John Kennedy — turned on how Nixon looked, that Nixon's makeup man "did him in." Whether or not this bit of conventional wisdom is true, there is no doubt that practical politicians are very much concerned with their appearance as they are projected on television. The rhetorical critic who limits himself or herself exclusively to studying the verbal text of such a speech may overlook a potentially significant part of the setting that could lead to distorted conclusions about what happened rhetorically.

## The Centrality of the Audience

Frequent mention has been made of the expectations of the audience. The audience for any message is one of the most important constituents of the rhetorical act with which a critic must deal. Speeches are, by their nature, audience centered. The understanding of the audience is absolutely vital to any critical inquiry.

As the critic reconstructs the context for a message or series of messages, much information about the nature of the audiences addressed will be uncovered. The critic must organize, systematize, and search out missing information to give as complete a picture as possible of those whom the speaker would influence. In order to do this, the critic must first identify immediate and potential audiences, then may want to consider secondary or implied audience, and finally must examine the primary variables that have a direct bearing on how audiences might receive and act on messages.

## Identifying Audiences

In some cases, identifying the audience or audiences is not too difficult; it may seem obvious that the primary audience is the one actually gathered to hear the speech. Certainly before the advent of mass media this was more likely to be the case. A speech given in the House of Commons in the eighteenth century, for example, was largely addressed to the members present. A speech given at a state convention called for the purpose of ratifying the new United States Constitution was primarily directed at the assembled delegates. But, even in historical cases, speeches were often designed with those in mind who would read about them later. Robert Emmet, the Irish revolutionary, spoke not for the English court that condemned him to hang, but to the larger Irish audience who would hear reports of what he said. Abraham Lincoln, delivering his first inaugural speech, did not address only the crowd assembled in Washington, or only Northern sympathizers. The people of the Southern states that had begun to secede from the Union and those in the border states who contemplated doing so were also in Lincoln's mind. William Seward's speech on the "irrepressible conflict" in Rochester, New York, had a profound effect on those who were not there and who judged the speech an "abolitionist" one. Depicted as a radical, Seward's chances of gaining the Republican nomination for president were thwarted, to the benefit of Lincoln.

For any speech, then, there is an immediate audience and a potentially larger one. This is true of messages given in the past, and it is certainly true of modern times when the mass media have the potential to disseminate a speaker's ideas rapidly, sometimes instantaneously, throughout the world. It is obvious, for example, that a major address by the president of the United States may be an attempt to communicate with the American people at large or with segments of the American public, with legislators who must act to effect presidential policy, with foreign governments in alliance with the United States, and with those who are seen as hostile to American interests and intentions. The immediate audience may be the Congress in joint session, students and faculty in a university convocation, television viewers, or the National Press Club. But a far wider audience is likely to be envisioned.

Both the text and the context will direct the critic's attention to the wider audience. The critic who has investigated the imperatives giving rise to rhetoric should know the political, social, and economic issues that are uppermost in the minds of potential listeners. Specific references to foreign policy, for example, alert the critic to the possibility that the speaker wishes to send a message to the leaders of other countries or to supporters or potential adversaries at home. Knowing the context, setting, and content of the speech, the critic can begin to make informed assumptions about the audience the speaker hoped or needed to reach.[12]

## Audience Variables

What a critic needs to know about an audience can be grouped under three essential variables. These elements are "variable" in that their impact and significance varies — they may differ in importance and relevance depending on the rhetorical characteristics of the situation. These variables are listeners' *knowledge*, their *group identification*, and their *receptivity* to the speech and the topic.

In order for a critic to begin to understand how an audience may respond to a speech, it is essential to understand what an audience knows about the subject under consideration, about current related events, and about the speaker. In addition to knowledge pertinent to the specific rhetorical event, audiences have general knowledge, which may or may not be relevant, that grows out of their educational background and personal experiences. The critic hopes to understand interactions and make reasonable judgments about how well and in what ways speakers have adapted such elements as language choice, basic arguments, supporting evidence, and the like, to audiences. In order to carry out an operational analysis that can lead to a sound judgment, the critic must know what the audience knows.

Take, for instance, the use of historical analogy. A speaker who compares American government policy in the Balkans with American actions in Vietnam could assume that the Vietnam experience — or, at least, the lessons of extreme caution generally drawn from it — is recent and general enough, and had such a profound impact on the American psyche, that most listeners would have a general knowledge of it. As a speaker delves further into the past, however, his or her audience's knowledge of history may be a function of their educational background. Furthermore, particular audiences can be expected to know more about particular subjects because of their cultural identity, their professional activities, or the perceived impact of the topic on their own lives. Some audiences may know more not only about a given subject but about current events in general because they tend to read newspapers, watch television documentaries and special reports, or discuss issues with other well-informed people. Also, some audiences will know more about the particular speaker than will other audiences. They may have been that speaker's constituents, or have read things that the speaker has written, or have belonged to the same social or religious organizations, and so forth. The ways in which a speaker either capitalized on or failed to take into account what an audience *knows* is an important critical concern, one that the critic can assess only if he or she is aware of audience knowledge.

What anyone knows is not only a function of his or her educational level and personal intellectual practices; knowledge is shaped partly by the *groups with which one identifies*. This group affiliation, in addition to furthering knowledge, also influences the way people interpret and use knowledge. Members of the Sierra Club, for example, probably know more about conservation than many other people do. They are likely to read publications, attend meetings, and generally gather specific information that will provide them with more detailed facts about such matters as federal land management policy, criteria for designating wilderness areas, or potential industrial uses of public lands. But along with this knowledge there is also a point of view that members of a group tend to share. Catholics, Presbyterians, Episcopalians, Pentecostal, and Jehovah's Witnesses may all "know" the Bible. They may all be able to quote passages or relate the essential ingredients of a particular scriptural narrative. They nevertheless hold widely divergent views of what the Bible means not only theologically but in very practical terms relating to day-to-day human relations. Association and identification with particular groups will predispose audience reactions to messages.

Other group identifications derive from less voluntary factors. One may elect to join the Sierra Club or to change one's religious affiliation, but one cannot so easily change one's age or sex or ethnic background. Also, it is much more difficult to modify one's social status or economic circumstances than it is to join or drop out of a particular interest group or formal organization. The critic must also be aware of how these group identifications may exert influence on audiences. Polish organizations in Chicago have a cultural and emotional relationship to Eastern Europe that is bound to affect their response to a speaker who addresses the problems of American foreign policy in that area. Blue-collar workers threatened with unemployment will view speeches on economic policy from that very personal perspective. Older Americans' real stake in the Social Security program will shape their reaction to speeches that deal with that issue. Because the speaker's task is to adapt to a variety of groups within audiences, often groups with *conflicting* orientations, the critic's job of sorting out the possible responses of audiences is likewise difficult. The effective critic must understand the problems that arise from the speaker's efforts to persuade heterogeneous elements within audiences in order to describe and evaluate the speaker's solutions to these rhetorical problems.

Just as listeners' knowledge about a given subject derives partly from the groups with which they identify, both the knowledge and the group identification have an impact on the *receptivity of an audience* to both subjects and speakers. The receptivity of an audience depends partly on salience.

An issue or topic is salient to a group when that group sees the subject as important to them, as impinging directly on their lives. The basic act of receiving a message takes some effort on the part of the receiver. To choose to listen to a speech or read a pamphlet or attend a meeting is an act based on some initial receptivity. Most open meetings of school boards, for example, will be sparsely attended. But if there is a threat of some schools being closed, or a plan to redistrict areas served by particular schools in order to change busing patterns, large crowds very likely will be present. Parents will attend these meetings, in spite of conflicting demands on their time and energy, because they believe that their children's education, safety, or social adjustment will be significantly affected by the outcomes of the meetings. Some audiences might not be disposed to take a serious or intense interest in foreign policy, but if they are farmers whose livelihood is affected by a grain embargo, or college students whose education could be interrupted by compulsory military service, certain aspects of foreign policy will be salient to them and will compel their receptivity to a discussion of the issue.

Receptivity in this sense concerns the listeners' willingness to engage themselves as a part of the communication process. The critic must realize that a speaker's rhetorical problem often involves the *creation of salience*. That is, there are times when audiences or potential audiences do not readily perceive the relevance of issues or do not see the relevance in the way the speaker wishes them to see it. For example, some listeners may see the "cleaning-up-the-environment" issue as remote to their personal experience, but to those who live on property contaminated by PCBs, pollution is a very real and harrowing threat. To those living in small towns or relatively nonindustrialized areas, the problem of pollution might be seen as a "big-city" issue that doesn't touch them directly. To some people, environmental controls have relevance because they believe that such controls can affect their health and the health of their children; others see relevance in the issue of government controls that increase manufacturing costs and thus affect them negatively in an economic way. The critic's task is to discern how audiences might answer the question, Is this issue relevant to me and in what ways? Then the critic will be better able to analyze the extent to which and the ways in which a speaker attempted to solve the salience problems of the situation.

In conjunction with salience, receptivity concerns the audience's disposition toward a subject or a speaker; it is important for the critic to understand listeners' attitudes so that he or she can better uncover rhetorical problems. Certain topics may be received by audiences in a hostile, friendly, or fearful way. (Likewise, audiences can be hostile or indifferent, respectful or suspicious toward a speaker. This point is developed more fully in the following chapter in the examination of the role of the speaker.) For example, a PTA audience may respond positively to a speech dealing with improving the quality of playground equipment. The same audience might approach a speech dealing with the need to reduce the local school budget with suspicion or even hostility. A conservative religious group might be negatively disposed to the subject of the church's role in promoting social action. The National Association of Broadcasters initially might be threatened by a discussion of the need for increased government regulation of broadcasting. The National Education Association would be inclined to receive positively a message that dealt with the increased use of national resources to improve the quality of instruction in the public schools.

A painstaking construction of audience variables in a given situation is fundamental to the critical process. In most circumstances, the critic will discover wide variations in the knowledge, group identifications, and receptivity of those who receive messages. But whether the audiences tend to be more homogeneous or more heterogeneous, the message that is designed for them must take into account who they are and where they stand. The speaker will have choices to make and will make them — consciously or unconsciously. The pattern of these choices will contribute to the formation of the speaker's strategy. Understanding precisely what those choices are and judging whether or not they are appropriate — strategically or ethically — is part of the critic's role.

## Summary

The critic should realize that the constituents of the rhetorical act discussed in this chapter are those over which the speaker exercises little direct control. A speaker cannot change the past, erase the traditions and values that are part of a culture, escape the technical limitations imposed by television, or convert workers who are fearful of losing their jobs into economically secure people. The context in which a message occurs and the audience or audiences to whom the message is addressed present rhetorical problems or rhetorical opportunities that delineate the boundaries within which a speaker must operate. Rhetoric is the process whereby values may be changed, traditions discarded, class distinctions erased or redefined, and future action shaped. But any given message, at a particular moment in time, is constrained by contextual and audience factors that are then operant. As a painter may be constrained by his or her canvas, a musician by the notes that instruments are capable of producing, and a dramatist by the technical possibilities of stage production, a speaker's possibilities are, in large measure, circumscribed by relevant events and relevant audience variables. The significant challenge for the speaker is to manipulate the factors over which he or she has some control — for example, the construction of arguments, the selection of evidence, the identification and appeal to values, the language employed, and the manner of delivery — so as to influence real audiences living in real contexts. The critic can only begin to appreciate a speaker's wisdom and skill, or lack of it, when the critic fully comprehends the constraints under which a speaker labors.

Perhaps the best way to epitomize the critic's task in regard to context and audience is to say that the critic must answer the fundamental question, What is there in the rhetorical situation that presents a clear indication of the rhetorical problems that a speaker must solve and the rhetorical opportunities that exist to be used? This chapter has suggested important elements to be dealt with by the critic as he or she goes about answering that overarching question. These elements can be summarized by directing the critic's efforts toward answering the following subsidiary questions:

1. What *political, social, or economic factors,* both historical and immediate, brought the issue into *rhetorical* being?
2. What *cultural values and practices* in the society were relevant to the issue?
3. What *varying perceptions of the issue* existed at the time the message was given?
4. What *rhetorical conventions* shaped audience expectations of how, in what circumstances, and within what limitations the message was to be sent and received?
5. What *prevailing ethical standards* were relevant to the message?
6. What were the particular *circumstances of the setting* for a speech, and in what ways did they determine what a speaker could or could not do?
7. What was the composition of the *immediate audience* to whom a message was addressed?
8. Who was the *larger audience,* or audiences, if any, to whom the message was addressed?
9. In what ways were the *audiences' knowledge, group identifications, and receptivity* relevant to the issue being addressed?

As the critic answers these questions, he or she will construct a framework within which analysis, interpretation, and evaluation of the message as it functions rhetorically can take place.

One other constituent of the rhetorical act must be considered before the critic can turn to an intensive investigation of the text of the message itself: The examination of the speaker as a unique constituent in the rhetorical act is the subject of the next chapter.

## *Notes*

1. The concept of "rhetorical imperatives" is discussed more fully and illustrated in James R. Andrews, "The Passionate Negation: The Chartist

Movement in Rhetorical Perspective," *Quarterly Journal of Speech,* 59 (1973), 196–208.

2. See the chapter entitled "The Unfinished Revolution," in Kurt W. Ritter and James R. Andrews, *The American Ideology: Reflections of the Revolution in American Rhetoric* (Falls Church, VA: SCA Bicentennial Monograph Series, 1978), pp. 93–117.
3. James R. Andrews has developed this point in some detail in "Reflections of the National Character in American Rhetoric," *Quarterly Journal of Speech,* 62 (1971), 316–324, and what follows draws extensively on that study.
4. Erik H. Erikson, *Childhood and Society,* 2d ed. (New York: W. W. Norton, 1963), p. 318.
5. See, for example, David M. Potter, *People of Plenty: Economic Abundance and the American Character* (Chicago: University of Chicago Press, 1954), p. 49.
6. Kenneth Keniston, *Young Radicals* (New York: Harcourt, Brace and World, 1968), p. 66.
7. Gabriel A. Almond, *The American People and Foreign Policy* (New York: Harcourt, Brace, 1950), p. 52.
8. John F. Kennedy, "Inaugural Address," January 20, 1961, *Inaugural Addresses of the Presidents of the United States* (Washington, DC: U.S. Government Printing Office, 1974), p. 268.
9. Robert T. Oliver, *History of Public Speaking in America* (Boston: Allyn & Bacon, 1965), p. 235.
10. Richard Hofstadter, *Great Issues in American History,* vol. 1 (New York: Vintage, 1958), p. 322.
11. "I Accept Your Nomination," *Voices of Crisis: Vital Speeches on Contemporary Issues,* ed. Lloyd W. Matson (New York: Odyssey Press, 1967), p. 125.
12. See Forbes Hill's discussion of "target audience" in "Conventional Wisdom — Traditional Forms: The President's Message of November 3, 1969," *Quarterly Journal of Speech,* 58 (1972), pp. 373–386.

# 3

# Constituents of the Rhetorical Act: The Speaker

## Defining Ethos

"Knowing" any person is an extremely difficult task. All of us present different pictures of ourselves to different people in different circumstances. The roles we play, the settings in which we find ourselves, the expectations of others, our own motives — all contribute to the extremely complex whole that makes up the "real" person. People have many sides, and no one can hope to see all those sides; we rarely understand or are even aware of every facet of our own personalities. When we communicate with others, most of us tend to manipulate, consciously or unconsciously, the aspects of ourselves that we wish others not to see, and those who communicate with us form impressions, intended or unintended, of who we are.

We know that we ourselves and those around us define us as students, or as friends, daughters, brothers, lovers, rivals, coworkers, and so forth. At the same time we may think of ourselves and be seen as Christians, or scientists, or Democrats, or vegetarians. And as situations change, what we and others think is most important about us, what is most relevant to the situation, also changes.

If we project these individual human circumstances into the public communication setting, we can see that speakers and audiences interact in such a way as to "define" the person who is sending the message. This "definition" is what is termed the speaker's *ethos,* or the composite *perception* an audience has of a speaker. This perception is not a complete, or in all ways accurate, reflection of a "real" person; it is what an audience *thinks* about a person at any given time. It is formed by a variety of factors to which the critic must turn his or her attention. Chief among these considerations are the context out of which the speech arises and into which it is designed to intrude; the speaker's prior reputation; the audience's needs, expectations, and priorities; the content and rhetorical characteristics of the message itself; and the manner in which the speech is given.

## Context and Ethos

Considerable attention was given in the last chapter to the elements in the context that can influence a rhetorical interaction. These factors can be viewed from the standpoint of their potential to influence an audience's perception of a speaker. Certain events or trends that gave rise to rhetoric in the first place may affect attitudes toward speakers.

Take, for example, what has come to be known as the Watergate scandal of the early 1970s. The revelations about the inner workings of government, the generally condemned unethical or even illegal actions of political figures, and the sense of violation of the public trust that arose from news accounts and congressional hearings created serious issues related to the honesty and integrity of government, the powers of the presidency, the balance of power between the branches of government, and a host of related issues that had to be dealt with rhetorically in subsequent political campaigns.

Part of the fallout from the Watergate experience was a profound suspicion of politicians, a suspicion that has intensified over the years and is seen in the attitudes of voters in the 1990s. Any speaker who was a professional politician faced potential hostility from an audience because he or she could be perceived as a part of the whole system that had produced Watergate. Indeed, one of Jimmy Carter's principal assets that contributed to his election as president might have been that he was not associated with the Washington establishment. In other circumstances, his lack of experience would have been a negative factor; given the context of the mid-1970s such a potentially harmful perspective could be turned to the speaker's advantage. Thus, the dissociation of former Governor Carter from professional politicians could have been a factor in shaping a positive ethos for many listeners.

Contrast this with the selection of Dan Quayle by George Bush as his running mate in 1988. The most persistent attacks on Senator Quayle dealt with his competence and experience. Charges that he was "just a pretty face," or a token conservative chosen to mollify the Republican right wing, or a young man who had used family influence to avoid the draft, were rooted in the conviction that he was not of potential presidential caliber. Given that everyone remembered that President Reagan had been shot in an unsuccessful assassination attempt and that the vice president was just "a heartbeat away" from the presidency, the experience factor became an important issue — especially when Quayle was contrasted with the older, politically astute Democratic vice presidential candidate, Senator Bentsen of Texas. So, what was a political plus for Jimmy Carter twelve years before — a lack of identification with the political establishment — became a negative for a candidate who was perceived as inexperienced because events altered the context in which the political ethos was formed.

In 1992, disillusion with professional politicians was again on the rise; Ross Perot was able to attract attention and votes in large measure because he was not part of the political establishment. Bill Clinton, too, though he had served for a total of twelve years as governor of Arkansas, positioned himself as a political "outsider." While this may have protected him, to some extent, from negative association with the Washington elite, it did not shield him from attacks on his character.

In particular, accusations surfaced in both the tabloid and mainstream press that Clinton had been unfaithful to his wife and had dodged the Vietnam draft. Both of these were salient with respect to Clinton's opponent, the incumbent George Bush, whose marriage seemed an archetype of stability and who was a decorated World War II veteran. The charge of infidelity may also have recalled for many voters the famous, campaign-ending photographs from 1988 of Gary Hart with Donna Rice. The way that Clinton handled these accusations illustrates some of the ways that speakers may craft ethos by inviting particular responses from their audience.

Responding to the charges of infidelity, Bill and Hillary Clinton appeared on a special edition of the CBS program "60 Minutes," following the 1992 Super Bowl. Clinton refused to deny directly the allegations regarding his alleged affair with Gennifer Flowers, but instead admitted to "causing pain in my marriage" and said that "I think most Americans who are watching this tonight — they'll know what we're saying, they'll get it." Apparently, Clinton and his campaign strategists were hoping that potential voters would accept his invitation to construct an image of Clinton as a fallible but honest candidate, one who perhaps was a lot like themselves.

Clinton responded to the "draft dodging" charges more directly but used a similar ethos-rebuilding strategy. He acknowledged that he had written a letter in 1969 to an official in the ROTC office at the University of Arkansas which seemed to suggest that Clinton used his enrollment in the ROTC as a way to evade the draft. However, on the ABC program "Nightline," Clinton invited potential voters to see the letter as one written long ago by a "deeply agitated 23-year-old boy." Clinton seems to take responsibility for his past actions while at the same time distancing himself from them. He is no longer a boy, and it might be presumed that he would make different decisions now if other circumstances were similar. Of course, he might indeed write a similar letter today, just as he might cause pain in his marriage in the future; remember that ethos is the image of the speaker as it is constructed through the interaction between speaker and audience.

Greta Marlow suggests that these examples from the 1992 presidential campaign show Clinton remaking himself, reestablishing his ethos through strategic speech. Rather than merely responding directly to accusations that he lacks character and consistency, Clinton builds a new character with the positive attributes of honesty and personal growth.[1] The potential viability of this new ethos may have contributed to the fact that the Whitewater scandal, a complex series of interrelated real estate ventures and bank loans that suggest the Clintons profited illegally while Bill Clinton was governor of Arkansas, largely has failed to become a credibility issue as did Watergate. Voters perhaps acknowledge that Clinton may have made some mistakes in the past, but, like infidelity and draft dodging, these mistakes were those of a younger and less sincere Bill Clinton.

In his 1996 reelection campaign, of course, Clinton could not run as a Washington outsider. Nevertheless, he was able to position himself as *more* of an outsider than his opponent, long-time senator Bob Dole. The public perception of Dole as one of Washington's career politicians may have been a factor in Clinton's reelection. Throughout the first half of 1997, reports surfaced that the Clintons used the White House illegally to solicit funds to finance his presidential reelection campaign. It is possible that such allegations may finally mark Clinton in public perception as an "insider" and thus as one who is just as tainted with the corruption of Washington politics as any other career politician.

Social and cultural elements within a context also can bear on ethos. Even though potential listeners may not know a speaker, they may associate him or her with a group or cause that suggests a network of values. For example, if an audience gathers for a speech in favor of reviving the Equal Rights Amendment, its members may identify the speaker as a feminist. To some audiences this label will suggest an interwoven fabric of positive values: the speaker is in favor of equality; the speaker believes in the right of women to determine their own destinies and control their own bodies; the speaker believes women should have confidence in and respect for themselves. For other listeners, a feminist represents threatening or negative values:

the speaker is too aggressive and competitive; the speaker scoffs at the values of home and family; the speaker hates men. Of course, neither set of perceptions is likely to be entirely true in any objective sense. What is important to understand is that the way a particular audience responds to the imperatives that have called forth the rhetoric can predispose that audience to view any speaker in a particular way and, accordingly, can influence the speaker's *ethos*.

Because of the impact of context on ethos, the critic of public addresses needs constantly to be reminded that perceptions of speakers *at the time they spoke* were influenced by that time and were not colored, as the critic's perceptions might be, by subsequent historical events. To have been an abolitionist before the Civil War, for example, was to be labeled a fanatic by most audiences and to ensure a negative ethos in most circumstances. Lincoln, whose popular image of "great emancipator" has come down to later generations, took great pains to dissociate himself from the abolitionists until well into his term of office. Speakers in England in the early nineteenth century who advocated reform of Parliament in order to enlarge the franchise vehemently denied the merest suggestion that they were "democrats." To be against slavery and for democracy may seem to the contemporary student automatically positive virtues; what the critic must realize is that the context helps determine what is virtuous and thus contributes to the speaker's ethos.

## The Speaker's Reputation

Our discussion of textual factors relates to a speaker's reputation. If a speaker is identified in a particular way with a particular issue, he or she takes on the generalized reputation that audiences may associate with other individuals who also identified in the same way with the same or similar issues. But many speakers are, or audiences believe them to be, known quantities. Listeners' awareness of anything that has occurred in a speaker's past can affect their prejudgment of the speaker.

One of the first matters about which an audience is likely to have information is the speaker's *issue orientation*. Because of other speeches, political actions, written works, or reports of positions the speaker has taken, the audience may have some awareness of the speaker's stand on the topic under consideration. Sometimes such information will be relatively concrete. The audience may know, for example, that the speaker voted against a constitutional amendment to prohibit school busing. Sometimes what is known is more vague: The speaker is a "conservative." And sometimes what the audience thinks it knows about the speaker is the result of labels attached by the speaker's opponents: She is a "big spender." The critic's task, then, is to assemble the available data about a speaker's actions or statements about a particular issue and assess the extent to which and the ways in which these positions were made public and were interpreted by others.

The speaker may also bring to the speaking situation a *public character*. His or her past actions, not only those associated with the specific issue being discussed, will contribute to audiences' impressions of the speaker's sincerity, trustworthiness, judgment, and ethical qualities. We have already mentioned Bill Clinton as a politician whose past actions continue to be an important influence on his public character. A good historical example of the impact of this aspect of ethos is that of General Dwight D. Eisenhower. Eisenhower, a hero of World War II, was generally regarded as an honest, trustworthy man who was used to solving massive problems. His political position on major issues was virtually unknown when he entered politics; indeed, most political leaders did not even know whether he was a Democrat or a Republican. In the 1990s, General Colin Powell appears to be similarly regarded by the American electorate, and he could prove to be a political force.

As the critic attempts to reconstruct the public character of a speaker, then much more is relevant than the speaker's identifiable stand on issues. The speaker's entire public life, as well as any part of his or her private life that is known or has been reported, is significant.

A speaker's reputation is also made up, in part, of an audience's beliefs about the speaker's *intelligence* and *experience*. It is apparent that for some listeners a speaker will be seen as someone who "knows what she's talking about." Aspects of the speaker's past will have established him or her as an authority on the question at hand. Simply being identified in an audience's mind as expert can enhance a speaker's ethos.

A noted medical researcher, for example, can expect to be regarded favorably by an audience gathered to hear a discussion of ways to prevent heart disease. Coaching clinics throughout the country attract eager young athletes who are willing to listen with great attention to a famous coach who has established authority by producing a string of winning teams. Eisenhower is an example of one whose favorable image makes him trustworthy. During the election campaign of 1952, he was able to strike a responsive chord in the American public by announcing, "I shall go to Korea." Eisenhower succeeded not because that statement revealed a specific plan for ending the war, but because he was viewed as an authority on military matters who could end a conflict that threatened to drag on endlessly.

During the 1992 campaign, Bill Clinton's lack of military experience became an important issue for many voters.

Eisenhower's statement about Korea was interpreted as signifying expertise because it was consistent with his known personal history as a successful general. An audience's perception of a speaker's integrity is also tempered by how consistent the members of that audience perceive a speaker to be, as well as the value they associate with that consistency. For example, a speaker who has changed his or her mind on issues can be seen as one who has grown and developed over the years, whose views have matured, or whose experiences have altered earlier convictions or attitudes. On the other hand, such a person may be viewed as an opportunist whose principles are easily adapted to prevailing popular currents of thought. In 1964, when Malcolm X left the Nation of Islam and repudiated the teachings of his long-time mentor, Elijah Muhammad, many of his followers rejected him because they suspected that he was affecting an attitude more acceptable to the dominant white culture. But, Malcolm X also gained many new followers from among those who interpreted his split with the Nation of Islam as a sign of growing personal and intellectual power. Malcolm himself emphasized his consistency, arguing that the rhetorical situation he faced had not changed and so neither, fundamentally, had his rhetoric: "How in the world can a white man expect a black man to change before *he* has changed?" he asked a reporter in 1965. "How do you expect us to change when the causes that made us as we are have not been removed?"[2]

Politicians often belabor one another with statements made in their past. In the New York primary in 1988, for example, Mayor Edward I. Koch, a supporter of Senator Albert Gore of Tennessee for the Democratic presidential nomination, was quick to remind the Jewish voters of New York City of what were construed as anti-Semitic remarks made four years earlier by Jesse Jackson, Gore's rival in the primary election. Congressmen from relatively conservative districts are frequently attacked for talking conservatively at home and voting liberally in Washington; such attacks clearly seem designed to call into question the sincerity and integrity of those officeholders.

Experience can relate not only to a speaker's expertise but also to his or her perceived interest in, and identification with, the audience. A speaker and an audience who have shared experiences and common tastes, similar backgrounds or even mutual prejudices, tend to be in sympathy with one another. A speaker who is seen as "one of us" may be viewed in a friendly light in comparison with a speaker about whom the audience is inclined to ask, "What does he know about what it's like to be poor?" — or to be black, or to work for a living, or to be lonely, or whatever. During the 1992 presidential campaign, for example, articles in several magazines suggested that many middle-class Americans were unlikely to vote for George Bush because they thought he was out of touch with their lifestyle. During the 1996 presidential campaign, perhaps sensing some similar popular sentiments, Bob Dole worked to establish himself as "Citizen Dole" during a summer speaking tour of the Midwest. Nonetheless, some commentators described his nomination acceptance speech as "nostalgic," focused on issues of past generations rather than on those that mattered to his immediate audience.

Audiences can be gullible; their yearnings for solutions to their problems can lead them to believe what and whom they want to believe. History abounds with examples of those who successfully courted audiences through appeals to their fears and desires in order to obtain power. But audiences can be suspicious, too. They can question the motivations of speakers who appear to have something to gain by soliciting their support. Certainly what the audience believes it knows about a speaker's motivations forms a part of the reputation that the speaker brings to a communicative situation. The used car salesman — fairly or unfairly — has become something of a symbol of the speaker whose word is to be discounted since he is perceived as one who has everything to gain and very little to lose in getting a car off the lot. What's in it for him? is a question that listeners can be expected to ask themselves as they listen to a speaker.

## Audience Priorities

A speaker's reputation, then, is made up of an audience's various perceptions of the speaker, based on what it knows or believes about the speaker. But in this case, the whole is certainly not equal to the sum of its parts. A critic cannot simply catalogue the speaker's strengths and weaknesses according to the speaker's character or intelligence or sincerity. What is *important* about a speaker's reputation, and how that reputation works for or against a speaker, is a function of the audience's needs, expectations, and priorities.

A speaker's character, for example, may be judged by his or her public actions, but whether those actions are interpreted favorably or unfavorably depends on the standards of the listeners. This point was made in the preceding chapter, but it is important to reemphasize it here. Some groups may judge a person to be of "good character" because he or she does not smoke or drink, whereas others would find such information largely irrelevant to whether the speaker would be, for example, a trustworthy manager of public funds. Other elements of a speaker's reputation, which are usually thought of as favorable, may not always be so. For example, there are those who like to believe that experts or intellectuals operate in a theoretical vacuum and lack "common sense." Many political incumbents have faced the charge that their experience in solving national problems flatly disqualifies them from leadership since the problems they addressed over their years in office remain unsolved; indeed, the movement to limit terms for political officeholders is a vivid reminder that many voters distrust those with too much political experience.

Furthermore, what constitutes an authority is a relative matter. Some listeners would pay close attention to a distinguished geologist or astronomer on the question of the age of the earth. Others would reject out-of-hand such persons as authorities and rely, instead, on the opinions of an evangelist who had no pretensions to scientific training or knowledge. Whether a Carl Sagan or a Jerry Falwell is the best authority on how the earth was formed depends on who is listening.

Authority can also be misplaced, and the critic needs to be aware of the fact that audiences are sometimes disposed to generalize widely. A distinguished physicist, who might rightly be regarded as an expert on certain scientific matters, may receive close attention when he is giving his opinion on political and social matters, on which he may have no more expertise than any well-informed, intelligent citizen. Audiences may have "heroes" — be they scientists, business leaders, or sports figures — whose authority, although logically limited to the field in which they have direct experience and in which they excel, is enlarged by listeners to include virtually any area in which such persons choose to express opinions. Such a phenomenon is the basis for much "endorsement" advertising, for example.

Authority can be spread and misplaced. It can also be disregarded by audiences when they perceive the basic issue as one lying outside the relevant area of authority. We have previously discussed the importance of understanding the ways in which issues are defined and focused. Take, for example, the issue of government regulation of the automobile industry. Some listeners may well concede that a scientist working for the Environmental Protection Agency is an authority on air pollution control, but audiences may dismiss the speaker's advocacy of strict regulation of emission control devices. Although audiences might grant that the speaker knows well the dangers to health and the scientific means of reducing those dangers, they might view the issue as economic, not scientific. Workers in Flint, Michigan, or Kokomo, Indiana, may be more responsive to a speaker whom they regard as an economic or political authority whose concern is with increasing automobile production. The critic, as a more dispassionate observer, may look at the welter of conflicting arguments and issues and reach a logical conclusion that our ultimate survival may depend on how well we learn to preserve our environment.

But the critic does not have to face stockholders who want more profits or a family whose standard of living depends on the wage earner's regular weekly check. What is crucial to listeners *as they see it* is what determines how an issue is focused, and this definition of an issue influences an audience's definition of an authority.

The crucial point here goes back to the definition of ethos. *The perception an audience has of a speaker* is what finally determines ethos. It ultimately rests not on a catalog of more or less objective personal qualities possessed by the speaker, but, rather, on what is known about those qualities and how they are interpreted by listeners.

## Ethos and the Message

Much of the discussion thus far has been concerned with what an audience knows (or believes it knows) about the speaker prior to a communication event. Part of the critic's task is to understand as fully as possible the ethos a speaker *brings to* a speaking situation. Yet it is also essential that the critic search for and explicate the ways in which the speaker both uses and *creates* ethos in his or her speech.

The text of the speech itself can reveal the *use of existing ethos* as a persuasive device. For instance, a general may use an example from his personal experience that reminds his listeners of his military expertise; a political leader may refer to the fact that she has served her constituents faithfully for a number of years; and a business executive may relate a personal anecdote that reveals her managerial skills. When President Lyndon Johnson presented his sweeping proposals for a new civil rights law that would effectively end political discrimination in the South, he reminded his audience that his own "roots go deeply into Southern soil," and, as a consequence, he knew "how agonizing racial feelings are."[3] The president was recommending to Congress a bill whose provisions would call forth bitter denunciation from southern political leaders. With this statement, Johnson identified himself not as an outsider who disparaged southern traditions, but as a southerner who could cherish his heritage and still demand serious and deep reform. When Prime Minister Winston Churchill, faced with an election challenge from the Labour Party, spoke to the British electorate near the end of World War II, he reminded voters of the situation when he had taken office and how he had led the country from "that memorable grim year when we stood alone against the might of Hitler with Mussolini at his tail. We gave all — and we have given all throughout to the prosecution of this war — and we have reached one of the great victorious haltingposts."[4] Speakers, then, will make efforts to exploit what they consider favorable elements of their ethos, and critics will attempt to discover the persuasive potential of such efforts.

It is also possible for speakers to strive to *create* favorable ethos within the speech itself. We have discussed previously some of the forces at work in the context and the audience that can dispose listeners to respond favorably or unfavorably to persuasive messages. As the speaker deals with such forces, he or she may enhance his or her ethos. A speaker with whom an audience can identify is a speaker for whom a positive ethos may be created.

The critic searches for the speaker's attempts to promote identification by discovering: (1) the ways in which the speaker associates himself or his position with an audience's values, and, conversely, pictures the opposition as linked to positions upon which an audience looks unfavorably; (2) the ways in which the speaker refutes or minimizes unfavorable aspects of his or her ethos; (3) the extent to which the speaker capitalizes on the positive ethos of those with whom the audience does identify; (4) the ways in which the speaker shows a grasp of the issues that are most important to the audience and a command of facts, information, and interpretations of those issues; (5) the ways in which the speaker seeks to convince audience members that she understands their problems and shares their aspirations and concerns; and (6) the ways in which the speaker reveals his motivations in order to counter impressions of self-interest.

A speaker may employ any or all of these tactics to enhance the listeners' image of her or him. In responding to speakers, as in so many aspects of life, we often find ourselves relying ultimately on very personal evaluations. On almost any given matter, there is such a welter of confusing and conflicting information that many feel too overwhelmed to make any sense of it. Others simply can't be bothered or are too busy with other things, or cannot begin to understand the meaning of masses of data and the many incompatible explanations of what those data mean. So we often resolve such difficulties by fixing on a *person* to save us or enlighten us or simply tell us what is best for us to do. Sometimes the results of such dependence are happy; sometimes they are disastrous. But there can be little doubt that reliance on persons we trust is a very potent force in shaping our behavior. The critic who would understand the persuasive impact implicit in a message must assess carefully and thoroughly the ways in which the speaker tries to promote such reliance by listeners.

## Ethos and Divergent Audiences

One very obvious problem for the speaker, and certainly for the critic, is that a speaker's ethos, by definition, varies with audiences and varies over time. That is to say, a speaker may have a positive ethos with one set of listeners and a negative ethos with another; a speaker who is highly regarded at one time may be considered a has-been ten years later. When speakers hope to address mass audiences, the difficulty posed by variable ethos is compounded.

Major political speeches, for example, must, of necessity, be addressed to people of different ages from different economic and racial backgrounds in different parts of the country. In the case of a major presidential address, not only are many different Americans listening, but people and governments throughout the world — some friendly, some unfriendly, some uncertain — are also potential auditors of the message. This complexity may well cause some speakers to attempt to say nothing that offends anyone and thus end up saying nothing at all. But what is of concern for the critic is the way in which any speaker balances the potential impact of the message on his or her ethos with different groups. In a later section of this book a case study of the varieties and problems of criticism is presented. A speech by then President Richard Nixon is reproduced, followed by several critical studies of that speech. One of the major issues that emerges from those studies is the question of how Nixon dealt with this very problem of audiences for whom he had divergent images. One solution to the dilemma of differing audiences is offered by a critic who argues, in effect, that Nixon did the most rhetorically wise thing by simply writing off those people whom he had no chance to persuade and concentrating instead on those who were susceptible to his efforts to convince. Another critic takes sharp issue with this assessment, arguing that it was the president's responsibility to answer his critics.[5] No matter what position the critic takes, the fact remains that he or she must grapple with the complexities of ethos, describing and explaining the many facets of the problem as it is faced — or ignored — by the speaker.

## The Speaker in Action: Assessing Delivery

For all that an audience may know or believe about a speaker, for all that a text might reveal about the speaker's efforts to exploit or create audience perceptions, a speech is, after all, actually delivered to an audience: it is performed. Much of what has been said thus far in this book relates to rhetorical artifacts in general, be they speeches, pamphlets, editorials, or polemical essays. But one of the most obviously unique qualities of a speech is that it is oral and that the audience receives it directly from its originator.

Many speeches are known through reports — either by the media or through accounts of other people, and many people will hear a two-minute summary of a major speech by a national figure and perhaps see and hear a forty-five-second excerpt from the speech. Nevertheless, a speaker who is actually giving a speech is intimately bound up with the persuasive message itself, and the potential impact of *how* a speaker says what he or she says is inevitably present. As communication researchers W. Barnett Pearce and Bernard J. Brommel observe, "A written message is not the same as the same words spoken aloud. . . ."[6]

The critic who wishes to come to a complete understanding of oral discourse must take delivery into account. Understanding delivery, like understanding everything else rhetorical, can best be done within a full knowledge of the limitations of the situation and the expectations of the audience.

Audiences can and do form impressions of a speaker that have the potential to influence a speaker's ethos on the basis of the speaker's delivery. Rhetorical critics have long assumed that answers to the three basic questions concerning delivery — How does the speaker sound? How does the speaker look? How does the speaker move? — will give us insights into the nature of a speaker's effectiveness and clues to the image he or she would project. Experimental evidence also points to the conclusion that nonverbal elements in a message have some influence on the audience's reception of the message, although research findings do not conclusively establish a precise cause-and-effect relationship between specific nonverbal action and audience responses.[7]

Empirical observations from our own experience further confirm the conclusion that nonverbal messages are considered as, and designed to be, persuasive. Advertisers go to great lengths to ensure that their products are promoted by, or seen to be used by, or even seen in the same picture with persons they believe will suggest the rugged or sexy or classy image they wish to project for those products. Political hucksters do the same thing, surrounding their candidate with his or her family, showing the candidate engaged in earnest conversation with factory workers, picturing the candidate in a friendly and confidential exchange with the president of the United States (if he's popular). It is only common sense to assume that such efforts seek to create the impression that the candidate holds traditional American family values and that he or she is a friend of working people and a confidant of the powerful.

What a speaker *does* in front of any audience almost always has some effect on that audience. For example, some listeners tend to respond stereotypically to regional dialects. Depending on where one is from, one may form immediate opinions of the intelligence, energy, and educational level of the speaker whose dialect demonstrates him or her to be from the hills of Kentucky or from Alabama or from

Brooklyn. Speakers whose monotonous voices bore audiences seem to have the added disadvantage of being less credible as well.

Correctly or incorrectly, a speaker's vocal qualities can suggest corresponding personality traits to audiences. The author of a highly publicized study of female sexual behavior came to speak at a large university campus. The speaker startled and dismayed some members of the audience because her breathy, "little girl" voice suggested to many that she could not be taken too seriously. Indeed, audiences tend to associate such vocal quality with immaturity. Though nothing the speaker said either strengthened or diminished the scientific validity of her published findings, some auditors may have felt uneasy about accepting those findings because the credibility of the speaker was tarnished by the immature image her voice helped to project. It seems safe to assume that when audiences judge a speaker's voice to be harsh, or nasal, or deviating in some way from "normal" quality, the speaker's ethos will suffer.

The way that speakers look and how they move also contribute to the formation of audience perceptions. Certainly President Carter's casual cardigans were meant to suggest an informality and directness when he gave his "fireside chats" to the American people. The famous smiles of popular politicians from Franklin Roosevelt to Dwight Eisenhower to Ronald Reagan suggested to some a warmth and sincerity that influenced their perceptions of the speaker's reliability and trustworthiness. We have all observed speakers whose tense, tiny movements seem to indicate tentativeness or whose exaggerated motions distract us or embarrass us.

In fact, delivery of which we are extremely conscious is likely to be delivery that does not help a speaker's ethos or contribute to the successful communication of that speaker's message. "Distracting" mannerisms do just that — they distract us from the message and irritate listeners.

Of greatest interest to the critic is the relationship between the qualities of a speaker's delivery and the content of the speaker's message. Audiences tend to be sensitive to whether a speaker's nonverbal behavior seems to contradict or deviate from the intended message. Thus, a speaker whose voice, gestures, and appearance convey the impression of remoteness while the message tries to say that the speaker cares about his or her audience, or a speaker who appears to take lightly a serious topic, will have his or her ethos impaired. Elements of delivery thus have the potential to interact with verbal elements. In 1988, for example, George Bush was plagued by the so-called "wimp factor." Questions about his ability to lead were implied by the suspicion that he was not "his own man," that he was a good "second banana," a man with an excellent résumé but not a striking personality. For his part, Michael

Dukakis was seen as dull — competent but not inspiring. For both men, their acceptance speeches became important to enhancing the "forceful," "dynamic," "inspirational" image considered essential to a credible presidential candidacy. To an inordinate extent, then, the way the speeches were delivered — as well as what was said in the speeches — became important as a measure of leadership. Both candidates took great pains preparing to deliver the speech (as well as preparing the text of the speech), and both seemed, through their delivery, to experience some measure of immediate success in improving their images.

The crucial point is that although delivery does seem to influence audience perceptions, it does not seem to be a critical determinant of audience perception in and of itself. What the critic tries to assess is the potential interactions between content and delivery in an effort to uncover aspects that could contribute to the overall perception formed by an audience, and, accordingly, could impact on the speaker's ethos.

## Summary

In this chapter, the fundamental question raised for the critic's consideration is: *What does the speaker bring to the communication situation, or capitalize on within the situation, that influences the audience's perception of that speaker?* The speaker's ethos can serve to help or hinder her or his persuasiveness, and the critic needs an accurate picture of what the speaker's ethos is for any given audience at any given time.

The following series of questions will help to summarize this chapter and will serve as a guide to the critic in reconstructing the ethos of the speaker.

1. What are the *historical and political factors* that can influence the audience's perception of the speaker?
2. What are the *social and cultural elements* within the context that bear upon ethos formation?
3. What is the speaker's *orientation toward the issue* under consideration?
4. How have the speaker's past actions served to form a *public character* perceived by the audience?
5. What is the audience's view of the speaker's *intelligence and experience*?
6. What does the speaker's past suggest to an audience about the speaker's *genuine interest* in its needs and concerns?

7. What factors in the speaker's background are most *salient* to the audience?
8. What devices, techniques, or strategies does the speaker *employ in the message itself* to enhance his ethos?
9. How does the speaker's ethos *vary among potential receivers* of his or her message?
10. What *distinguishing features in the speaker's delivery* can be described, and what is their potential for audience influence?
11. What potential for influencing ethos exists in the *relationship between the content of the speaker's message and his or her delivery*?

## Notes

1. See Greta R. Marlow, "Dodging Charges and Charges of Dodging," in *Bill Clinton on Stump, State, and Stage: The Rhetorical Road to the White House*, ed. Stephen A. Smith (Fayetteville: The University of Arkansas Press, 1994), pp. 150–162. We are indebted to Marlow's essay for much of the foregoing analysis. For another discussion of Clinton's alleged inconsistencies, see, in the same volume, Craig Allen Smith, "The Jeremiadic Logic of Bill Clinton's Policy Speeches."
2. Malcolm X, "Prospects for Freedom in 1965," (speech at Militant Labor Forum, Jan. 7, 1965), *Two Speeches by Malcolm X* (New York: Pathfinder Press, 1965), p. 22.
3. Lyndon B. Johnson, "We Shall Overcome," *Contemporary American Voices*, ed. James R. Andrews and David Zarefsky (New York: Longmans, 1992), p. 96.
4. Winston S. Churchill, "The Conservative Programme," *British Public Addresses, 1828–1960*, ed. James H. McBath and Walter R. Fisher (Boston: Houghton Mifflin, 1971), p. 469.
5. See the exchange between Campbell and Hill, pp. 175–200.
6. W. Barnett Pearce and Bernard J. Brommel, "Vocalic Communication in Persuasion," *Quarterly Journal of Speech*, 58 (1972), 305.
7. See, for example, W. Barnett Pearce and Forrest Conklin, "Nonverbal Vocalic Communication and Perception of a Speaker," *Speech Monographs*, 38 (1971), 235–241; John Waite Bowers, "The Influence of Delivery on Attitudes Toward Concepts and Speakers," *Speech Monographs*, 32 (1965), 154–158; David W. Addington, "The Relationship of Selected Vocal Characteristics to Personality Perception," *Speech Monographs*, 35 (1968), 492–503; David W. Addington, "The Effects of Vocal Variations on Ratings of Source Credibility," *Speech Monographs*, 38 (1971), 242–247.

# 4

# Constituents of the Rhetorical Act: The Text

## The Whole and Its Parts

As difficult as it is to understand the many complex forces at work in the rhetorical environment, beginning rhetorical critics often find the analysis of the text itself most baffling. Yet the text is at the heart of the critic's work: only through the careful analysis of its intricacies can the critic begin to interpret its overall functioning and judge its rhetorical worth. (This is not to say that the speech itself is always the most important single variable in a context. The critic should not fall into the trap of believing that the speech is the cause of whatever follows it.)

As was mentioned earlier, a careful and thoughtful reading of the text should precede examination of other elements in the rhetorical act. Some critics will prefer to carry out a more detailed textual analysis initially, turning then to contextual factors to enlarge their understanding of the text and to refine and enrich their interpretation and evaluation. As the critical process has been described here, the culmination is analysis, interpretation, and judgment. But, in either case, the text itself must be of central critical concern.

The text of a speech is an organic whole. It lives because its parts function together. No sensible student of rhetoric assumes that any persuasive message is produced additively, that is, that logic is added to emotion or that style is added to content in order to produce the final result. Nevertheless, in order to understand the physiology — how all the parts function together — the critic must study the anatomy — how each of the parts is constructed. To that end, the critic begins by systematically taking apart the text through an orderly analysis, studying the text closely and carefully.

## Analytical Categories

The critic begins to look for features that are fundamentally under the speaker's control. Though the speaker must take contextual features into account in constructing the message, such features cannot be readily modified or influenced. The speaker cannot, for example, change the age or sex of his or her listeners. He or she cannot alter historical events or refashion cultural values. (Although the speaker certainly can and does try to interpret events and values so as to give them particular meaning for an audience.) And whereas the speaker may be in part responsible for his or her own ethos and certainly can make efforts to manipulate his or her image, an audience's perception of the speaker is not entirely dependent on the speaker's choices. The text of the speech, however, does represent the speaker's choices — out of the range of possible material to be used and ways that the material might be put together, the speaker has selected certain material and certain arrangements to accomplish a purpose. In trying to identify these choices, the critic may be guided by certain categories that direct attention to crucial aspects of the discourse.

### *Argument*

Any speech makes certain assertions about reality. The speech grows out of a situation in which the speaker perceives the need to induce listeners to believe or feel or act in certain ways. The speaker has a conclusion he or she wishes to see accepted or a course of action he or she wishes taken. The principal conclusion of the speech, along with the reasons that sustain that conclusion, is the argument of the speech.

Studying the argument of the speech provides the critic with internal evidence of the speaker's purpose. What is the speaker really getting at? What is the speaker trying to do? These questions are best answered through an examination of the speaker's own ideas. The speaker may not clearly or directly state his or her purpose, but the speech itself will surely reveal the speaker's intention.

Perhaps the most famous speech in which the speaker's *stated* purpose is not the purpose revealed by the argument of the speech is Mark Antony's fictional funeral oration for Julius Caesar in Shakespeare's tragedy. The speech reveals that Mark Antony's explicitly stated purpose of simply providing the requisite forms for a decent burial — "I come to bury Caesar, not to praise him" — is not the same as his actual purpose, which is to incite the mob to take vengeful action against Caesar's assassins.

The overall argument of a speech is made up of a number of specific arguments, units that in themselves make assertions or draw conclusions. Taken together, arguments are designed to achieve the speaker's purpose. The critic who would understand how a speaker thinks and how that speaker wishes to direct the thinking of the audience must consider these units to illuminate the relationship between the fundamental parts of an argument. An argument is made up of specific bits of information or motivational material that can be called the *data*, a *conclusion*, and some form of *ideational link* between the two. Another way of describing an argument would be to say that it is the process whereby a speaker presents an idea which he or she wishes to have accepted, offers evidence that will promote acceptance, and demonstrates why or how the evidence is sufficient to warrant acceptance of the idea.

It is very important for the critic to realize that the parts of an argument do not dictate its organization and that the speaker will not always explicitly state all the parts of an argument. Indeed, one of the critic's tasks is to identify the implicit parts of an argument and to reconstruct the argument in its entirety in order to understand precisely the relationship between its parts. Only then will the critic uncover the hidden assumptions, the sometimes invisible links in the chain that the speaker hopes to forge. And only then will the critic have the precise data necessary to judge the worth of the argument.

To understand an argument more fully, let us take an example. The following is an excerpt from President Lyndon Johnson's speech on behalf of a civil rights bill that he was preparing to send to Congress in 1963:

> The history of this country in large measure is the history of expansion of that right to all of our people. Many of the issues of civil rights are very complex and most difficult. But about this there can and should be no argument: every American citizen must have an equal right to vote.
>
> There is no reason which can excuse the denial of that right. There is no duty which weighs more heavily on us than the duty we have to insure that right. Yet the harsh fact is that in many places in this country men and women are kept from voting simply because they are Negroes.
>
> Every device of which human ingenuity is capable has been used to deny this right. The Negro citizen may go to register only to be told that the day is wrong, or the hour is late, or the official in charge is absent.
>
> And if he persists and, if he manages to present himself to the registrar, he may be disqualified because he did not spell out his middle name, or because he abbreviated a word on the application. And if he manages to fill out an application, he is given a test.

> The registrar is the sole judge of whether he passes this test. He may be asked to recite the entire Constitution or explain the most complex provisions of state law.
>
> And even a college degree cannot be used to prove that he can read or write. For the fact is that the only way to pass these barriers is to show a white skin.
>
> Experience has clearly shown that the existing process of law cannot overcome systematic and ingenious discrimination. No law that we now have on the books, and I have helped to put three of them there, can insure the right to vote when local officials are determined to deny it. In such a case, our duty must be clear to all of us.
>
> The Constitution says that no person shall be kept from voting because of his race or his color. We have all sworn an oath before God to support and to defend that Constitution. We must now act in obedience of that oath.[1]

All the parts of an argument can be seen clearly in this passage. The conclusion of the argument is that African-Americans are wrongly being denied their constitutional right to vote simply because they are black. The data offered to support his conclusion are a series of specific examples of devices used to thwart African-Americans in their attempts to register. There are two explicit links between the data and the conclusion: the barriers to voting are based on race since "the only way to pass these barriers is to show a white skin," and to establish racial barriers to voting is wrong since "the Constitution says that no person shall be kept from voting because of his race or his color." Implicit links between data and conclusion are also to be found. The argument carries weight when there is a shared assumption that there is no justification for the violation of the Constitution and when there is a shared adherence to the value embodied by the concept of "equality under the law."

In the analysis of arguments, some critics find useful a model that has been adapted from the work of the philosopher Stephen Toulmin.[2] The Toulmin model can be useful because it offers a diagrammatic way of looking at the parts of an argument, at how they articulate, and particularly, at how the link between the data and the conclusion may be established — implicitly or explicitly. This is not a model that all critics will want to use; it is developed here merely as a way of illustrating the kinds of relationships between ideas and specific bits of content that can be uncovered in the text. The parts of the model are as follows:

(D) *Data*. These are the "facts" as the speaker sees them and presents them to the audience.

(C) *Claim*. This is the conclusion that the speaker draws from the facts.

(W) *Warrant*. This is a statement, whether explicit or implied, that justifies moving from the Data to the Claim.

(B) *Backing*. This is specific information, whether implicit or explicit, that supports the Warrant.

(R) *Reservation*. This is a statement that identifies possible areas of exception to the Warrant and Claim. (It need not appear in the speech.)

(Q) *Qualifier*. This is a statement that indicates the degree of certainty with which the Claim may be held.

Put in the form of a diagram, the model would look like this:

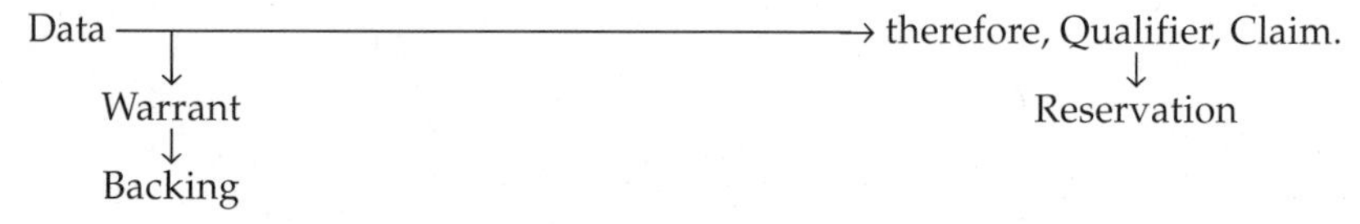


On first encounter, the model may seem somewhat complex to the beginning critic. But the subtleties of an argument are not always apparent on the initial reading, and the model is designed to illuminate complexities and uncover relationships. Let us consider the model using the Johnson passage once again. The Johnson argument might be diagrammed as follows:

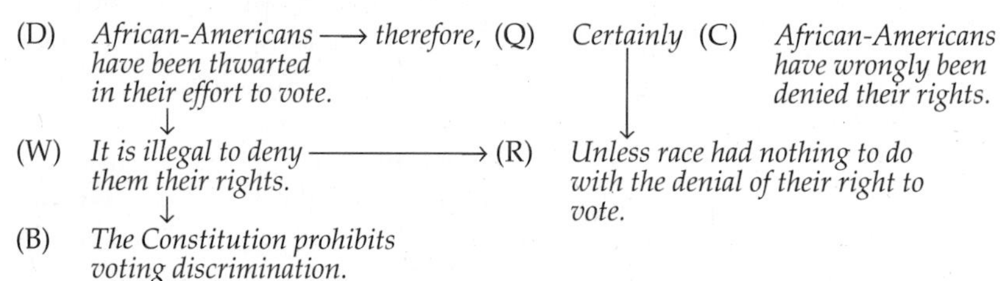


In light of this diagram, the Johnson argument might be restated like this: African-Americans have been thwarted in their efforts to vote; *since* it is illegal to do this *because* the Constitution prohibits discrimination; *therefore* African-Americans have been wrongly denied their rights *unless* it can be shown that they were not barred from voting because of their color.

Although the critic might initially feel that using the Toulmin model to lay out an argument is a somewhat intricate process, it is possible through practice to become more adept at diagramming. This approach to argument, however, is not suggested as *the* way to understand argument. It is merely an example of one way that a very careful reading of the text, guided by some systematic approach to each argument, can uncover the complex relationship between ideas and evidence.

Systematic analysis of arguments also can illuminate for the critic the ways in which individual arguments form links in the chain of reasoning that supports *the* argument of the speech. One might continue with an examination of the Johnson speech, for example, in which the Claim of the argument as diagrammed can be seen to become the Data for the argument that follows:

(D) *African-Americans have wrongly been denied their rights.* → therefore, (Q) *Certainly* (C) *Congress should pass a law that would guarantee the free exercise of these rights.*

↓ (from Q) (R) *Unless congressional action would be illegal or ineffective.*

(W) *It is immoral to deny persons their just rights in a democracy.* → (R)

↓

(B) *Americans traditionally value equality under the law.*

The separate arguments, and the way they relate to each other, form the building blocks of *the* argument of the speech. The careful analysis of these arguments will begin to uncover data that form the basis for the critical investigation of other analytical categories.

### *Supporting Materials*

Within any ideational unit of the speech, the speaker will make some effort to make the conclusion understandable and believable to the audience. The critic's task is to identify the forms of support used and to determine the role played by any supporting device in the development of an argument.

The basic forms of supporting material are generally known to students of rhetoric. Most supporting material could be classified as example, definition, analogy, testimony, statistical data, and scientific results. The analysis of the text leads the critic carefully to classify these forms and to note the extent and nature of their use.

It is of prime importance that the critic realize that whereas identification of forms of support is necessary, *merely* identifying them leads to no significant insights. To say only that a speaker used numerous examples or relied heavily on statistics does not, in itself, provide much illumination of the discourse. What is significant is the *function* that supporting material performs.

The critic seeks to uncover both logical and psychological dimensions in support for an idea. *Examples* that are specific and real may serve to demonstrate that actual cases do exist, yet, unless their typicality can also be demonstrated or is accepted, their psychological power is generally more formidable than their logical power. Examples help to make vivid and real generalizations that might otherwise be abstract;

thus they promote audience identification. *Definition* serves the logical foundation of explaining what terms mean. It is also basic to audience adaptation since it recognizes the possibility of audience members' technical or educational limitations. It has the potential to reassure an audience that the speaker has a psychologically positive concern for them and an awareness of their limitations. On the other hand, it could cause an informed audience to view the speaker as patronizing or pompous. *Analogy* is a means of comparing the known or experienced with the unknown or not experienced. To the extent to which the two ideas or things juxtaposed really are comparable in essential elements, analogies lead to logical predictions of what the unknown will be like. Analogies relate the familiar with the unfamiliar, providing listeners with an identification point from which to move on to what may be more complex or little known to them. The potentially threatening nature of the unknown may thus be reduced. *Testimony* by a relevant expert enhances the logical quality of the conclusions reached by the speaker. It may also serve to promote audience confidence in the speaker by allying him or her with recognized authority. *Statistical data,* when recent and accurate, may logically support conclusions related to such matters as how widespread a particular problem is or the rate at which a problem is increasing. It can also suggest to an audience that the problem is encompassing enough to be likely to affect them. *Scientific results* provide empirical evidence in support of generalizations. Like testimony, scientific results bring to bear the findings of experts in the field under discussion. Both scientific results and statistical data also possess a positive psychological appeal in a society such as ours, which places value on things that may be called "scientific."

The critic, then, examines the discourse to determine what kinds of supporting material were used and to discover *how* they were used. As an example of one procedure that the critic could employ in examining supporting material, let us consider a modified Toulmin model to uncover *function*. Using this approach, the critic could focus on a particular piece of support, determine the conclusion that support seeks to justify, and then speculate on the Warrant or Warrants that would be necessary to justify progress from the Data to the Claim. The two following examples, though not exhaustive or detailed, serve to illustrate the process.

(D) *Example*: John, who wants to go to medical school, needs an A− in his English lit course to maintain his high academic average. The final term paper counted 50 percent of his grade, so he got his roommate, → (C) The pressures to succeed are so great as to encourage cheating.

an English major, to
write it for him.

↓

(W) John could not have succeeded
without cheating.

(D) *Analogy*: When a bill cutting corporate taxes was passed before, prices remained the same while profits increased. → (C) The effect of the present bill to cut corporate taxes will be to increase profits while prices stay fixed.

↓

(W) Economic circumstances are similar, and the effect of similar bills on profits and prices will be the same.

These two illustrations show one way a critic can go about finding relationships; they demonstrate how the particular piece of evidence (example and analogy) is warranted as proof. Such an exercise could help the critic describe how supporting materials seem designed to serve the ends of the speaker. It also offers insights into how arguments may be working and will provide the critic with specific data upon which to base observations on the logical soundness and/or psychological appeal of the overall argument of the speech. Such judgments may occur to the critic as he or she proceeds with the analysis of the text. These judgments, however, must be tentative. Only when the analysis of the text is complete and the critic begins to discern patterns and relationships in the discourse itself and to relate these patterns to the context outside the discourse can the critic make more definitive judgments.

### *Structure*

As the critic analyzes the arguments that contribute to the goal of furthering the speaker's purpose, the critic will begin to discern the ways in which these arguments are put together in order to suggest relationships between them. Each idea developed by the speaker becomes the backdrop against which the next idea is painted. Thus, the ideas and supporting material of the speech form a pattern that the critic can identify and study to determine how the form in which the material is presented might help to move the audience toward acceptance of the persuasive purpose of the speech.

It is probably best for the critic to organize this phase of analysis by constructing a detailed outline of the speech. The critic should seek to identify the main ideas of the speech, arrange supporting material to discover the ways in which it serves to make the ideas understandable and believable to the audience, uncover the transitions and internal summaries that function to tie the ideas together, and isolate the ways in which the speaker sets the context for the speech in the introduction and gives direction to further audience thought and action in the conclusion. Such a reconstruction of the speech should point out for the critic the logical and psychological connections between the parts of the speech.

The critic is then in a position to understand the ways in which the speaker has arranged his or her ideas and material in order to promote such connections for the audience. That is, the critic, understanding how the speaker's ideas relate to each other, can describe the ways in which the speaker patterned those ideas into a meaningful sequence. The sequencing of ideas demonstrates how the speaker perceives, and/or wishes the audience to perceive, the nature of the issues under consideration. For example, if a speaker arranges his or her ideas in a *chronological* pattern, a historical view of the situation is suggested. This form will imply that what has happened in the past leads to the present state of events and provides clues with which to deal with present problems.

Several different patterns of organization are open to the speaker, and different patterns may predominate in different parts of the speech. These patterns are important to understand because they demonstrate the speaker's perspective on the problem and suggest the movement of ideas he or she wishes the audience to follow. A *topical* arrangement of ideas suggests independent ideas, which, taken together, show what the speaker thinks are the most relevant factors in the case. A speaker, for example, may develop economic, military, and political facets of a particular case, implying that moral or social considerations are not germane. A *cause-to-effect* or *effect-to-cause* development emphasizes the consequences of actions and events and can lead to the prediction of outcomes of actions taken by others as contrasted or compared with those advocated by the speaker. A *problem-solution* pattern defines the way the speaker perceives the problem, suggests criteria for the satisfactory solution of the problem, and shows how the speaker's solution meets those criteria. A *climactic* pattern may lead an audience from the most simple ideas to the most complex, or from ideas that are generally accepted and hence likely to be emotionally neutral to those that are more controversial and may generate highly intense emotional responses.

An investigation of the pattern or patterns that can be discerned in the speech point the critic's way to a fuller disclosure of the speaker's point of view with regard to the topic itself and to the speaker's conception of ways to motivate audiences. It should be understood, however, that the speaker may not *present* the speech in such a way that the pattern is immediately apparent. The critic's careful outline of the speech, for example, may show that when the speaker offers an idea that an audience might consider controversial or might react to with some initial antagonism, the speaker is using an indirect approach, carefully reviewing the evidence before fully disclosing the conclusion. In effect, the speaker turns the logical outline upside down, presenting the supporting material before disclosing the main idea that it supports. Another way of looking at this phenomenon might be to say that the critic, in order to see how ideas and evidence relate, prepares a *deductive* outline, whereas the speaker may choose to deliver the speech *inductively*.

### *Style*

Style is perhaps the most difficult single constituent of the rhetorical act for the critic. That is because the way in which a speaker uses language — from word choice to sentence construction to figurative devices — is so intimately bound up with the speaker's own personality and perspective, the audience's experiences and expectations, and the demands and constraints of the time that dictate "taste." The analysis of style is also complicated by the fact that it is very difficult to describe in such a way as to identify its unique qualities, and because it is so interwoven with meaning and argument.

Perhaps the overarching question for the critic to attempt to answer when considering style is the "fitness" of language. Traditionally, the test of good style is that it is clear, correct, appropriate, and exhibits pleasing aesthetic qualities. These criteria all depend on interaction among speaker, audience, and context. One way to approach the study of style is to separate its interdependent elements. Such a division must be artificial to some extent; no single aspect of a rhetorical act can stand alone in isolation from the whole. But, as we have said, for the purposes of analysis it is often necessary to "freeze" a complex, ongoing process so that its individual components might be examined.

The critic might begin with the various *external* factors that can influence the choice of an appropriate, or fitting, style. We discussed the context and audience of the rhetorical act at length in Chapter 2, and here need only suggest that the situation that the speech has been crafted to address, and the background and expectations of the audience, together suggest aspects of "fitness" that might be assessed by the critic. The language appropriate at an outdoor rally demanding that a redwood forest be spared from imminent logging would probably not "fit" an extended classroom lecture about the intricacies of the redwood forest ecosystem. The immediacy of the first situation invites a more emotionally charged rhetorical style than the relative distance of the second. A discussion of bridges that might be perfectly clear — and thus fitting — to an audience made up of structural engineers may not be clear at all to an audience with less technical expertise in that area.

The critic might next turn to an investigation of the ways that the *form* of the speech fits the *content*. Specifically, the critic's scrutiny of style may also include a search for the ways in which style is used to further the argument of the speech. By using a parallel construction, for instance, a speaker may suggest parallel ideas or consequences to his or her audience so that language construction furthers analogy and thus becomes "evidence" in and of itself. A speaker might allege that "The American determination to ensure liberty for all led us to found this nation. To ensure liberty we fought each other over the issue of whether or not men and women could be held as property by other men. To ensure liberty we twice sent our young men to die on the battlegrounds of Europe. To ensure liberty we must stand ready today to sacrifice our bounty and our blood in whatever part of the world that liberty is threatened." The parallel construction of this segment clearly implies that historical situations are comparable to the present situation; it acts as "proof" that what was done before must be done again. The critic, in this case, has the right to question whether such a stylistic construction is "fitting" support for the conclusion.

Another internal element of style that might engage the attention of the critic involves discerning the *tone* of the speech. Language signals the speaker's attitude — whether serious or light, comic or tragic, sympathetic or hostile, realistic or idealistic — toward the audience and the topic itself. A close study of style can reveal the *level of generality*, ranging from the abstract to the concrete, and the *level of complexity* evident in the choice of mono- or polysyllabic words, the length and configuration of sentences, and the like. The *diction* of the speech is indicated by the way the speaker's language suggests the level of formality with which he or she approaches the audience and the topic. The *texture* of the speech is uncovered by paying close attention to the speaker's stylistic devices; that is, by the way in which the speaker uses such schemes as parallelism or antithesis, figurative language such as similes or metaphors, and imagery.

The various external and internal elements of language style are not separate or autonomous. They constitute a complex matrix of interrelationships. Malcolm X is an example of a speaker who had a self-conscious sense of rhetorical style, altering his language depending on the relationship he wished to craft between himself, his audience, and his subject. For example, he spoke in a significantly different style when addressing predominantly white audiences than when addressing predominantly African-American audiences. Depending on the arguments he was making in his speeches to these various audiences, he used different analogies, examples, and types of supporting material and developed a different tone in each case. When addressing a regularly scheduled meeting of the Nation of Islam, for example, Malcolm often assumed the role of a teacher; his speech might resemble a lecture, a carefully reasoned and rather academically detached marshaling of various facts and anecdotes, perhaps to explicate and support in detail certain elements of the Nation's ideology. His vocabulary, tone, and degree of stylistic complexity all contributed to his role in this speech situation and to the attitude toward his subject that he wished to cultivate in his audience. In other words, Malcolm X negotiated a fitting relationship between the expectations of his audience and the stylistic qualities of his speech. If Malcolm was addressing a gathering of predominantly white college students, however, the expectations of the audience and the message that Malcolm desired to get across invited an altogether different style.[3]

The critical analysis of style, then, is guided by the careful examination of the *functions* of language in discourse. The critic's goal thus is to describe the ways in which language is *used* to promote the purpose of the speech and the potential influences of this use of language on listeners. The important thing for the critic to keep in mind in this analysis is that "fit" implies a *relationship*. The style of a speech is the result of the relationship between qualities and their potential to influence audiences. Merely examining a speech and identifying all of the metaphors, for example, does little to illuminate the text. It is the way that the various stylistic elements of a text are related to, correspond with, or undermine elements of the speech's context and subject matter that are of interest to the critic.[4]

## Interpretation

The analysis of a speech provides the critic with a mass of specific detail concerning the way in which the speech has been crafted by the speaker's choices. As the analysis proceeds, the critic will inevitably, if peripherally, begin to assess the meaning of these data and their interrelatedness. When the analysis is finished, the critic can devote full attention to drawing out and examining the patterns that have begun to emerge from the analysis.

After scrutinizing the argument, supporting material, structure, and style of a speech, the critic knows (if we may return to an earlier analogy) the anatomy of the discourse. Now the critic must make inferences about the physiology of the discourse. That is, now that the critic has ordered and arranged the parts, she or he must now investigate the ways that these parts work together to produce meaning. This process of inferring *how the discourse works* is interpretation.

Interpretation of a rhetorical work always involves the search for the meaning and function of the various parts of the text as they relate to the context. The critic's task is to explain how the text and context are mutually dependent and mutually effective. Only through such an explanation can the critic promote readers' understanding and appreciation for the speech.

Traditionally, critics have sought to interpret a speech by assessing the ways in which the data show that the speaker has identified his or her rhetorical problems and opportunities and has adapted the materials of the speech to meet these circumstances. The audience has assumed a central place in traditional criticism, and the critic has sought to find significance in the speaker's adaptations to a particular audience. This critical focus tends to bear most directly on a speech as a unique event, a situation in which a speaker has a specific purpose to accomplish with a specific group of auditors. A traditional critical interpretation would be addressed to this situation.

Perhaps one of the most potent forces in shaping the thinking of modern critics has been the work of Kenneth Burke.[5] Burke's *dramatic criticism* is based on his conception of human beings as symbol-using animals who act out the social drama that is life by inducing action and shaping attitudes in others through language. For Burke, rhetoric is a means of using language to overcome the divisions that exist between people. He sees "the use of language as a symbolic means of inducing cooperation in beings that by nature respond to symbols."[6] *Identification*, a key term in the Burkeian scheme, is promoted when language is used to reduce divisiveness and to bring the speaker and listener closer together in their conceptions and perceptions of the world around them, the ultimate achievement being a psychological fusion that Burke calls *consubstantiality*.

A rhetor's language choices form a pattern that Burke calls a *strategy*, which is not a term employed exclusively by Burkeian critics. Indeed, almost any critic who describes a pattern of choice make by a speaker could be said to be describing a strategy. A critic could look at a speaker's methods of adaptation to an audience and describe the way these methods work together to promote the speaker's purpose as a strategy. Generally, however, critics tend to consider strategy as a representation of a speaker's deliberate design in persuasion; choices have normally been thought of and written of as if they were *conscious* choices. Burke, who contends that identification "can include a partially 'unconscious' factor in appeal," conceives of strategies as the means of bringing about identification, and therefore admits the possibility that all strategies are not wholly intentional.[7] The critic who would draw on Burke in interpreting a rhetorical act would seek to discover and illuminate the strategies operating through language that promote the desired end of identification.

Traditionally, speeches have tended to be examined by critics as discrete entities, and in a sense they are — the way a century or historical period is discrete, the way a painting or a film is discrete, and the way a person's life is discrete. As we suggested in Chapter 3, speeches are performances, and like all performances they traditionally have been assigned beginnings and endings. Nevertheless, rhetorical events are part of a *process*; they are influenced by and can influence other events. To understand fully the circumstances surrounding a speech act, the critic will need to understand other speech acts that have a bearing on it. It would be absurd, however, to say that useful criticism cannot result from the intensive investigation of one speech, just as it would be ridiculous to assert that a critical analysis of *Hamlet* is not possible without a full analysis of all Shakespeare's works, of all Elizabethan drama, or of all drama for that matter. Even so, it surely must be recognized that rhetorical events can be shaped and directed by rhetorical events that have preceded them. Circumstances can circumscribe the limits of rhetorical options, or open new options to the rhetor, or mold audience expectations.

With this reality of the relatedness of rhetorical acts in mind, some critics have turned their attention to the ways in which situation can exert influence on discourse, that is, that similar contexts can evoke similar rhetorical responses. *Genre* denotes a similar grouping or species, and generic rhetorical criticism is a search for generalities that can be made about discourse in such matters as purpose, style, form, types of proof, and the like. Understanding generic features may lead the critic to a fuller comprehension of what an audience expects in certain situations and may lead to the formulation of a set of criteria whereby the critic can determine how well any speaker has met those expectations. Mohrmann and Leff, in their study of Lincoln, proposed Lincoln's Cooper Union address as an example of the genre of ingratiation,[8] arguing that political speeches are meant to ingratiate the speaker with significant audiences. Such an observation, if it is accepted, has implications for the understanding and evaluation of political speeches.

Acutely aware of the interrelatedness of rhetorical events, other critics have focused on units larger than the single speech and have studied the rhetorical processes involved in debates over important issues, political and other campaigns, and social movements. The obvious difficulty for the critic is in the almost overwhelming amount of rhetorical material that needs to be studied. Movement studies are a significant area of investigation in rhetoric, and ways of organizing, processing, and interpreting the rhetorical artifacts of these movements are constantly being refined.[9] But the critic of movement rhetoric assumes the task of interpreting a significant single rhetorical event in the light of rhetoric that precedes and follows it, seeking to find the meaning of rhetorical strategies in the way discourse progresses over time, the way it influences events, the way it is influenced by events, and how the whole process contributes ultimately to some resolution of the issue that called for movement in the first place.

It is not possible in the limited space available to describe, even as briefly as has been done previously, all the varieties of rhetorical criticism that are yielding useful perceptions of how rhetoric functions. A wide variety of methods and approaches are represented in the bibliographies at the end of this book. These perspectives and the theoretical stances they represent will influence critics' interpretations of texts.

Our intention in this book, however, is not to focus on any particular method. We hold that before all else, the beginning critic must learn to read and dissect the text. Careful study of the results of such inquiries can enlarge the novice critic's view of the possibilities of criticism.

Regardless of the method of interpretation that directs the critic's efforts, it should be recognized that a crucial function of interpretation is to isolate what the critic views as significant. No critique will evenhandedly discuss every aspect of the discourse that is capable of being discussed. The critic cannot, and should not feel obligated to, pay equally close attention to all of the material provided by an exhaustive analysis of a rhetorical act. Indeed, to consider the analytical categories as some kind of checklist of items that must be discussed is a move toward a sterile, formulaic description that submerges interpretation. On the basis of what she or he knows, the critic discovers (and can substantiate that discovery) what is most meaningful in the discourse under investigation. Interpretation, by examining and explaining the unique and the meaningful in discourse, is then a *creative process* that leads to insight and not a clerical chore that simply touches all the bases.

## Judgment

In the first chapter of this book criticism was defined as "the systematic process of illuminating and evaluating products of human activity." The final step in the process that has been described thus far is evaluation — reaching a reasoned judgment. "Reasoned" is to be emphasized. The rhetorical critic does not judge a speech on the basis of quick impressions; any critic who has gone through the analytical and interpretive stages of investigation has become intimately aware of the workings of the discourse in its context. It remains to reach a defensible conclusion on the quality of the speech.

A judgment may take different forms. Essentially, the judgment made on a rhetorical act or series of acts depends on the standards of judgment — the criteria — that are employed. In reaching a judgment and in evaluating the judgments reached by other critics, we must look to the criteria either advanced explicitly or suggested implicitly.

The criteria may derive from a variety of perspectives, depending on the critic's perception of his or her function, the nature of the evidence that has been uncovered in the examination of the discourse, or the demands — self- or situationally imposed — on the speaker. Basically, judgments are made on the grounds of audience receptiveness and potential audience effects, logical and intellectual validity, and social consequences. Some critics might wish to say that rhetoric can be judged as an art form; that is the *ultimate* judgment. An unflawed artistic work, however, is one that encompasses *all* the relevant possible criteria: rhetoric has truly reached the highest artistic pinnacle when it can be said to be effective, intellectually sound, and of benefit to humanity. That is the perfection toward which the best rhetoric strives, but which cannot frequently be reached.

Even though a speech may be flawed in one sense, it can still be judged positively with regard to the other elements that are subsumed under the overriding artistic evaluation. Critics, however, no matter how systematic they are and no matter how rigidly they adhere to the demand that their conclusions be based on soundly arguable conclusions, will differ in their values and in their views of both the nature and role of rhetoric. This being so, certain bases for judgment may be more important to some critics than to others.

Judgments based on audience receptiveness will be determined by the potential effect of the discourse. (We have already discussed in some detail the problems of determining effect.) If a speech is judged effective, it is, according to this criterion, a "good" speech. Judged on the basis of intellectual or logical validity, a speech may be determined to be "good" if the arguments advanced are sound, based on the best possible evidence available and leading to the conclusions that are warranted by that evidence. Using social consequences as a criterion, a critic would reach a positive judgment about a speech that promoted social welfare and contributed to furthering values that were most conducive to a full realization of the human and humane potential of listeners.

Depending on the critic's point of view, for example, he or she might consider the results of the analysis of a particular argument in different ways. A critic might look at an argument and determine that, since it so closely conformed to the prejudices and beliefs of the audience, it needed little development and was thus a good argument because the conclusion reached would be readily acceptable to the designated listeners. Another critic looking at the same argument might point to the fact that the example used was stereotypical, and even though the audience accepted its stereotypical quality as fact, it was not strong enough to support logically the conclusion drawn from it. A third critic could point out that the examples played on the darker prejudices of the audience and thus reinforced a conception of another group of individuals in such a way as to promote strife and divisiveness. A fourth critic might conclude that the text reinforced prevailing attitudes or practices that were oppressive to certain groups.

These perspectives are not mutually exclusive. The same critic might look at material in the speech and evaluate its worth with all four viewpoints in mind. Certain cases might make ethical considerations more relevant than logical ones, and vice versa. The paramount consideration for the critic is that he or she articulate criteria and demonstrate clearly and logically how the rhetorical effort under consideration meets them.

## Summary

Analysis, interpretation, and judgment are the principal means whereby the critic pursues his or her art. All these means are part of the process characterized by rigorous and careful examination in which the discourse and its context become the data out of which sound critical conclusions grow.

To summarize these steps and to help the beginning critic organize his or her approach to the rhetorical act, the following set of questions may serve as a guide:

1. What is the principal argument of the speech?
2. What is the implied purpose of the speech? How does it compare with the stated purpose?
3. What are the individual arguments? How are they constructed?
4. What specific forms of support can be identified? How do they function to promote conclusions?
5. What are the main ideas of a speech? How do they relate to the specific materials presented and to each other?
6. What functions do introduction, conclusion, and transitions play in promoting the movement of the speech?
7. Is a predominant pattern of development evident in the speech? Are there subpatterns within the speech?
8. What do the patterns suggest about the speaker's perspective on the issues involved and his or her perception of a desirable audience perspective?
9. How may the speech's tone, level of generality, level of complexity, diction, and texture be described?
10. What function does language appear to play in furthering the argument of the speech?
11. Given the analytical findings, what consistent patterns or strategies emerge in the areas of argument, supporting material, structure, and style?
12. How may these patterns be related to the entire rhetorical situation — context, audience, speaker — in which the rhetorical act took place?
13. What significant rhetorical meaning or meanings can be placed on this act within the rhetorical process of which it forms a part?
14. In what ways and to what extent does the speech engage the audience?

15. In what ways and to what extent does the speech exhibit sound intellectual and reasonable judgment?
16. What are the probable consequences to society of the speech's ideas and information, and the strategic patterns of ideas and information?

## *Notes*

1. *Congressional Record, House of Representatives,* March 15, 1963, 5059–5061.
2. Stephen E. Toulmin, *The Uses of Argument* (Cambridge: Cambridge University Press, 1958). See also Wayne Brockriede and Douglas Ehninger, "Toulmin on Argument: An Interpretation and Application," *Quarterly Journal of Speech,* 46 (1960), 44–53; and Charles Arthur Willard, "On the Utility of Descriptive Diagrams for the Analysis and Criticism of Arguments," *Communication Monographs,* 43 (1976), 308–319.
3. An instructive comparison in this regard can be drawn between "Black Man's History," which was delivered inside a Nation of Islam mosque, and "The Ballot or the Bullet," delivered to a racially mixed audience after Malcolm's split from the Nation of Islam. See *The End of White World Supremacy: Four Speeches by Malcolm X,* ed. Benjamin Karim (New York: Little, Brown and Company, 1971), pp. 23–66; and *Malcolm X Speaks,* ed. George Breitman (New York: Grove Press, 1965), pp. 23–44.
4. For an extended discussion of the relationship between the form and function of language, see Michael Leff, "Things Made by Words: Reflections on Textual Criticism," *Quarterly Journal of Speech,* 78 (1992), 223–231.
5. See particularly Kenneth Burke, *A Grammar of Motives and a Rhetoric of Motives* (New York: Meridian Books, 1962). An excellent example of Burke's own rhetorical criticism is "The Rhetoric of Hitler's 'Battle,'" in *The Philosophy of Literary Form* (New York: Vintage Books, 1957), pp. 164–189. See also Marie Hochmuth Nichols's essay on Burke, "Kenneth Burke and the 'New Rhetoric,'" *Quarterly Journal of Speech,* 38 (1952), 133–144.
6. Burke, *A Grammar of Motives and a Rhetoric of Motives,* p. 567.
7. Kenneth Burke, "Rhetoric — Old and New," *The Journal of General Education,* 5 (1951), 203. For an interesting and perceptive discussion of intentionality, see Robert L. Scott, "Intentionality in the Rhetorical Process," *Rhetoric in Transition: Studies in the Nature and Uses of Rhetoric,* ed. Eugene E. White (University Park: Pennsylvania State University Press, 1980), pp. 39–60.
8. Michael C. Leff and G. P. Mohrmann, "Lincoln at Cooper Union: A Rhetorical Analysis of the Text," *Quarterly Journal of Speech,* 60 (1974), 346–358.
9. One of the seminal articles regarding the rhetorical study of social movements is Leland M. Griffin, "The Rhetoric of Historical Movements," *Quarterly Journal of Speech,* 30 (1952), 184–188. A recent example of an excellent movement study is J. Michael Hogan's *The Nuclear Freeze Campaign: Rhetoric and Foreign Policy in the Telepolitical Age* (East Lansing: Michigan State University Press, 1994). Other discussions of movement rhetoric and studies of actual movements are cited in the bibliography.

# PART II • CRITICAL READINGS AND COMMENTARY

# 5

# Reading Abraham Lincoln's Young Men's Lyceum Address

## *Address to the Young Men's Lyceum of Springfield, Illinois*

ABRAHAM LINCOLN

### *The Perpetuation of Our Political Institutions*

As a subject for the remarks of the evening, *the perpetuation of our political institutions,* is selected.

In the great journal of things happening under the sun, we, the American People, find our account running, under date of the nineteenth century of the Christian era. We find ourselves in the peaceful possession, of the fairest portion of the earth, as regards extent of territory, fertility of soil, and salubrity of climate. We find ourselves under the government of a system of political institutions, conducing more essentially to the ends of civil and religious liberty, than any of which the history of former times tells us. We, when mounting the stage of existence, found ourselves the legal inheritors of these fundamental blessings. We toiled not in the acquirement or establishment of them — they are a legacy bequeathed us, by a *once* hardy, brave, and patriotic, but *now* lamented and departed race of ancestors. Their's was the task (and nobly they performed it) to possess themselves, and through themselves, us, of this goodly land; and to uprear upon its hills and its valleys, a political edifice of liberty and equal rights; 'tis ours only, to transmit these, the former, unprofaned by the foot of an invader; the latter, undecayed by the lapse of time, and untorn by usurpation — to the latest generation that fate shall permit the world to know. This task of gratitude to our fathers, justice to ourselves, duty to posterity, and love for our species in general, all imperatively require us faithfully to perform.

How, then, shall we perform it? At what point shall we expect the approach of danger? By what means shall we fortify against it? Shall we expect some transatlantic military giant, to step the Ocean, and crush us at a blow? Never! All the armies of Europe, Asia and Africa combined, with all the treasure of the earth (our own excepted) in their military chest; with a Buonaparte for a commander, could not by force, take a drink from the Ohio, or make a track on the Blue Ridge, in a trial of a thousand years.

At what point then is the approach of danger to be expected? I answer, if it ever reach us, it must spring up amongst us. It cannot come from abroad. If destruction be our lot, we must ourselves be its author and finisher. As a nation of freemen, we must live through all time, or die by suicide.

I hope I am over wary; but if I am not, there is, even now, something of ill-omen amongst us. I mean the increasing disregard for law which pervades the country; the growing disposition to substitute the wild and furious passions, in lieu of the sober judgement of Courts; and the worse than savage mobs, for the executive ministers of justice. This disposition is awfully fearful in any community; and that it now exists in ours, though grating to our feelings to admit, it would be a violation of truth, and an insult to our intelligence, to deny. Accounts of outrages committed by mobs, form the every-day news of the times. They have pervaded the country, from New England to Louisiana; — they are neither peculiar to the eternal snows of the former, nor the burning suns of the latter; — they are not the creature of climate — neither are they confined to the slaveholding, or the non-slaveholding States. Alike, they spring up among the pleasure hunting masters of Southern slaves, and the order loving citizens of the land of steady habits. Whatever, then, their cause may be, it is common to the whole country.

It would be tedious, as well as useless, to recount the horrors of all of them. Those happening in the State of Mississippi, and at St. Louis, are, perhaps, the most dangerous in example, and revolting to humanity. In the Mississippi case, they first commenced by hanging the regular gamblers: a set of men, certainly not following for a livelihood, a very useful, or very honest occupation; but one which, so far from being forbidden by the laws, was actually licensed by an act of the Legislature, passed but a single year before. Next, negroes, suspected of conspiring to raise an insurrection, were caught up and hanged in all parts of the State: then, white men, supposed to be leagued with the negroes; and finally, strangers, from neighboring States, going thither on business, were, in many instances, subjected to the same fate. Thus went on this process of hanging, from gamblers to negroes, from negroes to white citizens, and from these to strangers; till, dead men were seen literally dangling from the boughs of trees upon every road side; and in numbers almost sufficient, to rival the native Spanish moss of the country, as a drapery of the forest.

Turn, then, to that horror-striking scene at St. Louis. A single victim was only sacrificed there. His story is very short; and is, perhaps, the most highly tragic, of any thing of its length, that has ever been witnessed in real life. A mulatto man, by the name of McIntosh, was seized in the street, dragged to the suburbs of the city, chained to a tree, and actually burned to death; and all within a single hour from the time he had been a freeman, attending to his own business, and at peace with the world.

Such are the effects of mob law; and such are the scenes, becoming more and more frequent in this land so lately famed for love of law and order; and the stories of which, have even now grown too familiar, to attract any thing more, than an idle remark.

But you are, perhaps, ready to ask, "What has this to do with the perpetuation of our political institutions?" I answer, it has much to do with it. Its direct consequences are, comparatively speaking, but a small evil; and much of its danger consists, in the proneness of our minds, to regard its direct, as its only consequences. Abstractly considered, the hanging of the gamblers at Vicksburg, was of but little consequence. They constitute a portion of population, that is worse than useless in any community; and their death, if no pernicious example be set by it, is never matter of reasonable regret with any one. If they were annually swept, from the stage of existence, by the plague or small pox, honest men would, perhaps, be much profited, by the operation. Similar too, is the correct reasoning, in regard to the burning of the negro at St. Louis. He had forfeited his life, by the perpetration of an outrageous murder, upon one of the most worthy and respectable citizens of the city; and had he not died as he did, he must have died by the sentence of the law, in a very short time afterwards. As to him alone, it was as well the way it was, as it could otherwise have been. But the example in either case, was fearful. When men take it in their heads to day, to hang gamblers, or burn murderers, they should recollect, that, in the confusion usually attending such transactions, they will be as likely to hang or burn some one, who is neither a gambler nor a murderer as one who is; and that, acting upon the example they set, the mob of to-morrow, may, and probably will, hang or burn some of them, by the very same mistake. And not only so; the innocent, those who have ever set their faces against violations of law in every shape, alike with the guilty, fall victims to the ravages of mob law; and thus it goes on, step by step, till all the walls erected for the defence of the persons and property of individuals, are trodden down, and disregarded. But all this even, is not the full extent of the evil. By such examples, by instances of the perpetrators of such acts going unpunished, the lawless in spirit, are encouraged to become lawless in practice; and having been used to no restraint, but dread of punishment, they thus become, absolutely unrestrained. Having ever regarded Government as their deadliest bane, they make a jubilee of the suspension of its operations; and pray for nothing so much, as its total annihilation. While, on the other hand, good men, men who love tranquility, who desire to abide by the laws, and enjoy their benefits, who would gladly spill their blood in the defence of their country; seeing their property destroyed; their families insulted, and their lives endangered; their persons injured; and seeing nothing in prospect that forebodes a change for the better; become tired of, and disgusted with, a Government that offers them no protection; and are not much averse to a change in which they imagine they have nothing to lose. Thus, then, by the operation of this mobocratic spirit, which all must admit, is now abroad in the land, the strongest bulwark of any Government, and particularly of those constituted like ours, may effectually be broken down and destroyed — I mean the *attachment* of the People. Whenever this effect shall be produced among us; whenever the vicious portion of population shall be permitted to gather in bands of hundreds and thousands, and burn churches, ravage and rob provision stores, throw printing presses into rivers, shoot editors, and hang and burn obnoxious persons at pleasure, and with impunity; depend on it, this Government cannot last. By such things, the feelings of the best citizens will become more or less alienated from it; and thus it will be left without friends, or with too few, and those few too weak, to make their friendship effectual. At such a time and under such circumstances, men of sufficient talent and ambition will not be wanting to seize the opportunity, strike the blow, and overturn that fair fabric, which for the last half century, has been the fondest hope, of the lovers of freedom, throughout the world.

I know the American People are *much* attached to their Government; — I know they would suffer *much* for its sake; — I know they would endure evils long and patiently, before they would ever think of exchanging it for another. Yet, notwithstanding all this, if the laws be continually despised and disregarded, if their rights to be secure in their persons and property, are held by no better tenure than the caprice of a mob, the alienation of their affections from the Government is the natural consequence; and to that, sooner or later, it must come.

Here then, is one point at which danger may be expected.

The question recurs "how shall we fortify against it?" The answer is simple. Let every American, every lover of liberty, every well wisher to his posterity, swear by the blood of the Revolution, never to violate in the least particular, the laws of the country; and never to tolerate their violation by others. As the patriots of seventy-six did to the support of the Declaration of Independence, so to the support of the Constitution and Laws, let every American pledge his life, his property, and his sacred honor; — let every man remember that to violate the law, is to trample on the blood of his father, and to tear the character of his own, and his children's liberty. Let reverence for the laws, be breathed by every American mother, to the lisping babe, that prattles on her lap — let it be taught in schools, in seminaries, and in colleges; — let it be written in Primmers, spelling books, and in Almanacs; — let it be preached from the pulpit, proclaimed in legislative halls, and enforced in courts of justice. And, in short, let it become the *political religion* of the nation; and let the old and the young, the rich and the poor, the grave and the gay, of all sexes and tongues, and colors and conditions, sacrifice unceasingly upon its altars.

While ever a state of feeling, such as this, shall universally, or even, very generally prevail throughout the nation, vain will be every effort, and fruitless every attempt, to subvert our national freedom.

When I so pressingly urge a strict observance of all the laws, let me not be understood as saying there are no bad laws, nor that grievances may not arise, for the redress of which, no legal provisions have been made. I mean to say no such thing. But I do mean to say, that, although bad laws, if they exist, should be repealed as soon as possible, still while they continue in force, for the sake of example, they should be religiously observed. So also in unprovided cases. If such arise, let proper legal provisions be made for them with the least possible delay; but, till then, let them if not too intolerable, be borne with.

There is no grievance that is a fit object of redress by mob law. In any case that arises, as for instance, the promulgation of abolitionism, one of two positions is necessarily true; that is, the thing is right within itself, and therefore deserves the protection of all law and all good citizens; or, it is wrong, and therefore proper to be prohibited by legal enactments; and in neither case, is the interposition of mob law, either necessary, justifiable, or excusable.

But, it may be asked, why suppose danger to our political institutions? Have we not preserved them for more than fifty years? And why may we not for fifty times as long?

We hope there is no *sufficient* reason. We hope all dangers may be overcome; but to conclude that no danger may ever arise, would itself be extremely dangerous. There are now, and will hereafter be, many causes, dangerous in their tendency, which have not existed heretofore; and which are not too insignificant to merit attention. That our government should have been maintained in its original form from its establishment until now, is not much to be wondered at. It had many props to support it through that period, which now are decayed, and crumbled away. Through that period, it was felt by all, to be an undecided experiment; now, it is understood to be a successful one. Then, all that sought celebrity and fame, and distinction, expected to find them in the success of that experiment. Their *all* was staked upon it: — their destiny was *inseparably* linked with it. Their ambition aspired to display before an admiring world, a practical demonstration of the truth of a proposition, which had hitherto been considered, at best no better, than problematical; namely, *the capability of a people to govern themselves.* If they succeeded, they were to be immortalized; their names were to be transferred to counties and cities, and rivers and mountains; and to be revered and sung, and toasted through all time. If they failed, they were to be called knaves and fools, and fanatics for a fleeting hour; then to sink and be forgotten. They succeeded. The experiment is successful; and thousands have won their deathless names in making it so. But the game is caught; and I believe it is true, that with the catching, end the pleasures of the chase. This field of glory is harvested, and the crop is already appropriated. But new reapers will arise, and *they,* too, will seek a field. It is to deny, what the history of the world tells us is true, to suppose that men of ambition and talents will not continue to spring up amongst us. And, when they do, they will as naturally seek the gratification of their ruling passion, as others have *so* done before them. The question then, is, can that gratification be found in supporting and maintaining an edifice that has been erected by others? Most certainly it cannot. Many great and good men sufficiently qualified for any task they should undertake, may ever be found, whose ambition would aspire to nothing beyond a seat in Congress, a gubernatorial or a presidential chair; *but such belong not to the family of the lion, or the tribe of the eagle.* What! think you these places would satisfy an Alexander, a Caesar, or a Napoleon? Never! Towering genius disdains a beaten path. It seeks regions hitherto unexplored. It sees *no distinction* in adding story to story, upon the monuments of fame, erected to the memory of others. It *denies* that it is glory enough to serve under any chief. It *scorns* to tread in the footsteps of *any* predecessor, however illustrious. It thirsts and burns for distinction; and, if possible, it will have it, whether at the expense of emancipating slaves, or enslaving freemen. Is it unreasonable then to expect, that some man possessed of the loftiest genius, coupled with ambition sufficient to push it to its utmost stretch, will at some time, spring up among us? And when such a one does, it will require the people to be united with each other, attached to the government and laws, and generally intelligent, to successfully frustrate his designs.

Distinction will be his paramount object; and although he would as willingly, perhaps more so, acquire it by doing good as harm; yet, that opportunity being past, and nothing left to be done in the way of building up, he would set boldly to the task of pulling down.

Here then, is a probable case, highly dangerous, and such a one as could not have well existed heretofore.

Another reason which *once was;* but which, to the same extent, is *now no more,* has done much in maintaining our institutions thus far. I mean the powerful influence which the interesting scenes of the revolution had upon the *passions* of the people as distinguished from their judgment. By this influence, the jealousy, envy, and avarice, incident to our nature, and so common to a state of peace, prosperity, and conscious strength, were, for the time, in a great measure smothered and rendered inactive; while the deep rooted principles of *hate,* and the powerful motive of *revenge,* instead of being turned against each other, were directed exclusively against the British nation. And thus, from the force of circumstances, the basest principles of our nature, were either made to lie dormant, or to become the active agents in the advancement of the noblest of cause — that of establishing and maintaining civil and religious liberty.

But this state of feeling *must fade, is fading, has faded,* with the circumstances that produced it.

I do not mean to say, that the scenes of the revolution *are now* or *ever will be* entirely forgotten; but that like every thing else, they must fade upon the memory of the world, and grow more and more dim by the lapse of time. In history, we hope, they will be read of, and recounted, so long as the bible shall be read; — but even granting that they will, their influence *cannot be* what it heretofore has been. Even then, they *cannot be* so universally known, nor so vividly felt, as they were by the generation just gone to rest. At the close of that struggle, nearly every adult male had been a participator in some of its scenes. The consequence was, that of those scenes, in the form of a husband, a father, a son or a brother, a *living history was* to be found in every family — a history bearing the indubitable testimonies of its own authenticity, in the limbs mangled, in the scars of wounds received, in the midst of the very scenes related — a history, too, that could be read and understood alike by all, the wise and the ignorant, the learned and the unlearned. But *those* histories are gone. They *can* be read no more forever. They *were* a fortress of strength; but, what invading foemen could *never do,* the silent artillery of time *has done;* the levelling of its walls. They are gone. They *were* a forest of giant oaks; but the all resistless hurricane has swept over them, and left only, here and there, a lonely trunk, despoiled of its verdure, shorn of its foliage; unshading and unshaded, to murmur in a few more gentle breezes, and to combat with its mutilated limbs, a few more ruder storms, then to sink, and be no more.

They *were* the pillars of the temple of liberty; and now, that they have crumbled away, that temple must fall, unless we, their descendants, supply their places with other pillars, hewn from the solid quarry of sober reason. Passion has helped us; but can do so no more. It will in future be our enemy. Reason, cold, calculating, unimpassioned reason, must furnish all the materials for our future support and defence. Let those materials be moulded into *general intelligence, sound morality* and, in particular, *a reverence for the constitution and laws;* and, that we improved to the last; that we remained free to the last; that we revered his name to the last; that, during his long sleep, we permitted no hostile foot to pass over or desecrate his resting place; shall be that which to learn the last trump shall awaken our WASHINGTON.

Upon these let the proud fabric of freedom rest, as the rock of its basis; and as truly as has been said of the only greater institution, *"the gates of hell shall not prevail against it."*

*January 27, 1838*

## *Critical Reading and Commentary*
## *Abraham Lincoln's Young Men's Lyceum Address*

**Commentary.** *As we pointed out in the early chapters, rhetorical texts arise from the press of events. They respond to circumstances that affect the political and social world in which the speaker and the listeners live by attempting to give events meaning and to shape the course of future action. The critic begins the essay below with a succinct recounting of the murder of the abolitionist Elijah Lovejoy, he explains that that particular event gained widespread attention and took on great significance for American audiences at the time Lincoln gave his speech. The critic reminds us that abolition of slavery — something that, from our vantage point at the end of the twentieth century, we cannot imagine as being controversial — was highly controversial in the early nineteenth century. He also establishes that, in spite of the lack of direct references to the event, Lincoln's audience would surely have* *the Lovejoy incident clearly in their minds. Further, the critic believes that Lincoln's lack of direct engagement with the Lovejoy story enabled him to approach the matter from the perspective of his own principles for guiding political action.*

**Background, Sources, and Structure**

After graduating from Princeton Theological Seminary, Elijah Lovejoy returned to his native St. Louis, where he published a Christian newspaper. His antislavery editorials ignited strong protests, and in 1837, Lovejoy moved to Alton, Illinois. But violent opposition to his views continued, and Lovejoy's printing press was destroyed three times during that year. With financial aid from abolitionist groups, Lovejoy purchased a fourth press, and he and a group of supporters resolved to defend it in the warehouse where it was stored. On November 7, an angry crowd gathered outside the warehouse. Shots were exchanged, and Lovejoy was mortally wounded.

The incident immediately caused a storm of controversy, and even in the North opinions were divided. Some thought that it demonstrated the grave danger to public order occasioned by anti-slavery agitation and that it justified restrictions on abolitionist sentiment. Other citizens, although dubious about abolitionism in principle, were concerned about the peril to free speech, and coupled with earlier incidents of repression and intimidation, the violence at Alton made them more receptive to warnings about the tyranny of the slave-power in America. For the abolitionist, Lovejoy was a heroic figure, a martyr whose death required memorialization and offered an opportunity to drive home their message. In Illinois, where the event had occurred and where attitudes about slavery were especially diverse, the reaction was sharp and intense. The issue provoked not only heated debate but also a general fear about further violence.

It was in this turbulent atmosphere that Lincoln, then twenty-eight and a Whig member of the state legislature, addressed the Young Men's Lyceum in Springfield. Lincoln's topic was "the perpetuation of our political institutions," and he singled out mob violence and disregard for the law as the greatest dangers to American liberty. Remarkably, however, Lincoln referred to the abolitionist controversy only once, and that by way of example. He never mentioned Lovejoy's name and alluded clearly to the Alton incident only in a passage embedded in the middle of the speech. Nevertheless, as Harry Jaffa has said, no one can doubt that in composing the speech, Lincoln had in mind the "violence arising from abolitionism and the reaction to it." Nor would the point have been lost on the audience. As Roy Basler has commented, in one of the few substantive notes to his edition of

Lincoln's works, "members of the Lyceum who listened to Lincoln without sensing the specter of Lovejoy in their midst must have been very obtuse indeed." Lincoln, then, chose to engage the issue indirectly, adopting a perspective that allowed him rhetorical distance from immediate passions and that enabled him to encompass the matter at hand within a general network of principles. This stance corresponded precisely with one of the main themes of the speech — that political action should not stem from considerations of direct consequences but must respond to the less direct and more durable requirement of social order.

***Commentary.*** *The remainder of this section of the essay follows the speech itself as it unfolds. The critic's first concern is with the opening of the speech, in which Lincoln praises the founders for establishing the liberty that the present generation enjoys. Note how the critic studies Lincoln's language carefully, noting the metaphors in Lincoln's introduction and seeing in them a key to understanding Lincoln's political stance: liberty is associated with stability and is threatened by the progress of time. Then, what we have called "argumentative history" in an early chapter — or what might be referred to as the rhetorical history of ideas — surfaces as an important conception for the critic. The critic, you will read below, uncovers a "commonplace" of the time, namely, the idea that the generations following the founders had to protect the liberty that their forebears established. The critic then moves on to connect Lincoln's views with those of one of the greatest orators and most prominent politicians of the time — and Lincoln's fellow Whig — Daniel Webster, explaining their basic similarity and difference. The critic comes to a preliminary conclusion that Lincoln does not see liberty as dependent only on veneration of the past, a point that will become clearer as the essay is developed.*

The speech opens with a paean to America. The nation, Lincoln believes, is twice blessed — by the bounty of nature and by free political institutions. These blessings have not been gained by the current generation but come as a legacy from "a *once* hardy, brave, and patriotic, but *now* lamented and departed race of ancestors," who possessed "this goodly land" and upreared "a political edifice of liberty." The task for the living is to "transmit these, the former, unprofaned by the foot of an invader; the latter undecayed by the lapse of time, and untorn by usurpation." This is a task for "us faithfully to perform" in gratitude "to our fathers," in "justice to ourselves," in "duty to posterity," and in response to "love for our species in general."

The metaphors in this opening paragraph heavily mark Lincoln's political orientation. Liberty is an edifice; it is stable. That which works to build or maintain the edifice is good; that which decays or tears at its structure is bad. The main enemy is time. It has claimed the heroic builders of liberty, and it now threatens to decay the edifice that stands as their legacy.

This pattern recurs through the speech. Liberty is associated with walls, bulwarks, props, pillars, "hewn from the solid quarry of reason," and fortifications set against the ravages of time, the passions of the mob, and the will-to-power of talented and ambitious men. On the other side are symbols of destabilization: actions that tread down, strike blows against, overturn, and pull down institutions, and forces that decay, crumble, break down, or destroy their integrity. Time is portrayed consistently as an agency of decomposition; it causes the "living history" of national unity to fade from memory, and its "silent artillery" has leveled the generation that once was "a fortress of strength." "They *were* a forest of giant oaks; but the all-resistless hurricane has swept over them, and left, only here and there, a lonely trunk, despoiled of its verdure, shorn of its foliage. . . . They *were* the pillars of the temple of liberty," but now "they have crumbled away."

One other point about the opening paragraph deserves attention. The theme it articulates is a commonplace of the period. As early as 1817, President Monroe had asserted that the great object ahead was to preserve our government "in the essential principles and features that characterize it." During the next two decades, as the founding fathers passed away and as fears of disorder mounted, the theme of preservation intensified and became linked with the change of generations. The fathers had founded liberty; their successors faced the less heroic task of stabilizing free institutions. As George Forgie has shown, this sentiment was repeated at almost every appropriate opportunity.

The most notable opportunity, however, was occasioned by the fiftieth anniversary of the Declaration of Independence. In one of American history's most stunning coincidences, Thomas Jefferson and John Adams, the last survivors among the iconic personalities of the Revolution, both died on July 4, 1826. This was a "media event" of the highest order, and in the 1820s, epideictic oratory was a major medium of communication. Encomia were delivered throughout the country during the ensuing months, but Webster's eulogy delivered in Faneuil Hall undoubtedly attracted the greatest interest and had the most enduring influence.

The bulk of Webster's speech consists of a parallel biography of his two subjects. In the peroration, however, he turns to the "deep and solemn convictions of the duties which have devolved on us." Predictably, he develops the *topos* of the gift of the fathers and the obligations of their successor to preserve that gift. Yet, despite the commonplace status of the theme, the specific points Webster raises are so close to those that appear in Lincoln's exordium that a direct influence seems plausible. Webster's text includes the following:

(1) the fathers purchased the possessions we now enjoy; (2) these possessions refer both to the bounty of nature and the "glorious liberty" derived from a free government; (3) the present generation must preserve and transmit these possessions; and (4) in pursuing this task, the present generation is called by the fathers, by posterity, and by all the world to act "wisely" and "faithfully." As we have seen, Lincoln treats each of these points. There are also some significant verbal echoes. Lincoln's use of the adverb "faithfully" seems a close parallel to Webster. Webster admonishes his audience not to let the blood of our fathers be shed in vain; Lincoln (in the middle of his speech) warns against trampling on the blood of the fathers. Webster refers to Charles Carroll, the sole surviving signer of the Declaration of Independence, and calls him "an aged oak, standing alone on the plain, which time has spared a little longer after all its contemporaries have been leveled in the dust." Lincoln's description of the few survivors of the revolutionary generation, which I have quoted above, invokes a strikingly similar image. Finally, in the last few sentences of his speech, Webster invokes Washington, and Lincoln does the same.

I think it possible, then, that Lincoln had Webster's peroration in mind or at his elbow when he began composing the Lyceum speech. And if the evidence is insufficient to prove direct influence, the comparison between the two texts is, in any case, a matter of some interest. Obviously Lincoln and Webster share the same broad ideological space. But there is a crucial difference. Lincoln's fatalistic view of history has no counterpart in Webster. For the latter, the preservation of liberty is a straightforward business. The new generation has only to emulate the principles and virtues of the Fathers. Adams and Jefferson are dead, but their example is still before us and available for our purposes through an unimpeded line of transmission. For Lincoln, the passage of time erodes this connection. The virtues necessary for establishing liberty are not precisely the same as those required to maintain it, since the character of the polity changes as it matures. Thus, as we shall soon note, Lincoln must construct a more complex account of the linkage between the heroic past and the problems of his own age. Ordered liberty, in his version of the Whig ideology, cannot simply rest on veneration of the past and cannot hold the popular will within a single, continuous trajectory.

***Commentary.*** *Next, the critic considers the way the speech is structured, showing how one idea progresses to the next in demonstrating the problem and offering a solution. The critic shows how, outwardly, this "external frame" is rationally supportive of Lincoln's political beliefs. There is, however, more at work here: as we pointed out in Chapter 4, the critic examines a* *speaker's argument in order to uncover hidden assumptions and examines structure so as to understand the logical and psychological connections between the parts of the speech. From very careful and close reading of the text, the critic deduces that there is a subtle structure at work in the speech and suggests that understanding this structure will help us understand Lincoln as both a speaker and a political thinker.*

The body of the speech follows a well-ordered logical progression. Lincoln's remarks fall under three main headings: (1) consideration of the present danger to free institutions, (2) a proposed remedy to this danger, and (3) consideration of future dangers. Under the first heading, Lincoln argues that a tendency toward mob rule and disregard for the law now threatens American institutions. To establish the reality of the threat, he refers to two recent examples — lynchings that occurred in Vicksburg, Mississippi, and St. Louis. The examples are then examined in terms of their direct consequences (which are not necessarily unjust) and in terms of their indirect consequences (which are disastrous). This latter point is further subdivided as Lincoln explains that such violence encourages the lawless to act without restraint and subverts the attachment of the law-abiding to the government. The section ends with a strong assertion of the perils of the "mobocratic" spirit. The solution, Lincoln maintains, is to inculcate a spirit of reverence for the law, a commitment "never to violate in the least particular the laws of the country," which should become "the *political religion* of the nation." The position is then qualified, since Lincoln acknowledges the need for reform in the case of bad laws or the absence of laws needed to meet legitimate grievances. But such reforms must proceed through orderly channels, and until the proper remedies are enacted, problems, "if not too intolerable," should be "borne with." The final section argues that the dangers to free institutions will be greater in the future than they had been in the past. While the government had through its first fifty years "many props to support it," these have crumbled away. This point is then subdivided with respect to the leaders of the nation and its people. At the origin of the nation, leaders of talent and ambition turned their energy to support the experiment in self-government. Now, however, the experiment has proven successful, and the ambitious cannot find glory in adding on to an edifice already in place. Hence, they can achieve distinction only by dismantling the existing structure. As for the people, the circumstances of the Revolution smothered their passions or turned them to constructive ends. But as circumstances have changed and memories have faded, the passions have been freed to do their divisive work. The temple of liberty has lost the pillars that held through its first cycle of existence.

New ones must be fashioned, and since passion has already served its purpose, the temple must now stand on "cold, calculating, unimpassioned reason."

Such is the external frame of the speech, and its systematic divisions and subdivisions suggest a rational preoccupation consistent with the speaker's political agenda. But the internal operations of the speech reveal a more subtle and organic structure — a careful orchestration of parts and phrases designed to work upon the sentiments of the audience. Throughout the speech, transitional sentences soften Lincoln's assertions, anticipate possible objections, and make concessions to the audience. Moreover, the progression of argument is not strictly linear, for some parts of the speech seem to reverse direction, as Lincoln temporarily concedes to an opposing view or shifts focus in an unexpected way. These psychological tactics appear most notably in the first main section, and they tell us something important not only about Lincoln's persona as an orator, but also about his political thought.

***Commentary.*** *In the following section, notice how the critic examines the strategy, that is, the choices made by the speaker, by exposing the ways in which potential audience reactions and feelings direct the flow of Lincoln's argument. The critic argues that the way in which the speech unfolds demonstrates a keen awareness of the audience's responses and illustrates the strategic accommodations Lincoln made to his listeners. This is a strategy, the critic concludes, that exemplified and argued for Lincoln's own philosophy: "Self-government can survive only so long as the people govern their own passions through attachment to the rule of law."*

**The Mobocratic Spirit and Its Threat to Liberty**

Lincoln's first task is to convince his audience that disregard for law constitutes a significant threat. He begins with these words: "I hope I am over wary; but if I am not, there is, even now, something of an ill-omen among us." The speaker is hesitant, but, as Glen Thurow observes, "the hesitancy displayed must not make us believe that Lincoln is unsure of his analysis; it reflects that of his audience, not his own. Or, rather, Lincoln identifies himself with the audience through his rhetoric by accepting the audience's hesitancy as his own even at the moment of disagreement." This strategy occurs almost every time Lincoln punctuates the flow of his argument, and it functions to orient his own argument within the audience's frame of reference. He does not confront them with his rational argument, nor does he denounce them for their passions. Instead, he attempts to blend his views into the existing fabric of thought and sentiment.

Having announced his theme, Lincoln next proceeds to illustrate it. He narrates the two cases briefly but with considerable emotional force. The cases, he says, are "revolting to humanity." In Vicksburg, the mob first hanged "regular gamblers," men not following "a very useful" or "honest" pursuit, but one that was undoubtedly legal. And then the pattern of violence escalated: "Thus went the process of hanging, from gamblers to negroes, from negroes to white citizens, and from these to strangers; till, dead men were seen literally dangling from the boughs of trees upon every road." The St. Louis incident involved a single victim: "A mulatto man, by the name of McIntosh, was seized on the street, dragged to the suburbs of the city, chained to a tree, and actually burned to death; and all within a single hour from the time he had been a freeman, attending to his own business, and at peace with the world." "Such," Lincoln concludes, "are the effects of mob law."

Lincoln now considers the consequences of such violence, and his argument takes a rather unexpected turn. Rather than continue along the developing emotional curve, Lincoln seems to retreat, saying that "the direct consequences are, comparatively speaking, rather small; and much of its danger consists, in the proneness of our minds, to regard its direct, as its only consequences." Then, as if to enact the reality of this greater danger, he returns to the two cases and goes to some length to show that the immediate results might seem justified. The gamblers, who were described previously as engaged in a lawful, if disreputable, business, are called a "worse than useless" element of the community, and their deaths, other things being equal, would occasion "no regret with any one." "Similar too," Lincoln adds, "is the case of the negro at St. Louis." The man is, significantly enough, no longer a "mulatto," and it happens that he was not simply "attending to his own business, and at peace with the world," but that he had perpetrated "an outrageous murder." Had he not died by the lynching, he "must have died by the sentence of the law, in a very short time afterwards."

Lincoln here seems to discredit his own case and to yield "to the prejudices of his audience." But by enacting these prejudices, he prepares the audience to catch sight of his key point. Actions based on passions of the moment may seem right and serve our sense of immediate justice. They overcome the frustrations caused by resorting to the more remote processes of social order, which always refer to principles that extend beyond the immediate case. Nevertheless, these actions merely confirm our tendency to overlook indirect consequences and thus encourage arbitrary behavior that tears the fabric of the community. Hence, when Lincoln shifts direction again, his correction has special force: "But the example in either case was fearful."

Once set in motion, mob rule proceeds through its own momentum, punishing the innocent as well as the guilty, and continuing "step by step, till all the walls erected for the defense of the persons and property of individuals, are trodden down, and disregarded." Even worse, such examples cause the lawless in spirit "to become lawless in practice," and good men, who desire to abide by the law, lose their faith in government. "Thus, then, by the operation of this mobocratic spirit . . . the strongest bulwark of any Government, and particularly those constituted like ours, may effectually be broken down and destroyed — I mean the *attachment* of the people." And it is only at this point, after moving indirectly through a network of principles, that Lincoln can allude to the Lovejoy case: "Whenever this effect shall be produced among us; whenever the vicious portion of the population shall be permitted to gather in bands of hundreds and thousands, and burn churches, ravage and rob provision stores, throw printing presses into rivers, shoot editors, and hang and burn obnoxious persons at pleasure, and impunity; depend on it, this Government cannot last."

In this opening section, Lincoln does not simply present an argument; he takes his auditors through a sequence of moods. They first witness the inhumanity of mob rule, then vicariously participate in its energy, and finally are positioned to adopt a new and broader perspective. A purely emotional reaction against mob rule is hardly better than participating in it, for in both cases passion governs our response to a particular situation. What is needed is the discipline of reason and a habit of mind that enables us to look to the indirect and long-term consequences of our actions. Lincoln hesitates with and accommodates to his auditors until they can come to understand his main principles: The preservation of liberty depends not on the right emotional response to circumstances, but on the capacity to control emotion through reason and to respond as the good of the community requires. Self-government can survive only so long as the people govern their own passions through attachment to the rule of law.

***Commentary.*** *Now the critic comes to the heart of the speech wherein Lincoln tells his audience more exactly what he means by the rule of law. Here the critic recognizes Lincoln's burst of passion and explains why it is appropriate at this point, in spite of some reservations the critic has about how well this section fits with the rest of the speech. The critic then proceeds to show how Lincoln ties his views into the immediate issue of abolitionism, avoiding the moral issue. This, the critic points out, is consistent with popular opinion in Illinois at the time. However, the critic explains, this position presented problems for the Whig party as they tried to reconcile their* *principles with the ethical pressures that increased as the slavery controversy intensified.*

### Political Religion

In the center of the speech, Lincoln articulates his conception of the rule of law. Here he no longer hesitates or accommodates. He presents a very clear and forceful definition of this often vague doctrine: "Let every American, every lover of liberty, every well wisher to posterity, swear by the blood of the Revolution, never to violate in the least particular, the laws of the country; and never to tolerate their violation by others. As the patriots of seventy-six did to the support of the Declaration of Independence, so to the support of the Constitution and Laws, let every American pledge his life, his property, and his sacred honor." This commitment entails a nineteenth-century version of a sustained media blitz: "Let reverence for the laws, be breathed by every American mother, to the lisping babe, that prattles on her lap — let it be taught in the schools and seminaries, and in colleges; — let it be written in Primers, spelling books, and in Almanacs; — let it be preached from the pulpit, proclaimed in the legislative halls, and enforced in the courts of justice. And, in short, let it become a *political religion* of the nation." Should this campaign succeed "vain will be every effort, and fruitless every attempt, to subvert our national freedom."

At this point, Lincoln, who almost everywhere else in the speech appears as the apostle of reason, seems to give way to a burst of passion. Within the internal rhythm of the speech, Lincoln has picked the appropriate moment for this appeal. He has carefully waited until the audience is prepared to embrace the rule of law before working on its emotions. Moreover, as a number of commentators have observed, Lincoln's position is not logically inconsistent, since he does not preach a passion for justice that would apply to immediate situations. Rather, he advocates a reverence for law which clamps restraints on impassioned behavior. Nevertheless, Lincoln's reverence for law is itself passionate, and to my mind, the passage does not rest comfortably with the rest of the discourse. I wonder how "cold, calculating, unimpassioned reason" could induce an entire nation to swear by the blood of the Revolution and give unqualified fealty to the letter of the law. Lincoln has not yet found a sure point of balance; his prose lacks the ring of harmony, the powerful but controlled passion, that emanates from his later speeches. Here his moral passion for freedom strains against his austere conceptions of reason and procedural justice.

The near bathos of the praise of law immediately gives way to a sober, rather legalistic voice: "When I so pressingly urge a strict observance of all the laws, let me not be understood as saying there are no bad laws, nor that grievances might not arise, for the redress of which, no legal provisions have been made." Now well out of the clouds, Lincoln qualifies his position. Bad laws must be repealed and new laws fashioned. Thus, the rule of law admits change and reform. But reform must adhere to approved procedures, and while bad laws remain in force, we must avoid setting the wrong example and observe them "religiously," provided that they are "not too intolerable." This last phrase introduces an equivocal note, a point where hesitation might well have been in order, but it does not detain Lincoln as he presses to the immediate issue — the abolitionists and their right to free speech.

In concluding the middle section of the speech, Lincoln explicitly connects his neutral, procedural view of justice with the controversy about abolitionism. Earlier, he had signaled his neutrality on the matter: in reporting the growth of mob law, he noted that the problem was spread through the country from "New England to Louisiana" and was confined to neither "the slaveholding or the non-slaveholding states." Later, Lincoln would reinforce the point in more direct terms: when he warns about the destructive energy of great leaders, he says that their lust for distinction will realize itself "whether at the expense of emancipating slaves, or enslaving freemen." In the passage at hand, Lincoln grounds this attitude in his general argument, subsuming it under the principle of neutral legal process: "There is no grievance that is a fit object of redress by mob law. In any case that arises, as for instance, the promulgation of abolitionism, one of two positions is necessarily true; that is, the thing is right within itself, and deserves the protection of the law and all good citizens; or, it is wrong, and therefor proper to be prohibited by legal enactments; and in neither case, is the interposition of mob law, either necessary, justifiable, or excusable." The substantive moral issue is thus circumvented by its subordination to the larger problem of preserving ordered liberty.

Lincoln's position on the specific issue fitted well within the majority view that then prevailed in Illinois. What is remarkable is the way that he weaves the case at hand into the fabric of Whig ideology — or more properly, the way he weaves it into a Whig fabric bearing his own imprimatur. In general, the Whigs tilt strongly toward ordered liberty based on procedural justice and a rational commitment to the common good. Webster, for example, repeatedly asserts these values. But whenever Webster speaks in general terms about the nexus between liberty and the American social order, he practices an eloquence of studied vagueness. Lincoln interlaces the threads more tightly. He demystifies Webster's ideology by reducing it to a logic that values neutral processes over substantive moral claims. Seen in this clearer light, the cloth seems more fragile, less capable of holding together against sustained ethical pressure. Thus, in reading the Lyceum speech, we can better understand why the Whig party unraveled as the slavery issue hardened and why Lincoln would have to shift his political thought in a more ethically nuanced direction.

***Commentary.*** *In this final section the critic shows how Lincoln's language choice and adaptive tactics promote Lincoln's explanation of the differences between the founding generation and the present one. The critic describes the way in which Lincoln articulates his political philosophy, and points out that this philosophy draws from various sources but remains uniquely American. The critic is led finally to conclude that Lincoln not only speaks about his version of the Whig ideology, he virtually embodies it by the way in which the message is delivered.*

### Lions, Eagles, and the Temple of Liberty

The third section begins, as did the first, on a note of strategic hesitation. This time Lincoln wavers a bit longer:

> But it may be asked, why suppose danger to our political institutions? Have we not preserved them for more than fifty years? And why not fifty times as long?
>
> We hope there is no *sufficient* reason. We hope all dangers may be overcome; but to conclude that no danger may ever arise, would itself be dangerous. There are now, and will hereafter be, many causes, dangerous in tendency, which have not existed heretofore. . . .

This language announces and prepares the audience for a shift in the trajectory of the speech. Given Lincoln's commitment to maintaining stability and his invocation of the Founding Fathers, the audience might expect a straightforward recommendation that future conduct should follow directly in the path laid out by the earlier generation. Lincoln, however, argues that conditions have changed. Problems now exist that were unknown in the past, and Americans cannot use the past as a guide without doing hard interpretative work about its relationship to the current situation.

Lincoln contends that, through its first half-century, the maintenance of the government was relatively easy. It had powerful props for support that have now disintegrated. In founding the new nation, its leaders engaged in an "undecided experiment," and their hopes for "celebrity, fame, and distinction" were dependent on its success. The experiment has succeeded, and so "the game is caught," and "with the catching, end the pleasures of the chase." The edifice, in other words, is built, and men must look to other pursuits to achieve fame. Moreover, history instructs Lincoln that men of talent and ambition will "continue to spring up among us." Some may content themselves by occupying places of honor within the existing structure, but such are not of "family of the lion" or the "tribe of the eagle."

New Caesars will inevitably appear, and they will not be satisfied by adding "story to story" upon monuments built in the memory of others. Towering genius "disdains a beaten path," and to achieve distinction, a Caesar, finding that nothing is "left to be done in the way of building up," will "set boldly to the task of pulling down." To meet this almost inevitable scenario, the people must be "united with each other, attached to the laws, and generally intelligent."

By nineteenth-century standards, Lincoln's view of the founding fathers is almost iconoclastic. They were, on his account, eagles and lions goaded by the same motives that attach themselves to the ambitious as a species. Their public virtue, therefore, resulted not from special qualities peculiar to individual characters, but from the circumstances. Hence, since the circumstances have changed, the examples of the fathers no longer presents a paradigm for Lincoln's generation (at least not without modification). The leadership needed for founding a free nation is one thing; the task of preservation requires something else. In fact, it requires just the kind of leadership Lincoln provides in the speech. As he accommodates to his audience, Lincoln instructs it in the ways of political religion, and he bonds himself with it in a common network of social restraint. Such restraint was unnecessary for the leaders of the earlier generation, for circumstances allowed them to pursue fame and distinction without trampling on the common good. Lincoln, however, must accept this burden and demonstrate, both by precept and example, that liberty now depends upon the solidarity needed to withstand individuals possessed of exceptional talent and ambition.

In respect to popular sentiment, changed circumstances have also introduced new perils. The scenes of the revolution had a powerful influence upon the passions of the people. This influence counteracted "the jealousy, envy, and avarice incident to our nature. . . . And thus, from the force of circumstances, the basic principles of nature, were either made to lie dormant, or to become the active agents in the advancement of the noblest of causes — that of establishing and maintaining civil and religious liberty." But this "state of feeling" has faded. As the revolutionary generation has died away, the living history they represented no longer binds the nation. Memory dims as the "silent artillery" of time levels this generation. The "pillars of the temple of liberty" have crumbled away, and new pillars are needed — pillars "hewn from the solid quarry of sober reason." Passion has served its turn; the circumstances demand materials based on reason and molded into "reverence for the constitution and laws."

Lincoln's argument, both in respect to the leaders and the people, circles back to its point of origin and supports his program of political religion. At the same time, however, Lincoln articulates the rudiments of a political philosophy that rests on general assumptions about the nature of history and human character. The conception of history corresponds with a central tenet in classical civic humanism. Time is the enemy of republics, since it corrodes institutions and corrupts leaders.

For civic humanists, virtue stands as the bulwark against the destabilizing force of time. While humans naturally tend to act on the basis of narrow, self-interested motives, political activity can check this tendency by instilling a sense of prudential virtue. Circumstances, then, can affect and improve character, for republican politics can produce prudent leaders. On this matter, Lincoln parts company with the classical tradition and approaches the more austere view found in Madison. The passions always direct the individual toward self-interest. In the unfolding of history, circumstances sometimes allow self-interest to blend with the genuine interests of the community, but this is not the result of prudent control over the passions. It is a product of coincidence, of fortune. For Lincoln, then, the defense against time is not the agility of prudent leaders, who can bend principles to meet changing situations. Lincoln's somber view of human character does not allow that possibility. The republic must depend not on the virtue of its leaders but on the collective will of people — a will molded by the stable rule of law. Ordered liberty becomes an entirely social artifact, a product of a secular religion that instills reverence for the law within the community.

Lincoln's conception of ordered liberty incorporates a number of diverse strands in the political tradition: the neoclassical conception of time, the rational skepticism of the Enlightenment, the Whig doctrine of rights of property and persons, and, as the analogy between politics suggests, a thread of Calvinistic theology. The blend, however, is distinctive and uniquely American. Perhaps its most notable characteristic is its mode of articulation, for Lincoln not only provides a version of the Whig ideology, he also enacts it as he speaks. The relationship between speaker and audience becomes a microcosm of the preferred social order, and Lincoln thus fully embodies the republican/oratorical culture of the era: his performance is part of the message, and politics becomes as much a way of talking as it is a subject to be talked about.

# 6

# Reading W. E. B. Du Bois's "Of Mr. Booker T. Washington and Others"

Easily the most striking thing in the history of the American Negro since 1876 is the ascendancy of Mr. Booker T. Washington. It began at the time when war memories and ideals were rapidly passing; a day of astonishing commercial development was dawning; a sense of doubt and hesitation overtook the freedmen's sons, — then it was that his leading began. Mr. Washington came, with a simple definite programme, at the psychological moment when the nation was a little ashamed of having bestowed so much sentiment on Negroes, and was concentrating its energies on Dollars. His programme of industrial education, conciliation of the South, and submission and silence as to civil and political rights, was not wholly original; the Free Negroes from 1830 up to wartime had striven to build industrial schools, and the American Missionary Association had from the first taught various trades; and Price and others had sought a way of honorable alliance with the best of the Southerners. But Mr. Washington first indissolubly linked these things; he put enthusiasm, unlimited energy, and perfect faith into this programme, and changed it from a by-path into a veritable Way of Life. And the tale of the methods by which he did this is a fascinating study of human life.

It startled the nation to hear a Negro advocating such a programme after many decades of bitter complaint; it startled and won the applause of the South, it interested and won the admiration of the North; and after a confused murmur of protest, it silenced if it did not convert the Negroes themselves.

To gain the sympathy and coöperation of the various elements comprising the white South was Mr. Washington's first task; and this, at the time Tuskegee was founded, seemed, for a black man, well-nigh impossible. And yet ten years later it was done in the word spoken at Atlanta: "In all things purely social we can be as separate as the five fingers, and yet one as the hand in all things essential to mutual progress." This "Atlanta Compromise" is by all odds the most notable thing in Mr. Washington's career. The South interpreted it in different ways: the radicals received it as a complete surrender of the demand for civil and political equality; the conservatives, as a generously conceived working basis for mutual understanding. So both approved it, and to-day its author is certainly the most distinguished Southerner since Jefferson Davis, and the one with the largest personal following.

Next to this achievement comes Mr. Washington's work in gaining place and consideration in the North. Others less shrewd and tactful had formerly essayed to sit on these two stools and had fallen between them; but as Mr. Washington knew the heart of the South from birth and training, so by singular insight he intuitively grasped the spirit of the age which was dominating the North. And so thoroughly did he learn the speech and thought of triumphant commercialism, and the ideals of material prosperity, that the picture of a lone black boy poring over a French grammar amid the weeds and dirt of a neglected home soon seemed to him the acme of absurdities. One wonders what Socrates and St. Francis of Assisi would say to this.

And yet this very singleness of vision and thorough oneness with his age is a mark of the successful man. It is as though Nature must needs make men narrow in order to give them force. So Mr. Washington's cult has gained unquestioning followers, his work has wonderfully prospered, his friends are legion, and his enemies are confounded. To-day he stands as the one recognized spokesman of his ten million fellows, and one of the most notable figures in a nation of seventy millions. One hesitates, therefore, to criticise a life which, beginning with so little, has done so much. And yet the time is come when one may speak in all sincerity and utter courtesy of the mistakes and shortcomings of Mr. Washington's career, as well as of his triumphs, without being thought captious or envious, and without forgetting that it is easier to do ill than well in the world.

The criticism that has hitherto met Mr. Washington has not always been of this broad character. In the South especially has he had to walk warily to avoid the harshest judgments, — and naturally so, for he is dealing with the one subject of deepest sensitiveness to that section. Twice — once when at the Chicago celebration of the Spanish-American War he alluded to the color-prejudice that is "eating away the vitals of the South," and once when he dined with President Roosevelt — has the resulting Southern criticism been violent enough to threaten seriously his popularity. In the North the feeling has several times forced itself into words, that Mr. Washington's counsels of submission overlooked certain elements of true manhood, and that his educational programme was unnecessarily narrow. Usually, however, such criticism has not found open expression, although, too, the spiritual sons of the Abolitionists have not been prepared to acknowledge that the schools founded before Tuskegee, by men of broad ideals and self-sacrificing spirit, were wholly failures or worthy of ridicule. While, then, criticism has not failed to follow Mr. Washington, yet the prevailing public opinion of the land has been but too willing to deliver the solution of a wearisome problem into his hands, and say, "If that is all you and your race ask, take it."

Among his own people, however, Mr. Washington has encountered the strongest and most lasting opposition, amounting at times to bitterness, and even to-day continuing strong and insistent even though largely silenced in outward expression by the public opinion of the nation. Some of this opposition is, of course, mere envy; the disappointment of displaced demagogues and the spite of narrow minds. But aside from this, there is among educated and thoughtful colored men in all parts of the land a feeling of deep regret, sorrow, and apprehension at the wide currency and ascendancy which some of Mr. Washington's theories have gained. These same men admire his sincerity of purpose, and are willing to forgive much to honest endeavor which is doing something worth the doing. They coöperate with Mr. Washington as far as they conscientiously can; and, indeed, it is no ordinary tribute to this man's tact and power that, steering as he must between so many diverse interests and opinions, he so largely retains the respect of all.

But the hushing of the criticism of honest opponents is a dangerous thing. It leads some of the best of the critics to unfortunate silence and paralysis of effort, and others to burst into speech so passionately and intemperately as to lose listeners. Honest and earnest criticism from those whose interests are most nearly touched, — criticism of writers by readers, of government by those governed, of leaders by those led, — this is the soul of democracy and the safeguard of modern society. If the best of the American Negroes receive by outer pressure a leader whom they had not recognized before, manifestly there is here a certain palpable gain. Yet there is also irreparable loss, — a loss of that peculiarly valuable education which a group receives when by search and criticism it finds and commissions its own leaders. The way in which this is done is at once the most elementary and the nicest problem of social growth. History is but the record of such group-leadership; and yet how infinitely changeful is its type and character! And of all types and kinds, what can be more instructive than the leadership of a group within a group? — that curious double movement where real progress may be negative and actual advance be relative retrogression. All this is the social student's inspiration and despair.

Now in the past the American Negro has had instructive experience in the choosing of group leaders, founding thus a peculiar dynasty which in the light of present conditions is worth while studying. When sticks and stones and beasts form the sole environment of a people, their attitude is largely one of determined opposition to and conquest of natural forces. But when to earth and brute is added an environment of men and ideas, then the attitude of the imprisoned group may take three main forms, — a feeling of revolt and revenge; an attempt to adjust all thought and action to the will of the greater group; or, finally, a determined effort at self-realization and self-development despite environing opinion. The influence of all of these attitudes at various times can be traced in the history of the American Negro, and in the evolution of his successive leaders.

Before 1750, while the fire of African freedom still burned in the veins of the slaves, there was in all leadership or attempted leadership but the one motive of revolt and revenge, — typified in the terrible Maroons, the Danish blacks, and Cato of Stono, and veiling all the Americas in fear of insurrection. The liberalizing tendencies of the latter half of the eighteenth century brought, along with kindlier relations between black and white, thoughts of ultimate adjustment and assimilation. Such aspiration was especially voiced in the earnest songs of Phyllis, in the martyrdom of Attucks, the fighting of Salem and Poor, the intellectual accomplishments of Banneker and Derham, and the political demands of the Cuffes.

Stern financial and social stress after the war cooled much of the previous humanitarian ardor. The disappointment and impatience of the Negroes at the persistence of slavery and serfdom voiced itself in two movements. The slaves in the South, aroused undoubtedly by vague rumors of the Haytian revolt, made three fierce attempts at insurrection, — in 1800 under Gabriel in Virginia, in 1822 under Vesey in Carolina, and in 1831 again in Virginia under the terrible Nat Turner. In the Free States, on the other hand, a new and curious attempt at self-development was made. In Philadelphia and New York color-prescription led to a withdrawal of Negro communicants from white churches and the formation of a peculiar socio-religious institution among the Negroes known as the African Church, — an organization still living and controlling in its various branches over a million of men.

Walker's wild appeal against the trend of the times showed how the world was changing after the coming of the cotton-gin. By 1830 slavery seemed hopelessly fastened on the South, and the slaves thoroughly cowed into submission. The free Negroes of the North, inspired by the mulatto immigrants from the West Indies, began to change the basis of their demands; they recognized the slavery of slaves, but insisted that they themselves were freemen, and sought assimilation and amalgamation with the nation on the same terms with other men. Thus, Forten and Purvis of Philadelphia, Shad of Wilmington, Du Bois of New Haven, Barbadoes of Boston, and others, strove singly and together as men, they said, not as slaves; as "people of color," not as "Negroes." The trend of the times, however, refused them recognition save in individual and exceptional cases, considered them as one with all the despised blacks, and they soon found themselves striving to keep even the rights they formerly had of voting and working and moving as freemen. Schemes of migration and colonization arose among them; but these they refused to entertain, and they eventually turned to the Abolition movement as a final refuge.

Here, led by Remond, Nell, Wells-Brown, and Douglass, a new period of self-assertion and self-development dawned. To be sure, ultimate freedom and assimilation was the ideal before the leaders, but the assertion of the manhood rights of the Negro by himself was the main reliance, and John Brown's raid was the extreme of its logic. After the war and emancipation, the great form of Frederick Douglass, the greatest of American Negro leaders, still led the host. Self-assertion, especially in political lines, was the main programme, and behind Douglass came Elliot, Bruce, and Langston, and the Reconstruction politicians, and, less conspicuous but of greater social significance Alexander Crummell and Bishop Daniel Payne.

Then came the Revolution of 1876, the suppression of the Negro votes, the changing and shifting of ideals, and the seeking of new lights in the great night. Douglass, in his old age, still bravely stood for the ideals of his early manhood, — ultimate assimilation *through* self-assertion, and on no other terms. For a time Price arose as a new leader, destined, it seemed, not to give up, but to re-state the old ideals in a form less repugnant to the white South. But he passed away in his prime. Then came the new leader. Nearly all the former ones had become leaders by the silent suffrage of their fellows, had sought to lead their own people alone, and were usually, save Douglass, little known outside their race. But Booker T. Washington arose as essentially the leader not of one race but of two, — a compromiser between the South, the North, and the Negro. Naturally the Negroes resented, at first bitterly, signs of compromise which surrendered their civil and political rights, even though this was to be exchanged for larger chances of economic development. The rich and dominating North, however, was not only weary of the race problem, but was investing largely in Southern enterprises, and welcomed any method of peaceful coöperation. Thus, by national opinion, the Negroes began to recognize Mr. Washington's leadership; and the voice of criticism was hushed.

Mr. Washington represents in Negro thought the old attitude of adjustment and submission; but adjustment at such a peculiar time as to make his programme unique. This is an age of unusual economic development, and Mr. Washington's programme naturally takes an economic cast, becoming a gospel of Work and Money to such an extent as apparently almost completely to overshadow the higher aims of life. Moreover, this is an age when the more advanced races are coming in closer contact with the less developed races, and the race-feeling is therefore intensified; and Mr. Washington's programme practically accepts the alleged inferiority of the Negro races. Again, in our own land, the reaction from the sentiment of war time has given impetus to race-prejudice against Negroes, and Mr. Washington withdraws many of the high demands of Negroes as men and American citizens. In other periods of intensified prejudice all the Negro's tendency to self-assertion has been called forth; at this period a policy of submission is advocated. In the history of nearly all other races and peoples the doctrine preached at such crises has been that manly self-respect is worth more than lands and houses, and that a people who voluntarily surrender such respect, or cease striving for it, are not worth civilizing.

In answer to this, it has been claimed that the Negro can survive only through submission. Mr. Washington distinctly asks that black people give up, at least for the present, three things; —

First, political power,

Second, insistence on civil rights,

Third, higher education of Negro youth, —

and concentrate all their energies on industrial education, the accumulation of wealth, and the conciliation of the South. This policy has been courageously and insistently advocated for over fifteen years, and has been triumphant for perhaps ten years. As a result of this tender of the palm-branch, what has been the return? In these years there have occurred:

1. The disfranchisement of the Negro.
2. The legal creation of a distinct status of civil inferiority for the Negro.

3. The steady withdrawal of aid from institutions for the higher training of the Negro.

These movements are not, to be sure, direct results of Mr. Washington's teachings; but his propaganda has, without a shadow of doubt, helped their speedier accomplishment. The question then comes: Is it possible, and probable, that nine millions of men can make effective progress in economic lines if they are deprived of political rights, made a servile caste, and allowed only the most meagre chance for developing their exceptional men? If history and reason give any distinct answer to these questions, it is an emphatic *No.* And Mr. Washington thus faces the triple paradox of his career:

1. He is striving nobly to make Negro artisans business men and property-owners; but it is utterly impossible, under modern competitive methods, for workingmen and property-owners to defend their rights and exist without the right of suffrage.
2. He insists on thrift and self-respect, but at the same time counsels a silent submission to civic inferiority such as is bound to sap the manhood of any race in the long run.
3. He advocates common-school and industrial training, and depreciates institutions of higher learning; but neither the Negro common-schools, nor Tuskegee itself, could remain open a day were it not for teachers trained in Negro colleges, or trained by their graduates.

This triple paradox in Mr. Washington's position is the object of criticism by two classes of colored Americans. One class is spiritually descended from Toussaint the Savior, through Gabriel, Vesey, and Turner, and they represent the attitude of revolt and revenge; they hate the white South blindly and distrust the white race generally, and so far as they agree on definite action, think that the Negro's only hope lies in emigration beyond the borders of the United States. And yet, by the irony of fate, nothing has more effectually made this programme seem hopeless than the recent course of the United States toward weaker and darker peoples in the West Indies, Hawaii, and the Philippines, — for where in the world may we go and be safe from lying and brute force?

The other class of Negroes who cannot agree with Mr. Washington has hitherto said little aloud. They deprecate the sight of scattered counsels, of internal disagreement; and especially they dislike making their just criticism of a useful and earnest man an excuse for a general discharge of venom from small-minded opponents. Nevertheless, the questions involved are so fundamental and serious that it is difficult to see how men like the Grimkes, Kelly Miller, J. W. E. Bowen, and other representatives of this group, can much longer be silent. Such men feel in conscience bound to ask of this nation three things:

1. The right to vote.
2. Civic equality.
3. The education of youth according to ability.

They acknowledge Mr. Washington's invaluable service in counselling patience and courtesy in such demands; they do not ask that ignorant black men vote when ignorant whites are debarred, or that any reasonable restrictions in the suffrage should not be applied; they know that the low social level of the mass of the race is responsible for much discrimination against it, but they also know, and the nation knows, that relentless color-prejudice is more often a cause than a result of the Negro's degradation; they seek the abatement of this relic of barbarism, and not its systematic encouragement and pampering by all agencies of social power from the Associated Press to the Church of Christ. They advocate, with Mr. Washington, a broad system of Negro common schools supplemented by thorough industrial training; but they are surprised that a man of Mr. Washington's insight cannot see that no such educational system ever has rested or can rest on any other basis than that of the well-equipped college and university, and they insist that there is a demand for a few such institutions throughout the South to train the best of the Negro youth as teachers, professional men, and leaders.

This group of men honor Mr. Washington for his attitude of conciliation toward the white South; they accept the "Atlanta Compromise" in its broadest interpretation; they recognize, with him, many signs of promise, many men of high purpose and fair judgment, in this section; they know that no easy task has been laid upon a region already tottering under heavy burdens. But, nevertheless, they insist that the way to truth and right lies in straightforward honesty, not in indiscriminate flattery; in praising those of the South who do well and criticising uncompromisingly those who do ill; in taking advantage of the opportunities at hand and urging their fellows to do the same, but at the same time in remembering that only a firm adherence to their higher ideals and aspirations will ever keep those ideals within the realm of possibility. They do not expect that the free right to vote, to enjoy civic rights, and to be educated, will come in a moment; they do not expect to see the bias and prejudices of years disappear at the blast of a trumpet; but they are absolutely certain that the way for a people to gain their reasonable rights is not by voluntarily throwing them away and insisting that they do not want them; that the way for a people to gain respect is not by continually belittling and ridiculing themselves; that, on the contrary, Negroes must insist continually, in season and out of season, that voting is necessary to modern manhood, that color discrimination is barbarism, and that black boys need education as well as white boys.

In failing thus to state plainly and unequivocally the legitimate demands of their people, even at the cost of opposing an honored leader, the thinking classes of American Negroes would shirk a heavy responsibility, — a responsibility to themselves, a responsibility to the struggling masses, a responsibility to the darker races of men whose future depends so largely on this American experiment, but especially a responsibility to this nation, — this common Fatherland. It is wrong to encourage a man or a people in evil-doing; it is wrong to aid and abet a national crime simply because it is unpopular not to do so. The growing spirit of kindliness and reconciliation between the North and South after the frightful differences of a generation ago ought to be a source of deep congratulation to all, and especially to those whose mistreatment caused the war; but if that reconciliation is to be marked by the industrial slavery and civic death of those same black men, with permanent legislation into a position of inferiority, then those black men, if they are really men, are called upon by every consideration of patriotism and loyalty to oppose such a course by all civilized methods, even though such opposition involves disagreement with Mr. Booker T. Washington. We have no right to sit silently by while the inevitable seeds are sown for a harvest of disaster to our children, black and white.

First, it is the duty of black men to judge the South discriminatingly. The present generation of Southerners are not responsible for the past, and they should not be blindly hated or blamed for it. Furthermore, to no class is the indiscriminate endorsement of the recent course of the South toward Negroes more nauseating than to the best thought of the South. The South is not "solid"; it is a land in the ferment of social change, wherein forces of all kinds are fighting for supremacy; and to praise the ill the South is to-day perpetrating is just as wrong as to condemn the good. Discriminating and broad-minded criticism is what the South needs, — needs it for the sake of her own white sons and daughters, and for the insurance of robust, healthy mental and moral development.

To-day even the attitude of the Southern whites toward the blacks is not, as so many assume, in all cases the same; the ignorant Southerner hates the Negro, the workingmen fear his competition, the money-makers wish to use him as a laborer, some of the educated see a menace in his upward development, while others — usually the sons of the masters — wish to help him to rise. National opinion has enabled this last class to maintain the Negro common schools, and to protect the Negro partially in property, life, and limb. Through the pressure of the money-makers, the Negro is in danger of being reduced to semi-slavery, especially in the country districts; the workingmen, and those of the educated who fear the Negro, have united to disfranchise him, and some have urged his deportation; while the passions of the ignorant are easily aroused to lynch and abuse any black man. To praise this intricate whirl of thought and prejudice is nonsense; to inveigh indiscriminately against "the South" is unjust;

but to use the same breath in praising Governor Aycock, exposing Senator Morgan, arguing with Mr. Thomas Nelson Page, and denouncing Senator Ben Tillman, is not only sane, but the imperative duty of thinking black men.

It would be unjust to Mr. Washington not to acknowledge that in several instances he has opposed movements in the South which were unjust to the Negro; he sent memorials to the Louisiana and Alabama constitutional conventions, he has spoken against lynching, and in other ways has openly or silently set his influence against sinister schemes and unfortunate happenings. Notwithstanding this, it is equally true to assert that on the whole the distinct impression left by Mr. Washington's propaganda is, first, that the South is justified in its present attitude toward the Negro because of the Negro's degradation; secondly, that the prime cause of the Negro's failure to rise more quickly is his wrong education in the past; and, thirdly, that his future rise depends primarily on his own efforts. Each of these propositions is a dangerous half-truth. The supplementary truths must never be lost sight of: first, slavery and race-prejudice are potent if not sufficient causes of the Negro's position; second, industrial and common-school training were necessarily slow in planting because they had to await the black teachers trained by higher institutions, — it being extremely doubtful if any essentially different development was possible, and certainly a Tuskegee was unthinkable before 1880; and, third, while it is a great truth to say that the Negro must strive and strive mightily to help himself, it is equally true that unless his striving be not simply seconded, but rather aroused and encouraged, by the initiative of the richer and wiser environing group, he cannot hope for great success.

In his failure to realize and impress this last point, Mr. Washington is especially to be criticised. His doctrine has tended to make the whites, North and South, shift the burden of the Negro problem to the Negro's shoulders and stand aside as critical and rather pessimistic spectators; when in fact the burden belongs to the nation, and the hands of none of us are clean if we bend not our energies to righting these great wrongs.

The South ought to be led, by candid and honest criticism, to assert her better self and do her full duty to the race she has cruelly wronged and is still wronging. The North — her co-partner in guilt — cannot salve her conscience by plastering it with gold. We cannot settle this problem by diplomacy and suaveness, by "policy" alone. If worse come to worst, can the moral fibre of this country survive the slow throttling and murder of nine millions of men?

The black men of America have a duty to perform, a duty stern and delicate, — a forward movement to oppose a part of the work of their greatest leader. So far as Mr. Washington preaches Thrift,

Patience, and Industrial Training for the masses, we must hold up his hands and strive with him, rejoicing in his honors and glorying in the strength of this Joshua called of God and of man to lead the headless host. But so far as Mr. Washington apologizes for injustice, North or South, does not rightly value the privilege and duty of voting, belittles the emasculating effects of caste distinctions, and opposes the higher training and ambition of our brighter minds, — so far as he, the South, or the Nation, does this, — we must unceasingly and firmly oppose them. By every civilized and peaceful method we must strive for the rights which the world accords to men, clinging unwaveringly to those great words which the sons of the Fathers would fain forget: "We hold these truths to be self-evident: That all men are created equal; that they are endowed by their Creator with certain unalienable rights; that among these are life, liberty, and the pursuit of happiness."

## *Critical Reading and Commentary W. E. B. Du Bois's "Of Mr. Booker T. Washington and Others"*

**Commentary.** *In this essay, the critics begin by sampling the responses to what is generally regarded a landmark work, a turning point in African-American literature and in social and political thought. Examining the work of other critics and commentators, the authors of this essay describe the reactions of those who see in this work strong personal and poetic appeal derived from the intricate weaving of political and aesthetic strands. Noting the diversity in style and substance in Du Bois's collection, they comment on the pattern of unity in diversity that emerges. This leads them to raise an interesting critical question: How was such a powerful unified voice produced amid such diversity?*

Virtually from the moment of its publication in 1903, W. E. B. Du Bois's *The Souls of Black Folk* has exercised a unique and profound influence upon African-American intellectuals. After reading the book, Jessie Fauset wrote to Du Bois, praising him for voicing "the intricacies of the blind maze of thought and action along which the modern, educated colored man or woman struggles" (Rampersad, 1990, p. 68). John Daniels, a contemporary reviewer, celebrated the book for its "dominant spirituality"; it was, in his judgment, "a poem, a spiritual, not an intellectual offering," and its merit was not that of "a polemic, a transient thing, but that of a poem, a thing permanent" (Gates, 1989, p. xiv). Writing in 1912, James Weldon Johnson asserted that *Souls* was remarkable because, "in depicting the life, the ambitions, the struggles, and the passions of those who are striving to break the narrow limits of tradition," it began to give "the country something new and unknown" about the African-American experience (Gates, p. xiv). In later years, Johnson would recall that the book served as the rallying-point for "black radicals opposing [Booker T.] Washington" (Rampersad, p. 81) and judged that it had exerted a "greater effect upon and within the Negro race in America than any other single book published in this country since *Uncle Tom's Cabin*" (Gates, p. xiv). William Ferriss, in his *The African Abroad* (1913), referred to *Souls* as "the political Bible of the Negro race" (Gates, p. xiv), and he testified that it "came to me as a bolt from the blue" — an expression in "words of magic beauty of the worth and sacredness of human personality even when clothed in a black skin." In Du Bois, Ferriss discovered "a self-realization of the ideals of his own race" (Gates, pp. xvii–xviii). Among later generations of African-Americans, Langston Hughes reported that his "earliest memories of written words" were "those of Du Bois and the Bible" (Gates, p. xiv), and Henry Louis Gates found in the book "that special exhilarating feeling any reader gets when an author names things that the reader has felt very deeply but could not articulate" (Gates, p. xxii).

In drawing back from his own personal response and making a general assessment of the influence of the work, Gates holds that it has served as "a touchstone" for successive generations of black scholars and as "an urtext of the African-American experience" (p. xvii). And this judgment is consistent with the views of most other historians. David Levering Lewis contends that publication of *Souls* was an epochal event "dividing history into a before and after. Like fireworks going off in a cemetery, its fourteen essays were sound and light enlivening the inert and despairing. It was an electrifying manifesto, mobilizing a people for bitter, prolonged struggle to win a place in history" (1993, p. 277). Arnold Rampersad makes the equally strong claim that: "If all of a nation's literature may stem from one book, as Hemingway implied about *The Adventures of Huckleberry Finn*, then it can as accurately be said that all of Afro-American literature of a creative nature has proceeded from Du Bois's comprehensive statement on the nature of the people in *The Souls of Black Folk*" (p. 89).

All of these recollections and evaluations not only stress the importance of the book, but they also suggest the unified, almost electrical, effect it has had upon readers. In one great, comprehensive stroke, Du Bois seems to identify and give voice to a marginalized people; he creates what Gates calls a "narrative voice, a fictionalized 'I' " (p. xviii) that articulates "for the inarticulate insider and for the curious outsider . . . the cultural particularity of African-Americans" (xviii). Yet, this voice is complex and multi-faceted, and so readers and critics focus upon different dimensions of the book. *Souls* is a "poem," a "spiritual," a literary classic that influences a tradition of "creative" writing. And it is also a "manifesto," a "political bible," a polemic that serves as a "rallying-point" within a specific and heated controversy between African-Americans. The reception of *The Souls of Black Folk*, then, indicates an interesting pattern of unity in diversity; readers note and separate political and aesthetic strands within the text, while they testify to the deeply resonant unity that it conveys.

The diversity of response is hardly surprising, since as Arnold Rampersad had observed, *Souls* is "one of the more curious books of American Literature, a diverse mixture of styles and genres" (p. 69). The book consists of fourteen chapters — thirteen essays and one short story. Nine of the essays reprint or adapt previously published material, and the essays vary greatly both in subject-matter and tone, ranging from a scholarly study of the Freedmen's Bureau to an intensely personal and emotional reflection on the death of the author's son. Equally varied is Du Bois's style, which extends from simplicity to what Rampersad (p. 69) calls an "almost Ciceronian confabulation." On first inspection, the book seems to be a loose collection of occasional pieces, and the problem for critics is to explain how Du Bois could forge such a powerful, unified voice out of so many apparently disparate elements.

***Commentary.*** *In order to solve their critical problem, the critics must make a decision as to the focus of their study. In a work of this sort, particularly, the critics must focus their attention. Their survey of critical reactions reinforce the notion that the essay on Washington caused a serious ferment both in and outside of the African-American community; the controversy arising from this essay, the critics argue, is the result of Du Bois's clear efforts to develop and justify a political program, a successful attempt to inject his perspective into the public argument.*

*The difficulty the critics face is how to go about studying this intricate piece. Note how they identify recurrent themes that loop through the work and point to the contrast between the style of Du Bois's essay and that of Washington's works. Their careful reading of the text suggests to them that Du Bois is talking about "criticism" in different ways, combining, as he does so, scholarly and political motifs. The critics conclude that rhetorical action is the means whereby unity is achieved. Before explaining just how this rhetorical action works, they need first to sketch the historical context that demonstrates the tensions out of which the essay arose.*

In this paper, our inquiry focuses on only one chapter of the book, the essay "Of Mr. Booker T. Washington and Others." This chapter is of the most immediate and direct interest for students of public argumentation, for it is here that Du Bois explicitly develops and justifies a political program. Donald B. Gibson considers it the "most arresting chapter of the book" (1989, p. xix), and it is certainly Du Bois's "most controversial" essay (Rampersad, p. 69), and "the key to the book's political intent" (Rampersad, p. 81). Its effect was to make *Souls* "a contemporary bombshell" (Lewis, p. 287). In this polite but strong critique of Booker T. Washington, Du Bois established the argumentative ground for one of the most notable controversies in African-American political history — the "war between the Tuskegee Machine and the Talented Tenth" (Lewis, p. 277). And in the process, Du Bois set in motion rhetorical forces that would lead to the Niagara Movement and contribute significantly to the formation of the N.A.A.C.P. Surely, then, "Of Mr. Booker T. Washington and Others" occupies a crucial position not only in African-American literature but also in the tradition of American political rhetoric.

Belatedly, scholars in our discipline have begun to recognize the essay and its importance. It now appears with increasing frequency in course reading-lists and in anthologies of public address, where it is often paired with Washington's "Cotton States Exposition Address." Yet, within our disciplinary literature, we still cannot find a single sustained analysis of the essay, and our present purpose is to make amends for this omission. Our task, however, is complicated by a tension between prominent characteristics of the essay, which reflect the special and unconventional rhetoric of the book as a whole, and the conventional norms for argumentative analysis of political rhetoric.

Following the traditional disciplinary lines of inquiry, a rhetorical critic would stress the immediate historical context, define the issues dividing Du Bois and Washington, and study the essay from within this context. The result would be to isolate the essay from the rest of the book and to offer an analysis that abstracts its argumentative structures and strategies and assesses them in relation to a specific political debate. No doubt, a study of this kind would yield some useful results, but it would almost necessarily slight what we have noted as a special and crucial feature of Du Bois's book — its capacity to merge diverse elements into a unified voice. As Gates has argued, the history of the book's reception indicates its synthetic power: "That the sheer rhetorical force of Du Bois's text called attention to itself almost as often as his political positions did is testament to the author's knowledge of craft, to his sensitivity to the essay form. . . . Du Bois knew, above all else, that the noblest sentiment could not stand by itself, as it were, that form and content, manner and matter were one" (pp. xiii–xiv). Mindful of this point, we intend to approach the argumentation in "Of Mr. Booker T. Washington and Others" as something embedded within the larger rhetorical movement of the text — as something intimately and inseparably connected with the voice that Du Bois projects. Indeed, in our view, the construction of a distinctive and effective political voice for African-Americans was a central problem in the essay. Under the circumstances Du Bois confronted, what an African-American might argue was a less pressing issue than the question of how an African-American could make a public argument at all. And if we are to understand how Du Bois dealt with this fundamental problem, we must attend to the voice that he enacted within the text as well as to the specific political positions he articulated.

In taking this approach to the text, we need to qualify Rampersad's judgment that " 'Of Mr. Booker T. Washington and Others' is a rigidly unpoetic" essay (p. 69). Compared to other chapters in *The Souls of Black Folk*, this essay displays a more tightly structured sequence of linear argument and narrative, and it has none of the personal reflections or lyrical expressions that appear elsewhere. Yet, if, for these reasons, the essay might be considered "unpoetic" (or at least "less poetic" than other parts of the book), it hardly seems rigid or inartistic. Between and within its linear units, various recurrent themes loop through the essay, gathering force as they reverberate against one another; thus, for example, there is a subtly repeated contrast between Washington's narrow, single-minded posture and the "double movement" Du Bois describes and enacts. Moreover, Du Bois shifts his perspective agilely from South to North, and in almost rhythmic, chiastic sequence, back and forth from within the African-American community to the "environing" white society. Perhaps even more striking is the way that Du Bois blends the tonalities of academic inquiry with the rhetoric of advocacy. The essay begins with and sustains the "scholarly narrative posture or radical of presentation" that Stepto (1985, p. 149) finds typical of the book, but it develops into a pointed and controversial criticism of Washington's political program. Indeed, Du Bois uses and conceives "criticism" in several different ways; he not only criticizes Washington's politics, but he offers a seemingly distanced and objective critical account of Washington's rhetorical success, and he includes a rather philosophical disquisition about the role of criticism in a democratic society. In short, then, the essay hardly seems rigid. The coherence of the argumentative structure does not preclude a complex and lively interplay of themes, perspectives, and postures. And, as in the book as a whole, these diverse elements do not seem forced or discordant but are harmonized within the form of the essay and resonate through a single, finely balanced voice. In the interpretation of the essay that follows, we hope to explain how the rhetorical action of the text works to achieve this unity in diversity. But before we can turn to the text, we need to offer a brief account of its historical context.

At the dawn of the twentieth century, Booker T. Washington was the nation's preeminent black citizen. Working in the Deep South and constrained by the virulent racism of the post-reconstruction era, Washington managed to establish a successful school for industrial education at Tuskegee; and in 1895, he captured national attention through his "Cotton States Exposition Speech" — a masterpiece of rhetorical accommodation. Washington solidified and extended his influence through a network of personal and political alliances that came to be known as the "Tuskegee Machine," and he won support (both financial and political) from Northern white philanthropists. In 1901, his reputation was further magnified through his foundation of the National Negro Business League and the publication of his widely read and much acclaimed autobiography, *Up from Slavery*.

Meanwhile, Du Bois had embarked on a promising academic career. In 1898, after completing his Ph.D. at Harvard and his impressive sociological monograph, *The Philadelphia Negro*, Du Bois accepted a position at Atlanta University. His duties included, among other things, direction of the "Atlanta University Studies," an annual series devoted to scholarly inquiry into the condition of African-Americans. But the racism he experienced in Atlanta soon led him to reconsider his priorities. Reluctantly, Du Bois concluded that he could not wall himself off "in the ivory tower of race" (Lewis, p. 213). He had once thought that "knowledge based on scientific investigation" was sufficient to combat racism, but he had come to realize that the "cure wasn't simply telling people the truth, it was inducing them to act on the truth" (Lewis, p. 225). Thus, while he did not abandon his commitment to scholarship, Du Bois gradually became a political advocate.

Du Bois's growing reputation as a scholar and his quickening interest in politics inevitably brought him into contact with the "Wizard of Tuskegee." At first, relations between the two were cooperative and apparently cordial, but the changing political climate within the African-American community soon brought them into conflict (see Lewis, pp. 211–264). Washington, in fact, was a complex man, a shrewd politician, whose motives and actions often were more complicated than they appeared to be. Nevertheless, his public rhetoric was a simple and straightforward blend of the "politics of compromise and the mien of ingratiation" (Lewis, p. 238). Many middle and upper-middle class African-Americans found this stance uncomfortable and dangerous. Increasingly, they chafed under Washington's presumed leadership. They resented his obsequious posture before white authority and feared the consequences of a policy that accommodated to abridgements of political rights without self-assertive protest against them. By virtue of his background, education, and temperament, Du Bois was drawn into the orbit of this incipient revolt, and in 1901, his review of *Up from Slavery*, published in *The Dial*, "fired the opening salvo" (Lewis, p. 264) in the struggle to challenge Washington's hegemony. This review served as the basis for the essay that appeared two years later in *The Souls of Black Folk*, and the first half of the essay covers the same themes as the review and repeats much of its language verbatim. Nevertheless, "Of Mr. Booker T. Washington and Others" was "honed" and "expanded" to the point that, as Lewis has said, "it was virtually a new piece altogether" (p. 287).

***Commentary.*** *Now the critics come to grips with the rhetorical movement in the text. They identify the "voice" of the author, showing the more "impersonal," the "academic" voice that presents a sociological and historical diagnosis of the rise of Washington's leadership concurrent with the regression of African American rights. They show how Du Bois's analytical discussion points to the support of Washington's leadership by forces outside of the black community and thus results in the silencing of black voices.*

*Then the critics describe and explain the way in which a move is made as Du Bois makes the transition from diagnosis to the argumentative voice. Note the way the critics track the movement as the argument to end black silence first dissects polar racial reactions and then proceeds to a historical account of the patterns of black leadership and the implications of such styles of leadership in assessing Washington's role in limiting African-American self-determination through the silencing of the black voice. Now, the critics are able to demonstrate, Du Bois assumes the argumentative voice of the political activist. They go on to show how the first half of the text ends where it began by associating Washington with the surrounding forces that repress African-Americans and silence them. The critics in this section have shown the uses and effectiveness of the scholarly voice as it provides the tools necessary for the political voice to be expressed in the second half of Du Bois's essay.*

### First Movement: Diagnosis

The essay begins with these remarks:

> Easily the most striking thing in the history of the American Negro since 1876 is the ascendancy of Mr. Booker T. Washington. It began at the time when war memories and ideals were rapidly passing; a day of astonishing commercial development was dawning; a sense of doubt and hesitation overtook the freedmen's sons, — then it was that his leading began. Mr. Washington came, with a single definite programme, at the psychological moment when the nation was a little ashamed of having bestowed so much sentiment on Negroes, and was concentrating its energies on Dollars.

This passage deserves careful attention, since, in compact form, it illustrates the rhetorical precision of Du Bois's prose. In three sentences, Du Bois establishes a tone for the essay, suggests, but does not yet declare, an attitude toward Washington, and prefigures the structure of the first half of the essay.

The opening sentence establishes the author's narrative stance; his perspective is distanced, removed from the moment as it sweeps over a wider historical vista, and his voice is impersonal, academic, clinically diagnostic. From this perspective, what strikes Du Bois is not Washington as an agent, as an active leader, but his inert placement along the historical landscape — his emergence is not even an event, but a "thing." The impersonal and indirect construction of the sentence strongly suggests Washington's passivity. Consider how different the force of the sentence would be if it were cast in more active, and perhaps more normal, syntax, so that it would read: Mr. Booker T. Washington's ascendancy is easily the most striking thing in the history of the American Negro since 1876. In Du Bois's version, however, Washington's name emerges only at the end of the sentence, insulated from the verb by a preposition, and his ascendancy appears less as a force acting in history than as something that simply happened in history. Finally, the temporal frame that Du Bois uses is also rhetorically significant. Washington is viewed from within the context of events that have occurred since 1876 — that is, since the end of Reconstruction and during the era of Jim Crow — a low-point in African-American history. This suggests that his ascendancy as leader corresponds with a regression in the fate of his people.

Passing over the second sentence in our passage for the moment, we note that the third sentence presents Washington as a more active agent. Here his name appears at the beginning of the sentence and in the nominative case. But the stress falls not on what Washington did, but upon the moment when he came on the scene. He was simply in the right place at the right time, and insofar as he engaged in any independent action, it was to "put forward a single definite programme" that was suited to the circumstances. Washington, then, remains an essentially passive figure; his program reacts to external forces, but does nothing to resist or alter them.

These two sentences anticipate a number of key themes that persist through the essay: that Washington's program is a passive accommodation to external circumstances; that his leadership is rooted in sources outside the African-American community; that it is excessively narrow and single-minded; and that it has a decidedly regressive aspect.

The second sentence also suggests some of these themes, but its most prominent feature is the convoluted syntax; the word order is manipulated so that the sentence is encased by the verb "began" — which refers to Washington's leadership. This long, complex sentence, then, ultimately returns to its point of origin, since Washington's passive but inescapable presence binds it at either end. As we shall discover, the structure of this sentence prefigures the structure of the entire first half of the essay, which circles from and to Washington's hegemonic presence and develops a motif of entrapment.

Having acknowledged Washington's ascendancy, Du Bois next proposes to explain it. He approaches this issue in a distinctively academic voice. Washington's rise to prominence, Du Bois explains, commands attention because "the tale of the methods by which he did this is a fascinating study of human life." The tone here is not that of a political advocate, but of a scholar who finds the subject "fascinating" and who studies it from a distanced perspective so as to understand something about "human life." Except for a few short ironic comments, Du Bois maintains this scholarly voice throughout the first half of the essay, and the reader is invited to approach the text as historical and sociological diagnosis rather than as partisan argument.

As he assesses Washington's methods, Du Bois assumes a stance very like that of a neo-Aristotelian rhetorical critic. His interest focuses on instrumental effect, and the central question is: How did Washington succeed in persuading his audience by accommodating to it? The audience, however, is complex, and in his summary overview, Du Bois indicates its various components: Washington's program "startled and won the applause of the South, it interested and won the admiration of the North; and after a confused murmur of protest, it silenced if it did not convert the Negroes themselves." This technique of dividing and enumerating the parts of a subject is typical of Du Bois (see Rampersad, p. 73), and by giving the text a linear, analytic quality, it strongly reinforces the academic tone of the essay. In the analysis that follows, Du Bois begins with what seems a straightforward seriatim treatment of his sub-headings.

Concerning the South, Washington's achievement was remarkable, for he had to confront the "well-nigh impossible" task of gaining sympathy from the "various elements comprising" the white community. Yet, he won approval in a single speech — indeed in a single image comparing racial relations to the fingers of a hand. This "Atlanta Compromise," as Du Bois calls it, was the most "notable thing in Washington's career," since its ambiguity allowed both Southern conservatives and radicals to decode it to their own satisfaction, and it provided Washington with a secure base in his own region.

Concerning the North, Washington had gained place and consideration, where others "less shrewd and tactful" had failed to cross the sectional line. By a "singular insight," he "intuitively grasped the spirit of the age which was dominating the North" and was able to "learn the speech and thought of triumphant commercialism and the ideals of material prosperity" (p. 31).

Following the three-part division that Du Bois had outlined, we would now expect him to account for Washington's persuasive impact within the black community. But Du Bois does not discuss this matter directly — and for reasons that were implicit in his initial formulation. He had asserted that Washington "won the applause of the South" and the "admiration of the North," but his program had "silenced . . . the Negroes themselves." The earlier suggestion that Washington's leadership was imposed from the outside now becomes more explicit. By narrowing his vision and shaping it into oneness with the vision of his white audience, Washington has become the only "recognized spokesman of his ten million fellows." The tale of

Washington's methods, then, reveals leadership that silences a community through accommodation to forces external to it.

The critical diagnosis of Washington's rhetoric ends with the silence of African-Americans, and the problem Du Bois now confronts is how to generate a critical voice for the black community. He must open a space for criticism of Washington — a basis for an apparently loyal opposition. This task, Du Bois advises his readers, is not to be taken lightly, since "one hesitates to criticize a life which, beginning with so little, has done so much." Nevertheless the time has come to "speak in all sincerity and utter courtesy of the mistakes and shortcomings of Mr. Washington's career."

Such criticism, no matter how sincere or courteous, requires a partisan, argumentative voice that Du Bois has studiously avoided to this point and that he is still not ready to assume. Retaining his professorial demeanor, he defers direct criticism of Washington until he has added two more items to his social and historical diagnosis of the situation. First, assuming the role of social theorist, he considers existing criticisms of Washington, finds them inadequate, and sketches the general dimensions of an appropriate form of criticism. Second, assuming the role of historian, Du Bois crosses the veil and studies the African-American tradition in order to place Washington in context and to locate indigenous grounds for opposition to his leadership.

Just as he had reviewed the positive reception of Washington in the Southern, Northern, and African-American communities, so also Du Bois traces the critical response through the same divisions. In both North and South, criticism "has not failed to follow Mr. Washington, yet the prevailing public opinion of the land has been too willing to deliver the solution of a wearisome problem into his hands. . . ." "Among his own people," however, the situation is quite different. There he has "encountered the strongest and most lasting opposition, amounting at times to bitterness, and even today continuing strong and insistent even though largely silenced by the public opinion of the nation."

The difference represented here between these communities is not merely a matter of the breadth or strength of antagonism — there is a more fundamental distinction between criticism and opposition, between publicly voiced opinions and mute sentiments. However they differ in other respects, white Southerners and Northerners both are free to express critical judgments. But, on the other side of the veil there is no criticism; there is silent opposition. Du Bois's three-fold classification, then, reduces itself to two essential categories — to two worlds separated by race, the one critical and self-determining, the other mute and passive.

Du Bois rounds out this section of the essay with a brief but striking reflection about the function of criticism. "The hushing of criticism of honest opponents," he warns, "is a dangerous thing." It silences and paralyzes those who are well-intentioned, and it incites others "to burst into speech so passionately and intemperately as to lose listeners. Honest and earnest criticism from those whose interests are most nearly touched, — criticism of writers by readers, of government by those governed, of leaders by those who are led — this is the soul of democracy and the safeguard of modern society." If African-Americans fail to break the silence and accede to a leader because of "outer pressure," they gain something palpable. "Yet there is also an irreparable loss, — a loss of that peculiarly valuable education which a group receives when by search and criticism it finds and commissions its own leaders."

This disquisition on criticism emphasizes the extent to which Washington's hegemony limits authentic self-determination within the African-American world. The remedy to this problem is criticism, but not small-minded criticism based in envy or narrow partisanship. Du Bois sets for himself and his fellows a higher standard — criticism that is honest, courteous, and broad, and that serves as an instrument of social education. This form of criticism offers the vehicle for developing a vocal but loyal opposition to Washington and for constructive self-assertion. An effective critical voice, however, requires more than an appropriate form; it must also recognize options that exist within the life-world of the community; it must consider alternatives rooted in the history of the people addressed. Washington's monolithic leadership occludes recognition of such alternatives, and thus, Du Bois looks behind and beyond Washington and offers an historical account of the African-American experience in choosing group leaders.

Retaining his detached, analytical voice, Du Bois presents this account as a lesson in social history. The issue of group leadership, Professor Du Bois tell us, raises "the most elementary and the nicest problem of social growth." And the African-American experience is particularly "instructive" because it deals with "the leadership of a group within a group — that curious double movement where real progress may be negative and actual advance may be relative retrogression." At this point, Du Bois enacts the concept he names, for the essay itself becomes double as Du Bois takes the reader behind veil into the "black world."[1]

Du Bois's history identifies three patterns of African-American leadership, which are categorized in terms of the response to the dominant white society. At one extreme is a "feeling of revolt and revenge," and at the other is "an attempt to adjust all thought and action to the will of the greater group." The middle response is characterized by a "determined effort at self-realization and self-development despite environing opinion." These three positions correspond with the three reactions to Washington's leadership that Du Bois had listed earlier: intemperate outburst, silence, and, between them, broad-minded but self-assertive criticism. In the second half of the essay, Du Bois's move from diagnostic critique to political activism depends on the alignment of these two sets of categories. In both cases, Du Bois affiliates himself with the middle position.

Du Bois's narrative shows a complex but basically progressive development of the three leadership patterns up to 1876. There was, on his account, a general movement from "revenge and revolt" (the sole motive prior to 1750), to assimilation and amalgamation, and then, with the advent of the Abolition movement, to self-assertion and self-development. But the "Revolution of 1876" and the repressive measures that followed in its wake, blunted this progression, and after the death of Douglass and Price, the strategy of self-assertion became decrepit.

And then, as at the beginning of the essay, "came the new leader" — Washington. In this second coming, Washington remains just as Du Bois had described him at the outset of the essay — a "compromiser between the South, the North, and the Negro." And while African-Americans resented "signs of compromise which surrendered their civil and political rights," the circumstances seemed to offer no alternative. "Thus, by national opinion, the Negroes began to recognize Mr. Washington's leadership; and," Du Bois laments, "the voice of criticism was hushed." Thus, the first half of the essay ends where it begins — with Booker T. Washington reigning over a suppressed and silent black community.

The significance of the cyclical structure of the first half of the essay is clarified by comparing it with the review of *Up from Slavery* upon which it is based (Du Bois, 1901). The essay repeats most of the material in the review and often uses the same language, but there are two significant differences. First, Du Bois reverses the order of his two main topics in the later version. In the review, he begins with the history of African-American leadership and then describes Washington's reception among whites in the South and North. The piece, therefore, offers an unbroken chronological narrative, and the rise of Washington might seem an organic part of that history. In "Of Mr. Booker T. Washington and Others," Du Bois breaks the narrative; the analysis of Washington's reception, set in the context of post-Reconstruction history, comes first, and then Du Bois offers his account of African-American leadership — a narrative that stretches back to the early eighteenth century. In this revised sequence, Washington appears to be estranged from the organic history of the people he leads. Viewed from the perspective of events coming after the "Revolution of 1876," Washington's ascendancy might seem an advance for African-Americans, but viewed from a broader historical vista, his program seems atavistic — a regression to the point before black leaders advocated self-assertion and self-determination. Equally important, the reversal of topics allows Du Bois to position

Washington at either end of the whole historical development; Washington surrounds this section of the essay, and his omnipresence iconically represents the condition of a black community surrounded, suppressed, and silenced by outer forces.

Secondly, the essay contains one entirely new passage — the short but powerful disquisition on the role of criticism in a free society. Set squarely between the analysis of the outer white world and the inner world of black experience, these remarks about criticism as an educational process, an instrument of self-determination, and a safeguard for democracy at once emphasize the distance then existing between the two worlds and suggest a vehicle for reducing this distance. The hushing of criticism is the clearest sign of the disempowered and alienated condition of the black community, since a people who lack a critical voice cannot engage in self-determination or participate in a self-governing polity. Implicitly, it follows that Washington's program of assimilation, his rhetoric of silent acquiescence, cannot resolve the fundamental problem confronting his people. On the other hand, constructive criticism of Washington rooted within the black community and its traditions is an assertive act of self-determination; it breaks the wall of silence, and ultimately it suggests a means of participating in the outer world while retaining the group identity that African-Americans neither can nor should abandon.

Throughout the first half of the essay, Du Bois represents the condition of a black community repressed and silenced by external forces. Speaking within this frame, Du Bois refrains from direct criticism and political advocacy, as though this aspect of his own voice is hushed by the circumstances it describes. Yet, he takes a perspective and projects a voice that can transcend these limitations at a conceptual level. As a scholar positioned at some distance above the immediate context, he can see and describe things beyond the walls now surrounding his community. In a seemingly dispassionate narrative, he can diagnose Washington's hegemony and identify alternatives to it, since, when viewed against the sweep of African-American history, Washington's program seems neither inevitable nor unavoidable. The full record includes other, more active, possibilities for the black community. And thoughtful reflection indicates that constructive criticism can serve as the vehicle for realizing these possibilities. Thus, the scholarly voice of the first half of the essay offers the equipment needed for an effective political voice, and in the second half, Du Bois puts this equipment to use. In the unfolding development of the essay, advocacy grows out of diagnosis; narrative gives way to argument.

***Commentary.*** *As the critics turn to the second half of Du Bois's essay, they explain the refutational character of this section. As they explained earlier, the* *essay loops back on itself throughout. After making explicit Washington's attitudes (implicitly stated previously), Du Bois, as the critics demonstrate, aligns himself with the constructive critics and thus is able to offer a reflection of his earlier observations. His practice is consistent with the theory he has expounded on in the first half of the speech. Observe the ways in which the critics show that Du Bois returns to the identification of Washington with the white culture and describe Du Bois's move to reassert the need for — indeed, the positive good arising from — criticism in a democratic society.*

### Second Movement: Advocacy

Du Bois opens the second half of the essay by plainly asserting a point he had only implied earlier in the essay: "Mr. Washington represents in Negro thought the old attitude of adjustment and submission." A related series of equally pointed assertions follow in rapid sequence: Washington's program has become "a gospel of Work and Money to such an extent as apparently almost completely to overshadow the higher aims of life," and it "practically accepts the alleged inferiority of the Negro races." Washington "withdraws many of the high demands of Negroes as men and as American citizens," and he "distinctly asks that black people give up, at least for the present, three things, — First, political power, Second, insistence on civil rights, Third, higher education of Negro youth. . . ."

These three things serve as the basis for a refutational critique of Washington's program and for the alternative that Du Bois advocates. The refutation comes in the form of short, crisp ad hominem argumentation. Even if African-Americans accept Washington's goals, they cannot achieve them so long as they accept and act on his premises concerning political, social, and educational issues. Washington's position faces what Du Bois calls a "triple paradox": (1) Washington seeks to make Negro artisans "business men and property owners," but lacking the power to defend their rights and to vote, the goal is unattainable "under modern competitive methods"; (2) Washington wants to inculcate thrift and self-respect, but he also "counsels a silent submission to civic inferiority such as is bound to sap the manhood of any race in the long run"; and (3) he stresses the role of common schools in industrial training and de-emphasizes higher learning, but the common schools could not function without teachers educated "in the Negro colleges."

At this point, Du Bois breaks his line of argument and offers some reflections about his stance toward Washington. The "triple paradox of Mr. Washington's position," Du Bois observes, "is the object of attack by two classes of colored Americans." One of these classes represents the old attitude of revolt and revenge, and their criticism may be dismissed, since they offer nothing constructive. The other class dislikes "internal disagreements" and would not make "their just criticism of a useful and earnest man an excuse for a general discharge of venom. . . ." Nevertheless, the issues are so fundamental that representatives of this group can no longer hold their tongues. Du Bois, of course, belongs to this second class, which seeks to revivify the tradition of self-determination and self-assertion. The way he positions himself in this passage consistently reflects his earlier, more detached, observations about both criticism and African-American history. In confronting Washington's assimilationism, he cannot be silent, but he will not make intemperate outbursts. He offers constructive criticism rather than either of these extremes. Likewise, his political program of self-assertion and self-determination holds to the middle course between submission and revolt. In short, even as he engages in a sharp, clearly political attack against Washington, Du Bois recalls his earlier scholarly voice and attempts to demonstrate that his critical practice consistently enacts the balance and breadth that he had endorsed in theory.

As he closes this reflection, Du Bois turns to the constructive side of his own political argument. In substance, his program consists in the assertion of the three things Washington would ask African-Americans to deny: "1. The right to vote. 2. Civic equality. 3. The education of youth according to ability." More significant, perhaps, is the tone that emerges and its implicit contrast to Washington's carefully moderated voice of compromise. Du Bois's direct attacks on Washington represent self-assertion through criticism, and as he articulates them, Du Bois revivifies the African-American tradition of self-assertive protest — a tradition Washington had abandoned. The vitality of that tradition now makes itself apparent in the text. The group for whom he speaks, Du Bois asserts, is "absolutely certain that the way for a people to gain their reasonable rights is not by voluntarily throwing them away and insisting that they do not want them; that the way for a people to gain respect is not by continually belittling and ridiculing themselves; that, on the contrary, the Negroes must insist continually, in season and out of season, that voting is necessary to modern manhood, that color discrimination is barbarism, and that black boys need education as well as white boys."

Both the tone and direction of Du Bois's argument seem almost to propel him across the veil to a point where he can, and must, criticize the dominant white culture. The critique of Washington centers on his identity with that culture, on his accommodation to its values, interests, and prejudices. Thus, criticism of the one implies criticism of the other, and as the essay draws to its conclusion, Du Bois explicitly develops this connection. The second half of the essay, then, also exhibits a "double movement" between the white and black worlds. But the pattern of movement is chiastically reversed; the first half proceeds from the outer world of white culture to the inner world of black experience, while the second begins with a critique of Washington rooted in the black community and then spirals outward toward criticism of the surrounding white society.

Du Bois now argues that broad-minded, balanced criticism is a civic duty necessary for sustaining the larger culture. Thus, if the "thinking classes of American Negroes" fail to voice the legitimate demands of their people, they "shirk a heavy responsibility," not just "to themselves," but also to "the struggling masses," to the "darker races of men whose future depends largely on the American experiment," and especially "to this nation — this common Fatherland." This appeal to the greater good of the nation makes Washington's efforts to appease South and North dangerous not just for African-Americans but for the country as a whole. It is because of Washington's dual role as mediator and national black leader that African-Americans have been unable to find the critical voice required for participation in an active democracy, and so long as they are excluded, the American democratic ideal is at hazard. Patriotism and loyalty call upon black men to voice their disagreements with Washington, for they "have no right to sit silently by while the inevitable seeds of destruction are sown for a harvest of disaster to our children, black and white."

It is also the duty of black men to "judge the South discriminatingly" — to praise what is good in the region and "use the same breath" to denounce what is evil. "The South ought to be led," Du Bois argues, "by candid and honest criticism, to assert her better self and do her full duty to the race she has cruelly wronged and is still wronging." At the same time, the South needs this sort of criticism "for the sake of her own white sons and daughters, and the insurance of a robust, healthy mental and moral development."

As Du Bois moves across the veil, he does not enter the white world so completely that he abandons the black. His is not an assimilationist program. Thus, he turns his attention toward both Washington and the white world, and as the essay concludes, criticism of Washington and the white South is advanced by turns, almost in alternating passages. The criticism of the South relies upon a discriminating criticism of Washington, who himself "is especially to be criticized" for his failure to criticize the dominant white culture. But the assessment of Washington must be balanced. "It would be unjust," Du Bois notes, "not to acknowledge that in several instances he has opposed movements in the South which were unjust to Negroes." Yet, "it is equally true" that Washington's "propaganda" promotes only "a dangerous half-truth. The supplementary truths must never be lost sight of."

"The black men of America," Du Bois contends, "have a duty to perform, a duty stern and delicate, — a forward movement to oppose a part of the work of their greatest leader" (p. 42). Here, then, is a refiguring of the "double movement" that Du Bois mentioned at the end of the first section of the essay. Though Washington's leadership has resulted in some actual advance, and in these respects it should be supported, it has also resulted in some relative retrogression, and in these respects it must be criticized. Telling the difference is delicate, and the criticism must be stern.

***Commentary.*** *The critics here reiterate the movement of the text, explaining how the first half of the essay sets up the second half. They summarize how the rhetorical movement in the text allows Du Bois to find a way to break the silence created by Washington's dominance and offer a constructive alternative through his description and enactment of political argument.*

## Conclusion

In the first half of the essay, Du Bois discusses the function of criticism in abstract terms, but cannot apply it because of Washington's ruling presence — all voices except his have been hushed. Within this frame, with Washington looming on all sides, Du Bois diagnoses the characteristics of Washington's leadership and considers alternatives from the past, but he cannot offer direct, sharp criticism of Washington's program as an alternative that can compete with it. The rhetorical action of the text, however, moves from diagnosis to advocacy, and in the second half of the essay, Du Bois finds a critical voice that circumvents and challenges Washington's silencing hegemony. The movement from diagnosis to advocacy — from narrative analysis to political argument — develops through an interlocking pattern; the appropriate critical voice, which at first can only be described in abstract terms, because of white control (through Washington) of the black world, is used within the black world to unseat Washington, so that it can be applied to the white world as a vehicle for improving both worlds. This critical program, though it has negative elements, is not primarily negative. It is, instead, an engine for constructive self-determination in a plural world, a mechanism necessary for deliberation within a complex democratic nation.

Du Bois notes in his 1901 review of *Up from Slavery* that Washington's critics are not "unified by any single definite programme" (1901, p. 54). In "Of Mr. Booker T. Washington and Others," Du Bois sketches such a program, but its definite political premises are broad and rather thin, and they are derived from an inversion of key premises implicit in Washington's program. In fact, the contrast with Washington seems less a matter of political premises than of political sensibilities. Against Washington's monolithic and silencing politics of submission to external forces, Du Bois describes and enacts a politics of critical argument. The unity of Du Bois's program comes from its gathering of voices — from its evocation of the continuously moving, always multiple and complex, process of critical deliberation. Once set in motion, no one can predict or control its outcome, and since it invites rather than hushes opposing voices, the politics of criticism precludes a monolithic leader or a single, fixed program for a community. Thus, criticism, as Du Bois conceives it, not only is the tool to dislodge Washington's hegemony, but it is also the fitting alternative to the style and substance of his leadership.

## Notes

1. See Stepto (1991) for a discussion of the "black world" and the "white world" in *The Souls of Black Folk.*

## References

Du Bois, W. E. B. (1989). *The Souls of Black Folk.* New York: Bantam Books. (Originally published 1903)

Du Bois, W. E. B. (1901, July 16). "The evolution of Negro leadership" [Review of *Up from Slavery*]. *The Dial,* pp. 53–55.

Gates, H. L., Jr. (1989). "Introduction: Darkly, as through a veil." In W. E. B. Du Bois, *The Souls of Black Folk* (pp. vii–xxv). New York: Bantam Books.

Gibson, D. B. (1989). "Introduction." In W. E. B. Du Bois, *The Souls of Black Folk* (pp. vii–xxxv). New York: Penguin Books.

Lewis, D. L. (1993). *W. E. B. Du Bois: The Biography of a Race, 1868–1919.* New York: Henry Holt.

Rampersad, A. (1990). *The Art and Imagination of W. E. B. Du Bois.* New York: Schocken Books.

Stepto, R. B. (1985). "The quest of the weary traveler: W. E. B. Du Bois's *The Souls of Black Folk.*" In W. L. Andrews (Ed.), *Critical Essays on W. E. B. Du Bois* (pp. 139–173). Boston: G. K. Hall & Co. (Originally published 1979)

Stepto, R. B. (1991). *From Behind the Veil: A Study of Afro-American Narrative.* Urbana: University of Illinois Press.

# PART III • ALTERNATIVE READINGS

When critics read a text they will not always approach it from the same perspective or with the same purpose; they will not ask the same questions nor reach the same conclusions. Obviously, their interpretations will differ. Nevertheless, all critics will offer evidence to support the generalizations they make. This does not mean that every reading is just as good as any other, for obviously some critics will make more convincing arguments than others and some critiques will make more sense than others. But it does mean that critics can read texts differently and there need not be one "true" reading of the text. The following chapters contain studies of two important speeches that serve as examples of how critics can look at the same rhetorical text and come up with different insights and different explanations of the rhetorical forces at work.

The first speech, Richard M. Nixon's "Address to the Nation on the War in Vietnam," in Chapter 7, aroused controversy when it was given. It led to critical controversy, as well, when scholars attempted to assess the merits of the speech. The four critical studies presented here demonstrate how different critics can approach the same speech from varying perspectives, with contrasting methodologies, and can reach differing critical judgments. The exchange between two of these critics, Karlyn Campbell and Forbes Hill, affords an excellent illustration of divergent views on the nature, function, and method of rhetorical criticism held by two mature scholars. Chapter 8 presents alternative readings of a speech given in 1988 at the Democratic National Convention. These studies examine "Common Ground and Common Sense," a speech given by Jesse Jackson, the first African-American to make a serious bid to capture the presidential nomination of a major political party.

These studies point to a question of great importance to students of criticism: *Are all critical interpretations equally valid? Can they all be "right"?* By focusing attention on how critics construct arguments in support of their readings, students will learn a great deal about how to assess critical practice and how to begin to do criticism themselves.

# 7

# Alternative Readings of Richard Nixon's Address on Vietnam

## *Address to the Nation on the War in Vietnam*

RICHARD NIXON

*In 1968 Richard Nixon was elected President of the United States following a campaign in which America's involvement in Vietnam was a paramount issue. In the months following his inauguration pressure on President Nixon to solve the Vietnam problem continued to mount, and the protests that characterized the last years of the Johnson administration were unabated. President Nixon had publicly stated that protest would not influence his policy, but a national moratorium on the war held on October 15, 1969, secured intensive media coverage, and a second moratorium was scheduled for November 15. The President's speech on national television on November 3, 1969, was given extensive publicity prior to its delivery and was certainly one of the most important policy addresses of the decade.*

Good evening, my fellow Americans:

Tonight I want to talk to you on a subject of deep concern to all Americans and to many people in all parts of the world — the war in Vietnam.

I believe that one of the reasons for the deep division about Vietnam is that many Americans have lost confidence in what their Government has told them about our policy. The American people cannot and should not be asked to support a policy which involves the overriding issues of war and peace unless they know the truth about that policy.

Tonight, therefore, I would like to answer some of the questions that I know are on the minds of many of you listening to me.

How and why did America get involved in Vietnam in the first place?

How has this administration changed the policy of the previous administration?

What has really happened in the negotiations in Paris and on the battlefront in Vietnam?

What choices do we have if we are to end the war?

What are the prospects for peace?

Now, let me begin by describing the situation I found when I was inaugurated on January 20.

— The war had been going on for 4 years.

— 31,000 Americans had been killed in action.

— The training program for the South Vietnamese was behind schedule.

— 540,000 Americans were in Vietnam with no plans to reduce the number.

— No progress had been made at the negotiations in Paris and the United States had not put forth a comprehensive peace proposal.

— The war was causing deep division at home and criticism from many of our friends as well as our enemies abroad.

In view of these circumstances there were some who urged that I end the war at once by ordering the immediate withdrawal of all American forces.

From a political standpoint this would have been a popular and easy course to follow. After all, we became involved in the war while my predecessor was in office. I could blame the defeat which would be the result of my action on him and come out as the peacemaker. Some put it to me quite bluntly: This was the only way to avoid allowing Johnson's war to become Nixon's war.

But I had a greater obligation than to think only of the years of my administration and of the next election. I had to think of the effect of my decision on the next generation and on the future peace and freedom in America and in the world.

Let us all understand that the question before us is not whether some Americans are for peace and some Americans are against peace. The question at issue is not whether Johnson's war becomes Nixon's war.

The great question is: How can we win America's peace?

Well, let us turn now to the fundamental issue. Why and how did the United States become involved in Vietnam in the first place?

Fifteen years ago North Vietnam, with the logistical support of Communist China and the Soviet Union, launched a campaign to impose a Communist government on South Vietnam by instigating and supporting a revolution.

In response to the request of the Government of South Vietnam, President Eisenhower sent economic aid and military equipment to assist the people of South Vietnam in their efforts to prevent a Communist takeover. Seven years ago, President Kennedy sent 16,000 military personnel to Vietnam as combat advisers. Four years ago, President Johnson sent American combat forces to South Vietnam.

Now, many believe that President Johnson's decision to send American combat forces to South Vietnam was wrong. And many others — I among them — have been strongly critical of the way the war has been conducted.

But the question facing us today is: Now that we are in the war, what is the best way to end it?

In January I could only conclude that the precipitate withdrawal of American forces from Vietnam would be a disaster not only for South Vietnam but for the United States and for the cause of peace.

For the South Vietnamese, our precipitate withdrawal would inevitably allow the Communists to repeat the massacres which followed their takeover in the North 15 years before.

— They then murdered more than 50,000 people and hundreds of thousands more died in slave labor camps.

— We saw a prelude of what would happen in South Vietnam when the Communists entered the city of the Hue last year. During their brief rule there, there was a bloody reign of terror in which 3,000 civilians were clubbed, shot to death, and buried in mass graves.

— With the sudden collapse of our support, these atrocities of Hue would become the nightmare of the entire nation — and particularly for the million and a half Catholic refugees who fled to South Vietnam when the Communists took over in the North.

For the United States, this first defeat in our Nation's history would result in a collapse of confidence in American leadership, not only in Asia but throughout the world.

Three American Presidents have recognized the great stakes involved in Vietnam and understood what had to be done.

In 1963, President Kennedy, with his characteristic eloquence and clarity, said: ". . . we want to see a stable government there, carrying on a struggle to maintain its national independence."

"We believe strongly in that. We are not going to withdraw from that effort. In my opinion, for us to withdraw from that effort would mean a collapse not only of South Vietnam, but Southeast Asia. So we are going to stay there."

President Eisenhower and President Johnson expressed the same conclusion during their terms of office.

For the future of peace, precipitate withdrawal would thus be a disaster of immense magnitude.

— A nation cannot remain great if it betrays its allies and lets down its friends.

— Our defeat and humiliation in South Vietnam without question would promote recklessness in the councils of those great powers who have not yet abandoned their goals of world conquest.

— This would spark violence wherever our commitments help maintain the peace — in the Middle East, in Berlin, eventually even in the Western Hemisphere.

Ultimately, this would cost more lives.

It would not bring peace; it would bring more war.

For these reasons, I rejected the recommendation that I should end the war by immediately withdrawing all of our forces. I chose instead to change American policy on both the negotiating front and battlefront.

In order to end a war fought on many fronts, I initiated a pursuit for peace on many fronts.

In a television speech on May 14, in a speech before the United Nations, and on a number of other occasions I set forth our peace proposals in great detail.

— We have offered the complete withdrawal of all outside forces within 1 year.

— We have proposed a cease-fire under international supervision.

— We have offered free elections under international supervision with the Communists participating in the organization and conduct of the elections as an organized political force. And the Saigon Government has pledged to accept the result of the elections.

We have not put forth our proposals on a take-it-or-leave-it basis. We have indicated that we are willing to discuss the proposals that have been put forth by the other side. We have declared that anything is negotiable except the right of the people of South Vietnam to determine their own future. At the Paris peace conference, Ambassador Lodge has demonstrated our flexibility and good faith in 40 public meetings.

Hanoi has refused even to discuss our proposals. They demand our unconditional acceptance of their terms, which are that we withdraw all American forces immediately and unconditionally and that we overthrow the Government of South Vietnam as we leave.

We have not limited our peace initiatives to public forums and public statements. I recognized, in January, that a long and bitter war like this usually cannot be settled in a public forum. That is why in addition to the public statements and negotiations I have explored every possible private avenue that might lead to a settlement.

Tonight I am taking the unprecedented step of disclosing to you some of our other initiatives for peace — initiatives we undertook privately and secretly because we thought we thereby might open a door which publicly would be closed.

I did not wait for my inauguration to begin my quest for peace.

— Soon after my election, through an individual who is directly in contact on a personal basis with the leaders of North Vietnam, I made two private offers for a rapid, comprehensive settlement. Hanoi's replies called in effect for our surrender before negotiations.

— Since the Soviet Union furnishes most of the military equipment for North Vietnam, Secretary of State Rogers, my Assistant for National Security Affairs, Dr. Kissinger, Ambassador Lodge, and I, personally, have met on a number of occasions with representatives of the Soviet Government to enlist their assistance in getting meaningful negotiations started. In addition, we have had extended discussions directed toward the same and with representatives of other governments which have diplomatic relations with North Vietnam. None of these initiatives have to date produced results.

— In mid-July, I became convinced that it was necessary to make a major move to break the deadlock in the Paris talks. I spoke directly in this office, where I am now sitting, with an individual who had known Ho Chi Minh [President, Democratic Republic of Vietnam] on a personal basis for 25 years. Through him I sent a letter to Ho Chi Minh.

I did this outside of the usual diplomatic channels with the hope that with the necessity of making statements for propaganda removed, there might be constructive progress toward bringing the war to an end. Let me read from the letter to you now.

"Dear Mr. President:

"I realize that it is difficult to communicate meaningfully across the gulf of four years of war. But precisely because of this gulf, I wanted to take this opportunity to reaffirm in all solemnity my desire to work for a just peace. I deeply believe that the war in Vietnam has gone on too long and delay in bringing it to an end can benefit no one — least of all the people of Vietnam. . . .

"The time has come to move forward at the conference table toward an early resolution of this tragic war. You will find us forthcoming and openminded in a common effort to bring the blessings of peace to the brave people of Vietnam. Let history record that at this critical juncture, both sides turned their face toward peace rather than toward conflict and war."

I received Ho Chi Minh's reply on August 30, 3 days before his death. It simply reiterated the public position North Vietnam had taken at Paris and flatly rejected my initiative.

The full text of both letters is being released to the press.

— In addition to the public meetings that I have referred to, Ambassador Lodge has met with Vietnam's chief negotiator in Paris in 11 private sessions.

— We have taken other significant initiatives which must remain secret to keep open some channels of communication which may still prove to be productive.

But the effect of all the public, private, and secret negotiations which have been undertaken since the bombing halt a year ago and since this administration came into office on January 20, can be summed up in one sentence: No progress whatever has been made except agreement on the shape of the bargaining table.

Well now, who is at fault?

It has become clear that the obstacle in negotiating an end to the war is not the President of the United States. It is not the South Vietnamese Government.

The obstacle is the other side's absolute refusal to show the least willingness to join us in seeking a just peace. And it will not do so while it is convinced that all it has to do is to wait for our next concession, and our next concession after that one, until it gets everything it wants.

There can now be no longer any question that progress in negotiation depends only on Hanoi's deciding to negotiate, to negotiate seriously.

I realize that this report on our efforts on the diplomatic front is discouraging to the American people, but the American people are entitled to know the truth — the bad news as well as the good news — where the lives of our young men are involved.

Now let me turn, however, to a more encouraging report on another front.

At the time we launched our search for peace I recognized we might not succeed in bringing an end to the war through negotiation. I, therefore, put into effect another plan to bring peace — a plan which will bring the war to an end regardless of what happens on the negotiating front.

It is in line with a major shift in U.S. foreign policy which I described in my press conference at Guam on July 25. Let me briefly explain what has been described as the Nixon Doctrine — a policy which not only will help end the war in Vietnam, but which is an essential element of our program to prevent future Vietnams.

We Americans are a do-it-yourself people. We are an impatient people. Instead of teaching someone else to do a job, we like to do it ourselves. And this trait has been carried over into our foreign policy.

In Korea and again in Vietnam, the United States furnished most of the money, most of the arms, and most of the men to help the people of those countries defend their freedom against Communist aggression.

Before any American troops were committed to Vietnam, a leader of another Asian country expressed this opinion to me when I was traveling in Asia as a private citizen. He said: "When you are trying to assist another nation defend its freedom, U.S. policy should be to help them fight the war but not to fight the war for them."

Well, in accordance with this wise counsel, I laid down in Guam three principles as guidelines for future American policy toward Asia:

— First, the United States will keep all of its treaty commitments.

— Second, we shall provide a shield if a nuclear power threatens the freedom of a nation allied with us or of a nation whose survival we consider vital to our security.

— Third, in cases involving other types of aggression, we shall furnish military and economic assistance when requested in accordance with our treaty commitments. But we shall look to the nation directly threatened to assume the primary responsibility of providing the manpower for its defense.

After I announced this policy, I found that the leaders of the Philippines, Thailand, Vietnam, South Korea, and other nations which might be threatened by Communist aggression, welcomed this new direction in American foreign policy.

The defense of freedom is everybody's business — not just America's business. And it is particularly the responsibility of the people whose freedom is threatened. In the previous administration, we Americanized the war in Vietnam. In this administration, we are Vietnamizing the search for peace.

The policy of the previous administration not only resulted in our assuming the primary responsibility for fighting the war, but even more significantly did not adequately stress the goal of strengthening the South Vietnamese so that they could defend themselves when we left.

The Vietnamization plan was launched following Secretary Laird's visit to Vietnam in March. Under the plan, I ordered first a substantial increase in the training and equipment of South Vietnamese forces.

In July, on my visit to Vietnam, I changed General Abrams' orders so that they were consistent with the objectives of our new policies. Under the new orders, the primary mission of our troops is to enable the South Vietnamese forces to assume the full responsibility for the security of South Vietnam.

Our air operations have been reduced by over 20 percent.

And now we have begun to see the results of this long overdue change in American policy in Vietnam.

— After 5 years of Americans going into Vietnam, we are finally bringing American men home. By December 15, over 60,000 men will have been withdrawn from South Vietnam — including 20 percent of all our combat forces.

— The South Vietnamese have continued to gain in strength. As a result they have been able to take over combat responsibilities from our American troops.

Two other significant developments have occurred since this administration took office.

— Enemy infiltration, infiltration which is essential if they are to launch a major attack, over the last 3 months is less than 20 percent of what it was over the same period last year.

— Most important — United States casualties have declined during the last 2 months to the lowest point in 3 years.

Let me now turn to our program for the future.

We have adopted a plan which we have worked out in cooperation with the South Vietnamese for the complete withdrawal of all U.S. combat ground forces, and their replacement by South Vietnamese forces on an orderly scheduled timetable. This withdrawal will be made from strength and not from weakness. As South Vietnamese forces become stronger, the rate of American withdrawal can become greater.

I have not and do not intend to announce the timetable for our program. And there are obvious reasons for this decision which I am sure you will understand. As I have indicated on several occasions, the rate of withdrawal will depend on developments on three fronts.

One of these is the progress which can be or might be made in the Paris talks. An anouncement of a fixed timetable for our withdrawal would completely remove any incentive for the enemy to negotiate an agreement. They would simply wait until our forces had withdrawn and then move in.

The other two factors on which we will base our withdrawal decisions are the level of enemy activity and the progress of the training programs of the South Vietnamese forces. And I am glad to be able to report tonight progress on both of these fronts has been greater than we anticipated when we started the program in June for withdrawal. As a result, our timetable for withdrawal is more optimistic now than when we made our first estimates in June. Now, this clearly demonstrates why it is not wise to be frozen in on a fixed timetable.

We must retain the flexibility to base each withdrawal decision on the situation as it is at that time rather than on estimates that are no longer valid.

Along with this optimistic estimate, I must — in all candor — leave one note of caution.

If the level of enemy activity significantly increases we might have to adjust our timetable accordingly.

However, I want the record to be completely clear on one point.

At the time of the bombing halt just a year ago, there was some confusion as to whether there was an understanding on the part of the enemy that if we stopped the bombing of North Vietnam they would stop the shelling of cities in South Vietnam. I want to be sure that there is no misunderstanding on the part of the enemy with regard to our withdrawal program.

We have noted the reduced level of infiltration, the reduction of our casualties, and are basing our withdrawal decisions partially on those factors.

If the level of infiltration or our casualties increase while we are trying to scale down the fighting, it will be the result of a conscious decision by the enemy.

Hanoi could make no greater mistake than to assume that an increase in violence will be to its advantage. If I conclude that increased enemy action jeopardizes our remaining forces in Vietnam, I shall not hesitate to take strong and effective measures to deal with that situation.

This is not a threat. This is a statement of policy, which as Commander in Chief of our Armed Forces, I am making in meeting my responsibility for the protection of American fighting men wherever they may be.

My fellow Americans, I am sure you can recognize from what I have said that we really only have two choices open to us if we want to end this war.

— I can order an immediate, precipitate withdrawal of all Americans from Vietnam without regard to the effects of that action.

— Or we can persist in our search for a just peace through a negotiated settlement if possible, or through continued implementation of our plan for Vietnamization if necessary — a plan in which we will withdraw all of our forces from Vietnam on a schedule in accordance with our program, as the South Vietnamese become strong enough to defend their own freedom.

I have chosen this second course.

It is not the easy way.

It is the right way.

It is a plan which will end the war and serve the cause of peace — not just in Vietnam but in the Pacific and in the world.

In speaking of the consequences of a precipitate withdrawal, I mentioned that our allies would lose confidence in America.

Far more dangerous, we would lose confidence in ourselves. Oh, the immediate reaction would be a sense of relief that our men were coming home. But as we saw the consequences of what we had done, inevitable remorse and divisive recrimination would scar our spirit as a people.

We have faced other crises in our history and have become stronger by rejecting the easy way out and taking the right way in meeting our challenges. Our greatness as a nation has been our capacity to do what had to be done when we knew our course was right.

I recognize that some of my fellow citizens disagree with the plan for peace I have chosen. Honest and patriotic Americans have reached different conclusions as to how peace should be achieved.

In San Francisco a few weeks ago, I saw demonstrators carrying signs reading: "Lose in Vietnam, bring the boys home."

Well, one of the strengths of our free society is that any American has a right to reach that conclusion and to advocate that point of view. But as President of the United States, I would be untrue to my oath of office if I allowed the policy of this Nation to be dictated by the minority who hold that point of view and who try to impose it on the Nation by mounting demonstrations in the street.

For almost 200 years, the policy of this Nation has been made under our Constitution by those leaders in the Congress and the White House elected by all of the people. If a vocal minority, however fervent its cause, prevails over reason and the will of the majority, this Nation has no future as a free society.

And now I would like to address a word, if I may, to the young people of this Nation who are particularly concerned, and I understand why they are concerned, about this war.

I respect your idealism.

I share your concern for peace.

I want peace as much as you do.

There are powerful personal reasons I want to end this war. This week I will have to sign 83 letters to mothers, fathers, wives, and loved ones of men who have given their lives for America in Vietnam. It is very little satisfaction to me that this is only one-third as many letters as I signed the first week in office. There is nothing I want more than to see the day come when I do not have to write any of those letters.

— I want to end the war to save the lives of those brave young men in Vietnam.

— But I want to end it in a way which will increase the chance that their younger brothers and their sons will not have to fight in some future Vietnam someplace in the world.

— And I want to end the war for another reason. I want to end it so that the energy and dedication of you, our young people, now too often directed into bitter hatred against those responsible for the war, can be turned to the great challenges of peace, a better life for all Americans, a better life for all people on this earth.

I have chosen a plan for peace. I believe it will succeed.

It if does succeed, what the critics say now won't matter. If it does not succeed, anything I say then won't matter.

I know it may not be fashionable to speak of patriotism or national destiny these days. But I feel it is appropriate to do so on this occasion.

Two hundred years ago this Nation was weak and poor. But even then, America was the hope of millions in the world. Today we have become the strongest and richest nation in the world. And the wheel of destiny has turned so that any hope the world has for the survival of peace and freedom will be determined by whether the American people have the moral stamina and the courage to meet the challenge of free world leadership.

Let historians not record that when America was the most powerful nation in the world we passed on the other side of the road and allowed the last hopes for peace and freedom of millions of people to be suffocated by the forces of totalitarianism.

And so tonight — to you, the great silent majority of my fellow Americans — I ask for your support.

I pledged in my campaign for the Presidency to end the war in a way that we could win the peace. I have initiated a plan of action which will enable me to keep that pledge.

The more support I can have from the American people, the sooner that pledge can be redeemed; for the more divided we are at home, the less likely the enemy is to negotiate at Paris.

Let us be united for peace. Let us also be united against defeat. Because let us understand: North Vietnam cannot defeat or humiliate the United States. Only Americans can do that.

Fifty years ago, in this room and at this very desk,[1] President Woodrow Wilson spoke words which caught the imagination of a war-weary world. He said: "This is the war to end war." His dream for peace after World War I was shattered on the hard realities of great power politics and Woodrow Wilson died a broken man.

Tonight I do not tell you that the war in Vietnam is the war to end wars. But I do say this: I have initiated a plan which will end this war in a way that will bring us closer to that great goal to which Woodrow Wilson and every American President in our history has been dedicated — the goal of a just and lasting peace.

As President I hold the responsibility for choosing the best path to that goal and then leading the Nation along it.

I pledge to you tonight that I shall meet this responsibility with all of the strength and wisdom I can command in accordance with your hopes, mindful of your concerns, sustained by your prayers.

Thank you and goodnight.

## *Under the Veneer: Nixon's Vietnam Speech of November 3, 1969*

ROBERT P. NEWMAN

With the political honeymoon over, with his Congressional critics nipping at his heels and threatening full-scale attacks, and a major outpouring of antiwar sentiment probable on the October 15 Moratorium, Richard M. Nixon announced, on October 13, 1969, that he

[1] Later research indicated that the desk had not been President Woodrow Wilson's as had long been assumed but was used by Vice President Henry Wilson during President Grant's administration.

would make a major address about Vietnam November 3. The advance notice was unusually long for presidential addresses; the stakes in the burgeoning combat were unusually high. Vietnam had broken his predecessor, and Richard Nixon did not care to let himself in for the same treatment.

Part of the tension in October was due to the President's earlier incautious remark that he would not allow his program to be influenced by demonstrations in the streets. This gratuitous irritant to the peace forces guaranteed a massive turnout for the October 15 Moratorium, and it was partially to defuse the Moratorium that the President announced his speech so early. In this effort, the early announcement was perhaps successful; the size of the October 15 turnout remained impressive, but its tone was muted. All but the most violent of the protesters cushioned their stance with an anticipation that on November 3, when the President could speak without appearing to have yielded to pressure, he would announce major steps to end the war.

Even after the Moratorium, announcement of the coming address had its effect on the peace movement. From October 15 until Nixon spoke, plans for the November antiwar events were affected by anticipation of the Presidential speech. Had the prognosis for the November 3 speech been unfavorable, the peace forces would have strained every nerve to mount their greatest effort in mid-November. But Presidential aides let it be known that Nixon had attended to the Moratorium, even though he did not approve it, and the Washington gossip mills were rife with predictions that, on November 3, the President would produce good news for peace. For two weeks, the doves relaxed. Perhaps, thought many, Nixon has really got the word, and the November push won't be necessary after all.

Every channel of public intelligence built up the significance of the November 3 effort. The President was known to be "almost totally preoccupied" with drafting the speech during the last two weeks of October.[1] Whether in the White House, at Camp David, or on the road, he was writing, revising, reflecting. The speech had to "convey an authentic note of personal involvement," rather than appear as a run-of-the-mill ghost-written production; and for this reason, all ten drafts were pristine Nixon. Ray Price, one of the President's top writers, had no idea what was in it: "I contributed nothing — not even a flourish."[2] Evans and Novak, executive-watchers of more than usual competence, noted on the day of the speech: "In stark contrast to his last major speech on Vietnam, almost six months ago, Mr. Nixon's talk tonight has been written by one hand alone — the President's hand."[3]

Buildup? On the night of November 3, Caesar himself could not have upstaged Richard Nixon.

In retrospect, expectations were so high that not even the Sermon on the Mount could have fulfilled them. The President had focused the spotlight so long and so carefully that only rhetorical perfection would have been equal to the occasion.

**The Background**

One of the first questions to be raised about a major address by Nixon, who for years was dogged with the nickname "Tricky Dick," would be "Is he sincere?" Nixon did not survive the political wars by the simple-minded morality of a country parson. He had scuttled Helen Gahagan Douglas, done in Alger Hiss, run interference for Eisenhower, fought Jack Kennedy to a virtual draw, and outlasted Barry Goldwater. He is a politician, which is to say that he has run a gauntlet the parameters of which are set, not by the Marquis of Queensberry, but by the necessities of survival.[4] From such an old pol, some temporizing might be expected.

When, therefore, he claimed, on November 3, to have a plan for peace, which he must unfortunately keep secret due to the perverseness of the enemy, some scepticism was expressed. Did he mean it? Did he really have a secret plan? Did he intend to close out the war, or was this just another maneuver to justify the same old business?

The reaction of the peace forces was largely predictable. Few were more blunt than Nixon's erstwhile nemesis, Senator Kennedy, as quoted by the *Times*:

> *I do not wish to be harsh nor overly critical, but the time has come to say it: as a candidate, Richard Nixon promised us a plan for peace once elected; as chief executive, President Nixon promised us a plan for peace for the last 10 months. Last night he spoke again of a plan — a secret plan for peace sometime. There now must be doubt whether there is in existence any plan to extricate America from this war in the best interest of America — for it is no plan to say that what we do depends upon what Hanoi does.*[5]

But when it comes to judging the President's sincerity, by all the canons of truth, Mansfield of Montana and Fulbright of Arkansas are superior judges. After five years of dealing with LBJ, they can be counted on to smell a fraud. Both want rapid withdrawal from Vietnam. Both have registered profound opposition to the course of the war. When, after conferences with the President, and caveats about the pace of withdrawal, they nonetheless acknowledge that the President does intend to get out, one must believe them. Both want withdrawal to be programmed independently of what Hanoi does, but both accept as genuine the President's wish to wind down the war.[6]

Were the testimony of the two leading Democratic Senators not conclusive, the ever-watchful White House press contingent, and the major liberal columnists, might be cited in their support. James Reston, whom I shall quote later on matters less favorable to Nixon's cause, regarded Nixon's sincerity as "almost terrifying."[7] And Richard Harwood and Laurence Stern of *The Washington Post* accept as true "that the President, a veteran of the Korean War Settlement, is intent on liquidating the American involvement in Vietnam under a veneer of tough talk."[8] The veneer is highly visible, for all to see; but under it is the intention of winding down the American part of the war in Vietnam. What he said, he meant.

But what is the shape of his commitment to withdrawal? Has he now, after all these years of supporting the anticommunist effort in Indochina, decided that it was a mistake and that we *should* withdraw? Or is he merely bowing to political expediency, withdrawing because he can do no other and still retain power? An understanding both of his rhetoric and of his politics depends on answers to these questions.

There are those who maintain that the President is nonideological, a consummate politician and nothing more. This view is concisely expressed by Edwin Newman of NBC News: "But Mr. Nixon is as he is, and it is as well for him, and perhaps for the country, that he is so little ideological. He is neither embarrassed nor bound by having written in 1964 that the war in Vietnam was a life and death struggle in which victory was essential to the survival of freedom, and by having said in Saigon in April, 1967, that the great issue in 1968 would 'not be how to negotiate defeat but how to bring more pressure to bear for victory.' "[9]

There is indeed much evidence in Nixon's recent behavior to indicate that the anticommunist cold war ideology which he so powerfully embraced has now been modified: the SALT talks are underway with apparently serious intent; economic and travel restrictions applied to China for twenty years have been relaxed, and we are talking to the Chinese in Warsaw; germ warfare has been disavowed; and the military budget is, for the first time in years, on the way down. Does all this add up to a new Nixon, one who can willingly disengage from Vietnam?

Nixon's massive, sustained, vigorous hostility to Ho Chi Minh and his movement simply cannot be wiped out overnight. It was, after all, Nixon who as early as 1954 did his best to launch an American expeditionary force against Ho Chi Minh and in support of the French. On April 16, 1954, Nixon appeared for an off-the-record session before the American Society of Newspaper Editors, meeting in Washington, and said that "if France stopped fighting in Indo-China and the situation demanded it the United States would have to send troops to fight the Communists in that area."[10] This 1954 speech was the first sign that the battle to maintain a noncommunist government in Saigon, whether of French colonials or of French-trained Vietnamese generals, was precisely Richard Nixon's battle. And consistently since, with no exception until the campaign of 1968, he has supported that battle.

One must approach the Nixon rhetoric, then, entertaining the hypothesis that he is disengaging reluctantly, that his heart is not in it, that only the pressure of public opinion has caused him to embrace what he for fifteen years rejected. And one of the strong reasons for believing that the President does have a plan to phase out this war rapidly is the possibility that by late 1970 even the American Legion will be tired of fighting.

A second approach to understanding the President's speech lies in reflection on the various audiences to whom he was speaking.

There were at least three domestic audiences of consequence. First, his friends: the conservative Republicans who voted him into office and the Wallaceites he is now courting, largely a hawkish group, for whom he had the message, "Do not despair. I'm not heeding the demonstrators. We have to withdraw, but we don't have to give away a thing to the Viet Cong." Second, the "silent majority," some of whom had voted for him and some of whom had voted for Humphrey, many of them fence-straddlers on the war, all of them open, as Nixon saw it, to the plea, "I am winding down this war, but in a methodical and reasonable way which you ought to support." Third, the convinced doves, to whom he said, "Knock it off, I am the President, and disengaging from Vietnam is my bag. I respect your right to dissent, but don't carry it too far." In this latter group the youth, to whom he addressed a specific appeal, probably fit.

Abroad, he was concerned first with the South Vietnamese and other American client states: "We'll keep the faith, we won't desert you, and if the VC get tough again, we'll match them." There was also a clear word for Hanoi and other communist states: "You are going to have to come to terms with Thieu, or we will hang on forever; and if you escalate, the whole ball game is off."

One vital task of criticism is to decide which audience, and which message, was paramount. One is aided in making this decision by the recent publication of a startling book by a Nixon staffer, Kevin Phillips, an assistant to the Attorney General. In *The Emerging Republican Majority,*[11] Philips analyzes socioeconomic data to conclude that the white working-class voters who produced 9,906,473 votes for George Wallace in the last election can be turned into permanent Republicans. This can be done, says Philips, by taking over the Wallace message (which rejects peacenik and Black demands) and peddling it with enough sophistication to retain the present registered Republican clientele. Since the consevative, middle-class sun belt cities are growing at the expense of the Democratic cities in the East, this combination will give the Republicans a permanent majority.

The President has not, obviously, endorsed the book; but it fairly represents the strategy with which he fought the last election, and no repudiation of Phillips has been forthcoming: he assisted Attorney General Mitchell until February 1970. And it was to precisely this group, the Wallaceites, that the "veneer of tough talk" was directed. Nixon's rhetorical strategy was thus influenced by a political strategy: placate the doves not at all, appeal to the patriotism of the silent majority, but above all, show the "lower-middle-class clerks in Queens, steelworkers in Youngstown, and retired police lieutenants in San Diego"[12] *that you are their champion.* This is the rhetoric of confrontation.

It is a rhetoric which the Nixon administration, up to now, has largely delegated to the Vice-President. Careful scrutiny of Nixon's text will provide support for the thesis that he sought confrontation. He made numerous references to humiliation, disaster, and defeat, all of which outcomes he projects on to his opponents; these are fighting words. They were incorporated in the speech against the better judgment of Henry Kissinger,[13] and, according to columnists Evans and Novak, against the advice of Republican leaders in Congress to "give the doves something": "Mr. Nixon rejected that advice because he consciously wanted to split off what he regards as a small minority of antiwar activists from his 'great silent majority' of Americans. He was striving for a polarization of opinion isolating the dissenters and thereby dooming the extremist-led Nov. 15 march on Washington."[14]

This divide-and-isolate strategy was not dictated by the circumstances. The substance of President's plan could have been made palatable to many of his opponents. There were three crucial action programs: (1) avoid precipitate withdrawal; (2) keep the timetable secret; and (3) maintain a noncommunist government in Saigon. Given the division within the peace forces, who ranged from Friends to anarchists, he could easily have explained why the whole timetable could not be announced while announcing the next phase of withdrawal, which he did within six weeks anyway; he could have acknowledged the desirability of broadening the base of the Saigon government; and he could have put a higher priority on a cease fire. Had he done these things, he could have substantially alleviated the fears of many doves.

He not only failed to make these gestures of conciliation, he went far to agitate his opponents. He need not have injected the abrasive discussion of how the war started and how we got involved. He need not have talked as if all his opponents favored precipitate withdrawal. He need not have paraded before us again the controversial domino theory. He need not have done these things, that is, unless he had already decided to write off the dissenters and to start building his "emerging Republican majority" with Wallaceite support. But the decision was his. Anthony Lewis, Pulitzer Prize Winner of *The New York Times,* put it this way: "The puzzle is why he chose to speak as he did. He could so easily have expounded the same policy in less doom-laden rhetoric."[15]

**The Argument**

There were, according to the President, five questions on the minds of his listeners.

"How and why did America get involved in Vietnam in the first place?

"How has this Administration changed the policy of the previous Administration?

"What has really happened in the negotiations in Paris and the battlefront in Vietnam?

"What choices do we have if we are to end the war?

"What are the prospects for peace?"[16]

After a brief description of the "situation I found when I was inaugurated on Jan. 20th," he turns to what he claims is the "fundamental issue," why and how did we become involved in the first place. This is a surprising candidate for priority in any discussion today. One might have thought that the burning question was how to get out. The President's chief foreign policy advisors, his allies on Capitol Hill, and the memorandum he got from the Cabinet bureaucracy all urged him to skip discussions of the causes and manner of our involvement. Yet the history comes out with top billing. How and to what extent it is distorted is an interesting subject, but not our major concern here. This was a deliberative speech, and the President is arguing for a specific policy.

The substance of his policy argument, scattered throughout the speech, deals with four alternative plans for achieving disengagement. (The possibility of escalation is reserved as a club with which to scare the North Vietnamese into cooperating with Nixon's preferred plan for disengagement, but it is not offered as a full-fledged course of action in its own right.)

First, the President could "end the war at once by ordering the immediate withdrawal of all American forces. From a political standpoint, this would have been a popular and easy course to follow." But it is not Nixon's course; it is craven advice, and it draws his most concentrated fire.

It would, for one thing, constitute a defeat. Given Mr. Nixon's historic commitment to a noncommunist South Vietnam, and his visceral reaction to being bested by communists any time on any issue (as revealed in his autobiographical *Six Crises*)[17] it is not surprising that he makes much of this argument. Even though, as he claims, he could blame the defeat on his predecessor, this would not be an honorable course.

Whether acknowledging defeat in Vietnam would be a wise course is another matter. Mr. Nixon's mentor, Eisenhower, recognized that, in the much more defensible war in Korea, we sustained a substantial defeat of MacArthur's objectives of rolling back the communists to the Yalu River. Most Americans seemed to approve a less-than-satisfactory settlement; avoidance of defeat did not then commend itself as the greatest good.

Similarly, in the abortive Bay of Pigs invasion, American-trained troops and American strategy suffered great humiliation. But, as Theodore Draper says of John F. Kennedy, "the President knew how to end the misery, without deception or whimpering, in a way that made him seem to grow in defeat."[18] The trauma of defeat varies with the character of the captain, as de Gaulle proved once again in Algeria. But then Nixon is no Kennedy or de Gaulle.

When one asks, "How can the anguish and terror of a loss in Vietnam be mitigated?" the answer has to be something other than the repeated stress on the necessity of avoiding defeat which we heard from President Nixon November 3. There is a case to be made for the honesty and therapeutic value of admitting that we were in over our heads, that we cannot police the whole world, that we really should not, as the military once told us, become involved in a ground war on the Asian continent.

Nixon does not reject immediate withdrawal solely on the basis of its intrinsic evil as a symbol of defeat. It would also lead to a train of undesirable consequences, all of which he ticks off as reasons for repudiating such a policy. It would damage the credibility of other American commitments; encourage communist aggressiveness everywhere; lead not only to the collapse of South Vietnam but all of Southeast Asia; result in horrendous massacres when the Viet Cong take over; and cause us to lose confidence in ourselves, with "inevitable remorse and divisive recrimination."

It might, indeed, do all of these things. These are consequences which need to be considered, *but they need to be considered only if immediate withdrawal is a serious alternative plan which the President needs to refute.* It is hard to see that it had such status. The sharpest challenge to his policy came from Senator Goodell and those who favored phased but definite withdrawal, with a specific deadline by which all American troops, or at least all combat troops, would be out. The call for immediate and total withdrawal came from a minority faction of the peace movement; and in rebutting it as if it were the most serious challenge to his preferred course, Nixon was drawing a red herring across the trail of his opponents, attacking a straw man whose demolition he could portray as destruction of the dissenters generally. This argumentative strategy seems to have succeeded with the silent majority; it festers and repels when one attends to his rhetoric carefully.

The second alternative plan for disengagement is negotiation. Mr. Nixon holds open some slight hope that this might still be the road out; but after a long and frustrating year of meeting with the enemy in Paris, he does not put much faith in it. In this he is undoubtedly correct. North Vietnam has not now, and is not likely to acquire, any faith in negotiated agreements. For those who can remove the distorting lenses of national self-righteousness, which of course always reveal the other part as culprit in scuttling international agreements, the evidence points overwhelmingly to a justification of Hanoi's attitude.[19] But this need not concern us here. Aside from the debater's points Mr. Nixon makes by detailing the substance of U.S. negotiating proposals, and his claim that "Hanoi has refused even to discuss our proposals," this is a blind alley.

The third possible way to get out of Vietnam has the weightiest support behind it, both in the Senate and elsewhere; it is to withdraw steadily with a fixed terminal date. Here is the option upon which attention should have been focused. Here is the real challenge to presidential decision making. If the President were to reason with the most reasonable of his critics, he should have spent the bulk of his energies showing why this plan is disadvantageous compared to his; yet the emphasis it receives is minor.

The few swipes he takes at fixed-schedule withdrawal are instructive. "An announcement of a fixed timetable for our withdrawal would completely remove any incentive for the enemy to negotiate an agreement. They would simply wait until our forces had withdrawn and then move in." This attack is curious indeed. Have we not already written off the prospects for negotiation? Under what possible logic would the enemy be more likely to "wait until our forces had withdrawn and then move in" if they have a terminal point for that wait than if they do not? Is this not likely to happen whether the timetable is secret or public? Here is the core of the dispute between the President and his detractors, and he attends to it with a casual and obfuscating logic that defies belief.

The only other attack on the idea of a *terminus ad quem* for withdrawal is based on its alleged inflexibility; Mr. Nixon does not want to be "frozen in on a fixed timetable." One can accept that some flexibility in such an operation might be in order. This seems not to have deterred our officials from setting up, if not a rigid schedule, at least a terminal date for the accomplishment of other objectives. One must strain one's imagination somewhat to conceive Mr. Nixon incapable of extending a deadline for withdrawal in the face of Vietcong attacks which he defined as serious.

Here is the sum total of the President's refutation of the most serious challenge his program faces. It is hardly worth the candle.

So, finally, we come to alternative number four, the plan adopted and defended by the President. This scenario was worked up by Herman Kahn of the Hudson Institute. The July, 1968 *Foreign Affairs* carried an article by Kahn setting forth his plan for deescalation: build up Arvin, withdraw most American combat units, leave behind a reservoir of between 200,000 and 300,000 men to "deter a resumption of major hostilities."[20] This is now Nixon's plan, with the additional proviso that no long-range schedule be announced.

One needs, at this stage, to view the plan as a whole, inspecting the justifications for it, the reasons for preferring it to alternatives, the rhetoric in which it is clothed. A number of salient points need close scrutiny. As with any policy proposal, the pay off stage is the prediction of future consequences: how will the plan work?

Specifically, one needs to know whether it is probable that (1) the Vietcong and Hanoi will tolerate the presence of 450,000, 400,000 or 350,000 foreign troops while the hated Thieu regime attempts to develop combat effectiveness; (2) the Vietcong and Hanoi will beyond that tolerate the indefinite presence in the country of 250,000 or more occupation troops; (3) the shaky regime in Saigon will really develop political support and military muscle sufficient to keep the communists at bay; (4) the American public, including the great silent majority, the Emerging Republican Majority, and all the rest of us, will tolerate this kind of semi-permanent occupation even if combat casualties drop to zero; and (5) there will be less right-wing recrimination should this plan fail than if there is a fast, clean withdrawal.

The President's defense on all these points deserves the closest inspection. We need, in a situation where Mr. Nixon admits "that many Americans have lost confidence in what their Government has told them about our policy," some indication of the evidence on which these assumed consequences are based, whether it be from the CIA, the military, the State Department, Sir Robert Thompson, or wherever. We need some assurance that the President is capable of what social psychologists call "tough-minded empathy," or the ability to see this plan as Hanoi sees it, and not just from the compulsively optimistic viewpoint of the Department of Defense.

There is nothing. The plan is there, take it or leave it. There is a warning to Hanoi to go along or else. There is a recognition that "some of my fellow citizens disagree" with the plan he has chosen. There is a rejection of demonstrations in the street, an appeal to the young people of the nation to turn their energies to constructive ends, a call for patriotism, a reference to Woodrow Wilson (at whose desk he spoke). In defense of his plan, there is only a contemptible rhetorical device, "My fellow Americans, I am sure you can recognize from what I have said that we really have only two choices open to us if we want to end this war. I can order an immediate precipitate withdrawal of all Americans from Vietnam without regard to the effects of that action. Or we can persist in our search for a just peace through ... our plan for Vietnamization." Here it is, all over again, the false dilemma, the black or white position, the collapse of all alternative strategies into the one most offensive and easiest to ridicule. Only two choices: my plan, or the cut-and-run cowardice of the rioters in the streets.

It is, perhaps, a consummation to be expected of the politician who perfected the technique of "The Illusion of Proof."[21]

For the attentive public to accept the Nixon program of open-ended, no-deadline withdrawal, we have got to have answers which he does not provide. Literally dozens of his opponents have protested that he is giving Saigon the best excuse in the world for not broadening its base, for not coming to terms with the Buddhists and General Khanh, for not cracking down on corruption, for not accommodating to the demands of peasants in the countryside. As Reston put it, "For if his policy is to stick with the South Vietnamese until they demonstrate that they are secure, all they have to do is prolong their inefficiency in order to guarantee that we will stay in the battle indefinitely."[22] No defense of the President's plan could ignore the logic of this argument; yet ignore it is precisely what Mr. Nixon did.

### Consequences

The announcement that the President would speak about the war on November 3 had consequences in itself. The October Moratorium was weakened; an attitude of "let's wait and see" may have deterred many would-be doves from participating. But the significant consequences were of course after the speech.

The stock market, that sensitive barometer of America's morale and business health, dropped. At 10:30 on the morning of the 4th, prices were down 7.72 on the Dow-Jones industrial average. Stocks largely recovered later in the day, and closed mixed; but the people who handle the money clearly didn't think the President had pulled a coup.

One consequence of the speech, given Nixon's past debilitating relationship with the journalistic fraternity, was a serious lowering of his credibility. Reston put it this way: "The result is that the really important men reporting on the Presidency — not the columnists but the reporters and White House correspondents — are now wondering about the President after his Vietnam speech and his partisan reaction to the elections. He invited them to believe that he would not be like President Johnson, that he would be open and candid. But his approach and reaction to the elections have not been open and candid but personal and partisan. Like Johnson he has dealt with the politics of his problem but not with the problem of Vietnam."[23]

The effects in Saigon were electric. As the *Times* headline read on November 10, "Nixon's Impact: Thieu is Helped Through a Tight Spot."[24] The National Assembly had been raising hell, a motion of no confidence was being discussed in the lower house, and a petition calling for a nationwide referendum was being circulated. Nixon stopped all this. His reaffirmed commitment to stay until there was no more challenge to "freedom" strengthened Thieu's hand immeasurably. Not being one to bite the hand that upholds him, Thieu recorded his gratitude for the press: this was "one of the most important and greatest" speeches made by an American President.[25]

The three domestic audiences identified at the beginning of this essay reacted predictably. Nixon's supporters, the hawks and the Emerging Republican Majority, were delighted. Columnist Joseph Alsop rejoiced hugely: "Whether you agree or disagree with its content, this remarkable speech was one of the most successful technical feats of political leadership in many, many years."[26]

The silent majority was impressed. Gallup, who clocked them in by telephone immediately after the speech, found 77% approving. And in his regular survey of presidential performance, taken November 14–16, approval of the President generally rose 12% over the previous month, to a high of 68%.[27] Although as Gallup noted, there was some question as to the durability of this result, the speech did sell; the "terrifying sincerity" was just what the public wanted to see. But the long pull is yet ahead.

The doves were horror-struck. There had been much reason to believe that the speech would be conciliatory, that the rhetoric would be encouraging. One consequence of the toughness of the speech was that registrations for buses to Washington for the November 13–15 events flooded in;[28] and the ultimate crowd in Washington could be said to be a direct result of Nixon's challenge to the dissidents. The effete ones were not going to take it lying down.

The candid conclusion must be that the President cheered his friends and disheartened his enemies. The peace movement is in disarray, planning no more massive marches, resigned to campus and campaign activities — until the President slips, or Hanoi trips him. As of the end of December, Richard Starnes of Scripps-Howard put it succinctly: "Peace Marchers Give Round to Nixon."[29]

## Epilogue

The Nixon style in this speech has been characterized as "tough talk." But this is not the same as saying it was rough; Nixon did preserve the amenities. As Reston put it, "He put Spiro Agnew's confrontation language into the binding of a hymn book."[30] But hymn books are not the only score from which the Administration sings. The cruder, more abrasive tunes are coming steadily from the Vice-President; and it is worth inquiring as to whether the Nixon tune must be heard against the accompaniment of his second in command.

The arguments that have raged in Washington as to whether the Vice-President plays the role of hatchet man to Nixon's above-the-battle dignity just as Nixon was once the hatchet man for Eisenhower, has now largely been resolved. Agnew comes up with his own script. His purple-passioned prose is indigenous, and with the exception of his November 13 blast against the television networks, which according to Clark Mollenhoff "was developed in the White House,"[31] the ideas as well as the language are his.

But even when he is doing his own thing, Mr. Agnew represents the President's true gut feelings.[32] The relationship is one of willing supporter, not ventriloquist's dummy. If Agnew were not around to ventilate the President's pique, someone else would have to be commandeered to put out the purple-passioned prose. The President himself, of course, could do it very well; the summer of 1969 he reverted to a former style with his colorful speeches at General Beadle State College and the Air Force Academy; but the reaction to these by the President's staff was less than enthusiastic, and he has since then turned over the rough talk to the Vice-President.

What we have, then, in the President's speech, is the substance of toughness without the rough style. And the President's text is indeed sanitized. What he might have said, what his style would have been were he not consciously trying to retain the old Republican genteel clientele, one can discover by reading Agnew. The visceral language, the blunt insults, the uncompromising hostilities are missing.[33]

But a presidential address must meet higher standards than campaign oratory or the speeches of lesser figures. Nixon's speech did not meet them. Neither his rhetorical strategies nor his substantive argument were sound. Yet the most likely time for healing and realistic rhetoric has passed. The President's personal involvement in Government decisions will grow, his commitment to what we are doing now will increase, his access to noncongruent intelligence will decrease, the youth will become more alienated. Nixon is not LBJ, and the total closing of filters that occurred in the last days of the Johnson Administration probably will not happen again; but the prospect for improvement is slight. One can always hope that another Clark Clifford is waiting in the wings to restore sanity, or another Eugene McCarthy will appear in the hustings to startle a self-deluded establishment.

A fitting summary of the whole business is provided by Anthony Lewis:

> *The preeminent task of Richard Nixon's Presidency is to heal a nation torn apart by Vietnam. The President knew that when he took the oath of office, and it is no less urgently true today. Part of the process must be to help the American people know, and accept, the unpleasant truths about the war: that we got into it by stealth and for reasons at best uncertain; that the Government we defend in South Vietnam is corrupt and unrepresentative; that in the course of fighting we have killed people and ravaged a country to an extent utterly out of proportion to our cause, and that, in the old sense of dictating to the enemy, we cannot "win." In those terms, Mr. Nixon's speech to the nation last Monday evening was a political tragedy.*[34]

It was not just the speech that was a political tragedy; the speech merely made visible tragic policy decisions — to maintain the goals and propaganda of the cold war, to seek confrontation with those who want change, to go with a power base confined to white, nonurban, uptight voters. Given such decisions, the shoddy rhetoric, the tough talk, the false dilemmas are inevitable. Instant criticism, via the networks, while desirable, cannot begin to do justice to such policies and such rhetoric. They require more searching exploration. As the saying goes, presidential rhetoric is much too important to be left to presidents.

## *Notes*

1. Robert B. Semple, Jr., "Speech Took 10 Drafts, And President Wrote All," *The New York Times,* November 4, 1969, p. 17.
2. *Ibid.*

3. Rowland Evans and Robert Novak, "Nixon's Appeal for Unity," (Baltimore) *News-American,* November 3, 1969, p. 7B.
4. For a candid statement of the pressures operating on politicians, and the hard choices they make in the struggle for survival, see John F. Kennedy, *Profiles in Courage* (New York, 1956), ch. 1.
5. November 5, 1969, p. 10.
6. Mansfield has generally been more sympathetic to the President's position than Fulbright; the Majority Leader joined Minority Leader Hugh Scott in sponsoring a resolution expressing qualified support of the President on November 7. See UPI dispatch. "40 Senators Back Cease-Fire Plea," *The New York Times,* November 8, 1969, p. 10.
7. "Nixon's Mystifying Clarifications," *The New York Times,* November 5, 1969, p. 46.
8. "Polls Show the 'Silent Majority' Also Is Uneasy About War Policy," *The Washington Post,* November 5, 1969, p. A19.
9. "One Man Alone," *The New York Times Book Review,* November 23, 1969, p. 10.
10. Luther A. Huston, "Asian Peril Cited; High Aide Says Troops May Be Sent if the French Withdraw," *The New York Times,* April 17, 1954, p. 1. Someone in Paris is alleged to have blown his cover, and Nixon was identified as the "High Aide" the next day. See also Bernard Fall, *Hell in a Very Small Place: The Siege of Dien Bien Phu* (New York, 1966), ch. IX.
11. (New Rochelle, 1969).
12. The categories of Wallace supporters are those of Andrew Hacker in his sympathetic review of Phillips, "Is There a New Republican Majority?" *Commentary,* XLVIII (November 1969), 65–70.
13. Robert B. Semple, Jr., "Nixon's November 3 Speech: Why He Took the Gamble Alone," *The New York Times,* January 19, 1970, p. 23.
14. Rowland Evans and Robert Novak, "Nixon's Speech Wedded GOP Doves to Mass of Americans," *The Washington Post,* November 6, 1969, p. A23.
15. Anthony Lewis, "The Test of American Greatness in Vietnam," *The New York Times,* November 8, 1969, p. 32.
16. All quotations from the speech are from *The New York Times* text, carried November 4, 1969, p. 16.
17. *Six Crises* (Garden City, N.Y., 1962).
18. *The Dominican Revolt* (New York, 1968).
19. Probably the best source on American violations of the Geneva Agreement on Vietnam is George M. Kabin and John W. Lewis, *The United States in Vietnam,* rev. ed. (New York, 1969).
20. "If Negotiations Fail," XLVI, 627–641.
21. See Barnet Baskerville, "The Illusion of Proof," *Western Speech,* XXV (Fall 1961), 236–242.
22. James Reston, "Washington: The Unanswered Vietnam Questions," *The New York Times,* December 10, 1969, p. 54.
23. James Reston, "Washington: The Elections and the War," *The New York Times,* November 7, 1969, p. 46.
24. Terence Smith, *The New York Times,* November 10, 1969, p. 2.
25. Terence Smith, "Thieu Hails the Speech: 'One of the Most Important,' " *The New York Times,* November 5, 1969, p. 10.
26. Joseph Alsop, "Nixon Leadership is Underestimated," *The Washington Post,* December 29, 1969, p. A13.
27. George Gallup, "Nixon Support Soars to 68%," *The Washington Post,* November 24, 1969, p. A1.

28. David E. Rosenbaum, "Thousands Due in Capital in War Protest This Week," *The New York Times*, November 9, 1969, pp. 1, 56.
29. *The Pittsburgh Press*, December 26, 1969, p. 15.
30. James Reston, November 5, 1969.
31. E. W. Kenworthy, "Nixon Aide Says Agnew Stand Reflects White House TV View," *The New York Times*, November 16, 1969, p. 78.
32. Robert B. Semple, Jr., "Agnew: The Evidence is That He's Speaking for Nixon," *The New York Times*, November 2, 1969, Sec. 4, p. 3.
33. But the old debator's syndrome is very much present. A good capsule description of what this means is in Earl Mazo and Stephen Hess, *Nixon: A Political Portrait* (New York, 1968), p. 7.
34. *The New York Times*, November 8, 1969, p. 32.

## *The Quest Story and Nixon's November 3, 1969 Address*

HERMANN G. STELZNER

The Quest story is a literary genre in which the subjective experiences of life are central. The themes in such stories vary, but the genre is one of the oldest, hardiest, and most popular. Perhaps its persistent appeal is due to "its validity as a symbolic description of our subjective personal experience of existence as historical."[1] The Quest story describes a search for "something" the truth or falsity of which is known only upon the conclusion of the search.

Although the themes and the details change, the form or "the fixity" of Quest stories is fairly stable,[2] one reason why the Quest story is archetypal. When the essential elements of the story interact with the subjective experiences of individuals verbal transactions occur. Occasionally universal human reactions are elicited.

The practical world of political affairs shares many themes with the imaginative world of fiction. When a leader of a body politic and his people seek to resolve a problem, they may be engaged in a Quest. A leader speaks and orders a reality, a form; he offers an *objective* experience of the social, political, or moral life. However, to become viable it must interact with the *subjective* experiences of his listeners. If a given problem, war and peace, for example, occurs frequently enough, perhaps a close examination of all such speeches might yield an archetypal pattern. Thus far, however, the rhetorical criticism of speeches has not proceeded from this perspective. This exploratory effort centers on a single speech.

When President Richard M. Nixon spoke to the nation on November 3, 1969 about the war in Vietnam he indicated how central it was to him, his Administration, and his people: "I did not wait for my inauguration to begin my quest for peace."[3] The connotations of "quest" and Nixon's strong, personal identification with it — "my," not *our* or *the*, convey an orientation and a potential pattern of behavior that suggest that this speech and the archetypal Quest story share similarities.[4] To place the speech within the genre of the Quest story is merely to classify it. But the essential elements of the Quest story may then provide a way into the speech, and they may yield insights that other critical approaches do not obtain. The critical prism refracts light differently as a function of the way it is turned. The light refracted from this angle may be a different "color" from that obtained from some other facet of the prism.[5] Finally, the objective political experience of Vietnam structured by President Nixon and the listeners' subjective experiences of life should interact. What in the chosen and arranged language of the speech increases the probability of a verbal transaction? What goes on in the speech?

The five essential elements of a Quest story are stated here and developed below. These elements also function as a rhetorical partition, providing terms for the analysis and forcing the parts of the analysis to comment on one another. The essential elements are (1) a precious Object and/or Person to be found and possessed or married; (2) a long journey to find the Object, because its whereabouts are not originally known to the seekers; (3) a Hero; (4) the Guardians of the Object who must be overcome before it can be won; and (5) the Helpers who with their knowledge and/or magical powers assist the Hero and but for whom he would never succeed.

1. *A precious Object and/or Person to be found and possessed or married.* Because the conflict in Vietnam was central in the political scene Nixon inherited on his inauguration, he sketches its background in swift, broad strokes; it serves as a refresher for listeners and as a point of departure. He advances five questions that preview the direction his remarks will take: (1) "How and why did America get involved in Vietnam in the first place?" He terms it the "fundamental issue." (2) "How has this Administration changed the policy of the previous Administration?" Centering on this question allows Nixon to capitalize on the public frustration with the Johnson approach and to avoid any serious consideration of the "fundamental issue." (3) "What has really happened in the negotiations in Paris and the battlefront in Vietnam?" Nixon's reports are scattered throughout the speech (4) "What choices do we have if we are to end the war?" This is a central question but Nixon examines only two choices. (5) "What are the prospects for peace?"

Nixon does not make the precious Object immediately clear, withholding its precise nature and character. Instead he alludes to the October 15, 1969 Moratorium and comments briskly and adversely on a peace proposal endorsed by its leaders. Intending to unveil a new view, he weakens the old before announcing it, thus avoiding a direct conflict.

Nixon early makes clear that whatever the policy, it will be influenced by the long view of the national and international scene. He refers obliquely to the young, telling the Now and In generation they must yield to his "greater obligation" to think of the "next generation" and of the "future of peace and freedom in America and in the world." The view is global. Nixon's treatment of time and the next generation suggests that stability and settledness will emerge from the as yet undisclosed precious Object.

But Nixon's statements are not altogether consistent. He appears troubled as he searches for a view that will be acceptable to an anxious audience at home and to the international audience as well:[6] "I had to think of the effect of my decision on the next generation, and on the future of peace and freedom in America and in the world." Three sentences later he offers a view that restricts, if it does not altogether compromise, the breadth of his concern: "The great question is: How can we win America's peace?" If this is indeed the *great question*, what has happened to the world? Has there been a shift in perspective? A possible explanation for these contradictory emphases must be hazarded.

The first statement is not only global; it also emphasizes future time. The second statement is restricted and time is not specifically mentioned. Measured against the first statement the second suggests being accomplished in a shorter time. The second statement springs out of Nixon's need to recognize early emotional stresses and divisiveness at home. It suggests that they can be resolved sooner than later. The long war has often been justified as an international obligation. The national patience has worn thin. Nixon offers something to quiet the impatience. He centers on and satisfies self.

The prized Object is finally announced. It is a "just peace," a "just and lasting peace." Nixon makes clear that the peace his opponents seek cannot be prized. Their method of achieving it and the effects of it tarnish the Object. A just peace is more valuable than a pragmatic peace because it lies beyond men and the moment; it transcends both. Here, of course, is the higher peace of an Upper World and such an Object is potentially persuasive when the opponents in South Vietnam, the Communist North Vietnamese supported by Communist China and the Soviet Union, represent the demonic powers of a Lower World.

Further, if America achieves only an immediate peace, which Nixon defines as the "popular and easy course," she will not have set a goal worthy enough to meet the requirements of a "lasting peace," which concerns "many people in all parts of the world." Peace in Vietnam is not enough; peace in Vietnam must serve the "cause of peace . . . in the Pacific and the world." The prized Object has been located and defined.

2. *A long journey to find the Object, because its whereabouts are not originally known to the seekers.* The journey takes place in both time and space. For the United States it began "fifteen years ago" when North Vietnam "launched a campaign to impose a Communist government on South Vietnam." Nixon quickly summarizes the actions taken by Presidents Eisenhower, Kennedy, and Johnson who sent men and materials into the conflict.

Time is central in Nixon's analysis. It is partially because the war has been "long and bitter" that he rejects the policy of immediate withdrawal. His many references to its proponents are his open acknowledgment of their strength, but he is certain that a lengthy, bitter military and psychological effort cannot simply stop.

The fifteen long years also condition the peach he will accept. His opposition seeks a pragmatic peace. But the time already spent and still to be spent in the search will further dignify the Object. Nixon makes a "just peace" and an "immediate peace" via withdrawal into antithetical images, a timeless value versus a momentary value; the former has weight, the latter is weightless and ephemeral.

The search for a weightless ephemeral Object cannot be rewarding; it is a journey into Nowhere, a journey "to the end of the night," and the effect would be chaos, Nixon claims. He acknowledges his journey is into a "dangerous" Unknown. But in contrast to the gesture or policy of despair his opponents offer (Nixon resists calling it suicide), his policy has *significant form.* A policy of despair always lacks a reliable and objective narrator. Nixon stresses that the young are idealistic; idealism is antithetical to objectivity and reliability.

However valuable a "just peace" may be, Nixon understands that it must not appear to be beyond reach. Time is both a physical measure and a psychological state, and he senses that to satisfy his listeners he must make the timeless future somehow concrete and reasonably immediate. He announces some of the gains his approach has achieved: "Now we have begun to see the results of this long-overdue change in American policy in Vietnam." The results indicate that both the war and the battle with time can be won.

3. *A Hero.* The precious Object cannot be won by anybody, but only by the one person who possesses the right qualifications of breeding and character. Further, the Quest story presents a Test or a series of Tests by which the unworthy are screened out, and the Hero revealed.

There are two types of Quest Hero. The first has a superior arete manifest to all. No one doubts that he can win the Golden Fleece if anyone can. The second has a concealed arete. He turns out to be the Hero when his manifest betters have failed. His zeal is plodding and pedestrian. He enlists help because unlike his betters he is humble enough to take advice and kind enough to give assistance to people who, like himself, appear to be nobody in particular.

Hero images often appear in public addresses, and they are symbolic. In Nixon's speech both types of Hero appear and his portrayals of them build support for himself and his policy. The Heroes are structured in polar terms, but because they faced a common problem, Vietnam, the polarities are not in direct moral or ethical conflict. The portrayal is not developed as good-bad, strong-weak, right-wrong, but as practical-impractical, workable-unworkable, or feasible-unfeasible. For example, Nixon acknowledges that "many believe that President Johnson's decision to send American combat forces to South Vietnam was wrong." Nixon supports the decision, but observes: "And many others, I among them, have been strongly critical of the way the war has been conducted." His criticism of Woodrow Wilson also centers on practicality, workability and feasibility.

Early in the speech Nixon reports on the efforts of Presidents Eisenhower, Kennedy, and Johnson to achieve success in Vietnam. Immediately following the factual citations, Nixon employs Kennedy for support and refers to him in a special way. About one aspect of American policy, Kennedy spoke, Nixon states, with "characteristic eloquence and clarity," and these are attributes of men of superior arete.

If Kennedy, a Hero of superior arete, appears early in the speech, not until it is almost concluded does Nixon place another figure who is similarly described. Woodrow Wilson, says Nixon, had a "dream for peace." And he "spoke words which caught the imagination of a war-weary world . . . : 'This is the war to end wars'." Heroes of superior arete can express the affairs of state in apocalyptic terms. They have an imaginative conception of the whole of nature.

These two Heroes are much alike in another way. Kennedy died a tragic death while in office. Listeners need not be reminded. Wilson did not die in office, but Nixon says that he "died a broken man," and he stresses that Wilson's "dream" was "shattered on the hard reality of great power politics." These two examples remind listeners that the leadership offered by visionary Heroes may result in a "tragic fall" if an idealized goal cannot be achieved.

About his policy and himself, Nixon is emphatic; he does not offer a vision beyond his ability to produce: "I do not tell you that the war in Vietnam is the war to end wars." He hopes only to "increase the chance that . . . younger brothers and . . . sons" of the men in Vietnam "will not have to fight in some future Vietnam some place in the world."

Nixon knows that he is not a Kennedy or a Wilson, but he does not disassociate himself completely from them. He reports that he, too, is a statesman, aspiring to the title of peacemaker in the world. How? He tells listeners he speaks from the room, "in this room" where Wilson spoke about the "war to end wars." He tells them about Wilson's desk, "at this very desk" Wilson spoke. The desk is in the room and via television in the presence of listeners. Nixon has kept it and apparently works at it. A moral value is not only expressed; it is also displayed.

Nixon also emphasizes the kind of Hero he is by not taking advantage of a fallen Hero, his predecessor. If he supported immediate withdrawal, it would bring defeat, but he could "blame" it on Johnson and "come out as the peacemaker." To achieve peace at another's expense is a low form of honor. Nixon knows that many citizens mistrust Johnson, whose fall is partially explained in moral terms. More than a few citizens believe Johnson capable of the very action Nixon rejects as unworthy of a man of stature. He puts distance between himself and Johnson.

Nixon also equates many of the dissenting young people with the first type of Hero. He delivered this speech two weeks after the first Moratorium (October 15, 1969).[7] Another demonstration was planned for November. Nixon announced his speech far in advance (on October 13, 1969), strategically placing it between the two convocations. That the Moratorium was an eloquent and dramatic statement-act is a value judgment. That it was largely an expression by the young is fact.

That Nixon equates the young with the first type of Hero is clear from evidence in the address. He states that "some" people urged him to order "the immediate withdrawal of all American forces." In Quest stories Heroes of superior arete often ride straight up the golden path to win the prized Object. Nixon alludes to such activity; immediate withdrawal means "without regard to the effects of that action." Further, to ride straight up the path wins the applause of the multitude; it would have been a "popular . . . course to follow." Nixon acknowledges that the young have "energy and dedication." He also respects their "idealism," a term he specifically reserves for the young.

Nixon and his supporters are the second type of Hero. In 1960 he had jousted with a Hero of the first type, was defeated, and hovered near political death. Patiently and industriously he brought himself back to political health. He and his policy for Vietnam are counterbalances to the first type of Hero. Whatever is done must not risk death — political or any other kind. Withdrawal from Vietnam means "collapse" in all "Southeast Asia." Immediate withdrawal, equated with "defeat," would result in a "collapse of confidence" in America's leadership "not only in Asia but throughout the world." Our collapse would "promote recklessness" and "spark violence" which ultimately would "cost more lives" — more death. An idealistic policy, Nixon suggests, might create a Hell on Earth.

It is interesting to compare Nixon's personal political fortunes with those he has described for the state if the wrong course is chosen. Defeat in 1960 did not mean total collapse for him. Defeat again in California in 1962 did not mean total collapse. Affairs in the world of individual men are reversible. In affairs of state they are not. Or is it that the Hero who has suffered, and understands what to suffer means, wishes to protect his people from the agonies he has personally experienced? He must also know full well that if the nation emerges from Vietnam suffering as he has personally suffered, his place in the history books (the annals of the time) will be dimmed.

Nixon's policy for Vietnam is disciplined, cautious, and pragmatic. He will not go straight up the path. He has provided for options. Realizing that peace might not be achieved "through negotiation" he had ready "another plan." He will work earnestly; even before his inauguration he began his quest. For Nixon peace is not a vision. It is a "concern" and a "goal." Consistent with the type of Hero he is, he asks to be judged by the cumulative effects of his labors, not by the moral intensity of his strivings.

If Nixon's policy is disciplined, cautious, and pragmatic, the language that displays it is hard, rigid, and barren. Word choices are both familiar and unpretentious. Images are absent; the texture is flat.

Noticeably lacking are Biblical images. Yet the speech is directed largely to a silent majority, the generations nurtured on war and Biblical imagery. However, this is a secular war and God does not explicitly support our policy; nor is He explicitly on our side. Three rhetorical considerations explain the absence of such imagery. First, this speech is not so much a war message as it is a message about a war. Second, Vietnam is a small war that Presidents Eisenhower, Kennedy, and Johnson sought to localize and restrain. Nixon, too, aims to deflate it. Biblical images have magnitude, scope, and thrust. Thus, on both logical and aesthetic grounds they are simply "too large" for the problem. Third, Biblical images connote ethical and moral values. Keeping the war secular, and justifying it with political, military, and economic values, deprives the opposition of a potential issue. Further, Nixon does not give the silent majority an opportunity to consciously consider if the Biblical imagery and the Vietnam war are consistent. He avoids constructing for them a potentially disturbing dilemma.

Either type of Hero-president can use the power of the Office to further policies. Nixon reports on many of his efforts. He sent emissaries across the water (another part of the long journey) to the symbolic capital of the civilized — and thus safe — world, Paris, to meet with the North Vietnamese. He himself crossed the water to inspect the unsafe world and to receive firsthand reports about our efforts to stabilize it, a dimension of civilization. Then from Guam, that piece of secure United States territory nearest the conflict, he intoned from afar a shift in foreign policy. The policy is given a potentially potent name, Vietnamization. The phonetic similarities between Vietnamization and Americanization suggest our continued influence and concern. He also announces that other "significant initiatives which must remain secret to keep open some channels of communications" are in progress. Further, he sends a letter to Ho Chi Minh through an unnamed representative who had known Minh personally for 25 years; a dimension of intrigue is added to the effort. In some reports there are signs of hope. Nixon refers to the "deadlock" in negotiations, but perhaps new energies will come from this tired metaphor. He refers to the letter he received from Ho Chi Minh, "three days before his death." The letter says nothing new, but may not its writer's death be read as a hopeful harbinger of some new movement? Of what significance is the report of Minh's death, if not that? In deadlock and in death itself is the potential for rebirth.

Nixon's policy, language, and behavior reveal him as a Hero whose omnipotence and omniscience are limited.

4. *The Guardians of the Object who must be overcome before it can be won.* They may simply be a further test of the Hero's arete, or they may be malignant in themselves.

That the government of North Vietnam is both different from and in opposition to the United States is understood. In the popular mind, North Vietnam is malignant simply because it is communist; external motives are neither necessary to its behavior nor can they ever fully explain its behavior. Nixon does nothing to soften that view. Rather he emphasizes and develops it. An evil government will instigate and support revolutions: in the time past, in the present time, and in the future. Nixon's language is extremely severe: "murdered," "thousands . . . died in slave labor camps," "civilians were clubbed, shot, . . . and buried in mass graves," "a bloody reign of terror," and a "nightmare" in South Vietnam describe the North Vietnamese activities; the government is presented as being much worse than an undeveloped version of ourselves. Surely in an address about a war the image of the dual experience, a contest between two sides, friends and enemies, is expected. Nixon emphasizes animality and bestiality.

But the North Vietnamese also present further tests to the Hero and the American people. Nixon details the proposals the United States has advanced. We will work in common and will be open-minded. Except for the right of the people of South Vietnam to determine their own future "anything is negotiable." Again and again

Nixon remarks on the responses to such proposals. Hanoi has "refused even to discuss our proposals." In Paris a "deadlock" developed. Further negotiation "depends only on Hanoi's deciding to negotiate." The silent, uninvolved, nonparticipating North Vietnamese made success difficult. Nixon's tone is objective. But to stress his personal exasperation, he concludes with a folksy idiom consistent with his common-sense observation: "Well, now, who's at fault?"

A war message and the Quest story share the presupposition that one side is good, the other bad. But our *objective experience* of social and political life informs us otherwise. The moral ambiguities of political conflicts do not adhere to the proposition. But in war, men stereotype, reserving the good for their side and the bad for their opponents. And any virtues an enemy may possess are ignored.[8]

5. *The Helpers who with their knowledge and/or magical powers assist the Hero and but for whom he would never succeed.* Ideally, all citizens in a democracy will be Helpers, but in a "free society" dissent is recognized and tolerated. However, if dissenters take to the streets they might bind a president and circumscribe his options. In such a situation, what may be of greater danger than a dissenting Chorus is a confused, perplexed, and silent Chorus. To a Hero in need of support a formless and mute Chorus presents problems. How does a Hero-president "divine" what a silent majority will hear? Although Nixon can neither see it nor hear it, he has personal resources. His private vision furnishes him direction.

The rhetorical strategy emerges slowly and develops late. The approach to silent America is through young America, or for purposes of a rhetorical antithesis "shrill America." The young have been described. They are fervent, vocal, idealistic, energetic, and dedicated. These are positive virtues. Nixon counters them with a single negative particular that explains how the young have gone wrong. The positive virtues have been turned "into bitter hatred." Bitter hatred is irrational. It is, Nixon suggests, the tragic flaw in the character of the young.

If a democracy tolerates dissent and if men of station and experience have something to say to those (the young) who have achieved less, it is reasonable to assume that the young will attend to the President. It is also reasonable to assume that the President may speak directly to any audience. Yet when Nixon addresses the young, he casts doubt on these assumptions. He asks permission: "I would like to address a word, if I may, to the young people of this nation." The deliberately artificial idiom creates a cool and distant relationship. A superior depicts himself begging favors of an inferior and in the inversion Nixon discards the rhetorical mask of sociability. He comes close to portraying himself as a "silent American" or still better for his purposes a "silenced American." If the president approaches the young in this fashion, he suggests to others that the young people are a serious problem.

Nixon, however, had stated a policy. He had forcefully declared that he would not be "dictated" to "by the minority." Should other adults adopt his stance? If the connotations of the word "dictate" central to our involvement in Vietnam are extended, the answer is positive. If we are helping South Vietnam to avoid being dictated to by a belligerent minority, surely the people at home can also resist being dictated to.

The stance provides Nixon with an opportunity to give added force to nostalgic values: "I know it may not be fashionable to speak of patriotism or national destiny these days." The negative emphasizes the positive. These values are the beacon lights that confirm the reality of democratic form. They indicate that democracy is not yet, at least, invisible and unrecognizable. A citizenry and a nation unaware of their form live a death.

Together the discussion of the young and of values prepares that audience Nixon has yet to address directly: "So tonight, to you, the great silent majority of my fellow Americans, I ask for your support."[9] Silent America has been invited to speak; it need not ask permission. A formal fashion is preserved. Further, Nixon's private vision rhetorically developed before a public, creates a new form or audience, the "silent majority." The Helpers in the citizen Chorus who were confused are perplexed are made cohesive and real. They are no longer invisible and unrecognizable to themselves. They are also made visible and recognizable to others.

Nixon gives added meaning to patriotism and destiny by commenting on their history and heritage. "Two hundred years ago" America "was the hope of millions" and the "wheel of destiny" has now placed "any hope the world has for the survival of peace and freedom" squarely upon her. Survival suggests life; its absence, death. To his silent majority Nixon says: He who rejects his heritage rejects humanity, and thus himself. Rejection of self is a form of suicide that affects others. A conscious rejection of heritage, humanity, and self by Americans will cause the hopes of others (Vietnamese primarily, but other millions as well) "to be suffocated," still another form of death, perhaps even murder in the first degree.

If history and heritage are rejected, then further tragedy may be expected. Sooner or later we would have "more wars," which "would cost more lives." But Nixon carefully avoids an ultimate conclusion. He does not say that the United States would be overcome. If we desert Asia, we would "lose confidence in ourselves." As we "saw the consequences . . . inevitable remorse and divisive recrimination would scar our spirit as a people." Here, too, he avoids a final conclusion, but he describes a country people by "nameless strangers." The conclusions drawn from Nixon's objective statements are easily cast into images of self-extinction.

When the silent majority speaks, it participates. Constructive action may then occur at home and abroad. But the silent majority speaks not only because it has been asked to. Unless it speaks and participates, it will act much like the North Vietnamese who earlier had been portrayed as nonspeakers and uninvolved participants. The silent majority cannot or will not speak and act like the young; yet neither can it not speak and not act as the North Vietnamese have done. Where then should it place itself? The silent majority will take a middle position, out of choice perhaps, but not until choice has been suggested by the polarities of Nixon's rhetorical structure. For his policy Nixon has a public. He has Helpers.

The resolution of the Vietnam war Nixon terms a quest, a "big" word suggesting magnitude, great risks, and tremendous moments. A true quest has moments so large that they lack definite boundaries and risks of such magnitude that they cannot easily be faced or exactly described by those who must endure them. To look for a paper clip is not a true quest.

Nixon positions the word in the right place — early in the speech. But the word itself is wrong. His policy does differ from those of his predecessors. But it remains one of cautious, subtle modifications. He offers no new imaginative whole; indeed he blunts such considerations. Immediate withdrawal has magnitude, and potentially great risks and moments. Nixon rejects it. Those who call for a serious discussion of war as an important instrument of foreign policy ask fundamental questions of value. They are nearer to Wilson than to Nixon. To the call, Nixon is silent.

Nixon's political narrative also fails as a quest because he does not structure a direct confrontation between himself and the leader of the Guardians of the Object. It is Nixon who prophesies that immediate withdrawal means the loss of Asia and the loss of respect throughout the world. But has Ho Chi Minh or his successor claimed that great a victory growing out of the war? If yes, why doesn't Nixon confront them or him? Let him meet and overthrow the claims of his opponents and show that they are braggadocios. Nixon's prophecy may be correct. But he may also claim more for the Guardians than they claim for themselves. To that extent his political analysis is braggadocian.

Nixon's confrontation with the young is direct. And his listeners have both seen and heard the young. Many believe social unrest at home is an urgent matter. They have again been asked to be patient about Vietnam. Many seem willing, but their frustrations remain intense. Nixon directs them to satisfy them by meeting, testing, and overthrowing the claims of young loud, windy, braggadocios. The strategy adds little nobility or grandeur to his Quest.

Within the development of his Quest, Nixon illustrates how a Hero as one historical personage may move to larger Heroic groups.[10] There was the Great but Woolly Woodrow, Paternal Ike, Dashing John, and finally Black Lyndon. All had opportunities and moments. Now Somber Richard, a different Hero, appears to establish a new Heroic group, the silent majority.

The relationship between Nixon and the silent majority parallels in general outline a standard myth pattern. Nixon fought political battles, lost, and disappeared. He had fallen, becoming a part of the silent minority. During his absence various events caused his followers and others to wonder whether they and their world had fallen. Nixon's risen political body now speaks with a strong voice, uniting and reuniting others with him.

Listeners who sensed the Devil in all around them were assured, if not exhilarated. Traditional values such as the confident love of country, of personal and public honor, of pride in soldiership and citizenship were affirmed. This Hero does not believe that these values are sins. He will confront those who do.

Evaluated in literary terms Nixon's political narrative is obviously not a good Quest story. It is not altogether convincing. There are too many loose ends and too many unanswered questions. It is peopled by flat characters and its language is dull and unimaginative.

This speech was not offered to the public as a literary work. It deals with practical political problems and if evaluated accordingly it accomplishes some objectives. Although divisiveness in the political community remains, Nixon gains an audience and time. He finds listeners who will respond to his words and images. He gains a firmer possession of the policy he lays out before them and makes himself ready for the next series of events he must deal with in Vietnam.

## Notes

1. W. H. Auden, "The Quest Hero," *Texas Quarterly,* IV (Winter 1961), 82. This analysis borrows much from Auden. The essential elements of the Quest story are Auden's, slightly modified. General accounts of the Quest story and archetypal patterns can be found in numerous works. Maud Bodkin's *Archetypal Patterns in Poetry* (London, 1934) and Northrop Frye's *Anatomy of Criticism* (Princeton, 1957) and *Fables of Identity* (New York, 1963) are indispensable to a study of the method.
2. Wayne Shumaker, *Literature and the Irrational* (Englewood Cliffs, N.J., 1960), p. 135.

3. The text for this analysis is found in *Vital Speeches,* XXXVI (November 15, 1969), 66–70. Each paragraph of the text was numbered, 1–125. Thus this statement appears in paragraph 41 of the text.
4. This speech is the product of Nixon's mind and hand. He "solicited ideas from his large corps of speechwriters but did not order drafts from them . . . or otherwise use their literary talents." The speech went "through 10 drafts, all written by the President himself." Nixon felt the address "must convey an authentic note of personal involvement. He clearly felt that the speech would not carry such a message if someone else wrote it." These descriptions suggest other dimensions of a "quest." Robert B. Semple, Jr., "Speech Took 10 Drafts, and President Wrote All," *The New York Times,* November 4, 1969, p. 17.
5. For example, see Robert P. Newman, "Under the Veneer: Nixon's Vietnam Speech of November 3, 1969," *QJS,* LVI (April 1970), 168–178.
6. General Ky of South Vietnam is reported to have said before the speech was delivered that it would be addressed to the American audience. See James Reston, "Nixon's Mystifying Clarifications," *The New York Times,* November 5, 1969, p. 46.
7. Unnamed associates of Nixon offer a different interpretation for the timing of the speech. They say that the President had decided as early as August 1969 to give the country an accounting of the war and that he wanted to key "such an accounting . . . to the first anniversary of the bombing halt in early November." Further, in "the words of one high source," early announcement was necessary to "give Hanoi fair warning and a chance to turn around in Paris." Robert B. Semple, Jr., "Nixon's Nov. 3 Speech: Why He Took the Gamble Alone," *The New York Times,* January 19, 1970, p. 23.
8. Nixon's descriptions of the North Vietnamese are consistent with this observation. He does express emotion apart from intellect and there is a certain automatism in the analysis. However, it is inaccurate to use the metaphor of intoxication, which often designates the complete breakdown of rhetorical control. There is little doubt that what listeners are asked to embrace is in part a projection from Nixon's own emotional life. Insofar as the public scene is concerned, an obsessive repetition of verbal formulas may not stand up in objective discussions of public policy, and the audience may not become as cohesive as the speaker may like.
9. Associates report that Nixon had difficulty developing a satisfactory conclusion for the speech. He had jotted down numerous phrases he wanted to use but could not find room for. One read: "I don't want demonstrations, I want your quiet support." The line in the text seems to have emerged from such jottings. Semple, "Nixon's Nov. 3 Speech . . . ," p. 23.
10. I am indebted to Professor Ernest Bormann, University of Minnesota, who read a draft of this essay and suggested this insightful interpretation.

## *An Exercise in the Rhetoric of Mythical America*

KARLYN KOHRS CAMPBELL

This major policy address on the Vietnam War was, in part, a response to the October moratorium demonstration, despite Nixon's assertion that he would, under no circumstances, be affected by it.[1] The address was followed by an even larger moratorium demonstration in November and by Spiro Agnew's harsh attacks on the news media for their analyses and evaluations of the President's speech.[2] This criticism is an attempt to appraise this discourse primarily in terms of criteria suggested within the address by the President himself.

At the outset the President tells us that there is deep division in the nation partly because many Americans have lost confidence in what the government has told them about the war. In the President's opinion the people of the nation should be told the truth. The three criteria the President explicitly suggests are truth, credibility, and unity, and he later implies a fourth criterion based on responsibility and ethical principles. In other words Nixon tells us that the address is intended to relate the truth, increase the credibility of Administrative statements about the war, unify the nation, and remind us of our duties as Americans.

Two serious misrepresentations cast doubt on the truthfulness of the President. First, he misrepresents his opposition by treating them as a homogeneous group who seek immediate, precipitate withdrawal epitomized by the slogan "Lose in Vietnam; bring the boys home." Hence he also misrepresents the policy options available to him. As the President recognizes, somewhat indirectly, there are four alternatives to the policy of Vietnamization: escalation, immediate and precipitate withdrawal, disengagement through negotiation, and a scheduled withdrawal with a fixed date of termination. He mentions the possibility of escalation only as a threat to Hanoi, should increased enemy activity jeopardize the process of Vietnamization. The primary focus of the President's refutation is immediate, precipitate withdrawal — a justifiable argumentative stance only if the bulk of his opposition supported this policy. Instead most of his critics supported the fourth option — a scheduled withdrawal with a fixed date of termination, such as former Senator Charles Goodell's proposed disengagement plan, which called for total withdrawal of all American troops in a year's time but continued economic and military aid to South Vietnam at the discretion of Congress and the President.[3] A few critics, such as Eugene McCarthy, advocated a negotiated settlement. But only a small minority of the peace movement supported immediate, total withdrawal. The President's characterization of his opposition is designed to make the alternatives to Vietnamization appear as extreme as possible so that the voices urging them will not be heeded. The misrepresentation of the opposition and the consequent focus on immediate, total withdrawal as the most important alternative allow the President to transform a complex policy question into a simple either-or decision:

> *I am sure that you can recognize from what I have said that we have only two choices open to us if we want to end the war. I can order an immediate precipitate withdrawal of all Americans from Vietnam without regard to the effects of that action. Or we can persist in our search for a just peace through . . . Vietnamization . . .*

The misrepresentation of his opposition makes the only apparent alternative to his policy as unattractive and radical as possible. This strategy may gull the audience, and it may make his speech more persuasive for some listeners, but the technique violates his earlier promise to tell the truth.

The second misrepresentation occurs in relation to what the President calls the "fundamental issue. Why and how did the United States become involved in Vietnam in the first place?" He answers this question with a dubious description of the beginning of the war:

> *Fifteen years ago North Vietnam, with the logistical support of Communist China and the Soviet Union, launched a campaign to impose a Communist government on South Vietnam by instigating and supporting a revolution.*

Now "fifteen years ago" was 1954, the year of the Geneva Agreements that were to unify Vietnam through elections to be held in 1956. Those elections never occurred because the United States supported Diem, who refused elections and attempted to destroy all internal political opposition, Communist and otherwise. The Vietcong did not persuade Hanoi or Peking or Moscow to aid them against Diem until about 1959. By 1965 South Vietnam was clearly losing, the point at which President Johnson decided to send in United States combat forces.[4]

The surprising decision to give top priority to the historical question, in a policy address that perforce must concern itself with the best means of disengagement, merits consideration. The President's attempt to perpetuate the now largely discredited justifications for United States intervention serves at least two functions. First, it allows Nixon to appeal to history and historical values, to the prior decisions of Presidents Eisenhower, Kennedy, and Johnson and to Woodrow Wilson and his dream of a just peace. Nixon's policy becomes the logical outcome of the decisions and values of his predecessors, and Nixon's way become the American way. Second, emphasis on the origins of the war structures the argument so that the primary justifications for the policy can be ethical rather than pragmatic. The speech contains no information about how the plan will work, no evidence for the consequences predicted, and no analysis of how the Vietcong or Hanoi will view it. Instead almost all the justifications are ethical; Vietnamization is "the right way." Although the misrepresentation of the beginning of the war may be believed because of the authority of the speaker, the evasion of the hard questions of feasibility and costs is not consistent with the President's promise to tell the truth.

Two major contradictions damage the President's status as a truthteller. Early in the speech he tells the audience that immediate withdrawal would be the popular and easy course, enhancing the prestige of the Administration and increasing its chances of reelection. Yet at the end of the speech it is clear that the President believes his opposition is a "vocal minority" and that his policy represents the will of the "great, silent majority." If so, isn't his policy the popular and easy one with the best chance of returning him to the White House?

Similarly early in the speech Nixon explains that immediate and total withdrawal would be a disaster for the South Vietnamese because it would inevitably allow the Communists to repeat the massacres that followed their takeover of the North.[5] In response former Senator Goodell remarked that this argument rests on the assumption that the South Vietnamese army would be powerless to prevent a complete takeover of the South. Yet at the time of the address the South Vietnamese had over a million men under arms, while the Vietcong had about 100,000, and the North Vietnamese had about 110,000 in the South.[6] If these smaller armies could take over and massacre, then the president's proposed policy of Vietnamization is surely doomed because it assumes that the South Vietnamese army, with American equipment and training, can successfully take over the fighting of the war and defeat both the Vietcong and the North Vietnamese. The two notions seem somewhat contradictory.

The overwhelming questions concerning credibility are, of course, whether the President really had a secret plan for withdrawal and whether he really intended to end the war? The events that followed this address answered these questions for most Americans. Shortly after the address a Gallup poll reported that the Nixon Administration is facing the same crisis in public confidence on the war that confronted the Johnson administration: 69 percent of the Americans feel that the Administration is not telling the American people all they should know about the war, and 46 percent disapprove of the President's way of handling the Vietnam situation.[7] One critic, after careful analysis of the credibility issue, concludes that Nixon had a plan and sincerely intended to end the war. However, even this critic says "that his heart was not in it, that only the pressure of public opinion had caused him to embrace what he for fifteen years rejected,"[8] and that the address seriously lowered his credibility with newsmen.[9]

In an immediate sense the speech may be called highly credible but, at the same time, extremely divisive. Gallup reported that 77 percent of those who heard it gave the President a vote of confidence;[10] still the divisions over the war were not healed. In fact the address played an important part in exacerbating the bitter conflict between what the President termed the "silent majority" and a "vocal minority" fervently seeking to prevail "over reason and the will of the majority." He characterized dissenters as a small group trying to impose their views and dictate policy "by mounting demonstrations in the streets," terms that place them outside acceptable processes for change in a democratic society. He implied that the opposition was a partial cause for the continuation of the war when he said that "the more divided we are at home, the less likely the enemy is to negotiate." Finally he says that "only Americans," presumably only *dissenting* Americans, "can humiliate and defeat the United States." These statements belie the theme of unity and contradict his earlier assertion that "honest and patriotic Americans have reached different conclusions as to how peace should be achieved." In fact one critic has argued that the address was deliberately designed to isolate dissenters from the majority of opinion.[11] If this address is to unify Americans and fulfill the President's Inaugural promise to "bring us together," it will do so only to the degree that the speaker has silenced his opposition or shamed them into acquiescence.

The President also suggests a fourth criterion. The notion of responsibility or obligation appears frequently, and the President emphasizes that his policy is not the easy, but the right, way. An ethical principle seems implicit. However, despite his numerous protestations, the address does not call on Americans to assume responsibility. First, the President never holds the United States responsible in any way for its part in the war despite the role of the United States in undermining the Geneva Agreements. Instead he places all blame for the initiation and escalation of the war on North Vietnam, China, and Russia. Similarly he places all blame for the failure to negotiate a settlement on Hanoi. Praise and blame on such controversial and complicated questions can be assigned so simply and clearly only if the intent is to avoid all responsibility. Second, the President's repeated assertion of *his* responsibility, including his responsibility to choose the best path and lead the nation along it, becomes the individual citizen's *irresponsibility:* The President will decide, the President will lead, and the President will be responsible; while the "silent majority" of "forgotten Americans" will follow, patriotic and undissenting, in the sure knowledge that quiet acquiescence to his considered judgment is the path to victory, peace, and honor.

The powerlessness and frustration felt by dissenters and demonstrators in the face of this rhetoric should be mirrored to some extent in all of us. The President tells us, in effect, there is nothing we can do. By definition, if we are vocal and dissenting, we are the minority whose will must not prevail and to whom no heed will be paid. The only alternative is to join "the great, silent majority" in support of his policy.

In addition as many commentators have pointed out, the policy of Vietnamization, viewed at its worst, is war by proxy in which the Vietnamese supply the bodies while we supply guns, money, and advice.[12] In this sense the policy is a means to avoid the responsibility for making moral judgments about the war. Whether it is viewed as war by proxy or as a long, slow, costly process for ending American involvement, the policy of Vietnamization makes the pace of American withdrawal dependent on decisions made in Hanoi and Saigon and on factors almost wholly beyond United States control. Vietnamization may be "the right way," but it is also a way that limits United States' responsibility severely by placing the burden of decision on others. If the enemy is irresponsible, the threat, although disclaimed, is clear: Troop withdrawals will stop and military action will escalate; and it will be *their* responsibility. As a consequence Americans clearly are not asked to assume moral obligations.

From the point of view of the critic, the most intriguing statements in the speech are these:

> *I have chosen a path for peace. I believe it will succeed. If it does succeed, what the critics say now won't matter. If it does not succeed, anything I say then won't matter.*

The two statements about criticism are cryptic and more than a little mystifying. What does the President mean when he says, "If it does succeed, what the critics say now won't matter"? Presumably he expects the critics to be negative and dissatisfied as they have often been. If they point out weaknesses in the policy, in the arguments, in the truth of what he says, if they point out contradictions and inconsistencies, and if the policy does not succeed, then what? Is the criticism of no matter? Such criticism should provide a partial explanation of why the policy did not work and what was faulty in the decision-making process. The same is true of the criticism of a rhetorical discourse. If the rhetorical act fails, the critics' comments are important because criticism should give some reasons for the failure of the rhetoric. Clearly, however, the President is giving notice that under no circumstances will he be affected by what the critics say, and such warning is precisely the tragedy, for criticism is the mechanism by which to improve the quality of rhetoric and of decision making. But Nixon has been quite bitter about criticism, as was evident in his concession speech of the 1962 gubernatorial campaign in California.[13]

What does the President intend when he says, "If it does succeed, what the critics say now won't matter"? In such a case the President would have proved the critics wrong, vindicating himself and calling the critics' methods and assumptions into serious question. In all likelihood such a moment would be gratifying for the President. However, if we take the rhetorical act as an analogy, can we consider the critical comments inconsequential simply because the address was successful (at least in terms of the Gallup poll)? I think not. It may be futile to warn against the rhetorician who misrepresents, who is self-contradictory, who is divisive while asserting his desire for unity, or who disclaims responsibility while praising the idea of fulfilling moral obligations. But unless we become careful, discriminating critics, questioning and evaluating, we shall be constrained to make poor decisions and supporting policies destructive of ourselves, our society, and the world. In this respect Agnew's attacks on the concept of immediate critical analysis and evaluation are particularly ironic because his protest suggests that the policy and the address are both extremely fragile. The decision worth making and the policy deserving support, as well as the rhetorical act of quality, will withstand, even be strengthened by, critical scrutiny, and such criticism is the essence of democratic decision making.

Finally this address is an example of the perpetuation of American mythology. The President describes a mythical America whose business is the defense of freedom, whose strength has resulted from facing crises and rejecting the easy way, whose greatness has been the capacity to do what had to be done when it was known to be right. This mythical America is the last hope for the survival of peace and freedom in the world; this most powerful nation will not allow the forces of totalitarianism to suffocate the hopes of the peoples of the earth. This is a nation of destiny.

*Non*mythical America presents quite a different picture. *Non*mythical America supports totalitarian governments all over the world. *Non*mythical America is engaged in a war in South Vietnam in which it is systematically destroying the civilian population and agricultural capacity of the country it is ostensibly defending. *Non*mythical America practices a racism that makes a mockery of its mythic principles. The examples could go on and on. Concentrating so on the details of this address — whether this point or that is true or distorted — the critic can so easily forget that all these considerations rest on the speaker's assumption of a mythical America, which always seeks justice, freedom, and right despite difficulty and cost. These considerations become irrelevant and fragmented outside this mythic context.

One commentator has made the point that "the only salutary aspect of Vietnam [is] the fact that it is forcing us to examine the misconceptions about ourselves and the world on which postwar American foreign policy has been based."[14]

Although this speech fails to meet the President's criteria of truth, credibility, unity, and responsibility, the most significant criticism is that this rhetorical act perpetuates the myths about America, which must be debunked and shattered if we are to find solutions to the problems that threaten immediately to destroy us. The "silent majority" may want to get out of Vietnam and to save face; it cannot have both — at least not quickly.

To avoid Vietnams of the future we must make a concerted effort to discover and scrutinize *non*mythical America. If in that scrutiny we pay particular attention to the rhetorical discourses that thresh out and formulate ideas of ourselves and our society, we may begin to solve the problems of the *real* America and of this shrinking world. That President Nixon is unwilling or unable to face the *real* problems is precisely the reason why this address is doomed to be so disappointing. It is, as almost every commentator has recognized, just "more of the same."[15]

## Notes

1. Cited in "Beyond the Moratorium," *New Republic,* Vol. 161 (October 25, 1969), p. 7.
2. See Chapter 6 in Campbell, *Critiques of Contemporary Rhetoric.*
3. Charles E. Goodell, "Set a Deadline for Withdrawal," *New Republic,* Vol. 161 (November 22, 1969), p. 13.
4. "Nixon's Non-Plan," *New Republic,* Vol. 161 (November 15, 1969), p. 10; Tom Wicker, "In the Nation: Mr. Nixon Twists and Turns," *New York Times,* 9 November 1969, p. E15.

   For a detailed summary of the history of United States involvement in Vietnam, see "Historical Report on U.S. Aggression in Vietnam 1964 to 1967, Testimony by Charles Fourniau" and "Juridical Report on Aggression in Vietnam, Testimony by the Japanese Legal Committee," in John Duffett ed., *Against the Crime of Silence* (New York: O'Hare Books, 1968), pp. 79–90, 105–118.
5. For an analysis of the massacre issue, see Tran Van Dinh, "Fear of a Bloodbath," *New Republic,* Vol. 161 (December 6, 1969), pp. 11–14.
6. Goodell, "Set a Deadline for Withdrawal," p. 13.
7. *Los Angeles Times,* 7 March 1971, p. 11,
8. Robert P. Newman, "Under the Veneer: Nixon's Vietnam Speech of November 3, 1969," *Quarterly Journal of Speech,* Vol. 56 (April 1970), pp. 170–171.
9. *Ibid.,* p. 176.
10. *Los Angeles Times,* 5 November 1969, p. 125.
11. Newman, "Under the Veneer," p. 172.
12. "Nixon's Non-Plan," p. 10.

13. Richard Bergholz, "Nixon Admits Defeat, Indicates Intention to Give Up Politics," *Los Angeles Times*, 8 November 1962, p. 1.
14. Fred Warner Neal, "Government by Myth," *The Center Magazine*, Vol. 2 (November 1969), p. 2.
15. See, for example, Robert J. Donovan, "Verdict on President's Speech Up to 'Great Silent Majority,' " *Los Angeles Times*, 4 November 1969, p. 1; "The Legitimacy of Protest," *New York Times*, 9 November 1969, p. E14; John W. Finney, "The Critics: It is Not a Plan to End U.S. Involvement," *New York Times*, 9 November 1969, p. E1.

## *Conventional Wisdom — Traditional Form — The President's Message of November 3, 1969*

FORBES HILL

More than one critique of President Nixon's address to the nation on November 3, 1969 has appeared,[1] which is not remarkable, since it was the most obvious feature of the public relations machine that appears to have dammed back the flood of sentiment for quick withdrawal of American forces from Southeast Asia. To be sure, the dike built by this machine hardly endured forever, but some time was gained — an important achievement. It seems natural, then, that we should want to examine this obvious feature from more than one angle.

Preceding critiques have looked at Nixon's message from notably nontraditional perspectives. Stelzner magnified it in the lens of archetypal criticism, which reveals a non-literary version of the quest story archetype, but he concluded that the President's is an incomplete telling of the story that does not adequately interact with the listeners' subjective experiences. Newman condemned the message as "shoddy rhetoric" because its tough stance and false dilemmas are directed to white, urban, uptight voters. Campbell condemned it on the basis of intrinsic criticism because though its stated purposes are to tell the truth, increase credibility, promote unity, and affirm moral responsibility, its rhetoric conceals truth, decreases credibility, promotes division, and dodges moral responsibility. Then, stepping outside the intrinsic framework, she makes her most significant criticism: the message perpetuates myths about American values instead of scrutinizing the real values of America.

I propose to juxtapose these examinations with a strict neo-Aristotelian analysis. If it differs slightly from analyses that follow Wichelns[2] and Hochmuth-Nichols,[3] that is because it attempts a critique that re-interprets neo-Aristotelianism slightly — a critique guided by the spirit and usually the letter of the Aristotelian text as I understand it. What the neo-Aristotelian method can and should do will be demonstrated, I hope, by this juxtaposition.

Neo-Aristotelian criticism compares the means of persuasion used by a speaker with a comprehensive inventory given in Aristotle's

*Rhetoric.* Its end is to discover whether the speaker makes the best choices from the inventory to get a favorable decision from a specified group of auditors in a specific situation. It does not, of course, aim to discover whether or not the speaker actually gets his favorable decision; decisions in practice are often upset by chance factors.[4] First the neo-Aristotelian critic must outline the situation, then specify the group of auditors and define the kind of decision they are to make. Finally he must reveal the choice and disposition of three intertwined persuasive factors — logical, psychological, and characterological — and evaluate this choice and disposition against the standard of the *Rhetoric.*

### The Situation

The state of affairs for the Nixon Administration in the fall of 1969 is well known. The United States had been fighting a stalemated war for several years. The cost in lives and money was immense. The goal of the war was not clear; presumably the United States wanted South Viet Nam as a stable non-Communist buffer state between Communist areas and the rest of Southeast Asia. To the extent that this goal was understood, it seemed as far from being realized in 1969 as it had been in 1964. In the meantime, a large and vocal movement had grown up, particularly among the young, of people who held that there should have been no intervention in Viet Nam in the first place and that it would never be possible to realize any conceivable goal of intervention. The movement was especially dangerous to the Administration because it numbered among its supporters many of the elements of the population who were most interested in foreign policy and best informed about it. There were variations of position within the peace movement, but on one point all its members were agreed: the United States should commit itself immediately to withdraw its forces from Viet Nam.

The policy of the Nixon Administration, like that of the Johnson Administration before it, was limited war to gain a position of strength from which to negotiate. By fall 1969 the Administration was willing to make any concessions that did not jeopardize a fifty-fifty chance of achieving the goal, but it was not willing to make concessions that amounted to sure abandonment of the goal. A premature withdrawal amounted to public abandonment and was to be avoided at all costs. When the major organizations of the peace movement announced the first Moratorium Day for October 15 and organized school and work stoppages, demonstrations, and a great "March on Washington" to dramatize the demand for immediate withdrawal from Viet Nam, the Administration launched a counter-attack. The President announced that he would make a major address on Viet

Nam November 3. This announcement seems to have moderated the force of the October moratorium, but plans were soon laid for a second moratorium on November 15. Nixon's counter-attack aimed at rallying the mass of the people to disregard the vocal minority and oppose immediate withdrawal; it aimed to get support for a modified version of the old strategy: limited war followed by negotiated peace. The address was broadcast the evening of November 3 over the national radio and television networks.

### The Auditors and the Kind of Decision

An American President having a monopoly of the media at prime time potentially reaches an audience of upwards of a hundred million adults of heterogeneous backgrounds and opinions. Obviously it is impossible to design a message to move every segment of this audience, let alone the international audience. The speaker must choose his targets. An examination of the texts shows us which groups were eliminated as targets, which were made secondary targets, and which were primary. The speaker did not address himself to certain fanatical opponents of the war: the ones who hoped that the Viet Cong would gain a signal victory over the Americans and their South Vietnamese allies, or those who denied that Communist advances were threats to non-Communist countries, or those against any war for any reason. These were the groups the President sought to isolate and stigmatize. On the other hand, there was a large group of Americans who would be willing to give their all to fight any kind of Communist expansion anywhere at any time. These people also were not a target group: their support could be counted on in any case.

The speaker did show himself aware that the Viet Cong and other Communist decision-makers were listening in. He represented himself to them as willing and anxious to negotiate and warned them that escalation of the war would be followed by effective retaliation. The Communists constituted a secondary target audience, but the analysis that follows will make plain that the message was not primarily intended for them.

The primary target was those Americans not driven by a clearly defined ideological commitment to oppose or support the war at any cost. Resentment of the sacrifice in money and lives, bewilderment at the stalemate, longing for some movement in a clearly marked direction — these were the principal aspects of their state of mind assumed by Nixon. He solicited them saying "tonight — to you, the great silent majority of my fellow Americans — I ask your support."[5]

His address asks the target group of auditors to make a decision to support a policy to be continued in the future. In traditional terms, then, it is primarily a deliberative speech. Those who receive the message are decision-makers, and they are concerned with the past only as it serves as analogy to future decisions. The subjects treated are usual ones for deliberation: war and peace.[6]

### Disposition and Synopsis

The address begins with an enthymeme that attacks the credibility gap.[7] Those who decide on war and peace must know the truth about these policies, and the conclusion is implied that the President is going to tell the truth. The rest of the *proem* is taken up by a series of questions constructing a formal partition of the subjects to be covered. The partition stops short of revealing the nature of the modification in policy that constitutes the Nixon plan. The message fits almost perfectly into the Aristotelian pattern of *proem*, narrative, proofs both constructive and refutative, and epilogue. Just as *proem* has served as a general heading for a synoptic statement of what was done in the first few sentences, so the other four parts will serve us as analytical headings for a synopsis of the rest.

The narrative commences with Nixon's statement of the situation as he saw it on taking office. He could have ordered immediate withdrawal of American forces, but he decided to fulfill "a greater obligation . . . to think of the effect" of his decision "on the next generation, and on the future of peace and freedom in America, and in the world." Applicable here is the precept: the better the moral end that the speaker can in his narrative be seen consciously choosing, the better the *ethos* he reveals.[8] An end can hardly be better than "the future of peace and freedom in America, and in the world." The narrative goes on to explain why and how the United States became involved in Viet Nam in the first place. This explanation masquerades as a simple chronological statement — "Fifteen years ago . . . " but thinly disguised in the chronology lie two propositions: first, that the leaders of America were right in intervening on behalf of the government of South Viet Nam; second, that the great mistake in their conduct of the war was over-reliance on American combat forces. Some doubt has been cast on the wisdom of Nixon's choice among the means of persuasion here. The history, writes one critic, "is a surprising candidate for priority in any discussion today. . . . The President's chief foreign policy advisors, his allies on Capitol Hill, and the memorandum he got from the Cabinet bureaucracy all urged him to skip discussions of the causes and manner of our involvement. Yet history comes out with top billing."[9] This criticism fails to conceive the rhetorical function of the narrative: in the two propositions the whole content of the proofs that follow is foreshadowed, and foreshadowed in the guise of a non-controversial statement about the historical facts. Among traditional orators this use of the narrative to foreshadow proofs is common, but it has seldom been handled with more artistry than here.

Constructive proofs are not opened with an analytical partition but with a general question: what is the best way to end the war? The answer is structured as a long argument from logical division: there are four plans to end American involvement; three should be rejected so that the listener is left with no alternative within the structure but to accept the fourth.[10] The four plans are: immediate withdrawal, the consequences of which are shown at some length to be bad; negotiated settlement, shown to be impossible in the near future because the enemy will not negotiate in earnest; shifting the burden of the war to the Vietnamese with American withdrawal on a fixed timetable, also argued to have bad consequences, and shifting the burden of the war to the Vietnamese with American withdrawal on a flexible schedule, said to have good consequences, since it will eventually bring "the complete withdrawal of all United States *combat ground* forces," whether earnest negotiations become possible or not. Constructive proofs close with one last evil consequence of immediate withdrawal: that it would lead eventually to Americans' loss of confidence in themselves and divisive recrimination that "would scar our spirit as a people."

As refutative proof is introduced, opponents of the Administration are characterized by a demonstrator carrying a sign, "Lose in Viet Nam"; they are an irrational minority who want to decide policy in the streets, as opposed to the elected officials — Congress and the President — who will decide policy by Constitutional and orderly means. This attack on his presumed opponents leads to a passage which reassures the majority of young people that the President really wants peace as much as they do. Reassuring ends with the statement of Nixon's personal belief that his plan will succeed; this statement may be taken as transitional to the epilogue.

The epilogue reiterates the bad consequences of immediate withdrawal — loss of confidence and loss of other nations to totalitarianism — it exhorts the silent majority to support the plan, predicting its success; it evokes the memory of Woodrow Wilson; then it closes with the President's pledge to meet his responsibilities to lead the nation with strength and wisdom. Recapitulation, building of *ethos,* and reinforcing the right climate of feeling — these are what a traditional rhetorician would advise that the epilogue do,[11] and these are what Nixon's epilogue does.

Indeed, this was our jumping-off place for the synopsis of the message: it falls into the traditional paradigm; each frame of the paradigm contains the lines of argument conventional for that frame. The two unconventional elements in the paradigm — the unusual placement of the last evil consequence of immediate withdrawal and the use of the frame by logical division for the constructive proofs — are there for good rhetorical reasons. That last consequence, loss of confidence and divisive recrimination, serves to lead into the refutation which opens with the demonstrator and his sign. It is as if the demonstrator were being made an example in advance of just this evil consequence. The auditor is brought into precisely the right set for a refutation section that does not so much argue with opponents as it pushes them into an isolated, unpopular position.

Because of the residues-like structure, the message creates the illusion of proving that Vietnamization and flexible withdrawal constitute the best policy. By process of elimination it is the only policy available, and even a somewhat skeptical listener is less likely to question the only policy available. Approaching the proposal with skepticism dulled, he perhaps does not so much miss a development of the plan. In particular, he might not ask the crucial question: does the plan actually provide for complete American withdrawal? The answer to this question is contained in the single phrase, "complete withdrawal of all United States *combat ground* forces." It is fairly clear, in retrospect, that this phrase concealed the intention to keep in Viet Nam for several years a large contingent of air and support forces. Nixon treats the difference between plan three, Vietnamization and withdrawal on a fixed schedule, and plan four, Vietnamization and withdrawal on a flexible schedule, as a matter of whether or not the schedule is announced in advance. But the crucial difference is really that plan three was understood by its advocates as a plan of quick, complete withdrawal; plan four was a plan for partial withdrawal. The strategic reason for not announcing a fixed schedule was that the announcement would give away this fact. The residues structure concealed the lack of development of the plan; the lack of development of the plan suppressed the critical fact that Nixon did not propose complete withdrawal. Although Nixon's message shows traditionally conventional structure, these variations from the traditional show a remarkable ability at designing the best adaptations to the specific rhetorical situation.

## Logical and Psychological Persuasive Factors

Central to an Aristotelian assessment of the means of persuasion is an account of two interdependent factors: (1) the choice of major premises on which enthymemes[12] that form "the body of the proof" are based, and (2) the means whereby auditors are brought into states of feeling favorable to accepting these premises and the conclusions following from them. Premises important here are of two kinds: predictions and values. Both kinds as they relate to good and evil consequences of the four plans to end American involvement, will be assessed. The first enthymeme involving prediction is that immediate withdrawal followed by a Communist takeover would lead to murder and imprisonment of innocent civilians. This conclusion follows from the general predictive rule: the future will resemble the past.[13] Since the Communists murdered and imprisoned opponents on taking over North Viet Nam in 1954 and murdered opponents in the city of Hue in 1968, they will do the same when they take over South Viet Nam. Implied also is an enthymeme based on the value premise that security of life and freedom from bondage are primary goods for men,[14] a Communist takeover would destroy life and freedom and therefore destroy primary goods for men.

Presumably no one would try to refute this complex of enthymemes by saying that life and freedom are not primary goods, though he might argue from more and less,[15] more life is lost by continuing the war than would be lost by a Communist takeover, or American-South Vietnamese political structures allow for even less political freedom than the Communist alternatives. Nixon buries these questions far enough beneath the surface of the message that probably auditors in the target group are not encouraged to raise them. One could also attack the predictive premise: after all, the future is not always the past writ over again. But this kind of refutation is merely irritating; we know that the premise is not universally true, yet everyone finds it necessary to operate in ordinary life as if it were. People on the left of the target group, of course, reject the evidence — North Viet Nam and Hue.

A related prediction is that immediate withdrawal would result in a collapse of confidence in American leadership. It rests on the premise that allies only have confidence in those who both have power and will act in their support.[16] If the United States shows it lacks power and will in Viet Nam, there will be a collapse of confidence, which entails further consequences: it would "promote recklessness" on the part of enemies everywhere else the country has commitments, i.e., as a general premise, when one party to a power struggle loses the confidence of its allies, its enemies grow bolder.[17] The conclusion is bolstered by citations from former presidents. Eisenhower, Johnson, and Kennedy: the statement of the "liberal saint," Kennedy, is featured.

It is difficult to attack the related premises of these tandem arguments. They rest on what experience from the sandbox up shows to be probable. The target group consists of people with the usual American upbringing and experience. Someone will question the premises only if he questions the world-view out of which they develop. That view structures the world into Communist powers — actual or potential enemies — and non-Communist powers — allies. America is the leader of the allies, referred to elsewhere as the forces of "peace and freedom" opposed by "the forces of totalitarianism." Because of its association with freedom, American leadership is indisputably good, and whatever weakens confidence in it helps the enemies. Only a few people on the far left would categorically reject this structure.

The foregoing premises and the world-view fundamental to them are even more likely to be accepted if the auditors are in a state of fear. Fear may be defined as distress caused by a vision of impending evil of the destructive or painful kind.[18] This message promotes a state of fear by the nature of the evil consequences developed — murder and imprisonment of innocents, collapse of leadership in the free world, and reckless aggressiveness of implacable enemies. America is the prototype of a nation that is fearful; her enemies are watching their opportunities all over the globe, from Berlin to the Middle East, yes even in the Western Hemisphere itself. The enemies are cruel and opposed to American ideals. They are strong on the battlefield and intransigent in negotiations. Conditions are such that America's allies may lose confidence in her and leave her to fight these enemies alone. But these circumstances are not too much amplified: only enough to create a state of feeling favorable to rejecting immediate withdrawal, not so much as to create the disposition for escalation.

Nixon claims to have tried hard to make a negotiated settlement, but he could not make one because the Communists refused to compromise. The evidence that they would not compromise is developed at length: public initiatives through the peace conference in Paris are cited, terms for participation of the Communist forces in internationally supervised elections offered, and promises made to negotiate on any of these terms. Then there were private initiatives through the Soviet Union and directly by letter to the leaders of North Viet Nam, as well as private efforts by the United States ambassador to the Paris talks. These efforts brought only demands for the equivalent of unconditional surrender. The citation of evidence is impressive and destroys the credibility of the position that negotiations can bring a quick end to the war.

Nixon does not explicitly predict that the plan for negotiated settlement will not work ever; on the contrary, he says that he will keep trying. But if the auditor believes the evidence, he finds it difficult to avoid making his own enthymeme with the conclusion that negotiated settlement will never work; the major premise is the same old rule, the future will be like the past. Nixon gives another reason, too:

it will not work while the opposite side "is convinced that all it has to do is wait for our next concession, and our next concession after that one, until it gets everything it wants." The major premise — no power convinced that victory is probable by forcing repeated concessions will ever compromise — constitutes a commonplace of bargaining for virtually everyone.

Peace is seen in these arguments as almost an unqualified good. Although compromise through bargaining is the fastest way to peace, the other side must make concessions to assure compromise. Reasons for continuing the war, such as an ideological commitment, are evil. There is no glory in war and prolonging it is not justified by political gains made but only by a commitment to higher values like saving lives and preserving freedom. Prolonging the war is also justified as avoiding future wars by not losing Southeast Asia altogether and not promoting the spirit of recklessness in the enemies. "I want," states Nixon, "to end it [the war] in a way which will increase the chance that their [the soldiers'] younger brothers and their sons will not have to fight in some future Vietnam. . . ."

A listener is prone to reject the likelihood of a negotiated peace if he is angry with his opponents. Anger is a painful desire for revenge and arises from an evident, unjustified slight to a person or his friends.[19] People visualizing revenge ordinarily refuse compromise except as a temporary tactic. Nixon presents the American people as having been slighted: they value peace, and their leaders have with humility taken every peace initiative possible: public, private, and secret. The Communist powers wish to gain politically from the war; they have rebuffed with spite all initiatives and frustrated our good intentions by demanding the equivalent of unconditional surrender. Frustration is, of course, a necessary condition of anger.[20] Again, Nixon does not go too far — not far enough to create a psychological climate out of which a demand for escalation would grow.

Nixon announces that his plan for Vietnamization and American withdrawal on a flexible timetable is in effect already. Its consequences: American men coming home, South Vietnamese forces gaining in strength, enemy infiltration measurably reduced, and United States' casualties also reduced. He predicts: policies that have had such consequences in the past will have them in the future, i.e. the future will be like the past. Again, the undisputed value that saving lives is good is assumed. But in this case the argument, while resting on an acceptable premise, was, at the time of this speech, somewhat more doubtful of acceptance by the target group. The evidence constitutes the problem: obviously the sample of the past since the policy of Vietnamization commenced was so short that no one could really judge the alleged consequences to be correlated with the change in policy, let alone caused by it. There is, then, little reason why that audience should have believed the minor premise — that the consequences of Vietnamization were good.

A temporizing and moderate policy is best presented to auditors who while temporarily fearful are basically confident. Nothing saps the will to accept such a proposal as does the opposite state, basically fearful and only temporarily confident. Confidence is the other side of the coin from fear: it is pleasure because destructive and painful evils seem far away and sources of aid near at hand.[21] The sources of aid here are the forces of the Republic of South Viet Nam. They have continued to gain in strength and as a result have been able to take over combat responsibilities from American forces. In contrast, danger from the enemy is receding — "enemy infiltration . . . over the last three months is less than 20 per cent of what it was over the same period last year." Nixon assures his auditors that he has confidence the plan will succeed. America is the "strongest and richest nation in the world"; it can afford the level of aid that needs to be continued in Viet Nam. It will show the moral stamina to meet the challenge of free world leadership.

For some time rumors about gradual American withdrawal from Viet Nam had been discounted by the peace movement. The only acceptable proof of American intentions would be a timetable showing withdrawal to be accomplished soon. Thus the third plan: withdrawal on a fixed timetable. Nixon predicts that announcing of a timetable would remove the incentive to negotiate and reduce flexibility of response. The general premise behind the first is a commonplace of bargaining: negotiations never take place without a *quid pro quo;* a promise to remove American forces by a certain date gives away the *quid pro quo.* For most Americans, who are used to getting things by bargaining, this premise is unquestionable. Only those few who think that the country can gain no vestige of the objective of the war are willing to throw away the incentive. The premises behind the notion of flexibility — that any workable plan is adaptable to changes in the situation — is a commonplace of legislation and not likely to be questioned by anyone. Nixon adds to this generally acceptable premise a specific incentive. Since withdrawal will occur more rapidly if enemy military activity decreases and the South Vietnamese forces become stronger, there is a possibility that forces can be withdrawn even sooner than would be predicted by a timetable. This specific incentive is illusory, since it is obvious that one can always withdraw sooner than the timetable says, even if he has one; it is hard to see how a timetable actually reduces flexibility. Everyone makes timetables, of course, and having to re-make them when conditions change is a familiar experience. But the average man who works from nine to five probably thinks that the government should be different: when it announces a timetable it must stick to it; otherwise nothing is secure. This argument may seem weak to the critic, but it is probably well directed to the target group. The real reason for not announcing a timetable has already been noted.[22]

One final prediction is founded on the preceding predictions — whenever a policy leads to such evil consequences as movement of Southeast Asia into alliance with the enemy and a new recklessness on the part of enemies everywhere, it will eventually result in remorse and divisive recrimination which will, in turn, result in a loss of self-confidence. Guiltlessness and internal unity, the opposites of remorse and recrimination, are here assumed as secondary goods leading to self-confidence, a primary good. The enthymeme predicting loss of self-confidence consequent on immediate withdrawal is summary in position: it seems to tie together all previous arguments. It comes right after a particularly effective effort at *ethos* building — the series of statements developed in parallel construction about not having chosen the easy way (immediate withdrawal) but the right way. However, it rests on the assumption that the long term mood of confidence in the country depends on the future of Southeast Asia and the recklessness of our enemies. Since these two factors are only an aspect of a larger picture in which many other events play their parts, it is surely not true that they alone will produce a loss of confidence. The enthymeme based on this assumption, placed where it is, however, does not invite questioning by the target group. Doubtful though it may look under searching scrutiny, it has an important function for the structure of psychological proof in this message. It reinforces the value image of the danger of facing a stronger enemy in a weakened condition: America itself would be less united, less confident, and less able to fight in the future if this consequence of immediate withdrawal were realized.

Other things being equal, the more commonplace and universally accepted the premises of prediction in a deliberative speech, the more effective the speech. This is especially true if they are set in a frame that prepares the auditor psychologically for their acceptance. There is almost no doubt that given the policy of the Nixon Administration — Vietnamization and partial withdrawal on a flexible schedule not announced in advance — the message shows a potentially effective choice of premises. In some cases it is almost the only possible choice. Likewise the value structure of the message is wisely chosen from materials familiar to any observer of the American scene: it could be duplicated in hundreds of other messages from recent American history.

Several additional value assumptions are equally commonplace. Betraying allies and letting down friends is assumed to be an evil, and its opposite, loyalty to friends and allies the virtue of a great nation. This premise equates personal loyalty, like that a man feels for his friend, with what the people of the whole nation should feel for an allied nation. Many people think this way about international relations, and the good citizens of the target group can be presumed to be among them.

Policies endorsed by the people they are supposed to help are said to be better policies than those not endorsed by them. This statement undoubtedly makes a good political rule if one expects participation in the execution of policy of those to be helped. Policies that result from the operation of representative government are good, whereas those made on the streets are bad. This value is, of course, an essential of republican government: only the most radical, even of those outside the target group, would question it. Finally, Nixon assumes that the right thing is usually the opposite of the easy thing, and, of course, *he* chooses to do the right thing. Such a value premise does not occur in rhetorics by Aristotle or even George Campbell: it is probably a peculiar product of Protestant-American-on-the-frontier thinking. Its drawing power for twentieth-century urban youngsters is negligible, but the bulk of the target group probably is made up of suburbanites in the 35–50 category who still have some affinity for this kind of thinking.

Some shift from the traditional values of American culture can be seen in the tone of Nixon's dealing with the war: the lack of indication that it is glorious, the muted appeal to patriotism (only one brief reference to the first defeat in America's history), the lack of complete victory as a goal. But nowhere else does the culture of the post-atomic age show through; by and large the speech would have been applauded if delivered in the nineteenth century. That there has been a radical revolution of values among the young does not affect the message, and one might predict that Nixon is right in deciding that the revolution in values has not yet significantly infected the target group.

### Characterological and Stylistic Factors

Nixon's choice of value premises is, of course, closely related to his *ethos* as conveyed by the speech. He promises to tell the truth before he asks the American people to support a policy which involves the overriding issues of war and peace — phraseology that echoes previous Nixonian messages. He refrains from harsh criticism of the previous administration; he is more interested in the future America than in political gains; such an avowal of disinterestedness is the commonest topic for self-character building.

Nixon is against political murders and imprisonments and active pushing initiatives for peace. He is flexible and compromising, unlike the negotiators for the enemy. He chooses the right way and not the easy way. He is the champion of policy made by constitutional processes; his opponents conduct unruly demonstrations in the streets. But he has healthy respect for the idealism and commitment of the young; he pledges himself in the tradition of Woodrow Wilson to win a peace that will avoid future wars. He has the courage to make a tasteful appeal to patriotism even when it's unpopular. Such is the character portrait drawn for us by Richard Nixon: restrained not hawkish, hardworking and active, flexible, yet firm where he needs to be. He seems an American style democrat, a moral but also a practical and sensitive man. The message is crowded with these overt clues from which we infer the good *ethos* of political figures in situations like this. Any more intensive development of the means of persuasion derived from the character of the speaker would surely have been counter-productive.

The language of Nixon's message helps to reinforce his *ethos*. His tone is unbrokenly serious. The first two-thirds of the message is in a self-consciously plain style — the effort is clearly made to give the impression of bluntness and forthrightness. This bluntness of tone correlates with the style of deliberative argumentation:[23] few epideictic elements are present in the first part of the speech. Everything seems to be adjusted to making the structure of residues exceedingly clear.

About two-thirds of the way through, the message shifts to a more impassioned tone. The alternative plans are collapsed into two, thus polarizing the situation: either immediate withdrawal or Nixon's plan for Vietnamization and unscheduled withdrawal. From here on parallel repetitions are persistent, and they serve no obvious logical function, but rather function to deepen the serious tone. There is, in short, an attempt to rise to a peroration of real eloquence. The qualities aimed at in the last third of the message seem to be gravity and impressiveness more than clarity and forthrightness. The effort seems to tax the speechwriter's literary skill to the limit, and the only new phrases he comes up with are the "silent majority" and the description of the energies of the young as "too often directed to bitter hatred against those they think are responsible for the war." All else is a moderately skillful pastiche of familiar phrases.

### General Assessment

A summary answer can now be given to the question, how well did Nixon and his advisors choose among the available means of persuasion for this situation? The message was designed for those not ideologically overcommitted either to victory over Communism or to peace in any case while frustrated by the prolonged war. It operates from the most universally accepted premises of value and prediction; it buries deep in its texture most premises not likely to be immediately accepted. Enough of the means for bringing auditors into states of fear, anger, and confidence are used to create a psychological climate unfavorable to immediate withdrawal and favorable to Vietnamization. The goals — life, political freedom, peace, and self-confidence — are those shared by nearly all Americans, and connections of policies to them are tactfully handled for the target group. The structure is largely according to tradition: it can best be seen as falling into the four parts, and the right elements are contained in each of the parts. Two minor variations from the traditional are artfully designed to realize evident psychological ends. Conventional wisdom and conventional value judgments come dressed in conventional structure. The style of the narrative and proofs reflects adequately Nixon's reliance on clearly developed arguments from accepted premises; the style of the latter part of the message shows a moderately successful attempt at grandeur. In choice and arrangement of the means of persuasion for this situation this message is by and large a considerable success.

Neo-Aristotelian criticism tells a great deal about Nixon's message. It reveals the speech writer as a superior technician. It permits us to predict that given this target group the message should be successful in leading to a decision to support the Administration's policies. It brings into sharp focus the speechwriter's greatest technical successes: the choice of the right premises to make a version of the domino theory plausible for these auditors and the creation of a controlled atmosphere of fear in which the theory is more likely to be accepted. Likewise, the choice of the right means of making success for peach negotiations seems impossible and the building of a controlled state of anger in which a pessimistic estimate of the chances for success seems plausible. Also the finely crafted structure that conceals exactly what needs to be concealed while revealing the favored plan in a context most favorable to its being chosen.

What neo-Aristotelianism does not attempt to account for are some basic and long-run questions. For instance, it does not assess the wisdom of the speaker's choice of target audience as does Newman, who wanted the President to alleviate the fears of the doves. All critics observe that Nixon excludes the radical opponent of the war from his audience. Not only is this opponent excluded by his choice of policy but even by the choice of premises from which he argues: premises such as that the Government of South Viet Nam is freer than that of North Viet Nam, or that the right course is the opposite of the easy one. Radical opponents of the war were mostly young — often college students. The obvious cliché, "they are the political leadership of tomorrow," should have applied. Was it in the long run a wise choice to exclude them from the target? An important question, but a neo-Aristotelian approach does not warrant us to ask it. There is a gain, though, from this limitation. If the critic questions the President's choice of policy and premises, he is forced to examine systematically all the political factors involved in this choice. Neither Newman nor Campbell do this in the objective and systematic fashion required by the magnitude of the subject. Indeed, would they not be better off with a kind of criticism that does not require them to do it?

Nor does the neo-Aristotelian approach predict whether a policy will remain rhetorically viable. If the critic assumes as given the Nixon Administration's choice of policy from among the options available, he will no doubt judge this choice of value and predictive premises likely to effect the decision wanted. To put it another way, Nixon's policy was *then* most defensible by arguing from the kinds of premises Nixon used. It seems less defensible at this writing, and in time may come to seem indefensible even to people like those in the target group. Why the same arguments for the same policy should be predictably less effective to people so little removed in time is a special case of the question, why do some policies remain rhetorically viable for decades while others do not. This question might in part be answered by pointing, as was done before, to the maturing of the students into political leadership. But however the question might be answered, neo-Aristotelianism does not encourage us to ask it. As Black truly said, the neo-Aristotelian comprehends "the rhetorical discourse as tactically designed to achieve certain results with a specific audience on a specific occasion"[24] in this case that audience Nixon aimed at on the night of November 3, 1969.

Finally, neo-Aristotelian criticism does not warrant us to estimate the truth of Nixon's statements or the reality of the values he assumes as aspects of American life. When Nixon finds the origin of the war in a North Vietnamese "campaign to impose a Communist government on South Vietnam by instigating and supporting a revolution," Campbell takes him to task for not telling the truth. This criticism raises a serious question: are we sure that Nixon is not telling the truth? We know, of course, that Nixon oversimplifies a complex series of events — any speaker in his situation necessarily does that. But will the scholar of tomorrow with the perspective of history judge his account totally false? Campbell endorses the view that basically this is a civil war resulting from the failure of the Diem government backed by the United States to hold elections under the Geneva Agreements of 1954. But her view and Nixon's are not mutually exclusive: it seems evident to me that both the United States and the

Communist powers involved themselves from the first to the extent they thought necessary to force an outcome in their favor in Viet Nam. If a scientific historian of the future had to pick one view of the conflict or the other, he would probably pick Nixon's because it more clearly recognizes the power politics behind the struggle. But I am not really intending to press the point that Campbell commits herself to a wrong view, or even a superficially partial one. The point is that she espouses here a theory of criticism that requires her to commit herself at all. If anyone writing in a scholarly journal seeks to assess the truth of Nixon's statements, he must be willing to assume the burden of proving them evidently false. This cannot be done by appealing to the wisdom of the liberal intellectuals of today.[25] If the essential task were accomplished, would the result be called a *rhetorical* critique? By Aristotle's standards it would not, and for my part I think we will write more significant criticism if we follow Aristotle in this case. To generalize, I submit that the limitations of neo-Aristotelian criticism are like the metrical conventions of the poet — limitations that make true significance possible.

## *Notes*

1. Robert P. Newman, "Under the Veneer: Nixon's Vietnam Speech of November 3, 1969," *QJS*, 56 (Apr. 1970), 168–178; Hermann G. Stelzner, "The Quest Story and Nixon's November 3, 1969 Address," *QJS*, 57 (Apr. 1971), 163–172; Karlyn Kohrs Campbell, "An Exercise in the Rhetoric of Mythical America," in *Critiques of Contemporary Rhetoric* (Belmont, Calif.: Wadsworth, 1972), pp. 50–58.
2. Herbert A. Wichelns, "The Literary Criticism of Oratory," in Donald C. Bryant, ed., *The Rhetorical Idiom: Essays in Rhetoric, Oratory, Language, and Drama* (1925; rpt. Ithaca: Cornell Univ. Press, 1958), pp. 5–42.
3. Marie Hochmuth [Nichols], "The Criticism of Rhetoric," in *A History and Criticism of American Public Address* (New York: Longmans, Green, 1955) III, 1–23.
4. Aristotle, *Rhetoric* I. 1. 1355[b] 10–14. "To persuade is not the function of rhetoric but to investigate the persuasive factors inherent in the particular case. It is just the same as in all other arts; for example, it is not the function of medicine to bring health, rather to bring the patient as near to health as is possible in his case. Indeed, there are some patients who cannot be changed to healthfulness; nevertheless, they can be given the right therapy." (Translation mine.) I understand the medical analogy to mean that even if auditors chance to be proof against any of the means of persuasion, the persuader has functioned adequately as a rhetorician if he has investigated these means so that he has in effect "given the right therapy."
5. Text as printed in *Vital Speeches*, 36 (15 Nov. 1969), 69.
6. Aristotle *Rhetoric* I. 4. 1359[b] 33–1360[a] 5.
7. *Aristotle Rhetoric* III. 14. 1415[a] 29–33. Here Nixon functions like a defendant in a forensic speech. "When defending he will first deal with any

prejudicial insinuation against him . . . it is necessary that the defendant when he steps forward first reduce the obstacles, so he must immediately dissolve prejudice."

8. See Aristotle *Rhetoric* III. 16. 1417[a] 16–36.
9. Newman, p. 173.
10. See Aristotle *Rhetoric* II. 23. 1398[a] 30–31. This basic structure is called method of residues in most modern argumentation textbooks.
11. Aristotle *Rhetoric* III. 19. 1419[b] 10–1420[a] 8.
12. For the purpose of this paper the term enthymeme is taken to mean any deductive argument. Aristotle gives a more technical definition of enthymeme that fits into the total design of his organon; in my opinion it is not useful for neo-Aristotelian criticism.
13. Remarkably enough Aristotle does not state this general rule, though it clearly underlies his treatment of the historical example, *Rhetoric* II. 20.
14. See Aristotle *Rhetoric* I. 6. 1362[b] 26–27 for life as a good; I. 8. 1366[a] for freedom as the object of choice for the citizens of a democracy.
15. The subject for *Rhetoric* I. 7. Chaim Perelman and L. Olbrechts-Tyteca, commenting on this chapter, indicate that there is usually a consensus on such statements as 'life is good'; the dispute is over whether life is a greater good than honor in this particular situation. See *The New Rhetoric: A Treatise on Argumentation,* trans. John Wilkinson and Purcell Weaver (Notre Dame, Ind.: Univ. of Notre Dame Press, 1969), pp. 81–82.
16. See Aristotle *Rhetoric* II. 19. 1393[a] 1–3.
17. This principle follows from *Rhetoric* II. 5. 1383[a] 24–25.
18. Aristotle *Rhetoric* II. 5. 1382[a] 21–22. Aristotle treated the *pathe* as states of feeling that a man enters into because he draws certain inferences from the situation around him: he sees, for example, that he is the type of man who experiences pity when faced with this type of victim in these circumstances. The means of getting a man to draw inferences are themselves logical proofs; hence *pathos* does not work apart from the logical proofs in a message but through them. See Aristotle *Rhetoric* II. 1. 1378[a] 19–28 and my explication in James J. Murphy, ed. *A Synoptic History of Classical Rhetoric* (New York: Random House, 1972).
19. Aristotle *Rhetoric* II. 2. 1378[a] 30–32.
20. Aristotle *Rhetoric* II. 2. 1379[a] 10–18.
21. Aristotle *Rhetoric* II. 5. 1383[a] 16–19.
22. Since he gave this speech Nixon has made a general timetable for American withdrawal, thus, presumably, showing that he was not utterly convinced by his own argument. But he has never quite fixed a date for complete withdrawal of all American support forces from Viet Nam; he has been consistent in maintaining that withdrawal as a bargaining point for negotiation with the Viet Cong and North Vietnamese.
23. See Aristotle *Rhetoric* III. 12. 1414[a] 8–19.
24. Edwin B. Black, *Rhetorical Criticism: A Study in Method* (New York: Macmillan, 1965), p. 33.
25. Richard H. Kendall, writing a reply to Newman, "The Forum," *QJS,* 56 (Dec. 1970), 432, makes this same point, particularly in connection with Newman's implication that ex-President Johnson was a fraud. "If so, let us have some evidence of his fraudulent actions. If there is no evidence, or if there is evidence, but an essay on the rhetoric of President Nixon does not provide proper scope for a presentation of such evidence, then it seems to me inclusion of such a charge (or judgment) may fall into the category of gratuitous." Newman in rejoinder asks, "Should such summary

judgments be left out of an article in a scholarly journal because space prohibits extensively supporting them? Omission might contribute to a sterile academic purity, but it would improve neither cogency nor understanding." I would certainly answer Newman's rhetorical question, yes, and I would go on to judge that view of criticism which encourages such summary judgments not to be a useful one.

## *The Forum: "Conventional Wisdom — Traditional Form": A Rejoinder*

KARLYN KOHRS CAMPBELL

Professor Hill's analysis of Nixon's Vietnamization address in this issue of *QJS,* has added a neo-Aristotelian critique to the roster of criticisms of that speech already published. However, Professor Hill has invited controversy by attacking the methodologies of the other critics, chiefly Professor Robert Newman and myself. I have taken advantage of the opportunity to respond because I think the conflict highlights certain important issues in rhetorical criticism.

Professor Hill legitimates his methodology by appealing to the authority of Aristotle, but in the tradition of heretics, I must demur at several points from his interpretation of the "true faith." I am chiefly concerned with his exclusion of considerations of truth and ethical assessments and with his treatment of the "target audience."

In responding to the exclusion of the truth criterion, I am inclined to appeal to "conventional wisdom" and "traditional form" in interpreting Aristotelian methodology. Thonssen and Baird, for example, treat the evaluation of logical content as one of determining "how fully a given speech enforces an idea; how closely that enforcement conforms to the general rules of argumentative development; and how nearly the totality of the reasoning approaches a measure of truth adequate for purposes of action" (*Speech Criticism,* 1948, p. 334) and specifically call for the rigorous testing of evidence and argument (p. 341). Aristotle himself wrote that rhetoric is valuable "because truth and justice are by nature more powerful than their opposites; so that, when decisions are not made as they should be, the speakers with the right on their side have only themselves to thank for the outcome. . . . [A proper knowledge and exercise of Rhetoric would prevent the triumph of fraud and injustice.]" (*Rhetorica,* trans. Lane Cooper, I. 1. 1355$^a$ 21–24). These statements are at odds with Hill's assertion that "neo-Aristotelian criticism does not warrant us to estimate the truth of Nixon's statements or the reality of the values he assumes . . ." (p. 385). In fact, there is a puzzling inconsistency in Professor Hill's essay. On the one hand, Newman and I are chided for questioning the President's choice of policy and premises, on the other, Hill himself takes pains to justify the choice of premises, stating that an assessment of the choice of major premises is central to an Aristotelian account. He discussed the truth of the premises used, e.g., "we know that the premise is not universally true, yet everyone finds it necessary to operate in ordinary life as if it were," "they rest on what experience from the sandbox up shows to be probable," and so forth (pp. 378–379). Similarly, there are numerous comments indicating Hill's recognition of the highly deceptive nature of this speech in which Nixon said we were to be told the truth, e.g., "this explanation masquerades as . . . ," "but thinly disguised in the chronology . . . ," "this phrase concealed the intention . . . ," and finally, "the finely crafted structure that conceals exactly what needs to be concealed . . ." (pp. 376, 377, 384). As I see it, Hill is arguing for the truth and acceptability of the major premises while recognizing the deception central to the *logos* of this address. The final statement I have cited makes the point of this critique explicit in regard to questions of truth: what we are to applaud as critics is highly skillful deception and concealment. As a critic, that is a bitter pill I cannot swallow.

The issue I have raised not only involves considerations of truth but ethical assessments, and I propose that an amoral reading of Aristotle is open to question. In the section on deliberative rhetoric to which Hill directs us, Aristotle reiterates that rhetoric "combines the science of logical analysis with the ethical branch of political science . . ." (I. 4. 1359$^b$ 9–11). Similarly, immediately following the analogy to health care cited by Hill comes the statement that "sophistic dialectic, or sophistical speaking, is made so, not by the faculty, but by the moral purpose" (I. 1. 1335$^b$ 16–18). These statements are coherent parts of a teleology defining man as rational and an ethic stating that moral good consists in acting in obedience to reason (*Ethica Nicomachea,* trans. W. D. Ross, I. 13 1102$^b$ 13–28). It seems to me that Aristotle enables the critic to recognize the skillful use of the faculty, i.e., the best (most effective) choices from the inventory, and to condemn the moral purpose and the rhetorical act as sophistic, perhaps even "shoddy." And Aristotle's description of the nature of deliberative rhetoric provides an additional warrant for combining concerns for truth and ethics. He says that the aim of deliberation is determination of advantage and injury with primary emphasis on expediency (I. 3. 1358$^b$ 22–24), suggesting that questions of practically and feasibility are essential to rational decision-making in deliberative addresses. Consequently, I take it that even an Aristotelian critic, confronting a deliberative speech that seeks to avoid questions of expediency and conceals the true nature of the policy being advocated (which Hill admits), might be justified in making a negative assessment.

Finally, Aristotle says that the deliberative speaker must "know how many types of government there are; what conditions are favorable to each type; and what things . . . naturally tend to destroy it" (1. 4. 1360[a] 20–23), elements relevant to deliberative rhetoric which lead me to object to Hill's assessment of the speech in terms of a "target audience." As he recognizes, political factors and the political context are germane to criticism. There is no dispute that this was a major policy address by the President to the nation. But contrary to Hill's assertion that Aristotelian methodology does not warrant questioning whether or not Nixon should have chosen to ignore parts of his constituency, I submit that Aristotle encourages the critic to recognize that this was not simply a speech by Richard Nixon, but a deliberative address from the Presidency — as institution, symbol, and role — *to all citizens in this republic-democracy.* I am not satisfied that the kind of divisiveness created through this rhetorical act in this political context can be excused by delineating a "target audience." In my critique, I argued that the President eliminated the concept of a "loyal opposition" by creating a dichotomy between the "great silent majority" that supports administrative policy and a "vocal minority" seeking to prevail "over reason and the will of the majority." Aristotle said that the end of democracy is liberty, and if that ambiguous term is to mean anything, it has to include the liberty to dissent from policy without being labeled in terms that suggest that dissent is subversive, if not traitorous. I recognized that Nixon paid lip service to the idea of a loyal opposition ("Honest and patriotic Americans have reached different conclusions as to how peace should be achieved."), but the remainder of the address contradicts this strongly, e.g., "the more divided we are at home, the less likely the enemy is to negotiate" and "only Americans [presumably only *dissenting* Americans] can humiliate and defeat the United States." To assess the speech in terms of a "target audience" is to ignore the special kind of disunity created by the speech which, I believe, is a threat to the political processes of our system of government, particularly when propounded by its chief executive.

As I read Professor Hill's criticism of the analyses of Professor Newman and myself, it seems to me that he believes a major shortcoming of both is a lack of "objectivity." He implied that neo-Aristotelian methodology is "objective," genuinely rhetorical (rather than political or ideological), and, in fact, is the only legitimate methodology — it makes "true significance possible" (p. 386). However, as I understand it, Hill's conception of objectivity requires the critic to remain entirely within the closed universe of the discourse and the ideology or point of view it presents. No testing of premises or data is permitted except that determining the degree of *acceptability* to the immediate audience or, more narrowly, to that part of it that is the speaker's target. This is, of course, commendably consistent with his exclusions of considerations of truth and ethics, but it hardly qualifies as objectivity. It is, in fact, to choose the most favorable and partisan account a critic can render. For example, it is to accept the perspective of the advertiser and applaud the skill with which, say, Anacin commercials create the false belief that their product is a more effective pain reliever than ordinary aspirin. As a consequence, the methodology produces analyses that are at least covert advocacy of the point of view taken in the rhetorical act — under the guise of objectivity. Recognizing that anyone reading my critique of this address will know that I am politically liberal (the same, I think, is true of Professor Newman), my simple rejoinder is that anyone reading Hill's critique will know that he is politically conservative.

The particular point on which he takes me to task, my objections to Nixon's view of the origins of the war, is highly illustrative. Professor Hill writes, "When Nixon finds the origin of the war in a North Vietnamese 'campaign to impose a Communist government on South Vietnam by instigating and supporting a revolution,' Campbell takes him to task for not telling the truth" (p. 385). But Nixon said, "Fifteen years ago North Vietnam, *with the logistical support of Communist China and the Soviet Union,* launched a campaign . . ." (emphasis added). What I said was:

> *Now "fifteen years ago" was 1954, the year of the Geneva Agreements that were to unify Vietnam through elections to be held in 1956. Those elections never occurred because the United States supported Diem, who refused elections and attempted to destroy all internal political opposition, Communist and otherwise. The Vietcong did not persuade Hanoi or Peking or Moscow to aid them against Diem until about 1959. By 1965 South Vietnam was clearly losing, the point at which President Johnson decided to send in United States combat forces (Critiques of Contemporary Rhetoric,* 1972. p. 52).

Professor Hill has condensed both Nixon's and my own comments about the North Vietnamese campaign *with* alleged aid from China and Russia into the simpler notion of a North Vietnamese campaign to instigate revolution and impose a Communist regime on the South. This condensation, although understandably desirable from a conservative point of view and understandably unacceptable from a liberal viewpoint, hardly qualifies as an objective appraisal of Nixon's characterization of the origins of the war or of my response to it. My point was and is that Nixon wished to disclaim all U.S. responsibility for the events with which we now wrestle in Indochina and place all blame on a monolithic Communist conspiracy. I think it highly doubtful that the "scientific historian" to whom Hill refers would support that characterization.

It should also be evident that I do not agree with Professor Hill that neo-Aristotelianism is the only, or even the best, methodology for rhetorical criticism. As Hill's essay illustrates, such an approach has explanatory power for revealing how a speaker produced the effects that he did on one part of the audience, what Hill calls the "target audience," but it ignores effects on the rest of the audience, and it excludes all *evaluations* other than the speech's potential for evoking intended response from an immediate, specified audience. Because I do not believe that the sole purpose of criticism is an assessment of a discourse's capacity to achieve intended effects, I cannot accept Hill's monistic view of critical methodology. I am strongly çommitted to pluralistic modes of criticism, considering that the questions the critic asks have such a significant effect on the answers generated, I think we know more about Nixon's rhetorical act because a variety of critical approaches have been brought to it than if Professor Hill's critique stood alone.

The objections I have made so far to Professor Hill's views of criticism and of critical methodology have been, I believe, important ones, but my final objection is, for me, the most important. In describing and defending the uses of rhetoric, Aristotle says that we should be knowledgeable about both sides of a question so that "if our opponent makes unfair use of the arguments, we may be able in turn to refute them," and he continues, to remark that although rhetoric and dialectic, abstractly considered, "may indifferently prove opposite statements. Still, their basis, in the facts, is not a matter of indifference . . ." (I. 1. 1355$^{a}$ 30–37). If rhetoric is to be justified, then rhetorical criticism must also be justifiable. For criticism, too, is rhetoric. Its impulse is epideictic — to praise and blame; its method is forensic — reason-giving. But ultimately it enters into the deliberative realm in which choices must be made, and it plays a crucial role in the processes of testing, questioning, and analyzing by which discourses advocating truth and justice may, in fact, become more powerful than their opposites.

The analogy that Professor Hill draws between neo-Aristotelian methodology and metrical conventions as "limitations that make true significance possible" (p. 386) is an interesting one, particularly for an Aristotelian. After all, it was Aristotle who recognized that poetry could not be defined metrically: "though it is the way with people to tack on 'poet' to the name of a metre . . . thinking that they call them poets not by reason of the imitative nature of their work, but indiscriminately by reason of the metre they write in" (*De Poetica,* trans. Ingram Bywater, 1. 1447$^{b}$ 12–16). Perhaps a more apt analogy is that the strict application of a rhetorical inventory may make the critic a versifier, but not a poet.

## *The Forum: "Reply to Professor Campbell"*

FORBES HILL

Professor Campbell's rejoinder states clearly the positions opposed to mine on certain important issues in criticism. I mean the model neo-Aristotelian critique, embodying an ideal form of neo-Aristotelian methodology based on a closer reading of the *Rhetoric* than common to many following Thonssen and Baird, to raise just such issues. They may be grouped in the following three questions: 1) Does neo-Aristotelianism warrant a critic to praise a leader for addressing a target audience and pushing the citizens who are off-target into an isolated and helpless position? 2) Does Aristotle's text authorize excluding considerations of truth from rhetorical critiques, and should such considerations be excluded? 3) Does the text authorize excluding considerations of morality from rhetorical critiques, and should such considerations be excluded? To all parts of these questions I answer yes — though in some particulars it must be a qualified yes. I understand Professor Campbell to answer no in every particular.

Aristotle nowhere uses the concept of target audience. This adaptation of Aristotelian theory to modern conditions is necessary because Aristotle put together his lectures on rhetoric with a group of Athenian students in mind. For them, auditors of a deliberative speech suggested three to five thousand decision-makers gathered in the Pnyx within the sound of the orator's voice. All these decision-makers were male citizens born on that rocky coastland; none were very rich by any standard; few were well-traveled; few had allegiances abroad. In short, they were a highly homogeneous group. That is what Aristotle assumed when he made a demographic analysis into categories of young, old, rich, poor, well-born and powerful. He did not use categories like Greek-descent and non-Greek descent, educated and uneducated, or urban and rural. And he seemed to assume that a speaker will be able to get all sub-groups of auditors to shout assent as did the Achaeans in the epic.

Obviously an American president communicating through the electronic media makes no assumption about getting assent from all his auditors; the audience is not homogeneous enough to permit it. He must start the preparation of his message by trying to decide who his potential supporters are, that is by making a construct of a target audience. Such procedure is entirely in line with Aristotle's, which starts with the question: who is expected to make a decision for or against what? The group expected to make a decision in this case can be only part of that auditing the discourse. When we thus extend Aristotle's method to deal with the greater national audience of a modern country, we are working along Aristotelian lines, not following his *Rhetoric* like a slavish copyist.

Aristotle aside, is it reasonable to demand, as Professor Campbell does, that the President not declare certain groups off-target but promote unity in the nation? It is — up to a point. But if the critic demands that he win over everyone in a policy address to the nation — not a discourse in praise of freedom but a policy address — an unreasonable standard is being maintained. Not Truman, nor even Eisenhower ever met that standard; it was not met save perhaps when Roosevelt asked Congress to declare war after Pearl Harbor. But Roosevelt also derided the money-changers in the temple; was he not acting on the sound precept that someone has to be off-target, that every drama needs an antagonist? Only if the critic wants an American president to fail scrutiny, will he hold up such a standard.

What did Aristotle decree was the role of truth in rhetorical criticism? Professor Campbell interprets the passage about rhetoric being useful since when true and just causes do not win out that must be because of the inadequacy of their advocates' use of rhetoric[1] to mean that Aristotle demands us to determine the truth of an advocate's statements, as part of a critique of his rhetoric. That interpretation is in my opinion incorrect. The passage itself assumes that the same rhetoric used to advocate true and just causes is also used by the advocates of untrue and unjust ones. A little further on Aristotle says that though rhetoric persuades impartially to contrary conclusions, we (i.e., good people like us) should not use it to advocate bad causes (*Rhet.* I. 1. 1355ᵃ 29–33). A distinction is presupposed here between rhetoric — used to argue either to true conclusions or false — and how a good person uses it — only to argue conclusions he believes to be true. The means of persuasion themselves (enthymemes, examples, and the like) are considered free of truth value, but we who use them should be committed to truth. Rhetoric is the study of our use of the means, not our commitments to ends.

This notion that the means of persuasion are in themselves truth-indifferent fits with other Aristotelian doctrines. Take the well-known distinction between demonstrations and dialectical arguments. The former proceed from premises that are true, primary, immediate, better known than and prior to their conclusions (*Post An.* I. 1. 71ᵇ 20–25; *Top* I. 1. 100ᵃ 25–30) elsewhere called first principles. The latter assume as starting points premises chosen by the respondent from among those generally accepted (*Top.* I. 1. 100ᵇ 23–24). Now rhetoric is the counterpart not of demonstrative reasoning but of dialectic. Instead of assuming as premises statements accepted by a single respondent, it assumes those believed by the type of people who are in attendance as decision-makers. In a few cases these premises may be first principles, but they seldom are. That is because men debate about human affairs, which are in the realm of the contingent (*Rhet.* I. 2. 1357[a] 22–23). Indeed, the more accurately a rhetorician examines his premises, the more likely he is to light on the first principles of some substantive field, and then he will have left the field of rhetoric altogether (*Rhet.* I. 2. 1358[a] 23–26). Another way of putting the distinction between dialectic or rhetoric and the study of demonstrative reasonings is to say that the former argue from probable premises to probable conclusions (*Rhet.* I. 2. 1357[a] 27–28). What does probability mean in this statement? A common Aristotelian synonym is *ta endoxa* (what are today called subjective probabilities), defined in the *Topics* as propositions accepted by all, or by the majority, or by the most distinguished people (*Top.* I. 1. 100[b] 22–24).

It is easy to see from this review of Aristotelian doctrine that Aristotle positively commands the critic of demonstrative arguments to inquire whether or not premises are true, but he says that if a rhetorician examines accurately into this question he leaves the field, ceasing to be a rhetorician and becoming some other kind of scholar. Dialecticians are commanded to examine whether the premises are accepted by all or by the majority, or by the most distinguished people; rhetoricians, by implication, must examine whether the premises will be accepted by the type of people who are decision-makers in this particular case.[2]

A careful look at my critique shows that this is precisely the activity I engaged in. The generalization I worked from is that other things being equal, the more commonplace and universally accepted the premises of prediction and value in a deliberative discourse, the more effective the discourse will be. Applying this principle to Nixon's address, I remarked that "we [the reader, myself, and all other potential members of Nixon's target audience] know that the premise [the future will be like the past] is not universally true, yet everyone finds it necessary to operate in ordinary life as if it were." Professor Campbell accuses me of being inconsistent with my interpretation of what Aristotle demands of a critic by making a judgment about the truth of the premises Nixon used. My remark, taken in context, however, can clearly be seen as a prediction about the acceptability of the premise to potential decision-makers. So can all other comments that taken alone seem to be about the truth of premises or the reality of values.

Only once did I depart from this methodological limitation: when I wrote that Nixon's account of the origins of the war would be preferred by the historian of the future to Campbell's. I was indeed in violation of my own principles. This is, perhaps, as happy an example as could be found of the peril of entering into controversy over the truth of a contemporary speaker's statements.

What is at work in her analysis compelling the conclusion that the United States is responsible for what has happened in Viet Nam is the revisionist theory of the cold war, so popular now in New Left circles. The theory isolates America's militant support of the *status quo ante* as the key element disrupting world peace, in contrast to Communist reaction, which is largely defensive. It informs the whole of Professor Campbell's critique. Naturally Richard Nixon does not analyze the situation this way, and of course, that must mean he is guilty of gross misrepresentation.

If a critic will write of Nixon's address from any such point of view, he has the choice of two ways to treat his theme. He can carefully sift the evidence for the revisionist view as it relates to the war in Viet Nam, or he can simply assume statements reflecting this view — like "the truth is that America supports totalitarian governments all over the world" — are to be accepted by his reader. In either case he is not writing rhetorical criticism.

In the broadest sense rhetorical criticism of any kind primarily assesses how a message relates to some group of auditors. In doing this it may, and usually must, secondarily consider some questions about how the message relates to what is known about the external world. Whenever this secondary consideration becomes the greater part of a critique it ceases to be a rhetorical critique — unless, of course, rhetoric is defined to include the universe.

Criticism of any kind, however, rests on established principles of one sort or another. A discourse where many starting-points must be taken on trust is an epideictic speech, or to put it another way, a tract for the faithful. Readers not among the faithful are blocked off from whatever insights about structure and strategies the critique may present. To assess the truth of a contemporary speaker's claims is to take either the scholarly way or the partisan way out of the area of rhetorical criticism. Of course, a critic is just as certainly led out of the area if he judges Nixon accurate in his account of the origins of the war. I hereby apologize for my inconsistency in characterizing Nixon's statement of these origins as more adequate than Campbell's.

It is not always plain whether Professor Campbell thinks that President Nixon fails to tell the truth because he is mistaken or because he deliberately tries to give a false impression. Her rejoinder, though, charges me with applauding deception, which she finds central to the *logos* of the address. I said the finely crafted structure concealed what needs to be concealed, but I avoided using the word deception because it implies a wrongful intention to suppress what the suppressor knows to be true. It demands a judgment on Nixon's intentions, his knowledge of the truth in this case, and the wrongfulness in this case of suppressing the truth. When speaking to my neighbors for George McGovern (as I often have lately; Professor Campbell's inference to the contrary I am a liberal) I easily make these judgments, but when writing rhetorical criticism I avoid them. Both Aristotle and sound critical practice sanction avoidance.

I appeal first to the passage cited by Campbell. Aristotle develops his categorization of rhetoric as the counterpart of dialectic by saying

> *[rhetoric's] function is to examine both proof and counterfeit proof, just as dialectic's is [to examine] both real and counterfeit syllogism. For the sophistry is not in the art [*dynamics *in this context =* techne*], but in the moral purpose [*proairesis*]. Except here a man will be a* rhetor *whether in relation to his art or to his moral purpose, but there [in the case of dialectic] he will be classified as a sophist in relation to his moral purpose, but a dialectician not in relation to the moral purpose, but in relation to his art (*Rhet. *I. 1. 1355b 15–21).*

Professor Campbell interprets Aristotle as enabling "the critic to recognize the skillful use of the faculty and to condemn the moral purpose and the rhetorical act as sophistic." True, but this interpretation misses the important distinction here drawn: the distinction between artistic judgment and ethical judgment. Built into the language is the proper distinction about dialectic: viewed artistically someone is a dialectician if he understands dialectical method; viewed ethically he is a sophist if he uses this method to bad ends. Employing a non-Aristotelian technique, we might distinguish between $rhetor_1$, who understands the art of rhetoric, and $rhetor_2$, who uses it purely for self-serving ends. Judgments about $rhetor_1$ are rhetorical criticism; those about $rhetor_2$ are in the field of ethics.

What the text shows us here follows from an important Aristotelian preoccupation. Whereas Plato wished to bring all arts and sciences (*technai kai epistemai*) under a single deductive system unified by the idea of the good, Aristotle conceived of the arts and sciences as separate and distinct areas of study, each with its own first principles (or probable premises that serve the function of first principles). His great endeavor was to separate all human knowledge into these studies and outline for each the basic principles.[3] He also created hierarchies — political science is for him the architectonic study which coordinate subfields like ethics, the rationale of personal moral choice, and dialectic-rhetoric, the study of methods for arguing about political and ethical subjects (*Nic. Eth.* I. 1. 1094[a] 27–30.)

What I have just said about the Aristotelian doctrine of the moral neutrality of rhetoric as art and the consequent separation of ethical judgments and rhetorical judgments is not the whole truth; a large section of the *Rhetoric,* (I. 4. to I. 9) is devoted to the value premises from which a speaker may argue. In this section we find a hierarchy of goods — admitted and disputed. We might see the section as an objective description of what people believe — of the value consensus of Aristotle's time. But it clearly is not that; it consists of an adaptation to rhetoric of the rationalized value system of the *Nicomachean Ethics.* Aristotle here commits himself to his own value system. How can he, then, maintain the moral neutrality of rhetoric? Perhaps Campbell is right saying that "an amoral reading of Aristotle is open to question."

Professor Olion in an admirable article, which thoroughly establishes that the dominant thrust of the *Rhetoric* is amoral, maintains that we can see these sections as descriptive and not Aristotle's own value system just so long as we understand that he is describing the values of persons of breeding, wealth, and education (*hoi aristoi*) and not the values of the masses (*hoi polloi*)[4] I will not here attempt a complete examination of this sophisticated view. I only hazard the opinion that if one understands the full context of Aristotle's remarks about the best citizens he will judge that sound ethical principles are discovered by finding they are held by such citizens. But they are verified as being the true principles by an argument from the parts: alternative principles are demonstrably inferior so these must be the right principles. I think that Aristotle establishes by reasoning and not empirically that his value system is the right one.

Aristotle attempts to have matters both ways in the *Rhetoric.* His prologue makes rhetoric the counterpart of dialectic, i.e. amoral. But he introduces the section on value premises by calling it an offshoot (*paraphues*) of the ethical branch of politics. An even better translation might be "a graft onto the ethical branch of politics." He does not say that rhetoric is the mirror-image of ethics; its connection to ethics is not that intimate. But even this way of verbalizing the matter does not quite get him out of contradicting himself.

Friedrich Solmsen, in my opinion the greatest of the twentieth century interpreters of the *Rhetoric,* explained that the first draft of Aristotle's lectures maintained the moral neutrality of the art with consistency. Later drafts, however, introduced the value system precisely because it was needed in any treatment of the art that would be competitive with the completeness of rival sophistic rhetorics all of which laid claim to having ethical foundations.[5] The evidence for this explanation is skimpy, but it has some inherent probability.

As a practical matter it makes for better neo-Aristotelian criticism to interpret the *Rhetoric* as if it were consistently amoral. There are two reasons why. First, no critic can realistically commit himself to Aristotle's value system as a basic inventory of American values and their hierarchy. Aristotle omits thrift, hardworkingness, chastity, piety, honesty, and humility from the list of virtues. (As Lawrence Rosenfield once remarked to me, he does not know about the Protestant ethic.) He omits progress and efficiency from the list of goods. It is by no means plain that happiness in the Aristotelian sense of the term is or should be the ultimate goal for the rational mid-century American. If, then, we are forced to abandon the value system to which Aristotle was committed, what should we do when judging a discourse — commit ourselves to a value system of our own? Or should we try objectively to describe what we think are the value commitments of the target group — the decision-makers in this case?

The second reason why in practice a neo-Aristotelian critic should give an amoral reading to the *Rhetoric* is that if he judges a speaker's values not to match reality, he is inevitably driven to decide the truth on questions that are best avoided: e.g., "who is really responsible for the cold war?" It has already been argued that attempting to answer such questions leads us to take an indefinite leave of absence from rhetorical criticism.

One more minor point: I never advocated critical monism. The several critical methods applied to this address have each produced essays with considerable virtues. Stelzner, in particular, revealed facets of its artistry I had not dreamed of before. Nevertheless, I think neo-Aristotelianism can do more to render a comprehensive assessment on it than other methods. This has something to do with Nixon and his *logographers* being products of highly traditional training. Their tendency is ever to produce another brand of the conventional wisdom structured in traditional forms.

The same is emphatically not true of other discourses. In *Critiques of Contemporary Rhetoric* Campbell prints an essay of Eldridge Cleaver's. By neo-Aristotelian standards that essay must be judged childishly ineffective: the society at large constitutes the body of decision-makers in this case, and the decision-makers will predictably not respond favorably to this selection of means of persuasion from the available inventory. But experience with hundreds of discussions warns me that in some sense Cleaver's essay is a considerable work of art. If neo-Aristotelianism compels a quick negative judgment on it, that is probably because Cleaver plays another kind of ball game from a different game plan. A method that has more explanatory power for Cleaver's game can certainly be found, as Professor Campbell's critique of the essay well shows.

## Notes

1. Aristotle, *Rhetoric* I. 1. 1355[a] 21–24. This paraphrase, like Lane Cooper's translation (used by Campbell), construes a text that is here utterly ambiguous. Literal translation: "Rhetoric is useful because true and just

causes are by nature more powerful than their contraries, so that when decisions do not turn out according to what is fitting, necessarily [they] have been defeated through themselves." What does 'themselves' refer to in this passage? True and just causes? Their contraries? Or must we from our own minds supply 'advocates' of true and just causes' as subject of 'have been defeated' and antecedent of 'themselves'? 'Their contraries' has had defenders, e.g., Victorius and Spengel, cited by Edward Meredith Cope, *The Rhetoric of Aristotle with a Commentary*, rev. and ed. by John Edwin Sandys (Cambridge: at the University Press, 1877), Vol. I, p. 23. But Mr. Cope rightly asks why, if true and just causes are naturally superior, would they be defeated by their contraries? Making 'advocates of true and just causes' the subject brings sense to the argument, but these words certainly have to be supplied out of thin air. I mention this ambiguity because one who would maintain that Aristotle believed determining truth necessary to rhetorical criticism probably needs to give what I consider an incorrect reading of this passage, but he also needs to think the text as we have it here meaningful enough to bear a definitive interpretation. This is probably not the case.

2. See Lloyd F. Bitzer, "Aristotle's Enthymeme Revisited," *QJS*, 45 (Dec. 1959), 407.
3. I have drawn here, on a good popular treatment, John Herman Randall, Jr., *Aristotle* (New York: Columbia Univ. Press, 1960), pp. 32–58.
4. J. Robert Olian, "The Intended Uses of Aristotle's *Rhetoric*," *SM*, 35 (June 1968), 137.
5. Friedrich Solmsen, *Die Entwicklung der Aristotelischen Logik und Rhetorik, IV, Neue Philogische Untersuchungen* (Berlin: Weidmann, 1929). For English presentations of material from this book see Forbes I. Hill, "The Genetic Method in Recent Criticism on the Rhetoric of Aristotle," Diss. Cornell 1963, and George Kennedy, *The Art of Persuasion in Greece* (Princeton, N.J.: Princeton Univ. Press, 1963), pp. 82–85.

# 8

# Alternative Readings of Jesse Jackson's "Common Ground and Common Sense"

## *Common Ground and Common Sense*

JESSE JACKSON

Tonight we pause and give praise and honor to God for being good enough to allow us to be at this place at this time. When I look out at this convention, I see the face of America, red, yellow, brown, black and white, we're all precious in God's sight — the real rainbow coalition. All of us, all of us who are here and think that we are seated. But we're really standing on someone's shoulders. Ladies and gentlemen. Mrs. Rosa Parks.

The mother of the civil rights movement.

I want to express my deep love and appreciation for the support my family has given me over these past months.

They have endured pain, anxiety, threat and fear.

But they have been strengthened and made secure by a faith in God, in America and in you.

Your love has protected us and made us strong.

To my wife Jackie, the foundation of our family; to our five children whom you met tonight; to my mother Mrs. Helen Jackson, who is present tonight; and to my grandmother, Mrs. Maltilda Burns; my brother Chuck and his family; my mother-in-law, Mrs. Gertrude Brown, who just last month at age 61 graduated from Hampton Institute, a marvelous achievement; I offer my appreciation to Mayor Andrew Young who has provided such gracious hospitality to all of us this week.

And a special salute to President Jimmy Carter.

President Carter restored honor to the White House after Watergate. He gave many of us a special opportunity to grow. For his kind words, for his unwavering commitment to peace in the world and the voters that came from his family, every member of his family, led by Billy and Amy, I offer him my special thanks, special thanks to the Carter family.

My right and my privilege to stand here before you has been won — in my lifetime — by the blood and the sweat of the innocent.

Twenty-four years ago, the late Fanny Lou Hamer and Aaron Henry — who sits here tonight from Mississippi — were locked out on the streets of Atlantic City, the head of the Mississippi Freedom Democratic Party.

But tonight, a black and white delegation from Mississippi is headed by Ed Cole, a black man, from Mississippi, 24 years later.

Many were lost in the struggle for the right to vote. Jimmy Lee Jackson, a young student, gave his life. Viola Luizzo, a white mother from Detroit, called nigger lover, and brains blown out at point blank range.

Schwerner, Goodman and Chaney — two Jews and a black — found in a common grave, bodies riddled with bullets in Mississippi. The four darling little girls in the church in Birmingham, Ala. They died that we might have a right to live.

Dr. Martin Luther King Jr. lies only a few miles from us tonight.

Tonight he must feel good as he looks down upon us. We sit here together, a rainbow, a coalition — the sons and daughters of slave masters and the sons and daughters of slaves sitting together around a common table, to decide the direction of our party and our country. His heart would be full tonight.

As a testament to the struggles of those who have gone before; as a legacy for those who will come after; as a tribute to the endurance, the patience, the courage of our forefathers and mothers; as an assurance that their prayers are being answered, their work has not been in vain, and hope is eternal; tomorrow night my name will go into nomination for the presidency of the United States of America.

We meet tonight at a crossroads, a point of decision.

Shall we expand, be inclusive, find unity and power; or suffer division and impotence.

We come to Atlanta, the cradle of the old south, the crucible of the new South.

Tonight there is a sense of celebration because we are moved, fundamentally moved, from racial battlegrounds by law, to economic common ground, tomorrow we will challenge to move to higher ground.

Common ground!

Think of Jerusalem — the intersection where many trails met. A small village that became the birthplace for three great religions — Judaism, Christianity and Islam.

Why was this village so blessed? Because it provided a crossroads where different people met, different cultures, and different civilizations could meet and find common ground.

When people come together, flowers always flourish and the air is rich with the aroma of a new spring.

Take New York, the dynamic metropolis. What makes New York so special?

It is the invitation of the Statue of Liberty — give me your tired, your poor, your huddled masses who yearn to breathe free.

Not restricted to English only.

Many people, many cultures, many languages — with one thing in common, the yearn to breathe free.

Common ground!

Tonight in Atlanta, for the first time in this century we convene in the South.

A state where governors once stood in school house doors. Where Julian Bond was denied his seat in the state legislature because of his conscientious objection to the Vietnam War.

A city that, through its five black universities, has graduated more black students than any city in the world.

Atlanta, now a modern intersection of the new South.

Common ground!

That is the challenge to our party tonight.

Left wing. Right wing. Progress will not come through boundless liberalism nor static conservatism, but at the critical mass of mutual survival. It takes two wings to fly.

Whether you're a hawk or a dove, you're just a bird living in the same environment, in the same world.

The Bible teaches that when lions and lambs lie down together, none will be afraid and there will be peace in the valley. It sounds impossible. Lions eat lambs. Lambs sensibly flee from lions. But even lions and lambs find common ground. Why?

Because neither lions nor lambs want the forest to catch on fire. Neither lions nor lambs want acid rain to fall. Neither lions nor lambs can survive nuclear war. If lions and lambs can find common ground, surely, we can as well, as civilized people.

The only time that we win is when we come together. In 1960, John Kennedy, the late John Kennedy, beat Richard Nixon by only 112,000 votes — less than one vote per precinct. He won by the margin of our hope. He brought us together. He reached out. He had the courage to defy his advisors and inquire about Dr. King's jailing in Albany, Georgia. We won by the margin of our hope, inspired by courageous leadership.

In 1964, Lyndon Johnson brought both wings together. The thesis, the antithesis and to create a synthesis and together we won.

In 1976, Jimmy Carter unified us again and we won. When we do not come together, we never win.

In 1968, division and despair in July led to our defeat in November.

In 1980, rancor in the spring and the summer led to Reagan in the fall. When we divide, we cannot win. We must find common ground as a basis for survival and development and change and growth.

Today when we debated, differed, deliberated, agreed to agree, agreed to disagree, when we had the good judgment to argue our case and then not self-destruct, George Bush was just a little further away from the White House and a little closer to private life.

Tonight, I salute Governor Michael Dukakis.

He has run a well-managed and a dignified campaign. No matter how tired or how tried, he always resisted the temptation to stoop to demagoguery.

I've watched a good mind fast at work, with steel nerves, guiding his campaign out of the crowded field without appeal to the worst in us. I've watched his perspective grow as his environment has expanded. I've seen his toughness and tenacity close up. I know his commitment to public service.

Mike Dukakis' parents were a doctor and a teacher; my parents, a maid, a beautician and a janitor.

There's a great gap between Brookline, Massachusetts and Haney Street, the Fieldcrest Village housing projects in Greenville, South Carolina.

He studied law; I studied theology. There are differences of religion, region, and race; differences in experiences and perspectives. But the genius of America is that out of the many, we become one.

Providence has enabled our paths to intersect. His foreparents came to America on immigrant ships; my foreparents came to America on slave ships. But whatever the original ships, we're in the same boat tonight.

Our ships could pass in the night if we have a false sense of independence, or they could collide and crash. We would lose our passengers. But we can seek a higher reality and a greater good apart. We can drift on the broken pieces of Reaganomics, satisfy our baser instincts, and exploit the fears of our people. At our highest, we can call upon noble instincts and navigate this vessel to safety. The greater good is the common good.

As Jesus said, "Not my will, but thine be done." It was his way of saying there's a higher good beyond personal comfort or position.

The good of our nation is at stake — its commitment to working men and women, to the poor and the vulnerable, to the many in the world. With so many guided missiles, and so much misguided leadership, the stakes are exceedingly high. Our choice, full participation in a Democratic government, or more abandonment and neglect. And so this night, we choose not a false sense of independence, not our capacity to survive and endure.

Tonight we choose interdependency in our capacity to act and unite for the greater good. The common good is finding commitment to new priorities, to expansion and inclusion. A commitment to expanded participation in the Democratic Party at every level. A commitment to a shared national campaign strategy and involvement at every level. A commitment to new priorities that ensure that hope will be kept alive. A common ground commitment for a legislative agenda by empowerment for the John Conyers bill, universal, on-site, same-day registration everywhere — and commitment to D.C. statehood and empowerment — D.C. deserves statehood. A commitment to economic set-asides, a commitment to the Dellums bill for comprehensive sanctions against South Africa, a shared commitment to a common direction.

Common ground. Easier said than done. Where do you find common ground at the point of challenge? This campaign has shown that politics need not be marketed by politicians, packaged by pollsters and pundits. Politics can be a marvel arena where people come together, define common ground.

We find common ground at the plant gate that closes on workers without notice. We find common ground at the farm auction where a good farmer loses his or her land to bad loans or diminishing markets. Common ground at the schoolyard where teachers cannot get adequate pay, and students cannot get a scholarship and can't make a loan. Common ground, at the hospital admitting room where somebody tonight is dying because they cannot afford to go upstairs to a bed that's empty, waiting for someone with insurance to get sick. We are a better nation than that. We must do better.

Common ground. What is leadership if not present help in a time of crisis? And so I met you at the point of challenge in Jay, Maine where paper workers were striking for fair wages; in Greenfield, Iowa, where family farmers struggle for a fair price; in Cleveland, Ohio, where working women seek comparable worth; in McFarland, Calif., where the children of Hispanic farm workers may be dying from poison land, dying in clusters with cancer; in the AIDS hospice in Houston, Texas, where the sick support one another, 12 are rejected by their own parents and friends.

Common ground.

America's not a blanket woven from one thread, one color, one cloth. When I was a child growing up in Greenville, S.C., and grandmother could not afford a blanket, she didn't complain and we did not freeze. Instead, she took pieces of old cloth — patches, wool, silk, gabardine, crockersack on the patches — barely good enough to wipe off your shoes with.

But they didn't stay that way very long. With study hands and a strong cord, she sewed them together into a quilt, a thing of beauty and power and culture.

Now, Democrats, we must build such a quilt. Farmers, you seek fair prices and you are right, but you cannot stand alone. Your patch is not big enough. Workers, you fight for fair wages. You are right. But your patch labor is not big enough. Women, you seek comparable worth and pay equity. You are right. But your patch is not big enough. Women, mothers, who seek Head Start and day care and pre-natal care on the front side of life, rather than jail care and welfare on the back side of life, you're right, but your patch is not big enough.

Students, you seek scholarships. You are right. But your patch is not big enough. Blacks and Hispanics, when we fight for civil rights, we are right, but our patch is not big enough. Gays and lesbians, when you fight against discrimination and a cure for AIDS, you are right, but your patch is not big enough. Conservatives and progressives, when you fight for what you believe, right-wing, left-wing, hawk, dove — you are right, from your point of view, but your point of view is not enough.

But don't despair. Be as wise as my grandmama. Pool the patches and the pieces together, bound by a common thread. When we form a great quilt of unity and common ground we'll have the power to bring about health care and housing and jobs and education and hope to our nation.

We the people can win. We stand at the end of a long dark night of reaction. We stand tonight united in a commitment to a new direction. For almost eight years, we've been led by those who view social good coming from private interest, who viewed public life as a means to increase private wealth. They have been prepared to sacrifice the common good of the many to satisfy the private interest and the wealth of a few. We believe in a government that's a tool of our democracy in service to the public, not an instrument of the aristocracy in search of private wealth.

We believe in government with the consent of the governed of, for, and by the people. We must not emerge into a new day with a new direction. Reaganomics, based on the belief that the rich had too much money — too little money, and the poor had too much.

That's classic Reaganomics. It believes that the poor had too much money and the rich had too little money.

So, they engaged in reverse Robin Hood — took from the poor, gave to the rich, paid for by the middle class. We cannot stand four more years of Reaganomics in any version, in any disguise.

How do I document that case? Seven years later, the richest 1 percent of our society pays 20 percent less in taxes; the poorest 10 percent pay 20 percent more. Reaganomics.

Reagan gave the rich and the powerful a multibillion-dollar party. Now, the party is over. He expects the people to pay for the damage. I take this principled position — convention, let us not raise taxes on the poor and the middle class, but those who had the party, the rich and the powerful, must pay for the party!

I just want to take common sense to high places. We're spending $150 billion a year defending Europe and Japan 43 years after the war is over. We have more troops in Europe tonight than we had seven years ago, yet the threat of war is ever more remote. Germany and Japan are now creditor nations — that means they've got a surplus. We are a debtor nation — it means we are in debt.

Let them share more of the burden of their own defense — use some of that money to build decent housing!

Use some of that money to educate our children!

Use some of that money for long-term health care!

Use some of that money to wipe out these slums and put America back to work!

I just want to take common sense to high places. If we can bail out Europe and Japan, if we can bail out Continental Bank and Chrysler — and Mr. Iacocca makes $8,000 an hour, we can bail out the family farmer.

I just want to make common sense. It does not make sense to close down 650,000 family farms in this country while importing food from abroad subsidized by the U.S. government.

Let's make sense. It does not make sense to be escorting oil tankers up and down the Persian Gulf paying $2.50 for every $1.00 worth of oil we bring out while oil wells are capped in Texas, Oklahoma and Louisiana. I just want to make sense.

Leadership must meet the moral challenge of its day. What's the moral challenge of our day? We have public accomodations. We have the right to vote. We have open housing.

What's the fundamental challenge of our day? It is to end economic violence. Plant closing without notice, economic violence. Even the greedy do not profit long from greed. Economic violence.

Most poor people are not lazy. They're not black. They're not brown. They're mostly white, and female and young.

But whether white, black or brown, the hungry baby's belly turned inside out is the same color. Call it pain. Call it hurt. Call it agony. Most poor are not on welfare.

Some of them are illiterate and can't read the want-ad sections. And when they can, they can't find a job that matches their address. They work hard every day, I know. I live amongst them. I'm one of them.

I know they work. I'm a witness. They catch the early bus. They work every day. They raise other people's children. They work every day. They clean the streets. They work every day. They drive vans with cabs. They work every day. They change the beds you slept in these hotels last night and can't get a union contract. They work every day.

No more. They're not lazy. Someone must defend them because it's right, and they cannot speak for themselves. They work in hospitals. I know they do. They wipe the bodies of those who are sick with fever and pain. They empty their bedpans. They clean out their commode. No job is beneath them, and yet when they get sick, they cannot lie in the bed they made up every day. America, that is not right. We are a better nation than that. We are a better nation than that.

We need a real war on drugs. You can't just say no. It's deeper than that. You can't just get a palm reader or an astrologer; it's more profound than that. We're spending $150 billion on drugs a year. We've gone from ignoring it to focusing on the children. Children cannot buy $150 billion worth of drugs a year. A few high profile athletes — athletes are not laundering $150 billion a year — bankers are.

I met the children in Watts who are unfortunate in their despair. Their grapes of hope have become raisins of despair, and they're turning to each other and they're self-destructing — but I stayed with them all night long. I wanted to hear their case. They said, "Jesse Jackson, as you challenge us to say no to drugs, you're right. And to not sell them, you're right. And to not use these guns, you're right."

And, by the way, the promise of CETA — they displaced CETA. They did not replace CETA. We have neither jobs nor houses nor services nor training — no way out. Some of us take drugs as anesthesia for our pain. Some take drugs as a way of pleasure — both short-term pleasure and long-term pain. Some sell drugs to make money. It's wrong, we know. But you need to know that we know. We can go and buy the drugs by the boxes at the port. If we can buy the drugs at the port, don't you believe the federal government can stop it if they want to?

They say, "We don't have Saturday night specials any more." They say, "We buy AK-47s and Uzis, the latest lethal weapons. We buy them across the counter on Long Beach Boulevard." You cannot fight a war on drugs unless and until you are going to challenge the bankers and the gun sellers and those who grow them. Don't just focus on the children, let's stop drugs at the level of supply and demand. We must end the scourge on the American culture.

Leadership. What difference will we make? Leadership cannot just go along to get along. We must do more than change presidents. We must change direction. Leadership must face the moral challenge of our day. The nuclear war build-up is irrational. Strong leadership cannot desire to look tough, and let that stand in the way of the pursuit of peace. Leadership must reverse the arms race.

At least we should pledge no first use. Why? Because first use begat first retaliation, and that's mutual annihilation. That's not a rational way out. No use at all — let's think it out, and not fight it out, because it's an unwinnable fight. Why hold a card that you can never drop? Let's give peace a chance.

Leadership — we now have this marvelous opportunity to have a breakthrough with the Soviets. Last year, 200,000 Americans visited the Soviet Union. There's a chance for joint ventures into space, not Star Wars and the war arms escalation, but a space defense initiative. Let's build in space together, and demilitarize the heavens. There's a way out.

America, let us expand. When Mr. Reagan and Mr. Gorbachev met, there was a big meeting. They represented together one-eighth of the human race. Seven-eighths of the human race was locked out of that room. Most people in the world tonight — half are Asian, one-half of them are Chinese. There are 22 nations in the Middle East. There's Europe; 40 million Latin Americans next door to us; the Caribbean; Africa — a half-billion people. Most people in the world today are yellow or brown or black, non-Christian, poor, female, young, and don't speak English — in the real world.

This generation must offer leadership to the real world. We're losing ground in Latin America, the Middle East, South Africa, because we're not focusing on the real world, that real world. We must use basic principles, support international law. We stand the most to gain from it. Support human rights; we believe in that. Support self-determination; we'll build on that. Support economic development; you know it's right. Be consistent, and gain our moral authority in the world.

I challenge you tonight, my friends, let's be bigger and better as a nation and as a party. We have basic challenges. Freedom in South Africa — we've already agreed as Democrats to declare South Africa to be a terrorist state. But don't just stop there. Get South Africa out of Angola. Free Namibia. Support the front-line states. We must have a new, humane human rights assistance policy in Africa.

I'm often asked, "Jesse, why do you take on these tough issues? They're not very political. We can't win that way."

If an issue is morally right, it will eventually be political. It may be political and never be right. Fannie Lou Hamer didn't have the most votes in Atlantic City, but her principles have outlasted every delegate who voted to lock her out. Rosa Parks did not have the most votes, but she was morally right. Dr. King didn't have the most votes about the Vietnam war, but he was morally right. If we're principled first, our politics will fall in place.

Jesse, why did you take these big bold initiatives? A poem by an unknown author went something like this: We mastered the air, we've conquered the sea, and annihilated distance and prolonged life, we were not wise enough to live on this earth without war and without hate.

As for Jesse Jackson, I'm tired of sailing by little boat, far inside the harbor bar. I want to go out where the big ships float, out on the deep where the great ones are. And should my frail craft prove too slight, the waves that sweep those billows o'er, I'd rather go down in a stirring fight than drown to death in the sheltered shore.

We've got to go out, my friends, where the big boats are.

And then, for our children, young America, hold your head high now. We can win. We must not lose you to drugs and violence, premature pregnancy, suicide, cynicism, pessimism and despair. We can win.

Wherever you are tonight, I challenge you to hope and to dream. Don't submerge your dreams. Exercise above all else, even on drugs, dream of the day you're drug-free. Even in the gutter, dream of the day that you'll be up on your feet again. You must never stop dreaming. Face reality, yes. But don't stop with the way things are; dream of things as they ought to be. Dream. Face pain, but love, hope, faith, and dreams will help you rise above the pain.

Use hope and imagination as weapons of survival and progress, but you keep on dreaming, young America. Dream of peace. Peace is rational and reasonable. War is irrational in this age and unwinnable.

Dream of teachers who teach for life and not for living. Dream of doctors who are concerned more about public health than private wealth. Dream of lawyers more concerned about justice than a judgeship. Dream of preachers who are concerned more about prophecy than profiteering. Dream on the high road of sound values.

And in America, as we go forth to September, October and November and then beyond, America must never surrender to a high moral challenge.

Do not surrender to drugs. The best drug policy is a no first use. Don't surrender with needles and cynicism. Let's have no first use on the one hand, or clinics on the other. Never surrender, young America.

Go forward. America must never surrender to malnutrition. We can feed the hungry and clothe the naked. We must never surrender. We must go forward. We must never surrender to illiteracy. Invest in our children. Never surrender; and go forward.

We must never surrender to inequality. Women cannot compromise ERA or comparable worth. Women are making 60 cents on the dollar to what a man makes. Women cannot buy meat cheaper. Women cannot buy bread cheaper. Women cannot buy milk cheaper. Women deserve to get paid for the work that you do. It's right and it's fair.

Don't surrender, my friends. Those who have AIDS tonight, you deserve our compassion. Even with AIDS you must not surrender in your wheelchairs. I see you sitting here tonight in those wheelchairs. I've stayed with you. I've reached out to you across our nation. Don't you give up. I know it's tough sometimes. People look down on you. It took you a little more effort to get here tonight.

And no one should look down on you, but sometimes mean people do. The only justification we have for looking down on someone is that we're going to stop and pick them up. But even in your wheelchairs, don't you give up. We cannot forget 50 years ago when our backs were against the wall, Roosevelt was in a wheelchair. I would rather have Roosevelt in a wheelchair than Reagan and Bush on a horse. Don't you surrender and don't you give up.

Don't surrender and don't give up. Why can I challenge you this way? Jesse Jackson, you don't understand my situation. You be on television. You don't understand. I see you with the big people. You don't understand my situation. I understand. You're seeing me on TV but you don't know the me that makes me, me. They wonder why does Jesse run, because they see me running for the White House. They don't see the house I'm running from.

I have a story. I wasn't always on television. Writers were not always outside my door. When I was born late one afternoon, October 8th, in Greenville, S.C., no writers asked my mother her name. Nobody chose to write down our address. My mama was not supposed to make it. And I was not supposed to make it. You see, I was born to a teen-age mother who was born to a teen-age mother.

I understand. I know abandonment and people being mean to you, and saying you're nothing and nobody, and can never be anything. I understand. Jesse Jackson is my third name. I'm adopted. When I had no name, my grandmother gave me her name. My name was Jesse Burns until I was 12. So I wouldn't have a blank space, she gave me a name to hold me over. I understand when nobody knows your name. I understand when you have no name. I understand.

I wasn't born in the hospital. Mama didn't have insurance. I was born in the bed at home. I really do understand. Born in a three-room house, bathroom in the backyard, slop jar by the bed, no hot and cold running water. I understand. Wallpaper used for decoration? No. For a windbreaker. I understand. I'm a working person's person, that's why I understand you whether you're black or white.

I understand work. I was not born with a silver spoon in my mouth. I had a shovel programmed for my hand. My mother, a working woman. So many days she went to work early with runs in her stockings. She knew better, but she wore runs in her stockings so that my brother and I could have matching socks and not be laughed at at school.

I understand. At 3 o'clock on Thanksgiving Day we couldn't eat turkey because mama was preparing someone else's turkey at 3 o'clock. We had to play football to entertain ourselves and then around 6 o'clock she would get off the Alta Vista bus; then we would bring up the leftovers and eat our turkey — leftovers, the carcass, the cranberries around 8 o'clock at night. I really do understand.

Every one of these funny labels they put on you, those of you who are watching this broadcast tonight in the projects, on the corners, I understand. Call you outcast, low down, you can't make it, you're nothing, you're from nobody, subclass, underclass — when you see Jesse Jackson, when my name goes in nomination, your name goes in nomination.

I was born in the slum, but the slum was not born in me. And it wasn't born in you, and you can make it. Wherever you are tonight you can make it. Hold your head high, stick your chest out. You can make it. It gets dark sometimes, but the morning comes. Don't you surrender. Suffering breeds character. Character breeds faith. In the end faith will not disappoint.

You must not surrender. You may or may not get there, but just know that you're qualified and you hold on and hold out. We must never surrender. America will get better and better. Keep hope alive. Keep hope alive. Keep hope alive. On tomorrow night and beyond, keep hope alive.

I love you very much. I love you very much.

## *The Rhythm of Rhetoric: Jesse Jackson at the 1988 Democratic National Convention*

PAULA WILSON

Jesse Jackson is recognized for "florid oratory work" and what some have called his "brilliant use of the intimate stage of television" (*Washington Post,* 1988, p. C1). In the convention hall on July 19th, 1988, commentator Tom Brokaw proclaimed Jackson to be "clearly the most gifted orator in the Democratic Party today" (NBC, 1988). The *Wall Street Journal* opined that Jackson would be a more memorable figure than presidential aspirants, Michael Dukakis or George Bush, and that "twenty years from now, we'll still be talking about the speech Jesse Jackson gives tonight" (1988, p. 32).

But in order to know what makes a Jackson speech memorable, effective and unique one must look beyond the layers of style, content and occasion to rhetorical form. The central task of this essay is to understand the shape and form of Jackson's rhetoric.

Unlike conventional analyses of musicians which use melody to aid the rhetorical impact of a message, I will consider Jackson's use of melodic structure a form of rhetorical support. As such, I argue that rhetorical logic may be reinforced by certain laws of music so as to make manifest a rhetorical form otherwise undiscerned.

An analysis of Jackson's rhetoric without regard to his "whole" person would grievously misevaluate his form (Sullivan, 1993). Therefore, I will begin by offering the context for Black ministerial oratory and Jackson's role therein. I will then develop a methodology from a cross section of emergent ideas represented in the literature. This critical tool will be used to assay Jackson's rhetorical form. Finally, I will draw conclusions about Jackson's form and the use of music as an aid to rhetorical form.

*Black Ministerial Oratory* The musicality of Black Baptist rhetoric is obvious and acknowledged in the literature. Speech and music are symbiont in African-American culture. Audience participation itself is indicative of Black preacher oratory wherein "one becomes aware of the close relationship between speech and music" (Smith, 1970, p. 269). This relationship quite naturally forms an "oral-formulaic method" for explaining "residually oral composition which is decidedly different from literary composition" (Ong, 1982, p. 61).

Classifying Jackson as an oral composer is fitting and appropriate in this context, despite the fact that a major part of his audience is cathected to culture. Oral expression frees Jackson to embrace "a load of epithets and other formulary baggage which high literacy rejects as cumbersome . . ." (Ong, p. 38).

Those who examine forms of Black religious rhetoric acknowledge the importance of musical contexts as these constructs reveal "facts and nuances that would not be disclosed through histories that are not musicological" (Spencer, 1992, p. x). Nevertheless, the musical nature of sermons is commonly examined apart from the rhetoric (Harris, 1992).

In a discussion of Black preacher rhetoric and the context for Jackson's speech, two particular variables surface as poignant dimensions to Jackson's style: preachers as politicians and a musical or antiphonal style.

The central task of the Black preacher has always been to communicate as a spokesperson and a processor of communication for Black society (Thurber & Petelle, 1968, p. 275). Preachers have also been categorized as exceptional leaders, politicians and orators (Nelson, 1971, p. 30).

The Black preacher communicates from the pulpit in the antiphonal sermon, which is sung or chanted in alteration. An obvious skill of the trained minister is the use of ritualistic cadence in the sermon. Prosodic discourse, common in Black ministry, is "the performed word" (Lincoln & Mamiya, 1990, p. 346). Words are coupled with nonsynthetic sound. Din and versification can transform an "audience through the spontaneous exaggeration of sounds combined with the presentation of vital themes . . ." (Harris, p. 265). Moreover, in terms of improvisation, cadence and chanting, evangelical oratory has metrical quality (Harris, p. 154).

Indeed Black evangelical oratory conforms to oral formulae: Walter Ong explains, "Protracted orally based thought tends to be highly rhythmic" (p. 34). In fact, Ong continues,

> Fixed, often rhythmically balanced, expressions . . . can be found in print . . . , but in oral cultures they are not occasional. They are incessant. They form the substance of thought itself. Thought in any extended form is impossible without them, for it consists in them (p. 35).

A musical paradigm is conspicuously warranted in the attempt to discern Jackson's rhetorical form. Jackson is a preacher-orator. To analyze a Jackson speech apart from his musical form would, at best, only partially calibrate his form and effectiveness. His vast audience is not an oral culture per se, but it never-the-less appears to attend to the orality of the speech. After his 1988 convention speech, the *Washington Post* concluded,

> One could disagree strongly with some of Jackson's policies and still be swept up and swept away with the passionate musicality of the rhetoric and the eager participation of the crowd (1988, p. C1).

Jackson's propensity toward using music as a part of his form is obvious, what is less obvious is the collaborative nature of his musical and rhetorical form. (1)

*Musical and Rhetorical Theory* The body of ideas concerning the symbiotic relationship between music and rhetoric begin with the obvious connection between rhetorical and musical theory. This literature divides itself between concerns over the general influence of music on rhetorical form (Holmberg, 1985; Knupp, 1981; LeCoat, 1976 and Morhmann & Scott, 1976) and approaching music as a medium from a rhetorical standpoint, (Auld, 1984; Burns, 1988; Chaffee, 1985; Francesconi, 1986; Lull, 1985, 1987; McLaughlin, 1970; Rasmussen, 1994; Rickert, 1979, 1986 and Shepherd, 1985).

The essays addressing rhetoric and music typically analyze the lyrics and not the score of a song (Bloodworth, 1975; Booth, 1976; Chesebro, Foulger, Nachman and Yannelli, 1986; Desmond, 1987; Lewis, 1976; Jones and Shumacker, 1992 and Smith, 1980). However, lyric analyses alone are problematic in that they do not comprehensively account for musical forms in rhetoric. Irving Rein and Craig Springer (1986) warn, "ignoring the complete musical communication act clearly leads to incomplete and often misleading conclusions" (p. 253).

Finally, despite the thorough work of James Irvine and Walter Kirkpatrick (1972) on the theoretical considerations of musical form in rhetorical exchange, there remain few persuasive paradigms for the examination of discourse using melodic structure (Brockriede & Scott, 1970 and Gonzalez & Makay, 1983). Irvine and Kirkpatrick only consider songs that use discourse as an example of persuasive, reinforcive and expressive paradigms as opposed to examining discourse that uses melodic structure as a persuasive paradigm.

However, Irvine and Kirkpatrick do provide the ground work for the construction of such a theoretical model. Specifically, modifications and applications of Irvine and Kirkpatrick's observations in the areas of "ethical reputation of the source" and "instrumental source" could account for discourse using music as agentive archetype.

A key element in the analysis of rhetoric which invites musical form is credibility. In situations where rhetoric invites musical form for impact the speaker is judged by his/her reputation as a composer/performer. The ethical reputation of a source must include his/her knowledge of contemporary issues, an understanding of audience-held values and "a judgment of the spirit of the times which produced both the rhetorical message and the values of the audience" (Irvine & Kirkpatrick, p. 274). Ethical reputation of a source can be manifested through the performance itself; audience values are acknowledged and substantiated through style and instrumental source. Instrumental source, as the second level of activity, examines individual instruments according to musical composition. Instrumental technology does not fall neatly into rhetorical matters, but it must be reckoned within rhetorical/musical analyses. Rein and Springer observe that in addition to lyric content, "the communication researcher needs to account for musical arrangements, new recording and instrumental technology and aesthetic conventions of different styles" (p. 253).

Acknowledging cultivated practices of different styles is crucial to using musical form in rhetorical analyses (Gonzalez & Makay, 1983). It is within the realm of "aesthetic conventions of different styles" that we may consider Jackson's Black religious oratorical style as instrumental source. The combination of musical and rhetorical style may hierarchically reinforce the order of certain dimensions of values according to a humanistic dimension, maintenance and development and productive tendency.

According to Irvine and Kirkpatrick, in the "humanistic dimension" a rhetor may indicate a concern for certain classes or subgroups within the structure of the group he/she addresses. The sociological structure of the group can then be "maintained and developed" on two levels: "the orientation of the value structure of the sub-cultural group, and the subsequent polarization from the main cultural stream" (p. 275). The support and defense of one's own needs is then reflected in a "productive tendency." These three elements constitute the dimensions of a group's value structure. Jackson's rhetorical form will now be examined according to musical and rhetorical patterns which reinforce certain dimensions of value.

*Musical Patterns for Jackson* Jackson's amplificative meaning is arranged according to the metaphoric pattern suggested by Irvine and Kirkpatrick, "familiar patterns of musical variables with other familiar patterns" (p. 274). The "familiar musical variables" Jackson utilizes come from melodies Jackson has created based on certain constructs from the sonata.

A Sonata can be characterized as a piece of music which contains two to five movements related by congruity and contrast of tempo. Movements contain rhythm, tempo, key, mood, theme and style. Sonata form, sonata allegro or first movement form can have two themes and three basic sections: exposition, development and recapitulation.

Exposition has to do with exposure of theme; one of the two themes or sub-themes can be in a different key. Exposition can also function as a transition.

In the development phase, themes unfold as the result of faster and slower note durations and extensions of theme. Finally, recapitulation repeats the exposition section, but themes at this point are in the same key. A coda or passage may sometimes signify the formal ending of the piece.

The Sonata, as a musical form can be correlated with certain aspects of rhetorical form:

Rhythm = *a mode of syllogistic acceptance*

Tempo and Key = *a selected state of mind*

Mood and Theme = *creation and alteration of mood and theme through repetitive forms*

Style = *common or individual style*

Furthermore, as the sonata engages in congruity and contrast between its elements so may rhetorical forms overlap. Kenneth Burke (1940) observes, "As in musical theory, one chord is capable of various analyses, so in literature the appeal of one event may be explained by various principles" (p. 129). Jackson's musical patterns identify and bolster values aspired to by his audience. Ethical reputation of source and instrumental source combined function as a demarcation of value for Jackson and his audience.

*Rhetorical Patterns for Jackson* Other familiar patterns in Jackson's speech are rhetorical and are identified as syllogisms constructed and recognizable as a constant part of his political message. These rhetorical patterns will be examined in the ensuing textual analysis.

Credibility and instrumental source are developed through Jackson's Black ministerial oratorical style. Thus, style, as Irvine and Kirkpatrick claim, can be a structured linguistic and musical unit which functions as a coequal of value. The demarcation in Jackson's style as a Black preacher goes beyond "aesthetic condition," it is an embodiment of culture manifested through style. The sound Jackson produces magnifies the function of instrumental source, it embodies the persona of the Black preacher.

### The 1988 Democratic National Convention Address

Specific musical traditions appear in incremental layers in Jackson's speech and function as a distinguishable part of his rhetorical form. Therefore, Jackson's speech will be discussed according to its musical pattern and how the rhetoric is stratified over that musical pattern through 1) ethical reputation of source, 2) instrumental source and 3) style and value.

Jackson's speech contains three separate movements. Each movement relies heavily on repetitive form. Each movement can be considered a part of a series of repetitive forms which are constructed syllogistically. Each movement after the first movement, is anticipated by language, tempo, and mood of certain clusters of statements. These clusters of statements, which function as transitions, are comprised of a grouping of simple statements repeated in succession. These statements are higher in pitch than preceding phrases and quicker in tempo.

The language in the speech appears to mutually supplement the rhythmic form; it portrays two distinct postures for Jackson, the preacher posture and the political posture. Each posture is indicative of a separate melody or rhythm. Jackson's preacher posture is identified by sermonic rhetoric, while his political posture is associated with references to the political and social behavior of the status quo.

Each cluster functions as exposition and contains three short sentences and one longer conclusionary sentence. For instance, a rather calm discussion of economics ends with an enthusiastic conclusion where Jackson emphasizes the first duplicated word of each phrase:

> *Use* some of that money to build decent housing!
> *Use* some of that money to educate our children!
> *Use* some of that money for long-term health care!
> *Use* some of that money to wipe out these slums and put America back to work! (p. 651) (emphasis added).

As a plea for involvement, another cluster of this type is slightly varied. Rather than three short sentences and one long, this passage begins with a short sentence, has three longer sentences in the middle and concludes with a short sentence:

> *Dream* of teachers who teach for life and not for living.
> *Dream* of doctors who are concerned more about public health than private wealth.
> *Dream* of lawyers more concerned about justice than a judgeship.
> *Dream* of preachers who are concerned more about prophecy than profiteering.
> *Dream* on the high road of sound values (p. 653) (emphasis added).

Directly following this cluster is another cluster of similar form repeated after a discussion of inequality, "Women are making 60 cents on the dollar to what a man makes":

> *Women* cannot buy meat cheaper.
> *Women* cannot buy bread cheaper.
> *Women* cannot buy milk cheaper.
> *Women* deserve to get paid for the work that you do (p. 653) (emphasis added).

The common element to these clusters is the emphasis on the first word of each sentence. The predominate value expressed in the language is social justice. The discourse in these clusters is combined with higher pitches and the regular emphasis of certain words. The accelerated tempo creates intensity. This pattern signifies escalated exhortation indicative of the climax or conclusion to exposition.

These clusters do much toward articulating issues and developing oral memory, and yet certainly say nothing new. The potency of narrative originality, however, lies not in the creation of a new story, but "in managing a particular interaction with this audience at this time" (Ong, pp. 41–42). It is precisely the interaction between speaker and audience and the evanescence of the spoken word which gives way to the residual orality in Jackson's speech, typical in the conservative nature of his oral style.

Tempo and key alteration signal the transition to another movement of the speech. These clusters operate collaboratively to prepare the way for another movement and the acceptance of more complex melodic variations. Each movement, like the transitional clusters, possesses virtually the same rhythm, but elucidates a different theme.

In the development phase of the speech there occurs three distinct movements. Each movement is syllogistic in that it is comprised of a series of short sentences supporting a premise. Interwoven with the short forms of support are identical thematic statements meant to further support the conclusion. These short sentences then converge into slightly longer sentences. The longer phrases at the end of the verse move the auditor directly to the conclusion — the reiteration of a sub-theme.

The syllogistic nature of each movement is virtually the same in terms of its rhythm. It is a separate sub-theme, delineated by the discourse, wherein each movement becomes sequestered.

The first movement occurs immediately after Jackson's introductory remarks. A family quilt serves the sub-theme of the movement which is inclusive of the central theme of the address, "common ground." Jackson uses the term "common ground" twenty-one times before this section:

> Now, Democrats, we must build such a quilt. Farmers, you seek fair prices and you are right, but you cannot stand alone. **Your patch is not big enough.** Workers, you fight for fair wages. **You are right. But your patch is not big enough** (p. 651).

Jackson repeats the same phrase, "you are right, but your patch is not big enough," five more times, but changes the agent in each case to women, mothers, students, Blacks, Hispanics, Gays, Lesbians, conservatives and progressives.

Jackson then provides this section or movement of the speech with a climax, a conclusion:

> But don't despair. Be as wise as my grandmama. Pool the patches and pieces together, bound by a common thread. When we form a great quilt of unity and common ground we'll have the power to bring about health care and housing and jobs and education and hope to our nation. We the people can win (p. 651).

The syllogism — each minority group has a bonafide claim (premise one), but this claim cannot be actualized alone (premise two), though when all unite each group can become prosperous (conclusion) — becomes fully apparent to Jackson's audience near the middle of the progression. Camera sweeps of conventional hall faces show obvious recognition of and participation in the syllogism through both verbal and nonverbal forms of feedback.

This fairly simple form of logic makes clear the value system Jackson defends on behalf of his audience. This value system is defined according to dimensions of humanism, maintenance and development, and productiveness. Premise one has specifically to do with the humanistic dimension. Jackson enumerates his concern for the justice entitled to each minority group. In this part of the speech Jackson's Rainbow Coalition swells to bring into the minority fold the handicapped, students, those diagnosed with aids, women and homosexuals.

Thus, the subgroup is defined and its difficulties are clarified. The enumeration of humanism as a dimension of value acknowledges that Jackson's "concern is holistic and all-inclusive" and indicative of levels of ethos equal to that of Martin Luther King (Young, 1979, p. 126).

Maintenance and development are apparent in premise two as orientations for each of the subgroups Jackson names are validated and then polarized from the cultural mainstream. The clustering of each subgroup pivots on some form of social injustice particular to that group. For example, "Women, you seek comparable worth and pay equity. You are right. But your patch is not big enough." It is necessary to divide each subgroup in order to validate it and its orientations. This is the only way for the collective values articulated by each subgroup to become accepted by the larger group, the Democratic Party, and hopefully eventually by the cultural mainstream.

A productive tendency is the final dimension of value articulated by Jackson; it is the admonishment to coalesce and the opportunity to support and defend individual needs and wants: "When we form a great quilt of unity and common ground we'll have the power to bring about health care and housing and jobs and education and hope to our nation. We the people can win" (p. 751). Here is the use of linguistic and musical units to reinforce the dimensions of value articulated by the Rainbow Coalition.

While Jackson plays no musical instrument, his particular cadence functions as an instrumental source would, it lays the ground work for particular themes both musical and lyrical.

The cadence of this movement is distinctive from the rhythm which precedes it. The identical repetitive phrases, "But your patch is not big enough" are an interval lower than the short sentences that precede them, they contain no variation of pitch or intonation. Thus, Jackson's audience becomes obedient to (Burke 1940, p. 130) or relies on the rhythmic design, if not the rhetorical message.

The progression from low to higher tones and increased melodic activity creates the expectation of climax. This is a particular skill of the Black preacher, a variation of the pitch of certain words to create a pattern and provide form to the text (Harris 1992, p. 159). The characteristics of the climax for this movement incorporate the use of longer sentences which provide closure to the syllogism.

The pitch becomes elevated and more varied. Support for the theme common ground is built through the repetition of righteous justification, "you are right." The low key non-varied phrase "your patch is not big enough" follows and is a representation of untoward reality. The more varied and excited phrases are sermonic, "But don't despair," "We the people can win."

Jackson provides the "best" kind of climax in Black oratorical forms because it indicates a "celebration of the goodness of God and the standing of Black people in the kingdom, as these elements have been expressed in the message" (Niles, 1984, p. 49). Instrumental source combines sound, pitch and cadence, with antecedent ethical reputation of source and Black oratorical forms to develop ethos in a multidimensional way. However, while the conformities to Black ministerial oratory are abundant in the speech, unique unto de facto candidate Jackson is the political ethos of "Black Christendom" (Washington 1985, p. 94).

The second movement, which occurs about midway through the speech, is comparable to movement one: it is composed of short sentences, short identical sentences which are repeated and longer conclusionary sentences. The cadence for movement one and movement two is the same. The climax of movement two also incorporates the "goodness of God" idea.

The sub-theme developed in this movement is articulated as "economic violence" against the misconception of who the poor are in America, "mostly white, and female and young":

> Some of them are illiterate and can't read the want-ad sections. And when they can, they can't find a job that matches their address. **They work hard every day,** I know. I live amongst them. I'm one of them.

Similar to movement one, here the phrase "they work hard every day" is repeated five more times and is related to those who raise other's children, clean the streets, drive cabs and work in hotels. These short repetitive sentences function as premises to the conclusion that economic injustice is inequitable:

> They wipe the bodies of those who are sick with fever and pain. They empty their bedpans. They clean out their commode. No job is beneath them, and yet when they get sick, they cannot lie in the bed they made up every day. America, that is not right. We are a better nation than that. We are a better nation than that (p. 652).

The repetitive form "they work every day" underscores the reconception of the poor. This premise elicits the logical conclusion that economic violence is unfair, (the Protestant work ethic that if we work we will live reasonably well) and that America is above this inequity.

Indicative of development in the sonata, the rhythmic nature of this passage is different from the rhythm of the discourse that precedes it. The rhythmic variation is the same in this case as in the first movement. The phrase, "they work every day," is an interval below preceding sentences.

The sheer rhythm and sound of the words create meaning apart from the words and, as noted earlier, this meaning is denotative of the value structure held by Jackson's audience. The repetition of this cadence creates particular mood/theme for the passage. The low key non-variated phrase "they work every day" is a representation of pious reality as it relates to the human experience of particular subgroups. It is a representation of the way things are. The more variated and excited phrases are lofty representations of what ought to be, or what could be developed and maintained, "we are a better nation than that." Both statements of reality (they work every day) and expectation (we are a better nation than that) are illustrative of good standing with God. Ostensibly, no higher level of productivity could there be.

This particular meaning, a grandiose form of individual and collective productivity, becomes formed for audience members through the acuminations of oral memory. Ong explains:

> Thus, the noetic economy of its [oral memory] nature generates outsize figures, that is, heroic figures, not for romantic reasons . . . but for much

> more basic reasons: to organize experience in some sort of permanently memorable form (p. 70).

An experience which cannot wholly be expressed in words can be organized using rhythm and words to culminate a memorable form. This is Jackson's forte, creating permanent memorable form for abstract ideals.

The third and final movement of the speech comes at the end of the speech and is clearly the most climatic part of the address. It begins with Jackson's declaration, "I have a story." It is marked by the sub-theme, "I understand", therefore do not abandon personal struggle. "I understand" is uttered twelve times. Longer explanative sentences lead to the dual conclusion: Jackson embodies and has empathy for the down trodden and faith in the Constitution and equality as a reality. "I understand," a declaration of reality, is followed by longer sentences which are symbolic of what can be:

> Every one of these funny labels they put on you, those of you who are watching this broadcast tonight in the projects, on the corners, I understand. Call you outcast, low down, you can't make it, you're nothing, you're from nobody, subclass, underclass — when you see Jesse Jackson, when my name goes in nomination, your name goes in nomination. I was born in the slum, but the slum was not born in me. And it wasn't born in you, and you can make it (p. 653).

Legitimacy for Jackson's campaign reaches a new high as his symbolic nomination becomes the climax to the speech, not Dukakis' nomination.

The minor or incidental forms in Jackson's speech are manifested in his urbanization of the language, a form common to Black preaching which incorporates the "use of short, vivid words and an occasional long word . . . [and] the use of Biblical English, language familiar to the audience, repetition, and parallel construction" (Pipes, 1945, p. 19). Despite the fact that this particular incidental form is language based, it is rhythmic and as a module of Black oratory, it contributes significantly to Jackson's ethos as a part of instrumental source. Jackson's incidental form could also be termed Black political revivalism. This stylistic device is rooted in Black Christianity and "includes the use of sermonic folk discourse and a complex of cultural praxes" (Washington 1985, p. 92).

Recapitulation, in the very end of the speech, repeats and combines the three movements and transitions to create in the climax the most complicated melodic form yet. This conclusion is marked by higher tones and a quickened tempo. It combines the rhythm of the transitions with the rhythm of the movements. Sentences always end on uplifted notes. The key is the same. The language is vintage southern preacher. The emphasis Jackson places on words is indicated with bold print:

> Wherever you are tonight **you can make it. Hold** your head high, **stick** your chest out. **You can make it.** It gets **dark** sometimes, but the **morning** comes. **Don't surrender. Suffering** breeds character. **Character** breeds faith. In the end **faith** will not disappoint (p. 653).

Indicative of each of the movements are short sentences followed by identical sentences in lower octaves, "you can make it." The conclusion is syllogistic: suffering, character and faith enable us to avoid disappointment.

Exposition transitions place emphasis on first words in evangelical style. The emphasis on "dark" and "morning" conjures the negative before the positive. The rhythm itself is different from other previous forms; it incorporates both the rhythmic forms of the movements and their transitions.

Identification with Jackson's presentation could ostensibly come from the content of the speech or the cadence or movement of the speech or both. The combination of the sub-themes of the three movements and their clustered transitions provides certain rhetorical and musical structure to the speech.

The first movement transpires early after somber introductory phrases, sober tones and softened tempo, and statement of theme for the address, "Common Ground." This phrase is followed by a discussion of Reaganomics. There is little rhythmic variation in this section until the conclusion for the passage: "Use some of that money . . . " which signals the coming of the second movement "They work every day." More non-rhythmic discussion on the status quo leadership is then followed by the second transition: "Dream of the day. . . . " and "Women can't buy bread cheaper." This marks the beginning of the last movement, "I understand."

The sub-themes of the three movements and their transitions create a fairly simple syllogism. Once again the familiar pattern indicative of Jackson's style reinforces in order the dimensions of value for Jackson's cause:

PREMISE 1: "Common ground" is most important. (*humanistic dimension*)

SUPPORT: "Use some of that money" to create common ground.

PREMISE 2: Using money to create common ground is justified. (*maintenance and development*).

SUPPORT: Because "they (the people) work every day" and the people who support the country ("women") deserve better services and should "dream" of the day when social injustice is resolved. (*productive tendency*).

CONCLUSION: Jackson understands ("I understand") all of this.

Auditors of the speech construct meaning from the structural relationship of the movements and clusters as well as from the content of the speech. As Martin Medhurst and Thomas Benson (1981) conclude, rhythm combined with rhetoric "creates a poetic expectation in the viewer [or listener] and then satisfies the appetite by a formally 'correct' resolution" (p. 58).

The Democratic nominee, Michael Dukakis, is not the one who understands the people, but rather it is Jackson who understands. Jackson becomes a more credible spokesperson for the cause of humanity; he becomes elevated as a spiritual and political leader as the values he espouses become a coequal of his credibility. He is hailed by the media as "the most eloquent apostle of 'the politics of inclusion' " (*Commonweal,* 1988, p. 419) and more than "a lone, charismatic politico" (Washington 1985, p. 90). His presidential campaign is legitimized.

**Conclusion**

This rhetorical analysis has revealed peculiarities and competencies cached in Jackson's form. This analysis also raises some quandary about the utility of music in rhetorical analyses.

Jackson's rhetorical form can only be understood comprehensively when it is viewed from a musical standpoint. Jackson systematically builds layers of credibility through appeals to ethical reputation of source. Ethical reputation of source is then developed through instrumental source. Instrumental source, in the case of Jackson, is very complex. It includes style, which embodies Black preacher/politician postures, and dimensions of value articulated through both postures.

Jackson acknowledges audience held values in three ways. First, he identifies the humanistic dimension for each minority group and calls for economic justice on their behalf. Second he develops and maintains each sub-group from the cultural mainstream through validation and polarization by identifying the orientation of the value structure for all sub-groups. Finally, Jackson's productive tendency is to encourage sub-groups to coalesce and support individual needs and wants as a way of achieving economic justice. Ultimately Jackson achieves a very high level of ethos because he has successfully demonstrated his knowledge of contemporary issues and, in the very least, democratically held values.

It is important to note here that Jackson's competency, established through the relationship between ethical reputation of source and instrumental source, is not readily apparent or apparent at all until music is introduced as the guiding factor in Jackson's form. Furthermore, the conservative nature of orality and the culmination of his oral style creates impression and meaning for Jackson's audience beyond the vague terms of rhetorical/lyrical paradigms. Jackson's rhetorical form can only fully be understood from a musical/rhetorical perspective. Conventional and traditional standards for speech criticism fail to reveal completely Jackson's form because there is no paradigm from which to observe the whole rhetor or a rhetor who does not conform to linear standards for speech execution.

Music used as a rhetorical construct is an interesting and productive tool. Music is considered "a language of emotion" (Critchley & Henson, 1977, p. 142), and as such Jackson's form engages right (music) and left (speech) brain processing activity. Therefore the form itself, apart from the language, appeals to his audience. The rhetorical-logical message (liberal political ideology) occurs on one cognitive level and is underscored by the musical-emotional message (outrage and indignation for the opposition, hope and pride for Democratic Party and Rainbow Coalition) occurring on another cognitive level.

Musical form does provide messages and meanings beyond and apart from lyrics; musical forms are enjoyable, exciting and memorable with or without the discourse. We may disagree with what Jackson says, but we are enticed, like a familiar melody, to listen to the musical form which then communicates its own meaning. The rhythmic design of Jackson's speech balances the left and right brain creating a holistic rhetorical experience not present in forms of discourse which only engage left brain activity. Whether or not this kind of cognitive balance as a rhetorical experience is more effective than single hemisphere appeal is a question left for another study. However, this phenomenon can be distinguished as a particular part of Jackson's form.

## *Notes*

1. Jackson's rhetoric has not yet been examined according to its musical nature. Sullivan is correct in her assumption that much of the misinterpretation of Jackson's rhetoric was due to a misunderstanding of his form, the oral tradition he represented (p. 4). However, Sullivan's analysis stops short of identifying Black oral traditions in rhythm as a key component in the "magical potency" (p. 5) of oral cultures. Sullivan acknowledges that Jackson created "a rhythm that encouraged the audience to respond to his

statements" (p. 9), but rhythm is not defined or observed as the principle element in Jackson's form.

2. Lesley A. Di Mare (1987) argues a typical Jackson technique is to amass credibility inclusively through the paradoxical creation of certain intergroup alliances through "cohesiveness" stemming from "separateness" (p. 223).

## *References*


Auld, Louis. (1984). Review of: The Corded Shell: Reflections on Musical Expression (Peter Kivy). *Philosophy and Rhetoric, 17,* 47–55.

Black, John A. (1988, August 12). Higher Ground. *Commonweal, 115,* 419–420.

Bloodworth, John David. (1975). Communication in the Youth Counter Culture: Music as Expression. *Central States Speech Journal, 26,* 304–309.

Booth, Mark. (1976). The Art of Words in Songs. *Quarterly Journal of Speech, 62,* 242–249.

Brokaw, Tom. (1988, July 19). NBC Special Coverage of the 1988 Democratic National Convention [broadcast].

Brockriede, Wayne & Scott, Robert L. (1970). *Moments in the Rhetoric of the Cold War.* New York: Random House.

Burke, Kenneth. (1940). *Counterstatement.* Berkeley: University of California Press.

Burns, Gary. (1988). Popular Music and Communication by Lull. *Journal of Broadcasting and Electronic Media, 32,* 244–246.

Chaffee, Steven H. (1985). Popular Music and Communication Research: An Editorial Epilogue. *Communication Research, 12,* 401–411.

Chesebro, James, Foulger, Davis A., Nachman, Jay E., & Yannelli, Andrew. (1986). Musical Patterns and Particular Musical Experiences. *Critical Studies in Mass Communication, 2,* 115–135.

Critchley, Macdonald, & Henson, R. A. (1977). *Music and the Brain.* London: William Heimann Medical Books limited.

Desmond, Roger Jon. (1987). Adolescents and Music Lyrics: Implications of a Cognitive Perspective. *Communication Quarterly, 35,* 276–284.

Di Mare, Lesley A. (1987). Functionalizing Conflict: Jesse Jackson's Rhetorical Strategy at the 1984 Democratic National Convention. *Western Journal of Speech Communication, 51,* 218–226.

Francesconi, Robert. (1986). Free Jazz and Black Nationalism: A Rhetoric of Musical Style. *Critical Studies in Mass Communication, 3,* 36–49.

Gonzalez, Alberto, & Makay, John. (1983). Rhetorical Ascription and the Gospel According to Dylan. *Quarterly Journal of Speech, 69,* 1–14.

Harris, Michael W. (1992). *The Rise of Gospel Blues.* New York: Oxford University Press.

Holmberg, Carl Bryan. (1985). Toward the Rhetoric of Music: 'Dixie.' *Southern Speech Communication Journal, 51,* 71–82.

Hunt, Albert R. (1988, July 19). Jesse's Class Act will Transform Theater of the Dull. *Wall Street Journal,* p. 32.

Irvine, James R., & Kirkpatrick, Walter G. (1972). The Musical Form in Rhetorical Exchange: Theoretical Considerations. *Quarterly Journal of Speech, 58,* 272–284.

Jackson, Jesse. Common Ground and Common Sense. *Vital Speeches of the Day, 54,* 649–653.

Jones, Simon C., & Shumacher, Thomas G. (1992). Muzak: On Functional Music and Power. *Critical Studies in Mass Communication, 9,* 156–169.

Knupp, Ralph E. (1981). A Time for Every Purpose Under Heaven: Rhetorical Dimensions of Protest Music. *Southern Speech Communication Journal, 46,* 377–389.

LeCoat, Gerald G. (1976). Music and the Three Appeals of Classic Rhetoric. *Quarterly Journal of Speech, 62,* 157–166.

Lewis, George. (1976). Country Music Lyrics. *Journal of Communication, 26,* 37–40.

Lincoln, C. Eric, & Mamiya, Lawrence H. (1990). *The Black Church in the African American Experience.* Durham: Duke University Press. p. 346.

Lull, James. (1985). On the Communicative Properties of Music. *Communication Research, 12,* 363–372.

Lull, James (Ed.). (1987). *Popular Music and Communication.* Newbury Park: Sage.

McLaughlin, Terence. (1970). *Music and Communication.* New York: St. Martin's Press.

Medhurst, Martin J., & Benson, Thomas W. (1981). The City: The Rhetoric of Rhythm. *Communication Monographs, 48,* 54–72.

Morhmann, G. P., & Scott, Eugene F. (1976). Popular Music and World War II: The Rhetoric of Continuation. *Quarterly Journal of Speech, 62,* 145–156.

Nelsen, Hart M. (1971). *The Black Church in America.* New York: Basic Books, Inc.

Niles, Lyndrey A. (1984). Rhetorical Characteristics of Traditional Black Preaching. *Journal of Black Studies, 15,* 41–52.

Ong, Walter (1982). *Orality and Literacy.* New York: Methuen & Co. Ltd.

Pipes, William Harrison. (1945). Old-Time Negro Preaching: An Interpretative Study. *Quarterly Journal of Speech, 31,* 15–21.

Ramussen, Karen. (1994). Transcendence in Leonard Bernstein's Kaddish Symphony. *Quarterly Journal of Speech, 80,* 150–173.

Rein & Springer. (1986). Where's the Music? The Problems of Lyric Analysis. *Critical Studies in Mass Communication, 3,* 252–256.

Rickert, William E. (1979). Music and the Art of Prosody. *Communication Education, 28,* 60–67.

Rickert, William E. (1986). A Musical Test of Prosody. *Communication Education, 35,* 169–174.

Shales, Tom. (1988, July 20). The Jackson Triumph. *The Washington Post,* p. C1.

Shepherd, John C. (1985). Prolegomena for the Critical Study of Popular Music. *Canadian Journal of Communication, 11,* 17–34.

Smith, Arthur L. (1970). Socio-Historical Perspectives of Black Oratory. *Quarterly Journal of Speech, 58,* 264–269.

Smith, Stephen A. (1980). Sounds of the South: The Rhetorical Saga of Country Music Lyrics. *Southern States Speech Journal, 45,* 164–172.

Spencer, Jon Michael. (1992). *Black Hymnody: A Hymnological History of the African-American Church.* Knoxville: University of Tennessee Press.

Thurber, John H., & Petelle, John L. (1968). The Negro Pulpit and Civil Rights. *Central States Speech Journal, 19,* 275.

Washington, James Melvin. (1985). Jesse Jackson and the Symbolic Politics of Black Christendom. *The Annals of American Academy of Political and Social Science, 480,* 99–104.

Wiesman, Eric. (1985). The Good Man Singing Well: Stevie Wonder as 'Noble Lover.' *Critical Studies in Mass Communication, 2,* 136–151.

Young, Henry. (1979). *Major Black Religious Leaders.* Nashville: Abingdon.

## *Signification and African-American Rhetoric: A Case Study of Jesse Jackson's "Common Ground and Common Sense" Speech*

PATRICIA A. SULLIVAN

> I've known rivers:
> I've known rivers ancient as the world and older than the flow of human blood in human veins.
> My soul has grown deep like the rivers.
>
> — LANGSTON HUGHES, "The Negro Speaks of Rivers"

In April, after the 1988 Wisconsin primary, an article in *The New York Times* suggested that Jesse Jackson's success indicated how far we had come in terms of surmounting racial prejudice in this country. Although the Democratic party had not overcome all the racial divisions in the party, the reporter noted: "Still, let it be recorded that for at least a week in American history, in a middle-sized Midwestern state, a broad range of white voters took the Presidential candidacy of a black man with the utmost seriousness" (Dionne, 1988, p. E1).

However, for the most part, Jackson's campaign was greeted with frustration by media representatives and political pundits. This frustration was reflected in two *Newsweek* cover stories; one cover story termed Jackson "The Power Broker: What Jesse Jackson Wants" and the other trumpeted "The Democratic Battle: Can He Win" (March 21, 1988; April 11, 1988). A *New York Times Magazine* article concentrated on "Jesse Jackson Aims for the Mainstream" (Purnick & Oreskes, 1987, pp. 28–31, 34–36, 58–61). A cartoon (of uncertain origin) sent to me by a friend depicted a television reporter with a garbage can over his head. "Blinded," he says, "The big question remains, where's the Democratic banner carrier? Who has the message, the passion, the charisma to move a broad based following — I don't see him." Behind the "blinded" reporter, a rally was being held by a large group of Jackson supporters.

This essay addresses the "blindness" as symbolized by the cartoon. Although commentators recognized Jackson's difference in a negative sense — the what does he want, can he win sentiments — they failed to understand and acknowledge what his difference might mean in a positive sense. Negative assessments of Jackson's political discourse draw attention to the need to examine his statements in relation to studies that document differences in black and white communication styles.

Kochman (1981), for example, has identified problems that occur when blacks and whites fail to recognize differences in their communication styles. Holt (1972) has discussed "a linguistic survival process functionally related to the conflicts implicit in American caste, class, and race" (p. 81). Foeman and Pressley (1987) have called for the recognition of differences between black and white management skills. Their study implies that integration and recognition of black interaction styles would enhance the quality of corporate communication (pp. 293–307). Stanback and Pearce (1981) propose that the study of black communication calls into question traditional research assumptions concerning communication processes (pp. 21–30).

Thus, a number of studies have indicated that African-American discourse requires scholars to generate new theoretical frameworks. In analyzing Jackson's speech, "Common Ground and Common Sense," presented at the 1988 Democratic National Convention in Atlanta, this essay proposes such a framework. A case study reveals that, in some parts of his speech, Jackson relied on patterns of signification associated with African-American discourse. In generating a theoretical framework and mapping patterns of signification, I use as reference points studies of black communication styles, as well as commentaries on oral cultural traditions. Additionally, I assume that Jackson's black communication style was misunderstood by many white listeners.

First, I examine the mainstream media assumptions that framed the coverage of Jackson's campaign; these assumptions reveal biases concerning Jackson's candidacy. Next, I propose that in order to provide constructive commentary concerning Jackson's discourse, it is necessary to go beyond white standards for communication, and bring to bear an understanding of characteristics associated with oral traditions. This section of the essay establishes a theoretical framework for analyzing African-American patterns in Jackson's political discourse. Third, the theoretical framework is applied to "Common Ground and Common Sense" in order to illuminate elements associated with African-American political discourse. This section of the essay also addresses "Common Ground and Common Sense" as a response to a rhetorical situation that required Jackson to address a diverse audience. Finally, I set forth a list of questions that media commentators and rhetorical critics should ask when political candidates rely on African-American communication patterns.

### Mainstream Media Assumptions

Two explanations seemed to emerge for white discomfort with Jackson's candidacy. Charges were leveled that Jackson was dishonest and too emotional. The charge that he was overly emotional often was paired with comments concerning his ability to coin catchy phrases. With both explanations, the assumption seemed to be, "Why won't Jackson step aside and let the "real" candidates fight it out?" Commentators implied that he had no place on the political stage.

The stories concerning dishonesty centered on what two *New York Times Magazine* authors termed Jackson's tendency to "exaggeration, a persistent trait," in recounting "tales" from his past (Purnick & Oreskes, 1987, p. 36). For example, Jackson received a scholarship to play football at The University of Illinois, but left when he did not become the starting quarterback. He claims he left the school due to the racism he experienced; some former teammates claim he did not become the starting quarterback because he was not the strongest candidate for the position (Purnick & Oreskes, p. 36).

In another case where "it is often difficult to separate reality from reminiscence," Jackson has been accused of exaggerating the poverty he experienced as a child. An often quoted line from his speeches is "I was born in a slum, but the slum was not born in me. And it wasn't born in you, and you can make it" (1988, p. 653). However, some relatives and childhood friends have pointed out that Jackson grew up in "a comfortable home" and that he was not poor (Purnick & Oreskes, p. 34).

The tale most often cited to suggest Jackson's dishonesty is related to his conduct following the assassination of Dr. Martin Luther King, Jr. The authors of the *New York Times Magazine* article observe that "many of Mr. Jackson's efforts at exaggeration seem little more than innocent chapters in a revisionist autobiography," but the exaggeration of the King story has distressed many people, including many King followers (Purnick & Oreskes, p. 36). After the assassination, Jackson claimed to be the "last person in the world he [King] spoke to" (Purnick & Oreskes, p. 36). When the assassination occurred, Jackson was on the floor below the balcony where King was standing. Furthermore, Jackson had blood on his shirt when he spoke to reporters. He later appeared on the *Today Show* wearing the bloodstained turtleneck, and recounted how he had "cradled" King's head in the moments after the assassination. Now when he recounts his behavior following the assassination, Jackson usually does not use the term "cradled"; he simply says he reached out for King (Purnick & Oreskes, pp. 36, 58).

In addition to the accusation that he misrepresented events, Jackson also was charged with being overly emotional. This claim generally came in conjunction with the observation that Jackson was "a master of bumper-sticker rhetoric, chanting his message in simpled-down rhythms" (Martz, 1988, p. 22). Reporters expressed distrust of his oral communication skills. His spontaneity was unsettling for some listeners who were uncomfortable with the "dramatic, almost messianic fervor [which] still imbues his rhetoric" (Purnick & Oreskes, p. 34). Terms such as "wooing" and "chanting" were used to characterize Jackson's speaking style (Purnick & Oreskes, p. 34). The *New York Times Magazine* article described his relationship with an audience.

> The crowd is yelling, "Right on, Jesse!" and the applause is thunderous. Jesse Jackson has shown once again that he knows how to rouse an audience. He wields his words like javelins, hurling sleek, memorable phrases that pierce to the heart of complex issues.
>
> But if Mr. Jackson's way with words has brought him attention at every step of his life, it has also fueled reservations that, as a former captain of his college football team put it, "the guys felt maybe he talked more than he played" (Purnick & Oreskes, p. 34).

Such descriptions implied that Jackson's skills with oral communication were dangerous. The suggestion was that he was out of control, and that he would encourage others to lose control.

Reflected in this fear was doubt concerning Jackson's reasonableness — his commitment to detail and specific proposals for programs. Campaign 1988 was marked by complaints that candidates refused to address issues and supply detailed approaches to solving problems. However, the charge seemed to stick to Jackson in a way that it did not stick to the other candidates. Although a *Newsweek* article acknowledged that "Jackson is saying more than any other candidate for president, and saying it better . . . he's still not saying what to do about them [problems]" (Martz, p. 23). This article implied that although Jackson was saying more, he was not saying enough. Why were the expectations higher for Jackson? Why did he need to be more specific? Later the article hinted that Jackson owed audiences more specifics than the other candidates because of his power as an orator — his ability to coin "catch phrases" (p. 23). The same *Newsweek* article termed Jackson "a master of maneuver" (p. 25).

In sum, commentators questioned Jackson's ethical standards and charged that he was overly emotional, dishonest, and vague during presentations on the campaign trail. Ultimately, negative responses to Jackson centered on his extraordinary powers as an oral communicator.

**Jackson and African-American Patterns of Signification**

Such statements concerning Jackson's campaign revealed a fundamental misunderstanding of the oral tradition he represented. In *Orality and Literacy: The Technologizing of the Word* (1982), Walter J. Ong synthesizes research on oral traditions, identifies characteristics associated with primary oral traditions, and questions the privileging of written traditions in our culture. He cautions that scholars frequently have considered "oral organizations" of thought "naive" and "unsophisticated" (p. 57). These assumptions are unwarranted and reflect a misunderstanding of the patterns which characterize "oral thinking" (p. 57).

In describing patterns of "oral thinking," Ong refers to primary oral cultures as "oral cultures untouched by writing" or "a culture not far removed from orality" (pp. 31–32). Obviously, Jackson has been "touched" by writing; however, he does *value and embrace* "a culture not far removed from orality." Ong's observations concerning primary oral cultures parallel the finding of scholars who have mapped characteristics of African-American discourse. The African-American speech community values the culture of primary orality identified by Ong.

In *The Signifying Monkey: A Theory of African-American Literary Criticism* (1988), Henry Louis Gates, Jr. defines African-American patterns of signification; he explains that black authors attempt to "recover orality" in the written word through the "speakerly text" — a text that evokes characteristics associated with African-American oral culture. Gates argues that the folkloric trickster figure or signifying monkey represents the efforts of African-Americans to mediate between demands of the black world and the white world.[1]

In negotiating what W. E. B. Du Bois termed "double consciousness" (Quoted in Johnson, 1984, pp. 214–215), African-Americans developed their own signification patterns — black tropes. Gates refers to "double-voiced words and double-voiced discourse" (1988, p. 50). He notes: "Their complex act of language signifies upon both formal language uses and its conventions, conventions established, at least officially, by middle-class white people" (1988, p. 47). African-Americans were forced to name themselves — to develop a space for themselves in language — because their experiences were muted by the dominant white culture. Gates explains the catalyst for development of African-American tropes.

> What did/do black people signify in a society in which they were intentionally introduced as subjugated, as the enslaved cipher? Nothing on the X axis of white signification, and everything on the Y axis of blackness (1988, p. 47).

The black tropes thus name "everything on the Y axis of blackness." In identifying black patterns of signification, Gates turns to a number of African-American scholars whose findings support those of Ong's concerning primary oral cultures.

First, for primary oral cultures, utterances are "dynamic." The word has special power — a "magical potency" (Ong, p. 32). The "sounded word" is living and represents "power and action" (Ong, p. 31). This notion of the word as living is reflected in Mitchell-Kernan's explanation of "the Black concept of signifying [which] incorporates essentially a folk notion that dictionary entries for words are not always sufficient for interpreting meanings or messages, or that meanings go beyond such interpretations" (Quoted in Gates, 1984, p. 289). Listeners must be aware of context and have highly developed interpretive skills in order to unravel what an utterance signifies in a particular situation.

Although some audience members mistrusted the power of Jackson's words, he spoke as though his utterances were "magical," and signifying in vital ways for those who were connecting with them. His title as "a master of bumper-sticker rhetoric" and "simpled-down rhythms" suggests the "magical potency" identified by Ong.

Additionally, Ong argues that "sustained thought in an oral culture is tied to communication" (p. 34). "Rhythm aids recall" and is the key to the preservation of "memorable thoughts" (Ong, p. 32). Statements in *Orality and Literacy: The Technologizing of the Word* concerning "mnemonic patterns" seem especially applicable to Jackson's discourse. Ong notes:

> Your thoughts must come into being in heavenly rhythmic, balanced patterns, in repetitions or antitheses, in alliterations and assonances, in epithetic and other formulary expressions, in standard thematic settings (the assembly, the meal, the duel, the hero's 'helper,' and so on), in proverbs which are constantly heard by everyone so that they come to mind readily and which themselves are patterned for retention and ready recall, or in other mnemonic form. (p. 34)

Furthermore, Ong comments on the role of formulas in "rhythmic discourse." Such formulas serve as "set expressions circulating through the mouths and ears of all" (p. 35). I am reminded that Tom Brokaw commented after Jackson's 1988 Democratic National Convention speech that the speech did not contain new phrases, but relied on a litany of phrases from the campaign trail. Such a statement overlooks the importance of "set expressions circulating through the mouths and ears of all."

When we turn to the analysis of "Common Ground and Common Sense," we shall see that this speech was marked by "set expressions" which have been identified as "call response formulas" in the African-American oral tradition. As Sithole (1972) notes, preachers and soul performers "establish rapport" with the audience through the evocation of these formulas (p. 81). Such formulas are vital for the black speaker who represents an oral tradition. Sithole quotes one of the formulas from a Jackson speech at an Operation Breadbasket meeting in Chicago.

> I am, *somebody*
> I may be black
> But I am, *somebody*
> I may be poor
> But I am, *somebody*
> I may be unemployed
> But I am, *somebody*
> I may be on welfare
> But I am, *somebody*
> I'm black, and I'm proud
> I'm black and beautiful
> I am God's child. (p. 81)

Gates discusses the "intertextuality" of such "formulaic phrases" and observes that the skillful oral narrator bonds with the audience by playing on and creatively reinventing such phrases (1988, p. 60).

These patterns of repetition connote shared concerns for listeners. Holt (1972) comments that this strategy is a reminder that "*All* blacks are linked in a community of historical suffering which allows the preacher to switch his image for dual audiences" (p. 195).

The repetition of formulaic phrases and stories from context to context and from communication situation to communication situation also exemplifies another characteristic of oral traditions. The emphasis is on performance — reading an audience and adapting and retelling (even revitalizing) a story — for the listeners on hand. When Jackson was charged with misrepresenting the truth as related to his upbringing, his college football career, or the King assassination, he may have been the performer reshaping the moment to serve his purposes. Whereas this might constitute lying for those grounded in a written tradition, for those from an oral tradition such adjustments are appropriate. Ong, paraphrasing Goody, comments on this type of "originality" in oral cultures:

> Narrative originality lodges not in making up new stories but in managing a particular interaction with this audience at this time — at every telling the story has to be introduced uniquely into a unique situation, for in oral cultures an audience must be brought to respond, often vigorously. But narrators also introduce new elements into old stories. (pp. 41–42)

Jackson's effort to "introduce new elements into old stories" may parallel the folk tradition of lying and telling "tall tales." As I read the criticisms of Jackson's "dishonesty," I was reminded of the process Zora Neale Hurston (1978) recounts in her ethnographic study, *Mules and Men.* Storytellers gather on the porch and prepare to tell their "lies." Story follows story, and story blends with story; indeed, Hurston's collection seems like one continuous story. The storytellers, as performers, adapt to their audiences, and to the other tales. In other words, the shape of the subsequent tale is determined by the one which preceded it.

As Hurston explains, this adaptability in performance also stems from the subservient position blacks have occupied in American culture. The tales are difficult to interpret; Hurston explains the logic behind the black man's secrecy patterns of signification. She says:

> The white man is always trying to know into somebody else's business. All right, I'll set something outside the door of my mind for him to play

> with and handle. He can read my writing but he sho' can't read my mind. I'll put this play toy in his hand, and he will seize it and go away. Then I'll say my say and sing my song. (pp. 4–5)

In mapping Jackson's discourse, we must take into account this performance dimension. "Lying" within the context of the black oral tradition does not necessarily connote dishonesty or insincerity. Sithole comments that "leadership among black folk, in church, politics, band-directing, or even court defense, has always been based on the ability of the leader to improvise upon a given theme" (p. 82).

Furthermore, the ability of the leader in this African-American oral tradition hinges on her or his capacity to relate knowledge to human experiences. In oral traditions, knowledge is not grounded in statistics or facts; there is no knowledge divorced from human activity or the human life world. As Ong notes, "primary oral culture is little concerned with preserving knowledge or skills as an abstract, self-subsistent corpus" (p. 43). Knowledge does not exist for its own sake, or in the abstract, but exists as grounded in human experience. What is relevant is relevant because it makes a difference in people's lives.

This difference is reflected in observations by Kochman concerning variations in black and white debating styles. An ethnographic study reveals that white students as debaters supported their positions by relying on sources they perceived as authoritative (p. 25). For them, this represented the goal in the debate. In addition, "They do not see themselves as personally responsible for the idea itself" (p. 25). Debate does not mean they need to have a "personal position" concerning the point. Black students, on the other hand, "consider it essential for individuals to have personal positions on issues and assume full responsibility for arguing their validity" (p. 25). Within this frame of reference, individuals are not adequately committed to their positions and the "truth value" of them unless they have "a personal stake in the material" (p. 25).

Such a difference seems relevant to the response to Jackson that he was overly emotional. This response may have been rooted in Jackson's insistence that abstract proposals could not be made without references to real people. Possibly, as *Newsweek* noted, "Jackson's vision seems larger and more compelling than what other candidates are offering" (1988, p. 22) because his suggestions were made in reference to real people. Was he a master of "bumper-sticker rhetoric," or simply a speaker who considered how programs might affect listeners and helped them see how they might be affected? This essay proposes that the answer to this question depends on the critical lens applied to Jackson's discourse.

The next section of this essay applies a critical lens based on the African-American patterns of signification identified by a number of scholars. Elements of Jackson's speech, "Common Ground and Common Sense," illustrate these patterns of signification.

### "Common Ground and Common Sense"

When Jackson opened his speech at the 1988 Democratic National Convention, he acknowledged a diverse audience. His appeals to common ground and common sense served as calls to unite that diverse audience. Although the Democratic Party was divided, he saw an opportunity to unite listeners on the basis of their shared concerns. He noted: "when I look out at this convention, I see the face of America, red, yellow, brown, black and white, we're all precious in God's sight — the real rainbow coalition" (p. 649).

In "Common Ground and Common Sense," Jackson created "a rainbow coalition" by reminding listeners that, in spite of their differences, they shared common goals as members of the Democratic Party. He also emphasized that they were united in their outrage concerning "reverse Robin Hood" and "Reaganomics" (p. 651). Although Jackson knew he would not win the Democratic presidential nomination in 1988, "Common Ground and Common Sense" evoked his central campaign message — unity. As Gary Wills (1988) observed in his essay, "New Votuhs," in *The New York Review of Books,* Jackson played an important role in the 1988 campaign.

> His positions were the ones that brought a response in debate after debate, so that they were taken up by the other Democratic candidates. He won white votes in northern states. He took voting registrars to large crowds, or large crowds to the registrars. He built on the coalition that had been formed around the opposition to Bork. He began to make it seem possible for Democrats to cooperate with blacks without losing all the whites who have defected in the South since the Sixties. (p. 5)

Thus, Jackson's themes in his 1988 Democratic National Convention speech echoed messages that he had shared on the campaign trail.

In echoing such messages in "Common Ground and Common Sense" and appealing to "the real rainbow coalition," Jackson relied on mainstream English; however, he also turned to African-American patterns of signification that called for audience participation. In "Common Ground and Common Sense," African-American patterns of signification were used to draw listeners together and to remind them of the problems they shared as victims of Reaganomics. Just as participatory African-American patterns of signification historically drew black audiences together and reminded them of their "shared historical suffering," the same patterns used by Jackson in "Common Ground and Common Sense" drew together members of the 1988 Democractic National Conventional and reminded them of shared concerns.

Close analysis of "Common Ground and Common Sense," with a focus on African-American patterns of signification, reveals that, in Mitchell-Kernan's terms, Jackson's words are [were] not always sufficient for interpreting meanings or messages, or that meanings go beyond those interpretations" (Quoted in Gates, 1984, p. 289). By emphasizing the participatory elements associated with black patterns of signification, Jackson united a diverse audience. In uniting this diverse audience, he utilized the following tropes: set expressions/call response formulas, "lies"/tall tales, and stories grounded in common sense.

### Set Expressions/Call Response Formulas

The set expression or call response formula was the most apparent pattern of signification employed by Jackson in "Common Ground and Common Sense." Throughout the speech, he relied on mnemonic devices in the form of set expressions or call response formulas. Thematically, the ideas in the speech were woven together with the words, common ground and common sense. This speech defies labeling in terms of a traditional organizational pattern; the speech, for example, was not organized chronologically or topically. Rather, the speech was organized around repetitive set expressions that established a rhythm in the speech.

Jackson first brought the audience together through repetition of the phrase "common ground." Although audience members — a true rainbow coalition at the 1988 Democratic National Convention — were marked by differences, repetition of the term "common ground" emphasized shared dreams and goals. "Common ground" became a call response formula as Jackson created rhythmic chants that invited audience participation.

> *Common ground!*
> Think of Jerusalem — the intersection where many trails met. A small village that became the birthplace for the three great religions — Judaism, Christianity and Islam.
>
> Why was this village so blessed? Because it provided a crossroads where different peoples met, different cultures, and different civilizations could meet and find *common ground.*

> When people come together, flowers always flourish and the air is rich with the aroma of a new spring.
>
> Take New York, the dynamic metropolis. What makes New York so special?
>
> It is the invitation of the Statue of Liberty — give me your tired, your poor, your huddled masses who yearn to breathe free.
>
> Not restricted to English only.
>
> Many people, many cultures, many languages — with one thing in *common*, the yearn to breathe free.
>
> *Common ground!* (p. 650) [emphasis added]

Through such repetition, Jackson brought listeners together as a community. As Jackson continued, common ground became common good. However, the shift to common good was seamless; due to the sense of community created by the call response formula, Jackson's shift to common good was so natural that it was almost imperceptible.

Alliteration in the phrase, "The greater good is the common good" (p. 650), further reinforced the sense of connection; the phrasing made the link between common ground and common good seem logical. In this speech, the approach was especially effective because Jackson faced a number of dualities in the audience. Through his discourse, he reminded audience members — black and white — that they were united by shared concerns.

After Jackson had successfully woven together common ground and common good, he evoked a powerful metaphor to encourage the audience to visualize the common ground that is the common good. To illustrate how Americans from diverse backgrounds could come together, he noted that "America's not a blanket woven from one thread, one color, one cloth" (p. 651), but like a quilt created by his grandmother. His grandmother "took the pieces of old cloth — patches, wool, silk, gabardine, crockersack on the patches — barely good enough to wipe your shoes with . . . [and] sewed them together into a quilt, a thing of beauty and power and culture" (p. 651).

This metaphor led to Jackson's use of another call response formula, "your patch is not big enough," that emphasized unity. The call response formula, rooted in the quilt metaphor, created a powerful vision of common ground leading to common good.

> Now, Democrats, we must build such a quilt. Farmers, you seek fair prices and you are right, but you cannot stand alone. *Your patch is not big enough.* Workers, you fight for fair wages. You are right. But *your patch is not big enough.* Women, you seek comparable worth and pay equity. You are right. But *your patch is not big enough.* Women, mothers, you seek Head Start and day care and pre-natal care on the front side of life, rather

> than jail care and welfare on the back side of life, you're right, *but your patch is not big enough.* (p. 651) [emphasis added]

After Jackson established common ground and brought the audience together as a community, he turned to the second theme of the speech, common sense. According to Jackson, realization of the common good required common sense actions. He again turned to a call response formula in claiming that he wanted "to take common sense to high places" (p. 651). In arguing that Europe and Japan should fund their own defense expenditures, Jackson fostered audience participation by creating a rhythm that encouraged the audience to respond to his statements.

> Let them share some of the burden of their own defense — *use some of that money* to build decent housing!
>
> *Use some of that money* to educate our children!
>
> *Use some of that money* for long-term health care!
>
> *Use some of that money* to wipe out these slums and put America back to work! (p. 651) [emphasis added]

Thus, Jackson relied on call response formulas in providing good reasons for the audience to embrace his "common good and common sense" agenda. Form corresponded with content as the rhythmic call response formulas brought listeners together to visualize a better America — an America different from the one created by President Ronald Reagan.

The speech closed with a powerful variation on the call response formula as Jackson evoked a set expression grounded in his personal experiences. He turned to his own autobiography to encourage even the most discouraged of audience members to "Don't surrender and don't give up" because "You can make it" (p. 653). As he narrated his own experiences, "I understand" became the refrain that united listeners to pursue "common ground and common sense."

> *I understand* work. I was not born with a silver spoon in my mouth. I had a shovel programmed for my hand. My mother, a working woman. So many days she went to work early with runs in her stockings. She knew better, but she wore runs in her stockings so that my brother and I could have matching socks and not be laughed at at school.
>
> *I understand.* At 3 o'clock on Thanksgiving Day we couldn't eat turkey because mama was preparing someone else's turkey at 3 o'clock. We had to play football to entertain ourselves and then around 6 o'clock she would get off the Alta Vista bus; then we would bring up the leftovers and eat our turkey — leftovers, the carcass, the cranberries around 8 o'clock at night. *I really do understand.* (p. 653) [emphasis added]

"Common Ground and Common Sense" closed with Jackson emphasizing his triumphs, but also indicating that he "understood" adversity.

Through call response formulas, Jackson unified the speech and the audience. When Jackson opened the speech, he indicated that he was privileged to follow in the steps of Martin Luther King, Jr., Fanny Lou Hamer, and Rosa Parks. As the speech unfolded, he turned to the challenges facing America; he rallied the audience through call response formulas to face those challenges. Finally, he closed by using a call response formula to unite his experiences with those of audience members. After appealing to the audience on the basis of "I understand," he was in a position to urge the audience "not to surrender" (p. 653). His presence on the stage enacted the virtues associated with "common ground and common sense." Throughout the speech, the rhythmic refrains spoke to human possibilities. When Jackson chanted "keep hope alive," the speech came full circle. Call response formulas lived in the minds of listeners as reminders of how to "keep hope alive."

Set expressions/call response formulas constitute the most important trope in "Common Ground and Common Sense." However, Jackson also relied on additional African-American patterns of signification.

### "Lies"/Tall Tales

Earlier in this essay I discussed charges that Jackson was dishonest and misrepresented his life history. Some relatives, childhood friends, and commentators claimed that Jackson was not "born in a slum." In "Common Ground and Common Sense," he did tell his story. To inspire others, he emphasized: "My mama was not supposed to make it. And I was not supposed to make it. You see, I was born to a teen-age mother who was born to a teen-age mother" (p. 653). However, whereas many media commentators accused Jackson of "lying," from the standpoint of African-American patterns of signification, he was using "figurative discourse" (Gates, 1988, p. 56) or symbolically adapting his story for the audience. In performing and "improvising upon a given theme," in Sithole's terms, Jackson was doing what would be expected of a leader in an African-American speech community.

In "Common Ground and Common Sense," Jackson provided his own story as an enactment of the American dream. Although he "was not supposed to make it," he did make it and was addressing the Democratic National Convention. When his autobiographical account is viewed symbolically, it may be appreciated for what it is — an inspiring story.

> I understand. I know abandonment and people being mean to you, and saying you're nothing and nobody, and can never be anything. I understand. Jesse Jackson is my third name. I'm adopted. When I had no name, my grandmother gave me her name. My name was Jesse Burns until I was age 12. So I wouldn't have a blank space, she gave me a name to hold me over. I understand when nobody knows your name. I understand when you have no name. I understand.
>
> I wasn't born in the hospital. Mama didn't have insurance. I was born in the bed at home. I really do understand. Born in a three-room house, bathroom in the backyard, slop jar by the bed, no hot and cold running water. I understand. Wallpaper used for decoration? No. For a windbreaker. I understand. I'm a working person's person, that's why I understand you whether you're black or white. (p. 653)

When Jackson's story in "Common Ground and Common Sense" is framed as African-American signification and the trope of the tall tale, the critic does not assume that the candidate was telling "the truth" in a traditional sense; rather, the critic focuses on the symbolic import of the story.

During campaign 1988, when Jackson's veracity was questioned, one critic did rush to his defense in relation to details concerning the King assassination. Gary Wills's defense seems applicable to other instances when Jackson's ethics have been questioned. In an essay in *The New York Review of Books,* Wills (1988) explored the symbolic dimensions of Jackson's reshaping of the events on the day King was assassinated in Memphis. He accounted for Jackson's behavior in smearing some of the blood on his shirt as "a natural reaction to the death of a martyr" (p. 5). When viewed symbolically, his behavior does not seem outrageous. Wills compared Jackson's symbolic act to Jacqueline Kennedy's hesitation to change her blood-stained suit after the assassination of her husband (p. 5).

From the standpoint of African-American patterns of signification, Jackson's "tall tales" as performance invite listeners to go beyond words to interpret meaning. Jackson's "common sense" stories, on the other hand, ask listeners to use human logic as an interpretive filter.

### Stories Grounded in Common Sense

In "Common Ground and Common Sense," Jackson insisted that abstract proposals could not be made without references to real people. For example, he called into question a popular slogan from the Reagan administration. He challenged listeners to think about what it means to "just say no" to drugs. "Just say no" sounded like a simple solution when a politician chanted it to school children. Jackson questioned its validity.

> We need a real war on drugs. You can't just say no. It's deeper than that. You can't just get a palm reader or an astrologer; it's more profound than that. We're spending $150 billion on drugs a year. We've gone from ignoring it to focusing on the children. Children cannot buy $150 billion worth of drugs a year. A few high profile athletes — athletes are not laundering $150 billion a year — bankers are. (p. 652)

Human logic says meaningless chants will not solve drug problems, nor will consulting the stars. Furthermore, $150 billion dollar programs that ignore the realities of people's lives will not work. He made the audience wonder about bureaucratic logic — logic that was based on the authoritative sources Kochman's young debaters called into question.

Furthermore, Jackson used his own experiences as evidence to challenge stereotypes concerning poor people. He asked listeners to look around them and use their common sense to evaluate government policies. He noted that "Most poor people are not on welfare" and "They work hard every day" (p. 652). He gave testimony concerning their struggles and called on the audience to use common sense to understand the suffering of poor people.

> I know they work. I'm a witness. They catch the early bus. They work every day. . . . No more. They're not lazy. Someone must defend them because it's not right, and they cannot speak for themselves. They work in hospitals. I know they do. They wipe the bodies of those who are sick with fever and pain. They empty their bedpans. They clean out their commode. No job is beneath them, and yet when they get sick, they cannot lie in the bed they made up every day. America, that is not right. We are a better nation than that. We are a better nation than that. (p. 652)

Although Jackson has been accused of recounting such emotional stories to short-circuit reasoning and sway audiences, his approach may be evaluated differently when viewed from the standpoint of African-American patterns of signification.

Those who feared Jackson's emotional approach failed to recognize his vision of argumentation as grounding positions in common sense and personal experience. Criticism of Jackson privileged reason over emotion without recognizing that his approach called into question this dichotomy. Possibly if we look beyond this dichotomy, we shall see that Jackson's style of argumentation suggests that we should question traditional splits between reason and emotion. Positions grounded in experiences in the live world call us to new definitions of what constitutes reasonableness.

The African-American tropes or patterns of signification — set expressions/call response formulas, "lies"/tall tales, and common sense stories — invite media commentators and rhetorical critics to examine their assumptions concerning political communication. Many African-American voices, such as Jackson's, will continue to be marginalized and muted on the American political stage unless their patterns of communication are recognized and honored by popular and scholarly gatekeepers.

**Implications**

Although this study represents preliminary reflections on a major topic, two areas seem especially important for future study. The first area centers on how popular and scholarly commentators should approach political discourse that is marked by African-American patterns of signification. The misunderstandings associated with commentaries concerning Jackson's campaign suggest that we should examine our assumptions — the frameworks we use to analyze political discourse. The study of rhetoric — in the best sense of the word — proposes questions we might want to ask when we approach political discourse. In James Boyd White's (1985) terms, rhetoric can encourage us to move away from abstract standards concerning discourse.

> It [rhetoric] is contiguous to a ground that is common to us all. Rhetoric must deal with ordinary language because it is the art of speaking to people who already have a language, and it is their language you must speak to reach and to persuade them. This is the sense in which, as I suggested above, rhetoric is always culture-specific. You must take the language you are given and work with that. (p. 45)

Rhetoric, in other words, reminds us that when we speak we deal "with real communities, real values, and real politics" (White, p. 45). Those who misunderstood Jackson's discourse did not recognize that his rhetoric was "culture-specific" and represented "real communities, real values, and real politics."

If commentators had attempted to understand Jackson's discourse as emerging from an African-American speech community — a "real community" with "real values" and "real politics;" he might not have been misunderstood. White discusses questions lawyers should ask about each rhetorical situation they enter. These questions also seem applicable to approaching political rhetorical situations. If the following questions had been asked during Jackson's campaign, his discourse might have been appreciated by more listeners.

In this essay, I began to pose and answer some of these questions in relation to Jackson and African-American patterns of signification. First, White says questions must be asked concerning "the inherited language." "What is the language or culture with which this speaker works?" This question encompasses considerations concerning "natural and social facts," "human motives and values," and "persuasive motions of the mind that we call reason" (pp. 45–46). The second question concerns "the art of the text." "How, by what art and with what effect, is this language remade by the speaker in this written or oral text? Is the text internally coherent, and if so by what standards of coherence?" The final question concerns "the rhetorical community." This series of questions listed by White seems especially applicable to this study and further research. "What kind of person is speaking here, and to what kind of person does he or she speak? What kind of response does this text invite, or permit? What place is there for me, and for others, in the universe defined by this discourse, in the community created by this text? What world does it assume, what world does it create?" (pp. 45–46).

White proposes that when we fail to address these questions, we simply assume the speaker shares our cultural assumptions as reflected in our frameworks for discourse. Furthermore, we fail to recognize the richness of discourse which enlivens and shapes our community and culture. Rather than evaluating a speech such as "Common Ground and Common Sense" in terms of whether it represents an appropriate response to a rhetorical situation, White suggests that critics and audiences should evaluate and broaden their rhetorical frameworks to embrace diversity. From White's perspective, critics should question their own rhetorical frameworks — what they view as appropriate — when evaluating discourse. A rhetorical critical analysis relying on White's recommendations would recognize and value the African-American patterns of signification that Jackson relied on in "Common Ground and Common Sense." Furthermore, such an analysis would acknowledge that Jackson used those patterns to his advantage in addressing a diverse audience at the 1988 Democratic National Convention.

If rhetorical critics broaden their frameworks for analysis to embrace diversity, a second area emerges as essential for further research. If we follow White's suggestions and call into question our "persuasive motions of the mind that we call reason," new standards might emerge in our culture for what constitutes a good reason in a political context.

As I reflected on the criticisms leveled at Jackson's style and his emphasis on personal experience and emotion, I was reminded of the criticisms Geraldine Ferraro received when she ran as a vice-presidential candidate in 1984. I believe both Jackson and Ferraro represented a different approach to reasoning and moral decision making. In *In a Different Voice: Psychological Theory and Women's Development* (1982), Gilligan examines the privileging of reason over emotion in theories mapping the course of human development. Superior decision-making, as discussed by theorists such as Kohlberg, is marked by the ability to privilege the abstract, as embodied in the law, over personal experiences. In other words, the mature mind sees as authoritative what has been "published" (to return to Kochman) and accepted over time. Gilligan points out that women are more likely to ground their decision making in personal experience than in the law. Traditional theories of human development brand this approach to problem-solving as inferior. Gilligan's observations also seem applicable to the African-American patterns of signification outlined in this essay.

Furthermore, Gilligan proposes that if we overcome dichotomies proposed by traditional theorists, then we will be able to embrace an ethical system that bridges elements in human decision-making. She believes this would lead to a better world (pp. 72–73, 99–100, 101, 102–103). A recognition of differences in communication patterns might help us understand the shape of this new world. Jackson's political discourse may take us in the direction of the ethical system visualized by Gilligan. As I suggested earlier, Jackson's discourse was not unreasonable; it simply challenged, in White's terms, "persuasive motions of the mind that we call reason."

## Notes

1. Gates (1988) addresses the difficulty of relating the black linguistic sign, "signification," to the standard English sign, "signification" (p. 45). Therefore, he designates the white term as "signifying" and the black term as "Signifyin(g)" (p. 46). He notes: "The bracketed *g* enables me to connote the fact that this word is, more often than not, spoken by black people without the final *g* as signifyin'. This arbitrary and idiosyncratic convention also enables me to recall the fact that whatever historical community of Afro-Americans coined this usage did so in the vernacular as spoken, in contradistinction to the literate written usages of the standard English 'shadowed' term. The bracketed or aurally erased *g*, like the discourse of black English and dialect poetry generally, stands as the trace of black difference in a remarkably sophisticated and fascinating (re)naming ritual graphically in evidence here" (p. 46).

   Although this easy relies on Gates's definition of African-American "Signifyin(g)" as opposed to white "signifying," it seems unnecessary, for the purposes of this analysis, to map the two terms in this way. "Signifying" and patterns of signification refer to African-American tropes in this study.

## References

The Democratic battle: Can we win. (1988, April 11). *Newsweek* [cover].

Dionne, E. J. (1988, April 10). Black and white: How Jesse Jackson made history while losing Wisconsin. *The New York Times,* p. E1.

Foeman, A. K. & Presley, G. (1987). Ethnic culture: Using black styles in organizations. *Communication Quarterly, 35,* 293–307.

Gates, H. L. Jr. (1984). The 'blackness of blackness': A critique of the sign and the signifying monkey. In H. L. Gates Jr. (Ed.), *Black literature and literary theory* (pp. 285–321). New York: Methuen.

Gates, H. L. Jr. (1988). *The signifying monkey: A theory of African-American literary criticism.* New York: Oxford University Press.

Gilligan, C. (1982). *In a different voice: Psychological theory and women's development.* Cambridge: Harvard University Press.

Holt, G. S. (1972). Stylin' outta the black pulpit. In T. Kochman (Ed.), *Rappin' and stylin' out: Communication in urban black America* (pp. 81–95). Urbana: University of Illinois Press.

Houston, M. S. & Pearce, B. (1981). Talking to 'the man': Some communication strategies used by members of 'subordinate' social groups. *The Quarterly Journal of Speech, 67,* 21–30.

Hurston, Z. N. (1935; 1978). *Mules and men.* Bloomington: Indiana University Press.

Jackson, J. (1988, August 15). Common ground and common sense. *Vital Speeches of the Day,* pp. 649–653.

Johnson, B. (1984). Metaphor, metonymy, and voice in *Their eyes were watching god.* In H. L. Gates Jr. (Ed.), *Black literature and literary theory* (pp. 205–219). New York: Methuen.

Kochman, T. (1981). *Black and white styles in conflict.* Chicago: University of Chicago Press.

Martz, L. (1988, April 11). Jackson's big takeoff. *Newsweek,* pp. 23–25.

Mitchell-Kernan, C. (1972). Signifying, loud-talking, and marking. In T. Kochman (Ed.), *Rappin' and stylin' out* (pp. 315–335). Urbana: University of Illinois Press.

Mitchell-Kernan, C. (1973). Signifying. In A. Dundes (Ed.), *Mother wit from the laughing barrel* (pp. 313–325). Englewood Cliffs, NJ: Prentice-Hall.

Ong, W. J. (1982). *Orality and literacy: The technologizing of the word.* New York: Methuen.

The power broker: What Jesse Jackson wants. (1988, March 21). *Newsweek* [cover].

Purnick, J. & Oreskes, M. (1987, November 29). Jesse Jackson aims for the mainstream. *The New York Times Magazine,* pp. 28–31, 34–36, 58–61.

Sithole, E. T. (1972). Black folk music. In T. Kochman (Ed.), *Rappin' and stylin' out: Communication in urban black America* (pp. 81–95). Urbana: University of Illinois Press.

White, J. B. (1985). *Heracles' bow: Essays on the rhetoric and poetics of the law.* Madison: University of Wisconsin Press.

Wills, G. (1988, August 18). New votuhs. *The New York Review of Books,* pp. 3–5.

# PART IV

# CRITICAL READINGS: SAMPLE STUDIES

The following studies are examples of rhetorical criticism written by perceptive, mature critics who approach their tasks from various critical perspectives. These are not models that the beginning student can hope to emulate; rather, they are demonstrations of what serious critics can contribute to our understanding of rhetoric and communication. Beginning critics who study them carefully will begin to appreciate what kinds of questions can fruitfully be asked, what techniques of analysis and interpretation can begin to uncover answers to significant questions, how critical arguments are constructed, and what fresh insights can be generated.

# 9

# Critical Reading of Elizabeth Cady Stanton's "Solitude of Self"

## *Solitude of Self*

ELIZABETH CADY STANTON

Mr. Chairman and gentlemen of the Committee:

We have been speaking before Committees of the Judiciary for the last twenty years, and we have gone over all the arguments in favor of the sixteenth [ultimately, the nineteenth] amendment which are familiar to all you gentlemen; therefore, it will not be necessary that I should repeat them again. The point I wish plainly to bring before you on this occasion is the individuality of each human soul; our Protestant idea, the right of individual conscience and judgment; our republican idea, individual citizenship. In discussing the rights of woman, we are to consider, first, what belongs to her as an individual, in a world of her own, the arbiter of her own destiny, an imaginary Robinson Crusoe, with her woman Friday on a solitary island. Her rights under such circumstances are to use all her faculties for her own safety and happiness.

Secondly, if we consider her as a citizen, as a member of a great nation, she must have the same rights as all other members, according to the fundamental principles of our government.

Thirdly, viewed as a woman, an equal factor in civilization, her rights and duties are still the same; individual happiness and development.

Fourthly, it is only the incidental relations of life, such as mother, wife, sister, daughter, that may involve some special duties and training. In the usual discussion in regard to woman's sphere, such men as Herbert Spencer, Frederic Harrison and Grant Allen, uniformly subordinate her rights and duties as an individual, as a citizen, as a woman, to the necessities of these incidental relations, neither of which a large class of women may ever assume. In discussing the sphere of man, we do not decide his rights as an individual, as a citizen, as a man, by his duties as a father, a husband, a brother or a son, relations he may never fill. Moreover, he would be better fitted for these very relations, and whatever special work he might choose to do to earn his bread, by the complete development of all his faculties as an individual.

Just so with woman. The education that will fit her to discharge the duties in the largest sphere of human usefulness will best fit her for whatever special work she may be compelled to do.

The isolation of every human soul, and the necessity of self-dependence, must give each individual the right to choose his own surroundings.

The strongest reason for giving woman all the opportunities for higher education, for the full development of her faculties, forces of mind and body; for giving her the most enlarged freedom of thought and action; a complete emancipation from all forms of bondage, of custom, dependence, superstition; from all the crippling influences of fear — is the solitude and personal responsibility of her own individual life. The strongest reason why we ask for woman a voice in the government under which she lives; in the religion she is asked to believe; equality in social life, where she is the chief factor; a place in the trades and professions, where she may earn her bread, is because of her birthright to self-sovereignty; because, as an individual, she must rely on herself. No matter how much women prefer to lean, to be protected and supported, nor how much men desire to have them to do so, they must make the voyage of life alone, and for safety in an emergency, they must know something of the laws of navigation. To guide our own craft, we must be captain, pilot, engineer; with chart and compass to stand at the wheel; to watch the winds and waves, and know when to take in the sail, and to read the signs in the firmament over all. It matters not whether the solitary voyager is man or woman; nature, having endowed them equally, leaves them to their own skill and judgment in the hour of danger, and, if not equal to the occasion, alike they perish.

To appreciate the importance of fitting every human soul for independent action, think for a moment of the immeasurable solitude of self. We come into the world alone, unlike all who have gone before us; we leave it alone, under circumstances peculiar to ourselves.

No mortal ever has been, no mortal ever will be like the soul just launched on the sea of life. There can never again be just such a combination of prenatal influences; never again just such environments as make up the infancy, youth and manhood of this one. Nature never repeats herself, and the possibilities of one human soul will never be found in another. No one has ever found two blades of ribbon grass alike, and no one will ever find two human beings alike. Seeing, then, what must be the infinite diversity in human character, we can in a measure appreciate the loss to a nation when any large class of the people is uneducated and unrepresented in the government.

We ask for the complete development of every individual, first, for his own benefit and happiness. In fitting out an army, we give each soldier his own knapsack, arms, powder, his blanket, cup, knife, fork and spoon. We provide alike for all their individual necessities; then each man bears his own burden.

Again, we ask complete individual development for the general good; for the consensus of the competent on the whole round of human interests, on all questions of national life; and here each man must bear his share of the general burden. It is sad to see how soon friendless children are left to bear their own burdens, before they can analyze their feelings; before they can even tell their joys and sorrows, they are thrown on their own resources. The great lesson that nature seems to teach us at all ages is self-dependence, self-protection, self-support. What a touching instance of a child's solitude, of that hunger of the heart for love and recognition, in the case of the little girl who helped to dress a Christmas tree for the children of the family in which she served. On finding there was no present for herself, she slipped away in the darkness and spent the night in an open field sitting on a stone, and when found in the morning was weeping as if her heart would break. No mortal will ever know the thoughts that passed through the mind of that friendless child in the long hours of that cold night, with only the silent stars to keep her company. The mention of her case in the daily papers moved many generous hearts to send her presents, but in the hours of her keenest suffering she was thrown wholly on herself for consolation.

In youth our most bitter disappointments, our brightest hopes and ambitions, are known only to ourselves. Even our friendship and love we never fully share with another; there is something of every passion, in every situation, we conceal. Even so in our triumphs and our defeats. The successful candidate for the presidency, and his opponent, each has a solitude peculiarly his own, and good form forbids either to speak of his pleasure or regret. The solitude of the king on his throne and the prisoner in his cell differs in character and degree, but it is solitude, nevertheless.

We ask no sympathy from others in the anxiety and agony of a broken friendship or shattered love. When death sunders our nearest ties, alone we sit in the shadow of our affliction. Alike amid the greatest triumphs and darkest tragedies of life, we walk alone. On the divine heights of human attainment, eulogized and worshipped as a hero or saint, we stand alone. In ignorance, poverty and vice, as a pauper or criminal, alone we starve or steal; alone we suffer the sneers and rebuffs of our fellows; alone we are hunted and hounded through dark courts and alleys, in by-ways and highways; alone we stand in the judgment seat; alone in the prison cell we lament our crimes and misfortunes; alone we expiate them on the gallows. In hours like these we realize the awful solitude of individual life, its pains, its penalties, its responsibilities; hours in which the youngest and most helpless are thrown on their own resources for guidance and consolation. Seeing, then, that life must ever be a march and a battle, that each soldier must be equipped for his own protection, it is the height of cruelty to rob the individual of a single natural right.

To throw obstacles in the way of a complete education is like putting out the eyes; to deny the rights of property, like cutting off the hands. To deny political equality is to rob the ostracized of all self-respect; of credit in the market place; of recompense in the world of work; of a voice in those who make and administer the law; a choice in the jury before whom they are tried, and in the judge who decides their punishment. Shakespeare's play of "Titus Andronicus" contains a terrible satire on woman's position in the 19th century. Rude men (the play tells us) seized the king's daughter, cut out her tongue, cut off her hands, and then bade her go call for water and wash her hands. What a picture of woman's position! Robbed of her natural rights, handicapped by law and custom at every turn, yet compelled to fight her own battles, and in the emergencies of life to fall back on herself for protection.

The girl of sixteen, thrown on the world to support herself, to make her own place in society, to resist the temptations that surround her and maintain a spotless integrity, must do all this by native force or superior education. She does not acquire this power by being trained to trust others and distrust herself. If she wearies of the struggle, finding it hard work to swim up stream, and allows herself to drift with the current, she will find plenty of company, but not one to share her misery in the hour of her deepest humiliation. If she tries to retrieve her position, to conceal the past, her life is hedged about with fears lest willing hands should tear the veil from what she fain would hide. Young and friendless, *she* knows the bitter solitude of self.

How the little courtesies of life on the surface of society, deemed so important from man towards woman, fade into utter insignificance in view of the deeper tragedies in which she must play her part alone, where no human aid is possible!

The young wife and mother, at the head of some establishment, with a kind husband to shield her from the adverse winds of life, with wealth, fortune and position, has a certain harbor of safety, secure against the ordinary ills of life. But to manage a household, have a desirable influence in society, keep her friends and the affections of her husband, train her children and servants well, she must have rare common sense, wisdom, diplomacy, and a knowledge of human nature. To do all this, she needs the cardinal virtues and the strong points of character that the most successful statesman possesses. An uneducated woman trained to dependence, with no resources in herself, must make a failure of any position in life. But society says women do not need a knowledge of the world, the liberal training that experience in public life must give, all the advantages of collegiate education, but when for the lack of all this, the woman's happiness is wrecked, alone she bears her humiliation; and the solitude of the weak and the ignorant is indeed pitiable. In the wild chase for the prizes of life, they are ground to powder.

Imag[in]e when the pleasures of youth are passed, children grown up, married and gone, the hurry and bustle of life in a measure over, when the hands are weary of active service, when the old arm chair and the fireside are the chosen resorts, then men and women alike must fall back on their own resources. If they cannot find companionship in books, if they have no interest in the vital questions of the hour, no interest in watching the consummation of reforms with which they might have been identified, they soon pass into their dotage. The more fully the faculties of the mind are developed and kept in use, the longer the period of vigor and active interest in all around us continues. If, from a life-long participation in public affairs, a woman feels responsible for the laws regulating our system of education, the discipline of our jails and prisons, the sanitary condition of our private homes, public buildings and thoroughfares, an interest in commerce, finance, our foreign relations, in any or all these questions, her solitude will at least be respectable, and she will not be driven to gossip or scandal for entertainment.

The chief reason for opening to every soul the doors to the whole round of human duties and pleasures is the individual development thus attained, the resources thus provided under all circumstances to mitigate the solitude that at times must come to every one. I once asked Prince Kropotkin, a Russian Nihilist, how he endured his long years in prison deprived of books, pen, ink and paper. "Ah!" said he, "I thought out many questions in which I had a deep interest. In the pursuit of an idea, I took no note of time. When tired solving knotty problems, I recited all the beautiful passages in prose and verse I had ever learned. I became acquainted with myself, and my own resources. I had a world of my own, a vast empire, that no Russian jailer or Czar could invade." Such is the value of liberal thought and broad culture, when shut off from all human companionship, bringing comfort and sunshine within even the four walls of a prison cell.

As women ofttimes share a similar fate, should they not have all the consolation that the most liberal education can give? Their suffering in the prisons of St. Petersburg; in the long weary marches to Siberia, and in the mines, working side by side with men, surely call for all the self-support that the most exalted sentiments of heroism can give. When suddenly roused at midnight, with the startling cry of "Fire! Fire!" to find the house over their heads in flames, do women wait for men to point the way to safety? And are the men, equally bewildered, and half suffocated with smoke, in a position to do more than try to save themselves? At such times the most timid women have shown a courage and heroism, in saving their husbands and children, that has surprised everybody. Inasmuch, then, as woman shares equally the joys and sorrows of time and eternity, is it not the height of presumption in man to propose to represent her at the ballot box and the throne of grace, to do her voting in the State, her praying in the church, and to assume the position of High Priest at the family altar?

Nothing strengthens the judgment and quickens the conscience like individual responsibility; nothing adds such dignity to character as the recognition of one's self-sovereignty; the right to an equal place, everywhere conceded; a place earned by personal merit, not an artificial attainment by inheritance, wealth, family and position. Seeing, then, that the responsibilities of life rest equally on man and woman, that their destiny is the same, they need the same preparation for time and eternity. The talk of sheltering woman from the fierce storms of life is the sheerest mockery, for they beat on her from every point of the compass, just as they do on man, and with more fatal results, for he has been trained to protect himself, to resist, and to conquer. Such are the facts in human experience, the responsibilities of individual sovereignty. Rich and poor, intelligent and ignorant, wise and foolish, virtuous and vicious, man and woman; it is ever the same, each soul must depend wholly on itself.

Whatever the theories may be of woman's dependence on man, in the supreme moments of her life, he cannot bear her burdens. Alone she goes to the gates of death to give life to every man that is born into the world; no one can share her fears, no one can mitigate her pangs; and if her sorrow is greater than she can bear, alone she passes beyond the gates into the vast unknown.

From the mountain-tops of Judea long ago, a heavenly voice bade his disciples, "Bear ye one another's burdens" [Gal. 6:2]; but humanity has not yet risen to that point of self-sacrifice; and if ever so willing, how few the burdens are that one soul can bear for another! In the highways of Palestine; in prayer and fasting on the solitary mountain-top; in the Garden of Gethsemane; before the judgment-seat of Pilate; betrayed by one of his trusted disciples at his last supper; in his agonies on the cross, even Jesus of Nazareth, in those last sad days on earth, felt the awful solitude of self. Deserted by man, in agony he cries, "My God, my God, why hast thou forsaken me?" [Matt. 27:46; Mark 15:34]. And so it ever must be in the conflicting scenes of life, in the long, weary march, each one walks alone. We may have many friends, love, kindness, sympathy and charity, to smooth our pathway in everyday life, but in the tragedies and triumphs of human experience, each mortal stands alone.

But when all artificial trammels are removed, and women are recognized as individuals, responsible for their own environments, thoroughly educated for all positions in life they may be called to fill; with all the resources in themselves that liberal thought and broad culture can give; guided by their own conscience and judgment, trained to self-protection, by a healthy development of the muscular system, and skill in the use of weapons of defense; and stimulated to self-support by a knowledge of the business world and the pleasure that pecuniary independence must ever give; when women are trained in this way, they will in a measure be fitted for those hours of solitude that come alike to all, whether prepared or otherwise. As in our extremity we must depend on ourselves, the dictates of wisdom point to complete individual development.

In talking of education, how shallow the argument that each class must be educated for the special work it proposes to do, and that all those faculties not needed in this special walk must lie dormant and utterly wither for want of use, when, perhaps, these will be the very faculties needed in life's greatest emergencies! Some say, Where is the use of drilling girls in the languages, the sciences, in law, medicine, theology? As wives, mothers, housekeepers, cooks, they need a different curriculum from boys who are to fill all positions. The chief cooks in our great hotels and ocean steamers are men. In our large cities, men run the bakeries; they make our bread, cake and pies. They manage the laundries; they are now considered our best milliners and dressmakers. Because some men fill these departments of usefulness, shall we regulate the curriculum in Harvard and Yale to their present necessities? If not, why this talk in our best colleges of a curriculum for girls who are crowding into the trades and professions, teachers in all our public schools, rapidly filling many lucrative and honorable positions in life?

They are showing, too, their calmness and courage in the most trying hours of human experience. You have probably all read in the daily papers of the terrible storm in the Bay of Biscay, when a tidal wave made such havoc on the shore, wrecking vessels, unroofing houses, and carrying destruction everywhere. Among other buildings, the woman's prison was demolished. Those who escaped saw men struggling to reach the shore. They promptly, by clasping hands, made a chain of themselves, and pushed out into the sea, again and again, at the risk of their lives, until they had brought six men to shore, carried them to a shelter, and done all in their power for their comfort and protection.

What special school training could have prepared these women for this sublime moment in their lives? In times like this, humanity rises above all college curriculums, and recognizes nature as the greatest of all teachers in the hour of danger and death. Women are already the equals of men in the whole realm of thought, in art, science, literature and government. With telescopic vision they explore the starry firmament and bring back the history of the planetary spheres. With chart and compass they pilot ships across the mighty deep, and with skillful fingers send electric messages around the world. In galleries of art the beauties of nature and the virtues of humanity are immortalized by them on canvas, and by their inspired touch dull blocks of marble are transformed into angels of light. In music they speak again the language of Mendelssohn, Beethoven, Chopin, Schumann, and are worthy interpreters of their great thoughts. The poetry and novels of the century are theirs, and they have touched the keynote of reform, in religion, politics and social life. They fill the editor's and professor's chair, and plead at the bar of justice; walk the wards of the hospital, and speak from the pulpit and the platform. Such is the type of womanhood that an enlightened public sentiment welcomes to-day, and such the triumph of the facts of life over the false theories of the past.

Is it, then, consistent to hold the developed woman of this day within the same narrow political limits as the dame with the spinning-wheel and knitting-needle occupied in the past? No! no! Machinery has taken the labors of woman, as well as man, on its tireless shoulders, the loom and the spinning wheel are but dreams of the past; the pen, the brush, the easel, the chisel, have taken their places, while the hopes and ambitions of women are essentially changed.

We see reason sufficient in the outer conditions of human beings for individual liberty and development, but when we consider the self-dependence of every human soul we see the need of courage, judgment and the exercise of every faculty of mind and body, strengthened and developed by use, in woman as well as man.

Whatever may be said of man's protecting power in ordinary conditions, amid all the terrible disasters by land and sea, in the supreme moments of danger, alone woman must ever meet the horrors of the situation. The Angel of Death even makes no royal pathway for her. Man's love and sympathy enter only into the sunshine of our lives. In that solemn solitude of self, that links us with the immeasurable and the eternal, each soul lives alone forever. A recent writer says:

> I remember once, in crossing the Atlantic, to have gone upon the deck of the ship at midnight, when a dense black cloud enveloped the sky, and the great deep was roaring madly under the lashes of demoniac winds. My feeling was not of danger or fear (which is a base surrender of the immortal soul) but of utter desolation and loneliness; a little speck of life shut in by a tremendous darkness. Again I remember to have climbed the slopes of the Swiss Alps, up beyond the point where vegetation ceases, and the stunted conifers no longer struggle against the unfeeling blasts. Around me lay a huge confusion of rocks, out of which the gigantic ice peaks shot into the measureless blue of the heavens; and again my only feeling was the awful solitude.

And yet, there is a solitude which each and every one of us has always carried with him, more inaccessible than the ice-cold mountains, more profound than the midnight sea; the solitude of self. Our inner being which we call ourself, no eye nor touch of man or angel has ever pierced. It is more hidden than the caves of the gnome; the sacred adytum of the oracle; the hidden chamber of Eleusinian mystery, for to it only Omniscience is permitted to enter.

Such is individual life. Who, I ask you, can take, dare take on himself the rights, the duties, the responsibilities of another human soul?

## *Stanton's "The Solitude of Self": A Rationale for Feminism*

KARLYN KOHRS CAMPBELL

In 1892, near the end of her long career as a leader in the woman's rights movement,[1] Elizabeth Cady Stanton made her farewell address to the National American Woman Suffrage Association. The speech, "The Solitude of Self," is unlike the usual rhetoric of social activists of any period, and it is a startling departure from the typical speeches and arguments of nineteenth century feminists. The address is extraordinary because it is a philosophical statement of the principles and values underlying the struggle for woman's rights in the United States. It is also extraordinary because it is a social reformer's defense of humanistic individualism and because it is a rhetorical statement of the limits of those things which can be altered by words. In analyzing Stanton's address, I have two purposes: first, to use the speech as a means to discover and detail the ideology of nineteenth century feminism and, second, to examine its unusual features, particularly its lyric tone and its tragic perspective, to discover how and why it still has the power to speak to and move today's audience.

"The Solitude of Self" was delivered three times near the end of the long public career of Elizabeth Cady Stanton. It was first presented to the House Committee on the Judiciary on the morning of 18 January 1892. That afternoon Stanton delivered it to the twenty-fourth national convention of the National American Woman Suffrage Association as its retiring president. Two days later she repeated the speech at a hearing before the Senate Committee on Woman Suffrage.[2] The text of the speech was published subsequently in *The Woman's Journal*.[3] As presented to the congressional committees, the speech was part of the yearly lobbying effort of the association, made in conjunction with its national convention in Washington, D.C., to persuade Congress to pass a federal suffrage amendment.

Elizabeth Cady Stanton was a skilled rhetor who had spoken and testified frequently before legislative groups since her address to the New York State Legislature in 1854. Her earlier speeches demonstrate an ability to marshal evidence and to make cogent arguments and moving appeals. In 1892 she was seventy-six years old, and the wary contemporary critic may wonder whether the qualities of the speech reflect her rhetorical skills or her recognition of approaching death. Stanton lived for ten more years, however, and, in the period between the speech and her death, she published, with others, the two volumes of *The Woman's Bible*,[4] a work that is strong evidence of her energy, mental acuity, and continued dedication to social change. In sum, "The Solitude of Self" was addressed to policy makers and fellow activists by a highly skilled rhetor who, despite advanced age, was fully alert and actively engaged in efforts for reform.

Stanton was a prolific writer and speaker, but "The Solitude of Self" is unlike her other efforts. Although unusual, it was highly praised by her contemporaries. Susan Anthony, Stanton's close friend and co-worker, thought it "the speech of Mrs [sic] Stanton['s] life";[5] Anna Howard Shaw, an outstanding speaker in the early movement, called it "an English classic";[6] "it . . . is considered by many to be her masterpiece."[7] Rhetorically, the address violates nearly all traditional canons. It makes no arguments; it provides no evidence. The thesis, if it can be called that, is

> The strongest reason for giving woman all the opportunities for higher education, for the full development of her faculties, forces of mind and body; for giving her the most enlarged freedom of thought and action; a complete emancipation from all forms of bondage, of custom, dependence, superstition; from all the crippling influences of fear — is the solitude and personal responsibility of her own individual life.

It has no logical structure. It refers briefly at the outset to some shared values, but it makes no appeal to them. It has no proper introduction, and it ends abruptly with a pointed but poignant question. Yet, it retains still its power to speak, and, like John Chapman's address at Coatesville, it is "strange and moving."[8]

### The Lyric Mode

The speech is unusual, first, because it is a rhetorical act in the lyric mode. As a literary form, the lyric is defined as "a category of poetic literature that is distinguished from the narrative and dramatic . . . and is . . . characterized by subjectivity and sensuality of expression."[9] Lyric structure, in contrast to the narrative form of a novel or the climactic form of drama, is associative and develops through enumeration. Typically, the lyric poem attempts to explore and express all facets of a feeling or attitude in a series of statements related by the fact that they are all about a single subject; the parts are related to each other as the spokes of a wheel are related to the axle. A paradigmatic case is Elizabeth Barrett Browning's "How do I love thee? Let me count the ways." In addition, the lyric is intimate in tone, relies on personal experience, and uses sensual or aesthetic materials, including metaphor, to induce participation by the audience. The tone of the lyric is so subjective that it seems rhetorically inappropriate, as if one were washing emotional linen in public. For this reason, the lyric is described as a kind of indirect address that is "overheard" by the audience.

Stanton's speech exhibits these lyric qualities. It explores a single concept — the solitude of the human self, the idea that each person is unique, responsible, and alone. It begins with a string of associations: "The point I wish plainly to bring before you on this occasion is the individuality of each human soul; our Protestant idea, the right of individual conscience and judgment, our republican idea, individual citizenship" (p. 1). It develops by presenting a hierarchy in terms of which to discuss the rights of woman. Most fundamental is what belongs to her as an individual; next are her rights as a citizen; third are her rights which arise from the "incidental relations of life such as mother, wife, sister, daughter" (p. 1). The speech concerns itself exclusively with the most basic of these, her rights as an individual. Structurally, the speech is an exhaustive enumeration of human solitude in all its dimensions — through the stages of one's life from childhood to old age; in the varied roles of wife, mother, and widow; and in the extremities of poverty, childbirth, old age, catastrophe, and death. To encounter the speech is to experience the magnitude of human solitude.

Consistent with its lyric structure, the tone of the speech is intimate, and its language is sensual and figurative. As a member of the audience one confronts the existential reality of one's lonely life through imagery: Life is a solitary voyage that each makes alone; each person is a soldier who requires provisions from society but bears the burdens of fighting alone. The human condition is like the terrible solitude of Jesus — fasting and tempted on the mountain top, praying alone in Gethsemane, betrayed by a trusted intimate, and, in the agonies of death, abandoned even by God. In a concluding series of figurative comparisons, Stanton says,

> And yet, there is a solitude which each and every one of us has always carried with him, more inaccessible than the ice-cold mountains, more profound than the midnight sea; the solitude of self. Our inner being which we call ourself, no eye nor touch of man or angel has ever pierced. It is more hidden than the caves of the gnome: the sacred adytum of the oracle; the hidden chamber of Eleusinian mystery, for to it only Omniscience is permitted to enter.

Another paragraph illustrates the lyric tone and style, the appeal to personal experience and to the emotions engendered by extreme situations:

> Alike amid the greatest triumphs and darkest tragedies of life, we walk alone. On the divine heights of human attainment, eulogized and worshipped as a hero or saint, we stand alone. In ignorance, poverty and vice, as a pauper or criminal, alone we starve or steal; alone we suffer the sneers and rebuffs of our fellows; alone we are hunted and hounded through dark courts and alleys, in by-ways and highways; alone we stand in the judgment seat; alone in the prison cell we lament our crimes and misfortunes; alone we expiate them on the gallows. In hours like these we realize the awful solitude of individual life, its pains, its penalties, its responsibilities.

Repetition and parallelism are much used; the structure is associative; the evidence is the evocation of personal experiences. Consistent with other lyrical elements, Stanton's relationship to the audience is a kind of indirect address. Only the opening and closing sentences betray an unambiguous awareness of an immediate audience. The implied audience of the address is not composed of the delegates at the convention or the members of the congressional committees; it includes all persons. Stanton appears to be "musing aloud" about what it means to be a human being, and the audience is permitted to eavesdrop.

How does the lyric become rhetoric? How do these materials become instrumental to achieving woman's rights? The experience of the "solitude of self" breathes new life into the ideas of religious and political individualism. That individuals are unique, responsible, and alone is the philosophical basis for the Protestant concept of the priesthood of believers and the republican notion that rights are not granted by governments but inhere in persons. Members of the audience affirm these values more intensely because of the evocation of the experience of human solitude which underlies them.

Despite the universal appeals of such ideas, Stanton creates a sharp contrast between the condition of all humans and the special nature of woman's place. At one point the discrepancy is expressed in a vivid allusion:

> Shakespeare's play of "Titus Andronicus" contains a terrible satire on woman's position in the 19th century. Rude men (the play tells us) seized the king's daughter, cut out her tongue, cut off her hands, and then bade her to go call for water and wash her hands. What a picture of woman's position! Robbed of her natural rights, handicapped by law and custom at every turn, yet compelled to fight her own battles, and in the emergencies of life to fall back on herself for protection.

Stanton's speech tells one that woman, in all stages and conditions of life, is handicapped and yet responsible for her life. Woman's solitude of self becomes a dramatic refutation of the argument that woman is dependent on man or that she can be protected by man:

> Whatever the theories may be of woman's dependence on man, in the supreme moments of her life, he cannot bear her burdens. Alone she goes to the gates of death to give life to every man that is born into the world; no one can share her fears, no one can mitigate her pangs; and if her sorrow is greater than she can bear, alone she passes beyond the gates into the vast unknown.

Similarly, the unique quality of each individual is a refutation of the inferiority of woman, and individual solitude and responsibility entail the right to education and to other opportunities for development and the exercise of choice. Stanton comments, "The talk of sheltering woman from the fierce storms of life is the sheerest mockery, for they beat on her from every point of the compass, just as they do on man, and with more fatal results, for he has been trained to protect himself, to resist, and to conquer" (p. 32). The concept of self-sovereignty refutes the view that man can act for woman at the ballot box, in legislatures, on juries. Stanton's conclusion is a pointed question: "Who, I ask you, can take, dare take on himself, the rights, the duties, the responsibilities of another human soul?" (p. 32). That each person is unique, responsible, and alone refutes the view of woman as property; it implies her right to her wages, to own property, to sue and contract, to have a role in the custody of her children. Despite its associative structure, subjective tone, figurative language, and rather indirect address, the speech is a forceful rationale for the specific rights claimed by nineteenth century feminists.

### The Tragic Perspective

The form of the speech and its modes of expression are lyric, but its perspective is tragic, a philosophical stance common in literature but rare in rhetoric. Many analysts of literature see distinctions between comedy and tragedy as fundamental and significant. Langer describes them as the basis for two great artistic rhythms, and Frye treats them as two fundamental literary modes *(mythoi).*

As literary forms, comedy and tragedy have certain distinctive characteristics. The focus of tragedy is destiny or fate. Ordinarily, the protagonist is a hero or leader whose end is the inevitable outcome of a situation. Tragedy typically isolates the individual from the community whereas comedy incorporates the protagonist into society, and its happy, unifying ending is often related to the cleverness of the protagonist. Langer summarizes these differences:

> Destiny . . . as a future shaped essentially in advance and only incidentally by chance happenings, is Fate; and Fate is the "virtual future" created in tragedy. The "tragic rhythm of action". . . is the rhythm of man's life at its highest powers in the limits of his unique, death-bound career. Tragedy is the image of Fate, as comedy is of Fortune. . . . [T]ragedy is a fulfillment, and its form therefore is closed, final and passional. Tragedy is a mature art form . . . Its conception requires a sense of individuality which some religions and some cultures — even high cultures — do not generate.[10]

Briefly, then, tragedy emphasizes the isolation of the individual; comedy emphasizes integration into the community. Tragedy focuses on beginnings and endings, comedy on continuity. Tragedy reflects self-actualization — the individual at moments of greatest testing and achievement — whereas comedy affirms the cyclical survival of the species. Tragedy develops through inexorable fate; comedy involves fortune, which persons may influence through their wits. Langer,

Frye, and Burke all recognize the relationship between these modes and philosophical perspectives. Langer notes the relationship between tragedy and individualism; Frye speaks of a tragic philosophy of fate and a comic philosophy of providence;[11] Burke identifies the "tragic frame of acceptance" as the perspective which sets in motion what he calls the iron law of history.[12]

The tragic perspective in Stanton's speech is evident. Like tragedy, the speech focuses on the life of the individual. It emphasizes beginnings and endings; in fact, it reminds one vividly that suffering and death are the inevitable lot of humans. It isolates the individual from the community, focuses on fate as an element in human affairs, and emphasizes the crises in human experience. The tragic perspective limits rhetorical acts severely. Rhetoric usually is comic because, given its commitment to the efficacy of deliberation and social action, it must opt to emphasize rationality, the community, cyclical survival, and progress. In Stanton's tragic view, feminism cannot change the human condition. If all the laws are passed and all the changes made, humans, both male and female, will remain unique, responsible, and solitary individuals, forced to confront their inevitable trials in the solitude of their selves:

> But when all artificial trammels are removed, and women are recognized as individuals, responsible for their own environments, thoroughly educated for all positions in life they may be called to fill; with all the resources in themselves that liberal thought and broad culture can give; guided by their own conscience and judgment, trained to self-protection, by a healthy development of the muscular system, and skill in the use of weapons of defense; and stimulated to self-support by a knowledge of the business world and the pleasure that pecuniary independence must ever give: when women are trained in this way, they will in a measure be fitted for those hours of solitude *that come alike to all, whether prepared or otherwise.*

Stanton's tragic perspective limits her appeal although it offers some rhetorical advantages. For supporters, her tragic view of life dampens enthusiasm and lessens motivation for social reform as it reminds women of the limits of what can be achieved through the movement for women's rights. As depicted here, human life is a pain-filled struggle, a condition no reform can alter. Philosophically, Stanton denies the traditional American view of "progress," but her perspective has an important advantage. If one accepts the human ontology articulated in this speech, woman's rights are not a matter for justification or argument; they are entailed by the human condition.

For legislators and the public, her point of view has similar advantages and disadvantages. Her perspective has some force because it is fresh and unusual. Similarly, the speech indicates that women do not expect legislators to enact laws to usher in the golden age; as redefined by Stanton, legislation extending woman's rights simply provides an opportunity for individual effort. However, Stanton's perspective has the potential to intensify conflict. To deny Stanton's claims is to reject the concept of humankind affirmed by the dominant political philosophy and system of religious beliefs. One who disagrees is compelled to argue that women are not persons who may rightfully claim their rights as citizens or as children of God. Arguments based on such fundamental values polarize the audience and heighten disagreement.

However, it is not sufficient to describe Stanton's viewpoint as tragic, for her perspective is also existential, an emphasis which serves to qualify and modify the attitudes expressed in the speech.

### Humanism: The Lyric Modification of Tragedy

The interrelationship between form and substance in rhetoric is illustrated in this speech by the ways in which the qualities of lyric form, particularly its emphasis on the subjective and sensual, come to modify Stanton's tragic perspective.

Stanton's apparent choice of individualism as a philosophical posture could be rhetorically as well as axiologically problematic. Individualism can take the form of a malign social Darwinism used to blame individuals, including women, for their own oppression,[13] a point of view which rejects all reform efforts. Political individualism can become an anarchism that precludes social movements; and religious individualism, at its extreme, produces what Kierkegaard described as the "tragic hero," who acts on the dictates of his conscience to transcend the ethical rules of the community and whose reasons for actions are incommunicable to others.[14]

Stanton avoids these extremes because she opts, not for the philosophy or doctrine of individualism, but for a humanistic concern for the existential individual — the experience of the living person in the here and now. The changes Stanton seeks will alter the individual lives of real persons in the present, but there is in the speech no dream of progress toward a utopian state. In fact, as Stanton describes it, there is an element of absurdity in all reform efforts. No matter what is done to alter the circumstances of women and of men, they will continue to be unique, responsible, and alone; reforms may ease the struggles of individuals, but they cannot change the givens of every human life.[15] As she expresses it, "Rich and poor, intelligent and ignorant, wise and foolish, virtuous and vicious, man and woman; it is ever the same, each soul must depend wholly on itself" (p. 32). Stanton's tragic perspective is modified by an existential emphasis on the individual and an absurdist recognition of the limits of social change. These modifications produce a perspective that is philosophically humanistic.

As many of the citations have indicated, the speech concerns the conditions of humans, not just the concerns of females. The inclusion of and the appeals to males are both strategically desirable and philosophically consistent. Strategically, the agents of change in her immediate audience were males who held virtually all political and economic power. In this circumstance, there appears to be little conflict between pragmatic requirements and Stanton's principles. Early in the speech, as Stanton dismisses the significance of "social roles" as a basis for woman's rights, she uses the male as the standard from which the conclusion is drawn:

> In discussing the sphere of man, we do not decide his rights as an individual, as a citizen, as a man, by his duties as a father, a husband, a brother or a son, relations he may never fill. Moreover, he would be better fitted for these very relations, and whatever special work he might choose to do to earn his bread, by the complete development of all his faculties as an individual.
>
> Just so with woman.

Similarly, when she refers to the uniqueness of the individual, she says, "There can never again be just such . . . environments as make up the infancy, youth and manhood of this one," and she illustrated the need to rely on one's own resources with the example of Prince Piotr Alekseyevich Kropotkin's experiences in a Russian prison. Although nearly all of the examples in the speech are applicable to females in particular, one passage is noteworthy for its understanding of the constraints created by the male role:

> When suddenly roused at midnight, with the startling cry of "Fire! Fire!" to find the house over their heads in flames, do women wait for men to point the way to safety? And are the men, equally bewildered, and half suffocated with smoke, in a position to do more than try to save themselves?

In other words, not only are men incapable of protecting women from the vicissitudes of life, but it is unjust to demand that they should attempt to do so. Clearly, the philosophical bases of feminism are, for Stanton, humanistic, and the goals of the movement are goals for persons, for human beings. In Stanton's words, "We see reason sufficient in the outer conditions of human beings for individual liberty and development, but when we consider the self-dependence of every human soul we see the need of courage, judgment and the exercise of every faculty of mind and body, strengthened and developed by use, *in woman as well as man*" (p. 32; emphasis added).

As Stanton addressed male legislators and her brothers and sisters in the National American Woman Suffrage Association, she reminded them of the common philosophical precepts which are alike the foundations of Protestantism, republicanism, and feminism — the principles of humanism. She also reminded them of the wider meaning of feminism; it is a movement not solely aimed at the vote for women, but at equality and opportunity in all areas of life and for all persons. This is a speech for woman's rights broadly conceived; more properly, it is a speech for human rights.

In her first public speech at the convention in 1848 at Seneca Falls, New York, Stanton said:

> Woman herself must do this work; for woman alone can understand the height, the depth, the length, and the breadth of her own degradation. Man cannot speak for her, because he has been educated to believe that she differs from him so materially, that he cannot judge of her thoughts, feelings, and opinions by his own. Moral beings can only judge of others by themselves.[16]

Now, at the end of her speaking career, Stanton demonstrates her moral preeminence as one who can see and feel the conditions of others through herself. As a result, she speaks for all women, of all ages, in all roles, and in all conditions of life; indeed, she speaks for all persons, rich and poor, male and female, educated and uneducated. What she expresses and evokes is the nature of the human condition, and what her audience experiences is the lonely and troubled solitude of the individual for which each person requires all of the opportunities that can be provided by society.

Reformers, especially those who seek significant social change, are more than a little threatening. One fears the changes they seek and their energetic, sure-minded persistence. Rarely, if ever, do they show that they know the limits of the benefits that can be wrought through political, social, and economic reform. Although Stanton's depiction of the human condition is a terrifying one, it is reassuring to discover that a determined activist understood the inevitable and immutable elements of human life. As presented by Stanton, feminism is a humanistic movement for individual opportunity and choice, but it will not solve the problems of human life.

## Conclusion

"The Solitude of Self" is a statement about the meaning of feminism. Philosophically, it reminds us of the conditions of every human life:

that each of us is unique, responsible, and alone. These conditions entail the republican principle of natural rights and the religious principle of individual conscience. If women are persons, they merit access to every opportunity that will assist them in the human struggle. Stanton's speech enables us to understand why, by its nature and from its inception, feminism is grounded in humanism.

The address is also a rhetorical act that achieves its ends through poetic means. In contrast to more familiar forms of logical argumentation, the speech is nondiscursive and nonpropositional. However, as we encounter the solitude of human life as evoked through imagery, description, and example, we recall and reaffirm the bases for our most fundamental beliefs.

Stanton's speech is a rare moment in the protest rhetoric of a social movement. The address hardly mentions, and quickly abandons, the specific justifications for woman suffrage. There is mention made of, but only the slightest emphasis placed upon, the need to grant women the vote, educational and economic opportunity, and legal equality. It might seem that the speech would fail because it had lost sight of its purpose, but, in fact, the speech succeeds because it has set forth a new and deeper purpose. No matter what else is true of the oppression of women, whenever the right to vote and to legal, educational, and economic equality are denied them, men are presuming, out of motives malign or benign, to take responsibility for those women. And it is just here that Stanton's argument, lyric and tragic though it is, attains its full power. Men cannot take responsibility for women, as Stanton's examples so simply demonstrate. Men can take responsibility only for themselves, and, of course, women are the only ones who can be responsible for themselves. As presented in the speech, the rights of women are not achieved at the cost of the rights of others; woman's rights are a natural and necessary part of the human birthright.

Although the laws that interfere with this individual responsibility must be changed, Stanton was entirely aware that such changes will mean only that men and women will face the crucial moments of their lives in equal solitude. The reforms Stanton desired would result in precious little change, but how precious that little.

## *Notes*

1. The best history of the woman's rights movements in the United States is Eleanor Flexner, *Century of Struggle,* rev. ed. (Cambridge: Harvard Univ. Press, 1975). See, also, Andrew Sinclair, *The Better Half: The Emancipation of the American Woman* (New York: Harper, 1965). Stanton's leadership is

demonstrated in many ways: She was one of the five women who organized the Seneca Falls, N.Y., Convention in 1848; she edited *The Revolution* (1868–1870); and she was president of the National Woman Suffrage Association (1869–1890) and of the combined National American Woman Suffrage Association (1890–1892).

2. The speech was read for Stanton before the House Committee on the Judiciary, but she delivered it herself before the convention and before the Senate Committee on Woman Suffrage. See Aileen S. Kraditor, *The Ideas of the Woman Suffrage Movement, 1890–1920* (New York: Columbia Univ. Press, 1965), p. 46. The speech was favorably received by the congressional committees: "The Senate Committee made a favorable majority report. The House Committee were so impressed by her speech that they had 10,000 copies reprinted from the Congressional Record and sent throughout the country." See Alma Lutz, *Created Equal: A Biography of Elizabeth Cady Stanton, 1815–1902* (New York: John Day, 1940), p. 290.
3. *The Woman's Journal*, 23 January 1892, pp. 1 and 32. All citations from the speech are from this source, and all subsequent references will be in the text.
4. Elizabeth Cady Stanton and others, *The Woman's Bible*, Two parts (New York: European Publishing Co., 1895, 1898). In addition to Stanton, seven persons wrote commentaries for volume one, eight persons for volume two. Altogether twenty women collaborated on what was called "The Revising Committee" that produced these works. The volumes were reprinted in 1972 by Arno Press, New York.
5. Susan B. Anthony to Elizabeth Boynton Harbert, 12 August 1901, Harbert Papers, Radcliffe Women's Archives, cited by Kraditor, p. 46, n. 4.
6. Lutz, p. 290.
7. Susan B. Anthony and Ida Husted Harper, eds., *History of Woman Suffrage*, IV, 1883–1900 (Rochester, N.Y.: Charles Mann, 1902), 186.
8. Edmund Wilson's assessment of Chapman's speech is cited by Edwin Black, *Rhetorical Criticism: A Study in Method* (New York: Macmillan, 1965), p. 83.
9. *The American Heritage Dictionary of the English Language* (Boston: Houghton Mifflin, 1969).
10. Susanne K. Langer, *Feeling and Form* (New York: Scribner's, 1953), pp. 333–34.
11. Northrop Frye, *Anatomy of Criticism* (Princeton: Princeton Univ. Press, 1957), p. 64.
12. Kenneth Burke, *The Rhetoric of Religion: Studies in Logology* (Boston: Beacon, 1961), pp. 4–5.
13. See particularly the speech of the Reverend Antoinette Brown Blackwell in the debate on resolutions concerning marriage and divorce at the National Woman's Rights Convention, New York, 1860, in Elizabeth Cady Stanton, Susan B. Anthony, and Mathilda Joslyn Gage, eds., *The History of Woman Suffrage*, I, 1848–1861 (Rochester, N.Y.: Charles Mann, 1887), 724–29.
14. Soren Kierkegaard, *Fear and Trembling: A Dialectical Lyric*, trans. Walter Lowrie (1941; rpt. New York: Anchor, 1954), pp. 64–77, 91–129.
15. The philosophy of individualism is one which places the interests of the individual above those of the society or social group, and it is illustrated in the political philosophy of Thomas Hobbes or the views currently expressed by Ayn Rand. In contrast, humanism is a philosophy or attitude concerned with the achievements, interests, and welfare of human beings

rather than with abstract beings or theoretical concepts. Stanton's humanism is quite similar to the existential and absurdist humanism articulated by Jean-Paul Sartre in "Existentialism is a Humanism," in *Existentialism from Dostoevsky to Sartre,* ed. Walter Kaufmann (Cleveland: Meridian, 1956), pp. 287–311, and in "Introduction to *Les Temps Modernes,*" trans. Françoise Ehrmann, in *Paths to the Present: Aspects of European Thought from Romanticism to Existentialism,* ed. Eugen Weber (New York: Dodd, Mead, 1962), 432–41. Sartre there wrote that human life is limited by certain givens, "the necessity of being born and dying, of being *finite,* and existing in a world among other men" (p. 438).

16. *Proceedings of the Woman's Rights Conventions, Held at Seneca Falls & Rochester, N.Y., July & August, 1848* (New York: Johnston, 1870), p. 3.

# 10

# Critical Reading of Abraham Lincoln's Cooper Union Address

## *The Cooper Union Address*

ABRAHAM LINCOLN

*Mr. President and Fellow-citizens of New York:* The facts with which I shall deal this evening are mainly old and familiar; nor is there anything new in the general use I shall make of them. If there shall be any novelty, it will be in the mode of presenting the facts, and the inferences and observations following that presentation. In his speech last autumn at Columbus, Ohio, as reported in the "New-York Times," Senator Douglas said:

> Our fathers, when they framed the government under which we live, understood this question just as well, and even better, than we do now.

I fully indorse this, and I adopt it as a text for this discourse. I so adopt it because it furnishes a precise and an agreed starting-point for a discussion between Republicans and that wing of the Democracy headed by Senator Douglas. It simply leaves the inquiry: What was the understanding those fathers had of the question mentioned?

What is the frame of government under which we live? The answer must be, "The Constitution of the United States." That Constitution consists of the original, framed in 1787, and under which the present government first went into operation, and twelve subsequently framed amendments, the first ten of which were framed in 1789.

Who were our fathers that framed the Constitution? I suppose the "thirty-nine" who signed the original instrument may be fairly called our fathers who framed that part of the present government. It is almost exactly true to say they framed it, and it is altogether true to say they fairly represented the opinion and sentiment of the whole nation at that time. Their names, being familiar to nearly all, and accessible to quite all, need not now be repeated.

I take these "thirty-nine," for the present, as being "our fathers who framed the government under which we live." What is the question which, according to the text, those fathers understood "just as well, and even better, than we do now"?

It is this: Does the proper division of local from Federal authority, or anything in the Constitution, forbid our Federal Government to control as to slavery in our Federal Territories?

Upon this, Senator Douglas holds the affirmative, and Republicans the negative. This affirmation and denial form an issue; and this issue — this question — is precisely what the text declares our fathers understood "better than we." Let us now inquire whether the "thirty-nine," or any of them, ever acted upon this question; and if they did, how they acted upon it — how they expressed that better understanding. In 1784, three years before the Constitution, the United States then owning the Northwestern Territory, and no other, the Congress of the Confederation had before them the question of prohibiting slavery in that Territory; and four of the "thirty-nine" who afterward framed the Constitution were in that Congress, and voted on that question. Of these, Roger Sherman, Thomas Mifflin, and Hugh Williamson voted for the prohibition, thus showing that, in their understanding, no line dividing local from Federal authority, nor anything else, properly forbade the Federal Government to control as to slavery in Federal territory. The other of the four, James McHenry, voted against the prohibition, showing that for some cause he thought it improper to vote for it.

In 1787, still before the Constitution, but while the convention was in session framing it, and while the Northwestern Territory still was the only Territory owned by the United States, the same question of prohibiting slavery in the Territory again came before the Congress of the Confederation; and two more of the "'thirty-nine" who afterward signed the Constitution were in that Congress and voted on the question. They were William Blount and William Few; and they both voted for the prohibition — thus showing that in their understanding no line dividing local from Federal authority, nor anything else, properly forbade the Federal Government to control as to slavery in Federal territory. This time the prohibition became a law, being part of what is now well known as the ordinance of '87.

The question of Federal control of slavery in the Territories seems not to have been directly before the convention which framed the original Constitution; and hence it is not recorded that the "thirty-nine," or any of them, while engaged on that instrument, expressed any opinion on that precise question.

In 1789, by the first Congress which sat under the Constitution, an act was passed to enforce the ordinance of '87, including the prohibition of slavery in the Northwestern Territory. The bill for this act was reported by one of the "thirty-nine" — Thomas Fitzsimmons, then a member of the House of Representatives from Pennsylvania. It went through all its stages without a word of opposition, and finally passed both branches without ayes and nays, which is equivalent to a unanimous passage. In this Congress there were sixteen of the thirty-nine fathers who framed the original Constitution. They were John Langdon, Nicholas Gilman, Wm. S. Johnson, Roger Sherman, Robert Morris, Thos. Fitzsimmons, William Few, Abraham Baldwin, Rufus King, William Patterson, George Clymer, Richard Bassett, George Read, Pierce Butler, Daniel Carroll, and James Madison.

This shows that, in their understanding, no line dividing local from Federal authority, nor anything in the Constitution, properly forbade Congress to prohibit slavery in the Federal territory; else both their fidelity to correct principle, and their oath to support the Constitution, would have constrained them to oppose the prohibition.

Again, George Washington, another of the "thirty-nine," was then President of the United States, and as such approved and signed the bill, thus completing its validity as a law, and thus showing that, in his understanding, no line dividing local from Federal authority, nor anything in the Constitution, forbade the Federal Government to control as to slavery in Federal territory.

No great while after the adoption of the original Constitution, North Caroline ceded to the Federal Government the country now constituting the State of Tennessee; and a few years later Georgia ceded that which now constitutes the States of Mississippi and Alabama. In both deeds of cession it was made a condition by the ceding States that the Federal Government should not prohibit slavery in the ceded country. Under these circumstances, Congress, on taking charge of these countries, did not absolutely prohibit slavery within them. But they did interfere with it — take control of it — even there, to a certain extent. In 1798 Congress organized the Territory of Mississippi. In the act of organization they prohibited the bringing of slaves into the Territory from any place without the United States, by fine, and giving freedom to slaves so brought. This act passed both branches of Congress without yeas and nays. In that Congress were three of the "thirty-nine" who framed the original Constitution. They were John Langdon, George Read, and Abraham Baldwin. They all probably voted for it. Certainly they would have placed their opposition to it upon record if, in their understanding, any line dividing local from Federal authority, or anything in the Constitution, properly forbade the Federal Government to control as to slavery in Federal territory.

In 1803 the Federal Government purchased the Louisiana country. Our former territorial acquisitions came from certain of our own States; but this Louisiana country was acquired from a foreign nation. In 1804 Congress gave a territorial organization to that part of it which now constitutes the State of Louisiana. New Orleans, lying within that part, was an old and comparatively large city. There were other considerable towns and settlements, and slavery was extensively and thoroughly intermingled with the people. Congress did not, in the Territorial Act, prohibit slavery; but they did interfere with it — take control of it — in a more marked and extensive way than they did in the case of Mississippi. The substance of the provision therein made in relation to slaves was:

1st. That no slave should be imported into the Territory from foreign parts.

2d. That no slave should be carried into it who had been imported into the United States since the first day of May 1798.

3d. That no slave should be carried into it, except by the owner, and for his own use as a settler; the penalty in all the cases being a fine upon the violator of the law, and freedom to the slave.

This act also was passed without ayes or nays. In the Congress which passed it there were two of the "thirty-nine." They were Abraham Baldwin and Jonathan Dayton. As stated in the case of Mississippi, it is probable they both voted for it. They would not have allowed it to pass without recording their opposition to it if, in their understanding, it violated either the line properly dividing local from Federal authority, or any provision of the Constitution.

In 1819–20 came and passed the Missouri question. Many votes were taken, by yeas and nays, in both branches of Congress, upon the various phases of the general question. Two of the "thirty-nine" — Rufus King and Charles Pinckney — were members of that Congress. Mr. King steadily voted for slavery prohibition and against all compromises, while Mr. Pinckney as steadily voted against slavery prohibition and against all compromises. By this, Mr. King showed that, in his understanding, no line dividing local from Federal authority, nor anything in the Constitution, was violated by Congress prohibiting slavery in Federal territory; while Mr. Pinckney, by his votes, showed that, in his understanding, there was some sufficient reason for opposing such prohibition in that case.

The cases I have mentioned are the only acts of the "thirty-nine," or of any of them, upon the direct issue, which I have been able to discover.

To enumerate the persons who thus acted as being four in 1784, two in 1787, seventeen in 1789, three in 1798, two in 1804, and two in 1819–20, there would be thirty of them. But this would be counting John Langdon, Roger Sherman, William Few, Rufus King, and George Read each twice, and Abraham Baldwin three times. The true number of those of the "thirty-nine" whom I have shown to have acted upon the question which, by the text, they understood better than we, is twenty-three, leaving sixteen now shown to have acted upon it in any way.

Here, then, we have twenty-three out of our thirty-nine fathers "who framed the government under which we live," who have, upon their official responsibility and their corporal oaths, acted upon the very question which the text affirms they "understood just as well, and even better, than we do now"; and twenty-one of them — a clear majority of the whole "thirty-nine" — so acting upon it as to make them guilty of gross political impropriety and wilful perjury if, in their understanding, any proper division between local and Federal authority, or anything in the Constitution they had made themselves, and sworn to support, forbade the Federal Government to control as to slavery in the Federal Territories. Thus the twenty-one acted; and, as actions speak louder than words, so actions under such responsibility speak still louder.

Two of the twenty-three voted against congressional prohibition of slavery in the Federal Territories, in the instances in which they acted upon the question. But for what reasons they so voted is not known. They may have done so because they thought a proper division of local from Federal authority, or some provision or principle of the Constitution, stood in the way; or they may, without any such question, have voted against the prohibition on what appeared to them to be sufficient grounds of expediency. No one who has sworn to support the Constitution can conscientiously vote for what he understands to be an unconstitutional measure, however expedient he may think it; but one may and ought to vote against a measure which he deems constitutional if, at the same time, he deems it inexpedient. It, therefore, would be unsafe to set down even the two who voted against the prohibition as having done so because, in their understanding, any proper division of local from Federal authority, or anything in the Constitution, forbade the Federal Government to control as to slavery in Federal territory.

The remaining sixteen of the "thirty-nine," so far as I have discovered, have left no record of their understanding upon the direct question of Federal control of slavery in the Federal territories. But there is much reason to believe that their understanding upon that question would not have appeared different from that of their twenty-three compeers, had it been manifested at all.

For the purpose of adhering rigidly to the text, I have purposely omitted whatever understanding may have been manifested by any person, however distinguished, other than the thirty-nine fathers who framed the original Constitution; and, for the same reason, I have also omitted whatever understanding may have been manifested by any of the "thirty-nine" even on any other phase of the general question of slavery. If we should look into their acts and declarations on those other phases, as the foreign slave-trade, and the morality and policy of slavery generally, it would appear to us that on the direct question of Federal control of slavery in Federal Territories, the sixteen, if they had acted at all, would probably have acted just as the twenty-three did. Among that sixteen were several of the most noted antislavery men of those times, — as Dr. Franklin, Alexander Hamilton, and Gouverneur Morris, — while there was not one now known to have been otherwise, unless it may be John Rutledge, of South Carolina.

The sum of the whole is that of our thirty-nine fathers who framed the original Constitution, twenty-one — a clear majority of the whole — certainly understood that no proper division of local from Federal authority, nor any part of the Constitution, forbade the Federal Government to control slavery in the Federal Territories; while all the rest had probably the same understanding. Such, unquestionably, was the understanding of our fathers who framed the original Constitution; and the text affirms that they understood the question "better than we."

But, so far, I have been considering the understanding of the question manifested by the framers of the original Constitution. In and by the original instrument, a mode was provided for amending it; and, as I have already stated, the present frame of "the government under which we live" consists of that original, and twelve amendatory articles framed and adopted since. Those who now insist that Federal control of slavery in Federal Territories violates the Constitution, point us to the provisions which they suppose it thus violates; and, as I understand, they all fix upon provisions in these amendatory articles, and not in the original instrument. The Supreme Court, in the Dred Scott case, plant themselves upon the fifth amendment, which provides that no person shall be deprived of "life, liberty, or property without due process of law"; while Senator Douglas and his peculiar adherents plant themselves upon the tenth amendment, providing that "the powers not delegated to the United States by the Constitution" "are reserved to the States respectively, or to the people."

Now, it so happens that these amendments were framed by the first Congress which sat under the Constitution — the identical Congress which passed the act, already mentioned, enforcing the prohibition of slavery in the Northwestern Territory. Not only was it the same Congress, but they were the identical, same individual men who, at the same session, and at the same time within the session, had under consideration, and in progress toward maturity, these constitutional amendments, and this act prohibiting slavery in all the territory the nation then owned. The constitutional amendments were introduced before, and passed after, the act enforcing the ordinance of '87; so that, during the whole pendency of the act to enforce the ordinance, the constitutional amendments were also pending.

The seventy-six members of that Congress, including sixteen of the framers of the original Constitution, as before stated, were preeminently our fathers who framed that part of "the government under which we live" which is now claimed as forbidding the Federal Government to control slavery in the Federal Territories.

Is it not a little presumptuous in any one at this day to affirm that the two things which that Congress deliberately framed, and carried to maturity at the same time, are absolutely inconsistent with each other? And does not such affirmation become impudently absurd when coupled with the other affirmation, from the same mouth, that those who did the two things alleged to be inconsistent, understood whether they really were inconsistent better than we — better than he who affirms that they are inconsistent?

It is surely safe to assume that the thirty-nine framers of the original Constitution, and the seventy-six members of the Congress which framed the amendments thereto, taken together, do certainly include those who may be fairly called "our fathers who framed the government under which we live." And so assuming, I defy any man to show that any one of them ever, in his whole life, declared that, in his understanding, any proper division of local from Federal authority, or any part of the Constitution, forbade the Federal Government to control as to slavery in the Federal Territories. I go a step further. I defy any one to show that any living man in the whole world ever did, prior to the beginning of the present century (and I might almost say prior to the beginning of the last half of the present century), declare that, in his understanding, any proper division of local from Federal authority, or any part of the Constitution, forbade the Federal Government to control as to slavery in the Federal Territories. To those who now so declare I give not only "our fathers who framed the government under which we live," but with them all other living men within the century in which it was framed, among whom to search, and they shall not be able to find the evidence of a single man agreeing with them.

Now, and here, let me guard a little against being misunderstood. I do not mean to say we are bound to follow implicitly in whatever our fathers did. To do so would be to discard all the lights of current experience — to reject all progress, all improvement. What I do say is that if we would supplant the opinions and policy of our fathers in any case, we should do so upon evidence so conclusive, and argument so clear, that even their great authority, fairly considered and weighed, cannot stand; and most surely not in a case whereof we ourselves declare they understood the question better than we.

If any man at this day sincerely believes that a proper division of local from Federal authority, or any part of the Constitution, forbids the Federal Government to control as to slavery in the Federal Territories, he is right to say so, and to enforce his position by all truthful evidence and fair argument which he can. But he has no right to mislead others, who have less access to history, and less leisure to study it, into the false belief that "our fathers who framed the government under which we live" were of the same opinion — thus substituting falsehood and deception for truthful evidence and fair argument. If any man at this day sincerely believes "our fathers who framed the government under which we live" used and applied principles, in other cases, which ought to have led them to understand that a proper division of local from Federal authority, or some part of the Constitution, forbids the Federal Government to control as to slavery in the Federal Territories, he is right to say so. But he should, at the same time, brave the responsibility of declaring that, in his opinion, he understands their principles better than they did themselves; and especially should he not shirk that responsibility by asserting that they "understood the question just as well, and even better, than we do now."

But enough! Let all who believe that "our fathers who framed the government under which we live understood this question just as well, and even better, than we do now," speak as they spoke, and act as they acted upon it. This is all Republicans ask — all Republicans desire — in relation to slavery. As those fathers marked it, so let it be again marked, as an evil not to be extended, but to be tolerated and protected only because of and so far as its actual presence among us makes that toleration and protection a necessity. Let all the guaranties those fathers gave it be not grudgingly, but fully and fairly, maintained. For this Republicans contend, and with this, so far as I know or believe, they will be content.

And now, if they would listen, — as I suppose they will not, — I would address a few words to the Southern people.

I would say to them: You consider yourselves a reasonable and a just people; and I consider that in the general qualities of reason and justice you are not inferior to any other people. Still, when you speak of us Republicans, you do so only to denounce us as reptiles, or, at the best, as no better than outlaws. You will grant a hearing to pirates or murderers, but nothing like it to "Black Republicans." In all your contentions with one another, each of you deems an unconditional condemnation of "Black Republicanism" as the first thing to be attended to. Indeed, such condemnation of us seems to be an indispensable prerequisite — license, so to speak — among you to be admitted or permitted to speak at all. Now can you or not be prevailed upon to pause and to consider whether this is quite just to us, or even to yourselves? Bring forward your charges and specifications, and then be patient long enough to hear us deny or justify.

You say we are sectional. We deny it. That makes an issue; and the burden of proof is upon you. You produce your proof; and what is it? Why, that our party has no existence in your section — gets no votes in your section. The fact is substantially true; but does it prove the issue? If it does, then in case we should, without change of principle, begin to get votes in your section, we should thereby cease to be sectional. You cannot escape this conclusion; and yet, are you willing to abide by it? If you are, you will probably soon find that we have ceased to be sectional, for we shall get votes in your section this very year. You will then begin to discover, as the truth plainly is, that your proof does not touch the issue. The fact that we get no votes in your section is a fact of your making, and not of ours. And if there be fault in that fact, that fault is primarily yours and remains so until you show that we repel you by some wrong principle or practice. If we do repel you by any wrong principle or practice, the fault is ours; but this brings you to where you ought to have started — to a discussion of the right or wrong of our principle. If our principle, put in practice, would wrong your section for the benefit of ours, or for any other object, then our principle, and we with it, are sectional, and are justly opposed and denounced as such. Meet us, then, on the question of whether our principle, put in practice, would wrong your section; and so meet us as if it were possible that something may be said on our side. Do you accept the challenge? No! Then you really believe that the principle which "our fathers who framed the government under which we live" thought so clearly right as to adopt it, and indorse it again and again, upon their official oaths, is in fact so clearly wrong as to demand your condemnation without a moment's consideration.

Some of you delight to flaunt in our faces the warning against sectional parties given by Washington in his Farewell Address. Less than eight years before Washington gave that warning, he had, as President of the United States, approved and signed an act of Congress enforcing the prohibition of slavery in the Northwestern Territory, which act embodied the policy of the government upon that subject up to and at the very moment he penned that warning; and about one year after he penned it, he wrote Lafayette that he considered that prohibition a wise measure, expressing in the same connection his hope that we should at some time have a confederacy of free States.

Bearing this in mind, and seeing that sectionalism has since arisen upon this same subject, is that warning a weapon in your hands against us, or in our hands against you? Could Washington himself speak, would he cast the blame of that sectionalism upon us, who sustain his policy, or upon you, who repudiate it? We respect that warning of Washington, and we commend it to you, together with his example pointing to the right application of it.

But you say you are conservative — eminently conservative — while we are revolutionary, destructive or something of the sort. What is conservatism? Is it not adherence to the old and tried, against the new and untried? We stick to, contend for, the identical old policy on the point in controversy which was adopted by "our fathers who framed the government under which we live"; while you with one accord reject, and scout, and spit upon that old policy, and insist upon substituting something new. True, you disagree among yourselves as to what that substitute shall be. You are divided on new propositions and plans, but you are unanimous in rejecting and denouncing the old policy of the fathers. Some of you are for reviving the foreign slave-trade; some for a congressional slave code for the Territories; some for Congress forbidding the Territories to prohibit slavery within their limits; some for maintaining slavery in the Territories through the judiciary; some for the "gur-reat pur-rinciple" that "if one man would enslave another, no third man should object," fantastically called "popular sovereignty"; but never a man among you is in favor of Federal prohibition of slavery in Federal Territories, according to the practice of "our fathers who framed the government under which we live." Not one of all your various plans can show a precedent or an advocate in the century within which our government originated. Consider, then, whether your claim of conservatism for yourselves, and your charge of destructiveness against us, are based on the most clear and stable foundations.

Again, you say we have made the slavery question more prominent than it formerly was. We deny it. We admit that it is more prominent, but we deny that we made it so. It was not we, but you, who discarded the old policy of the fathers. We resisted, and still resist, your innovation; and thence comes the greater prominence of the question. Would you have that question reduced to its former proportions? Go back to that old policy. What has been will be again, under the same conditions. If you would have the peace of the old times, readopt the precepts and policy of the old times.

You charge that we stir up insurrections among your slaves. We deny it; and what is your proof? Harper's Ferry! John Brown!! John Brown was no Republican; and you have failed to implicate a single Republican in his Harper's Ferry enterprise. If any member of our party is guilty in that matter, you know it, or you do not know it. If you do know it, you are inexcusable for not designating the man and proving the fact. If you do not know it, you are inexcusable for asserting it, and especially for persisting in the assertion after you have tried and failed to make the proof. You need not be told that persisting in a charge which one does not know to be true, is simply malicious slander.

Some of you admit that no Republican designedly aided or encouraged the Harper's Ferry affair, but still insist that our doctrines and declarations necessarily lead to such results. We do not believe it. We know we hold no doctrine, and make no declaration, which were not held to and made by "our fathers who framed the government under which we live." You never dealt fairly by us in relation to this affair. When it occurred, some important State elections were near at hand, and you were in evident glee with the belief that, by charging the blame upon us, you could get the advantage of us in those elections. The elections came, and your expectations were not quite fulfilled. Every Republican man knew that, as to himself at least, your charge was a slander, and he was not much inclined by it to cast his vote in your favor. Republican doctrines and declarations are accompanied with a continual protest against any interference whatever with your slaves, or with you about your slaves. Surely, this does not encourage them to revolt. True, we do, in common with "our fathers who framed the government under which we live," declare our belief that slavery is wrong; but the slaves do not hear us declare even this. For anything we say or do, the slaves would scarcely know there is a Republican party. I believe they would not, in fact, generally know it but for your misrepresentations of us in their hearing. In your political contests among yourselves, each faction charges the other with sympathy with Black Republicanism; and then, to give point to the charge, defines Black Republicanism to simply be insurrection, blood, and thunder among the slaves.

Slave insurrections are no more common now than they were before the Republican party was organized. What induced the Southampton insurrection, twenty-eight years ago, in which at least three times as many lives were lost as at Harper's Ferry? You can scarcely stretch your very elastic fancy to the conclusion that Southampton was "got up by Black Republicanism." In the present state of things in the United States, I do not think a general, or even a very extensive, slave insurrection is possible. The indispensable concert of action cannot be attained. The slaves have no means of rapid communication; nor can incendiary freemen, black or white, supply it. The explosive materials are everywhere in parcels; but there neither are, nor can be supplied, the indispensable connecting trains.

Much is said by Southern people about the affection of slaves for their masters and mistresses; and a part of it, at least, is true. A plot for an uprising could scarcely be devised and communicated to twenty individuals before some one of them, to save the life of a favorite master or mistress, would divulge it. This is the rule; and the slave revolution in Hayti was not an exception to it, but a case occurring under peculiar circumstances. The gunpowder plot of British history, though not connected with slaves, was more in point. In that case, only about twenty were admitted to the secret; and yet one of them, in his anxiety to save a friend, betrayed the plot to that friend, and, by consequence, averted the calamity. Occasional poisonings from the kitchen, and open or stealthy assassinations in the field, and local revolts extending to a score or so, will continue to occur as the natural results of slavery; but no general insurrection of slaves, as I think, can happen in this country for a long time. Whoever much fears, or much hopes, for such an event, will be alike disappointed.

In the language of Mr. Jefferson, uttered many years ago, "It is still in our power to direct the process of emancipation and deportation peaceably, and in such slow degrees, as that the evil will wear off insensibly; and their places be, *pari passu,* filled up by free white laborers. If, on the contrary, it is left to force itself on, human nature must shudder at the prospect held up."

Mr. Jefferson did not mean to say, nor do I, that the power of emancipation is in the Federal Government. He spoke of Virginia; and, as to the power of emancipation, I speak of the slaveholding States only. The Federal Government, however, as we insist, has the power of restraining the extension of the institution — the power to insure that a slave insurrection shall never occur on any American soil which is now free from slavery.

John Brown's effort was peculiar. It was not a slave insurrection. It was an attempt by white men to get up a revolt among slaves, in which the slaves refused to participate. In fact, it was so absurd that the slaves, with all their ignorance, saw plainly enough it could not succeed. That affair, in its philosophy, corresponds with the many attempts, related in history, at the assassination of kings and emperors. An enthusiast broods over the oppression of a people till he fancies himself commissioned by Heaven to liberate them. He ventures the attempt, which ends in little else than his own execution. Orsini's attempt on Louis Napoleon, and John Brown's attempt at Harper's Ferry, were, in their philosophy, precisely the same. The eagerness to cast blame on old England in the one case, and on New England in the other, does not disprove the sameness of the two things.

And how much would it avail you, if you could, by the use of John Brown, Helper's Book, and the like, break up the Republican organization? Human action can be modified to some extent, but human nature cannot be changed. There is a judgment and a feeling against slavery in this nation, which cast at least a million and a half of votes. You cannot destroy that judgment and feeling — that sentiment — by breaking up the political organization which rallies around it. You can scarcely scatter and disperse an army which has been formed into order in the face of your heaviest fire; but if you could, how much would you gain by forcing the sentiment which created it out of the peaceful channel of the ballot-box into some other channel? What would that other channel probably be? Would the number of John Browns be lessened or enlarged by the operation?

But you will break up the Union rather than submit to a denial of your constitutional rights.

That has a somewhat reckless sound; but it would be palliated, if not fully justified, were we proposing, by the mere force of numbers, to deprive you of some right plainly written down in the Constitution. But we are proposing no such thing.

When you make these declarations you have a specific and well-understood allusion to an assumed constitutional right of yours to take slaves into the Federal Territories, and to hold them there as property. But no such right is specifically written in the Constitution. That instrument is literally silent about any such right. We, on the contrary, deny that such a right has any existence in the Constitution, even by implication.

Your purpose, then, plainly stated, is that you will destroy the government, unless you be allowed to construe and force the Constitution as you please, on all points in dispute between you and us. You will rule or ruin in all events.

This, plainly stated, is your language. Perhaps you will say the Supreme Court has decided the disputed constitutional question in your favor. Not quite so. But waiving the lawyer's distinction between dictum and decision, the court has decided the question for you in a sort of way. The court has substantially said, it is your constitutional right to take slaves into the Federal Territories, and to hold them there as property. When I say the decision was made in a sort of way, I mean it was made in a divided court, by a bare majority of the judges, and they not quite agreeing with one another in the reasons for making it; that it is so made as that its avowed supporters disagree with one another about its meaning, and that it was mainly based upon a mistaken statement of fact — the statement in the opinion that "the right of property in a slave is distinctly and expressly affirmed in the Constitution."

An inspection of the Constitution will show that the right of property in a slave is not "distinctly and expressly affirmed" in it. Bear in mind, the judges do not pledge their judicial opinion that such right is impliedly affirmed in the Constitution; but they pledge their veracity that it is "distinctly and expressly" affirmed there — "distinctly," that is, not mingled with anything else — "expressly," that is, in words meaning just that, without the aid of any inference, and susceptible of no other meaning.

If they had only pledged their judicial opinion that such right is affirmed in the instrument by implication, it would be open to others to show that neither the word "slave" nor "slavery" is to be found in the Constitution, nor the word "property" even, in any connection with language alluding to the things slave, or slavery; and that wherever in that instrument the slave is alluded to, he is called a "person"; and wherever his master's legal right in relation to him is alluded to, it is spoken of as "service or labor which may be due" — as a debt payable in service or labor. Also it would be open to show, by contemporaneous history, that this mode of alluding to slaves and slavery, instead of speaking of them, was employed on purpose to exclude from the Constitution the idea that there could be property in man.

To show all this is easy and certain.

When this obvious mistake of the judges shall be brought to their notice, is it not reasonable to expect that they will withdraw the mistaken statement, and reconsider the conclusion based upon it?

And then it is to be remembered that "our fathers who framed the government under which we live" — the men who made the Constitution — decided this same constitutional question in our favor long ago: decided it without division among themselves when making the decision; without division among themselves about the meaning of it after it was made, and, so far as any evidence is left, without basing it upon any mistaken statement of facts.

Under all these circumstances, do you really feel yourselves justified to break up this government unless such a court decision as yours is shall be at once submitted to as a conclusive and final rule of political action? But you will not abide the election of a Republican president! In that supposed event, you say, you will destroy the Union; and then, you say, the great crime of having destroyed it will be upon us! That is cool. A highwayman holds a pistol to my ear and mutters through his teeth, "Stand and deliver, or I shall kill you, and then you will be a murderer!"

To be sure, what the robber demanded of me — my money — was my own; and I had a clear right to keep it; but it was no more my own than my vote is my own; and the threat of death to me, to extort my money, and the threat of destruction to the Union, to extort my vote, can scarcely be distinguished in principle.

A few words now to Republicans. It is exceedingly desirable that all parts of this great Confederacy shall be at peace, and in harmony one with another. Let us Republicans do our part to have it so. Even though much provoked, let us do nothing through passion and ill temper. Even though the Southern people will not so much as listen to us, let us calmly consider their demands, and yield to them if, in our deliberate view of our duty, we possibly can. Judging by all they say and do, and by the subject and nature of their controversy with us, let us determine, if we can, what will satisfy them.

Will they be satisfied if the Territories be unconditionally surrendered to them? We know they will not. In all their present complaints against us, the Territories are scarcely mentioned. Invasions and insurrections are the rage now. Will it satisfy them if, in the future, we have nothing to do with invasions and insurrections? We know it will not. We so know, because we know we never had anything to do with invasions and insurrections; and yet this total abstaining does not exempt us from the charge and the denunciation.

The question recurs, What will satisfy them? Simply this: we must not only let them alone, but we must somehow convince them that we do let them alone. This, we know by experience, is no easy task. We have been so trying to convince them from the very beginning of our organization, but with no success. In all our platforms and speeches we have constantly protested our purpose to let them alone; but this has had no tendency to convince them. Alike unavailing to convince them is the fact that they have never detected a man of us in any attempt to disturb them.

These natural and apparently adequate means all failing, what will convince them? This, and this only: cease to call slavery wrong, and join them in calling it right. And this must be done thoroughly — done in acts as well as in words. Silence will not be tolerated — we must place ourselves avowedly with them. Senator Douglas's new sedition law must be enacted and enforced, suppressing all declarations that slavery is wrong, whether made in politics, in presses, in pulpits, or in private. We must arrest and return their fugitive slaves with greedy pleasure. We must pull down our free-State constitutions. The whole atmosphere must be disinfected from all taint of opposition to slavery, before they will cease to believe that all their troubles proceed from us.

I am quite aware they do not state their case precisely in this way. Most of them would probably say to us, "Let us alone; do nothing to us, and say what you please about slavery." But we do let them alone, — have never disturbed them, — so that, after all, it is what we say which dissatisfies them. They will continue to accuse us of doing, until we cease saying.

I am also aware they have not as yet in terms demanded the overthrow of our free-State constitutions. Yet those constitutions declare the wrong of slavery with more solemn emphasis than do all other sayings against it; and when all these other sayings shall have been silenced, the overthrow of these constitutions will be demanded, and nothing be left to resist the demand. It is nothing to the contrary that they do not demand the whole of this just now. Demanding what they do, and for the reason they do, they can voluntarily stop nowhere short of this consummation. Holding, as they do, that slavery is morally right and socially elevating, they cannot cease to demand a full national recognition of it as a legal right and a social blessing.

Nor can we justifiably withhold this on any ground save our conviction that slavery is wrong. If slavery is right, all words, acts, laws, and constitutions against it are themselves wrong, and should be silenced and swept away. If it is right, we cannot justly object to its nationality — its universality; if it is wrong, they cannot justly insist upon its extension — its enlargement. All they ask we could readily grant, if we thought slavery right; all we ask they could as readily grant, if they thought it wrong. Their thinking it right and our thinking it wrong is the precise fact upon which depends the whole controversy. Thinking it right, as they do, they are not to blame for desiring its full recognition as being right; but thinking it wrong, as we do, can we yield to them? Can we cast our votes with their view, and against our own? In view of our moral, social, and political responsibilities can we do this?

Wrong as we think slavery is, we can yet afford to let it alone where it is, because that much is due to the necessity arising from its actual presence in the nation; but can we, while our votes will prevent it, allow it to spread into the national Territories, and to overrun us here in these free States? If our sense of duty forbids this, then let us stand by our duty fearlessly and effectively. Let us be diverted by none of these sophistical contrivances wherewith we are so industriously plied and belabored — contrivances such as groping for some middle ground between the right and the wrong: vain as the search for a man who should be neither a living man nor a dead man; such as a policy of "don't care" on a question about which all true men do care; such as Union appeals beseeching true Union men to yield to Disunionists, reversing the divine rule, and calling, not the sinners, but the righteous to repentance; such as invocations to Washington, imploring men to unsay what Washington said and undo what Washington did.

Neither let us be slandered from our duty by false accusations against us, nor frightened from it by menaces of destruction to the government, nor of dungeons to ourselves. Let us have faith that right makes might, and in that faith let us to the end dare to do our duty as we understand it.

## *Lincoln at Cooper Union: A Rhetorical Analysis of the Text*

MICHAEL C. LEFF AND GERALD P. MOHRMANN

When Abraham Lincoln spoke at the Cooper Union on the evening of February 27, 1860, his audience responded enthusiastically, and the speech has continued to elicit praise throughout the intervening years. Biographers, historians, and literary scholars agree that it was "one of his most significant speeches,"[1] one that illustrated "his abilities as a reasoner,"[2] and one to which posterity has ascribed his "subsequent nomination and election to the presidency."[3] Ironically, however, this model of "logical analysis and construction"[4] has failed to generate a critical response in kind. Most of what has been written treats of the background, and, too often, the man as myth has intruded; caught up in the drama of the performance, writers find no bit of information too trivial to report, whether it be the price of tickets or the fit of Lincoln's new shoes.[5] Such details can deepen our appreciation of the event, but they do not illuminate the speech as a speech.

Unhappily, little light is shed by those who do comment on the speech text. Nicolay and Hay assert, for example, that Lincoln's conclusions "were irresistibly convincing,"[6] but their sole piece of supporting evidence is a four-hundred word excerpt. And if they happen to be "firmly in the hero-worshipping tradition,"[7] those of sterner stuff fare no better. Basler makes the curious claim that the rhetorical "high-water mark" occurs toward the end of the first section;[8] Nevins mistakenly argues that the speech "fell into two halves";[9] reputable scholars equate summary and quotation with explication;[10] and it is generally accepted that Lincoln demonstrated a conciliatory attitude toward the South.[11]

Certainly all is not dross in previous studies, but wherever one turns in the literature, no satisfying account of the speech is to be found.[12] We are convinced that a systematic rhetorical analysis can help rectify the situation, and what follows is our attempt to accomplish such an analysis. In that attempt, we center on the text of the speech, but our purpose demands some preliminary remarks about the rhetorical context.

Although it was not until after the speech that Lincoln frankly admitted his presidential aspirations, saying, "The taste *is* in my mouth a little,"[13] he had been savoring the possibility for months. The preceding November, he had written that the next canvas would find him laboring "faithfully in the ranks" unless "the judgment of the party shall assign me a different position,"[14] but even as he wrote, Lincoln was grasping for a different assignment, "busy using the knife on his rivals . . . and doing all he could to enhance his reputation as an outstanding Republican leader."[15] Small wonder that he decided early to "make a political speech of it" in New York.[16] Here was the opportunity to make himself more available to Republicans in the East. The appearance alone would make for greater recognition, but political availability required more: Lincoln had to be an acceptable Republican, and he had to be an attractive alternative to the Democratic candidate.

William A. Seward and Stephen A. Douglas were the presumptive nominees, and they, patently, were Lincoln's antagonists. Moreover, their views on slavery created an intertwining threat that menaced his conception of the party and his personal ambitions. When Seward spoke about a "higher law" and an "irrepressible conflict," he strained Lincoln's sense of moral and political conservatism; these pronouncements smacked too much of radicalism.[17] Douglas, meanwhile, exacerbated the situation with his doctrine of popular sovereignty. Lincoln feared that this siren song would cause wholesale apostacy in Republican ranks, an eventuality all the more likely if the party nominee was tinctured with radicalism. He knew, however, that a middle ground existed, and he long had occupied it with his insistence that slavery should be protected but not extended. Consequently, when Lincoln addressed the Eastern Republicans, both principle and expediency permitted, even dictated, that he speak for party and for self and that he maintain party and self in a position between those taken by Seward and Douglas.

That he took such a course is revealed by an examination of the speech text, but all the external evidence shows a man running hard, if humbly, for political office, and while Lincoln spoke for his party, he spoke first for his own nomination. In fact, the Cooper Union Address is best characterized as a campaign oration, a speech designed to win nomination for the speaker. This identification of genre is basic to our analysis, and the nature of the genre is suggested by Rosenthal's distinction between nonpersonal and personal persuasion;[18] in the former, the speaker attempts to influence audience attitudes about a particular issue, and ethos is important insofar as it lends credence to the substance of the argument. In the latter the process is reversed. The focal point is the speaker, and the message becomes a vehicle for enhancing ethos. Campaign orations, on this basis, tend to be examples of personal persuasion, for while "the ostensible purpose of a given speech may be to gain acceptance of a particular policy, . . . the actual purpose is to gain votes for the candidate."[19] In other words, the ultimate goal of the campaign orator is to promote himself as a candidate. Both policies and character are in question, but the treatment of issues is subsidiary to the purpose of creating a general identification between the speaker and the audience. The objective, then, in a campaign oration is ingratiation.

With genre and purpose in mind, we can approach the speech through familiar topics. Addressing himself first to the people of New York, then to the South and finally to the Republican Party, Lincoln divides his speech into three sections, and this pattern of organization invites seriatim analysis of the major dispositional units. Furthermore, argument and style immediately loom as important elements, since they disclose essential characteristics in and significant interrelationships among the main units of the discourse. Consequently, our critique will follow Lincoln's pattern of organization and will have special reference to matters of argument and style. This approach, however, is not without its hazards. The convenience of tracing the natural sequence of the argument may foster fragmentary analysis and obscure the dominant rhetorical motive. Yet to be mindful of the genre is to find a corrective. The central concern is ingratiation, and recognition of this purpose unifies the elements of analysis by giving them a more precise focus; awareness of the ultimate goal becomes shuttle to the threads of structure, argument, and style.

In the address, Lincoln deals exclusively with slavery, and although this inflammatory issue might seem a shaky bridge to ingratiation, the choice is a fitting response to the rhetorical problem. What better point of departure than the paramount issue of the day, the issue with which he was most closely identified, and the issue that had spawned the Republican Party?[20] And Lincoln starts with the very motivation that had driven men to Ripon only a few years before, the question of slavery in the territories. Capitalizing on these initial associations, he counters the emotionalism inherent in the topic by assuming a severely rational posture and enunciating a moderate but firm set of principles. The approach distinguishes him from his chief rivals and solicits an intensified association from Eastern Republicans. These objectives govern the matter and manner of the opening argument, and this argument lays a foundation for subsequent developments in the speech. In the opening section and throughout, Lincoln associates himself and Republicans with the founding fathers and Constitutional principle, and he dissociates rival candidates and factions from those fathers and that principle.

Acknowledging his "fellow citizens of New York," Lincoln begins by adopting a "text for this discourse."[21] The text is a statement in which Stephen A. Douglas had asserted, "Our fathers, when they framed the government under which we live, understood this question just as well and even better than we do now." Defining terms in catechistic sequence, Lincoln maintains that "the frame of government under which we live" consists of the Constitution and the "twelve subsequently framed amendments" and that "our fathers" are "the 'thirty-nine' who signed the original instrument." He then asks, what is the question "those fathers understood 'just as well and even better, than we do now'?" The answer "is this: Does the proper division of local from Federal authority, or anything else in the Constitution, forbid our Federal Government to control as to slavery in our Federal Territories?" The question joins the issue because it is a matter upon which "Senator Douglas holds the affirmative, and the Republicans the negative."

That Douglas should play the foil is most fitting. National newspaper coverage of the 1858 senatorial campaign had linked the two men together, and the debates were to be published in March.[22] Moreover, Lincoln had continued the argument during 1859, worrying whether the Republican Party would "maintain it's [sic] identity, or be broken up to form the tail of Douglas' new kite.[23] Nevertheless, Lincoln knew that Douglas was vulnerable. The Freeport Doctrine had convinced many in the North that the man was only too "willing to subordinate moral considerations to political expediency."[24] Douglas, then, was an established rival, one whom Lincoln perceived as a threat to party unity, and one whose strategic position was open to attack from principle.

On a tactical level, the "text" quoted from Douglas affords Lincoln an ideal starting point. The allusion to the fathers is a symbolic reference with the potential for universal respect, and Douglas' implicit attack upon the principles that had generated the Republican Party creates an antithesis binding speaker and audience together in opposition to a common enemy. This antithesis is a channel for ingratiation; Lincoln makes Republicanism the voice of rational analysis, and the precise terms of Douglas' assertion form the premises of logical inquiry. Moving into the inquiry, Lincoln pursues a vigorous *ad hominem* attack.[25] He accepts Douglas' logic and then turns it against him.

The argument of the first section develops out of a single hypothetical proposition: if the better understanding evinced by our fathers shows that they believed nothing forbade federal control of slavery in the territories, then such regulatory power is inherent in the governmental frame. Lincoln affirms the antecedent with an elaborate chain of inductive evidence. Instances in the induction consist of actions by the fathers before and after they signed the Constitution because the question "seems not to have been directly before the convention."[26] From the Northwest Ordinance of 1784 to the Missouri Compromise of 1820, Lincoln enumerates seven statutes regulating slavery in the territories, and he accounts for votes by twenty-three of the fathers.[27] Twenty-one voted in favor of such regulation. Since these men were bound by "official responsibility and their corporal oaths" to uphold the Constitution, the implication of their affirmative votes is beyond question. To conclude that the twenty-one would have condoned federal regulation if they thought it unconstitutional would be to accuse these fathers of "gross political impropriety and willful perjury," and "as actions speak louder than words, so actions under such responsibility speak still louder."

Emphasizing deeds and "adhering rigidly to the text," Lincoln cannot offer in evidence "whatever understanding may have been manifested by any person" other than the thirty-nine, nor can he cite the sixteen who left no voting records. But the latter include the likes of Franklin, Hamilton, and Morris, and he believes that this group "would probably have acted just as the twenty-three did." In any event, "a clear majority of the whole" understood that nothing "forbade the Federal Government to control slavery in the Federal Territories," and with the remaining fathers probably agreeing, there can be little doubt about "the understanding of our fathers who framed the original Constitution; and the text affirms that they understood the question 'better than we.' "

Lincoln now uses this understanding to discredit arguments based on the fifth and tenth amendments; he says it is "a little presumptuous" to suggest that the fathers embraced one principle when writing the Constitution and another when writing the amendments. And does not this suggestion "become impudently absurd when coupled with the other affirmation, from the same mouth, that those who did the two things alleged to be inconsistent, understood whether they really were inconsistent better than we — better than he who affirms that they are inconsistent?" The touch of sarcasm reveals a more aggressive attitude, but it is justified by the inductive process; Douglas' own criterion forces the conclusion that he does not comprehend the understanding of the fathers. Lincoln will become even more combative before he brings the first section to a close, but some comments on style are merited, and they will lead us into his conclusion.

The style of this section is entirely consistent with Lincoln's severely rational approach. The audience probably did not expect the "rhetorical fireworks of a Western stump-speaker,"[28] but Lincoln is most circumspect. There are none of the "many excuses" that made him a Uriah Heep to some of his opponents,[29] and he avoids all display, indulging neither in anecdotes nor figurative language. The syntax is complex at times, but the complexity is that of legal rather than literary prose, as is evidenced in the following sentence: "It, therefore, would be unsafe to set down even the two who voted against the prohibition as having done so because, in their understanding, any proper division of local from Federal authority, or anything in the Constitution, forbade the Federal Government to control as to slavery in Federal territory."

The preceding quotation, with its echo of the text, points to a noteworthy stylistic element: repetition. Lincoln includes fifteen extended citations of the issue and an equal number from the "text," repetitions that accentuate the single line of argument. He adds to the emphasis by stressing certain key words and phrases. For example, there are over thirty uses of the root "understand," usually in the participial "understanding," and Lincoln alludes to the "fathers" more than thirty-five times. None of these repetitions is blatant or forced because he weaves them into the fabric of the inductive process. Furthermore, the repetitions concomitantly reinforce and control the emotional association with the fathers and their understanding of the Constitution. This point is crucial to an appreciation of Lincoln's rhetorical method. Both the direction of the argument and the symbols expressing it are fiercely emotional; yet, all is enmeshed in an incisive logical and linguistic structure, and while the tone remains rationalistic and legalistic, it also creates a subtle emotive nexus between the Republican audience and the founding fathers.

As noted above, style and argument shift in the concluding paragraphs, after Lincoln already has established his logical credentials. The argument becomes bolder, and the style alters appropriately. When developing the induction, Lincoln refers to the framers of the Constitution as the "thirty-nine," but they become "our fathers" again in the conclusion of the long first section of the speech. And there periods become more polished and sophisticated.

> If any man at this day sincerely believes that a proper division of local from Federal authority, or any part of the Constitution, forbids the Federal Government to control as to slavery in the Federal Territories, he is right to say so, and to enforce his position by all truthful evidence and fair argument which he can. But he has no right to mislead others, who have less access to history, and less leisure to study it, into the false belief that 'our fathers who framed the government under which we live' were of the same opinion — thus substituting falsehood and deception for truthful evidence and fair argument.

This passage completes the negative phase of Lincoln's argumentation. Both matter and manner drive a rational wedge between the speaker and his rivals. Clearly, Lincoln suggests that Douglas may be guilty of deliberate "falsehood and deception," and just as clearly, his own position represents "truthful evidence and fair argument." Lincoln, one of those with "access to history" and some "leisure to study it," attempts to set the record straight. Another direct slash at Douglas, the very source of the text and issue. At the same time, Lincoln indirectly differentiates himself from Seward and his radical posture. Lincoln's position is more to the right, closer to the demands of objective inquiry, closer also to the demands of political availability, and it is important to remark that he achieves this dissociation without recourse to divisive rhetoric. The foray against the man and his position is patent, but it is completely inferential.

Although less obtrusive than the refutation, an equally important constructive movement exists within this part of the oration. Not only does Lincoln distinguish himself from his opponents, he nurtures Republican unity because he makes himself and party the vessels for transmitting the faith of the fathers. Avoiding self-references, he presents himself as the voice of Republicanism, and he caps this appeal with words both to and from the party.

> But enough! Let all who believe that 'our fathers who framed the government under which we live understood this question just as well, and even better, than we do now,' speak as they spoke, and act as they acted upon it. This is all Republicans ask — all Republicans desire — in relation to slavery. As those fathers marked it, so let it be again marked, as an evil not to be extended, but to be tolerated and protected only because of and so far as its actual presence among us makes that toleration and protection a necessity. Let all the guarantees those fathers gave it be not grudgingly, but fully and fairly, maintained. For this Republicans contend, and with this, so far as I know or believe, they will be content.

At this point in the speech, Lincoln has associated himself and his audience with the spirit, the principles and the actions of the founding fathers, and in doing so, he has taken the first steps toward ingratiation.

Comprising nearly half the speech, this initial section is so clearly logical that it regularly is cited as a demonstration of Lincoln's powers as a reasoner, but to say no more is to grossly underestimate his achievement. The next section, too, is remarkable for its logical development, and all that follows in the speech is anticipated and controlled by the attack upon Douglas. Failure to appreciate this unity has confounded commentators, and their confusion is strikingly illustrated in the generally accepted conclusion that Lincoln follows his attack with remarks "conciliatory toward the South."[30]

The second section does begin with an ostensible change in audience: "And now, if they would listen, — as I suppose they will not, — I would address a few words to the Southern people." But we learn more about the beholders than the object when we are told that the next twenty-six paragraphs are filled with "words of kindly admonition and protest,"[31] words of "sweet reasonableness to allay Southern fears."[32] Presuming that he will not be heard, Lincoln notes that "our party gets no votes" in the South, and he flatly asserts later that "the Southern people will not so much as listen to us." These are not idle reservations. They represent the realistic assessment of an astute politician who knows that the coming election will be won or lost in the North; it is hardly plausible that this man would detract from his ultimate purpose by directing nearly forty per cent of his speech to an unavailable audience.

In truth, the audience does not change. Lincoln merely casts the second section of the speech in the form of a *prosopopoeia,* a figure he had rehearsed five months earlier in Cincinnati.[33] The device suits his purposes admirably. It enables him to create a mock debate between Republicans and the South, a debate in which he becomes spokesman for the party. In this role, Lincoln can strengthen the identification between himself and the available Republican audience. He is careful to extend the refutation of Douglas into the second section and thus carry over the lines of association and disassociation begun earlier in the discourse. If Lincoln leaves Douglas with little ground on which to stand, he performs the same argumentative service for the South, and the debate he manufactures is far from being conciliatory.

The *prosopopoeia* develops into another *ad hominem* argument. This time, however, the presentation is complicated by the need to deal with the collective contentions of a collective opposition. To provide control, Lincoln again begins by stressing reason, saying to the South, "I consider that in the general qualities of reason and justice you are not inferior to any other people." Yet, in the specific case, rational discourse is stymied because the Southerners never refer to Republicans except "to denounce us as reptiles, or, at the best, as no better than outlaws." Such responses are unjust to both sides. The proper course would be to "bring forward your charges and specifications, and then be patient long enough to hear us deny or justify." Obviously, the South is unwilling and unable to follow this procedure, and becoming persona for both Republicanism and reason, Lincoln reconstructs the charges and specifications; these include sectionalism, radicalism, agitation of the slavery question, and slave insurrections.

The putative debate begins: "You say we are sectional. We deny it. That makes an issue; and the burden of proof is upon you." The crux of the matter is whether Republicans repel the South with "some wrong principle." Republican principle, however, is based in the beliefs and actions of the fathers, and Lincoln challenges the South to respond to this fact. "Do you accept the challenge? No! Then you really believe that the principle which 'our fathers who framed the government under which we live' thought so clearly right as to adopt it, and indorse it again and again, upon their official oaths, is in fact so clearly wrong as to demand your condemnation without a moment's consideration." Closing and reinforcing this line of reasoning Lincoln refers to the pre-eminent father: "Some of you delight to flaunt in our faces the warning . . . given by Washington in his Farewell Address," but if he were to speak for himself "would he cast the blame of that sectionalism upon us, who sustain his policy, or upon you, who repudiate it? We respect that warning of Washington, and we commend it to you, together with his example pointing to the right application of it."[34] Thus, the South claims to be the injured party, but analysis of the charge proves that the wounds are self-inflicted.

Lincoln uses the same refutational method for each of the other issues: first defining the charge with a series of rhetorical questions, he then turns the argument against the adversary. The South proclaims itself the bastion of conservatism and denounces Republican radicalism, but "what is conservatism? Is it not adherence to the old and tried, against the new and untried? We stick to, contend for, the identical old policy . . . which was adopted by 'our fathers who framed the government under which we live'; while you with one accord reject, and scout, and spit upon that old policy, and insist upon substituting something new." The South alleges that Republicans have made the slavery issue more prominent. True, the issue is more prominent, but this situation arose because the South "discarded the old policy of the fathers." Finally, Southerners complain that Republicans foment insurrection among the slaves, but they can adduce no evidence to support this allegation, cannot "implicate a single Republican" and ignore that "Republican doctrines and declarations are accompanied with a continual protest against any interference whatever" with the institution in the slave states. Indeed, were it not for the loud and misleading protestations of Southern politicians, the slaves would hardly know that the Republican Party existed. Worse yet, the South refuses to acknowledge a simple truth contained in Republican doctrine, a truth articulated "many years ago" when Jefferson indicated that the cause of slave insurrections was slavery itself. Like Jefferson, Republicans would not interfere with slavery where it exists, but Republicans do insist, as the fathers did, that the federal government "has the power of restraining the extension of the institution — the power to insure that a slave insurrection shall never occur on any American soil which is now free."

Finishing his treatment of specific charges, Lincoln builds to a more forceful and aggressive tone, just as he did at the end of the first section. His arrangement of responses to Southern allegations is itself climatic, the issue of insurrections being both last and most critical.

Always volatile, this issue had become extremely explosive in the wake of the Harper's Ferry raid and the trial of John Brown, and Lincoln understandably chooses this matter as the instrument for his most extensive defense of party and principle. He is not content, however, to assume a merely defensive posture; the entire pattern of his argumentation reveals a movement from reply to attack that gathers momentum as the discourse proceeds. Thus, having disposed of the insurrection controversy, Lincoln assails the very character of the Southern position, and he concludes this section with an examination of threats emanating from the South.

The South hopes to "break up the Republican organization." That failing, "you will break up the Union rather than submit to a denial of your constitutional rights." This is a course of "rule or ruin"; the union will be destroyed unless people are permitted to take slaves into the federal territories. But no such right exists in the Constitution, and Southern threats are fruitless. Neither the Constitution nor the Republican Party are so malleable as to bend at the touch of Southern fancy. Not even the Dred Scott decision offers a refuge. That verdict was made "in a divided court, by a bare majority of the judges, and they not quite agreeing with one another in the reasons for making it." The decision rests upon "the opinion that 'the right of property in a slave is distinctly and expressly affirmed in the Constitution,' " but careful analysis shows that this right is not even implied. Surely it is reasonable to expect the Court to retract "the mistaken statement" when apprised of its error. Furthermore, the verdict runs contrary to the judgment of the fathers, those who decided the same question long ago "without division among themselves when making the decision," without division "about the meaning of it after it was made," and without "basing it upon any mistaken statement of facts." Having thus contrasted the babel of the Court with the unity of the fathers and their lineal descendants, Lincoln builds to a striking analogy:

> Under these circumstances, do you really feel yourselves justified to break up this government unless such a court decision as yours is shall be at once submitted to as a conclusive and final rule of political action? But you will not abide the election of a Republican president! In that supposed event, you say, you will destroy the Union; and then, you say, the crime of having destroyed it will be upon us! That is cool. A highwayman holds a pistol to my ear, and mutters through his teeth, 'Stand and deliver, or I shall kill you, and then you will be a murderer!

Adding that the highwayman's threat can "scarcely be distinguished in principle" from "the threat of destruction to the Union," Lincoln completes his *ad hominem* assault against the Southern position, and the *prosopopoeia* ends.

The parallels and interrelationships between the first and the second sections of the speech are evident. Some shifts in invention and style between the two sections are occasioned by the change of antagonist, but it is more significant that Lincoln elects to argue against adversaries in both and that he uses the same fundamental argument to dispatch them all. In both sections, he strives to become spokesman for the party by demonstrating that he is a man of reason and that this characteristic melds himself and party with the principles of the founding fathers. In addition, the same characteristic distinguishes him from other candidates. Finally, each section is based on a severely rational framework and builds to a terminal climax that unifies and heightens logical and emotional dimensions.

Merging style and argument within and between parts of the discourse, Lincoln unquestionably remains in touch with his immediate audience, and he unquestionably has his eye on ingratiation. In the first movement, he separates himself and party from Douglas and Seward; in the second, he favorably contrasts the position of the party with that of its most vociferous opponent.[35] But one further step remains. To this juncture, the identification of speaker, party, and principle has been closely tied to a series of negative definitions. A positive gesture seems necessary, and in the final section of the speech, Lincoln fuses his audience together through more directly constructive appeals.

He begins by saying he will address "a few words now to Republicans," and though he puts aside both text and issue, his remarks evolve naturally from what has proceeded. Once more reason is the point of departure. Having, in the highwayman metaphor, implied a contrast between cool reason and hot passion, Lincoln urges Republicans to "do nothing through passion and ill-temper" that might cause discord within the nation, and, as he draws out the ultimate implications of the Southern position, antithesis becomes the dominant mode of argument and style. The section centers on a contrast between the Republicans and the South (between "we" and "they"); it extends and amplifies the distinction between word and deed that is present throughout the speech; and the argument is couched in and reinforced by antithetical syntax.

Recognizing Southern intransigence, Lincoln still wants his party to "calmly consider their demands" and reach conclusions based on all "they say and do." Pursuing the inquiry, he asks, "Will they be satisfied if the Territories be unconditionally surrendered to them? We know they will not." And "will it satisfy them if, in the future, we have nothing to do with invasions and insurrections? We know it will not." It will not because past abstention has not exempted "us from the charge and the denunciation." To satisfy them, "we must not only leave them alone, but we must somehow convince them that we do let them alone." Experience shows that this is no easy task because Republican policy and actions have been misconstrued consistently. The only recourse seems to be "this and only this: cease to call slavery wrong, and join them in calling it right. And this must be done thoroughly — done in acts as well as words. Silence will not be tolerated — we must place ourselves avowedly with them." Republicans must suppress all "declarations that slavery is wrong," must return "fugitive slaves with greedy pleasure," and must pull down all free state constitutions "before they will cease to believe that all their troubles proceed from us."

Most Southerners, Lincoln admits, would not put the argument in this extreme form. Most would simply claim that they want to be left alone, but "we do let them alone." Consequently, it is apparent that "they will continue to accuse us of doing, until we cease saying." Given the nature of their arguments and the character of their actions, the Southerners cannot stop short of the demand that all Republicans desist from speaking and acting out of conviction. Those who hold that "slavery is morally right and socially elevating" must necessarily call for its recognition "as a legal right and a social blessing." Stripped of its veneer and examined in the cold light of reason, the Southern position reveals the disagreement governing the entire conflict; it also underscores the principle from which Republicans cannot retreat. Lincoln expresses both points in a final antithesis that reduces the issue of slavery to a matter of right and wrong, to a matter of moral conviction:

> Their thinking it right and our thinking it wrong is the precise fact upon which depends the whole controversy. Thinking it right, as they do, they are not to blame for desiring its full recognition as being right; but thinking it wrong, as we do, can we yield to them? Can we cast our votes with their view, and against our own? In view of our moral, social, and political responsibilities, can we do this?

Providing no answers because they are only too obvious, Lincoln moves on to merge self and party with the fathers, and Washington is the exemplar.

Style changes appropriately as Lincoln makes his final call for unity. Antithetical elements appear in the penultimate paragraph, but the opposed clauses are subordinated within the long, periodic flow of the final sentence, a flow that builds emotionally to a union with Washington's words and deeds. Lincoln repeats that slavery can be left alone where it exists, but he insists that there can be no temporizing when it comes to the extension of slavery:

> If our sense of duty forbids this, then let us stand by our duty fearlessly and effectively. Let us be diverted by none of those sophistical contrivances wherewith we are so industriously plied, and belabored — contrivances such as groping for some middle ground between the right and the wrong: vain as the search for a man who should be neither a living man nor a dead man; such as a policy of 'don't care' on a question about which all true men do care; such as Union appeals beseeching true Union men to yield to Disunionists, reversing the divine rule, and calling, not the sinners, but the righteous to repentance: such as invocations to Washington, imploring men to unsay what Washington said and undo what Washington did.
>
> Neither let us be slandered from our duty by false accusations against us, nor frightened from it by menaces of destruction to the government, nor of dungeons to ourselves. Let us have faith that right makes might, and in that faith let us to the end dare to do our duty as we understand it.

This short third section, constituting less than fifteen per cent of the text, is a fitting climax to Lincoln's efforts. Rational principle develops into moral conviction, and the resulting emotional intensity emerges from and synthesizes all that has gone before. Yet the intensity is controlled. Speaker and audience are resolute and principled, but at the same time, they are poised and logical. Others may indulge in "false accusations" and "menaces of destruction," but Lincoln and Republicans will have faith in right and in their understanding.

With this closing suggestion of antithetical behavior, Lincoln harks back to all he has said, and with it, he completes his exercise in ingratiation. Douglas is a pitiful example of one who argues misguided principle in maladroit fashion, and Seward's notion of an irrepressible conflict is at odds with the true spirit of the Republican Party, a party whose words and deeds follow from what the framers of the government said and did. Neither opponent measures up to the new and higher self-conception that the speaker has created for his audience. Furthermore, Lincoln has, by this very performance, demonstrated that he is the one who will best represent party and principle. Starting with reason and principle, he has shunted aside opposition, differentiated between Republicans and the South, and pushed on to unite the party in the faith that will "let us to the end dare to do our duty as we understand it."

The very wording of the concluding paragraphs reflects the organic quality of Lincoln's quest for unity. "Understand" echoes the "text"; Washington is a synecdochic reminder of the fathers; and the antithetical language recalls dissociations that are fundamental. In examining the discourse, we have attempted to explicate this internal coherence by tracing the sequence of arguments and images as they appear in the text, by dealing with the speech on its own terms. We are satisfied that the analysis has produced a reading that is more accurate than those previously available, a reading that goes farther toward explaining why the Cooper Union Address was one of Lincoln's most significant speeches.

Our interpretation is at odds, of course, with the conventional wisdom concerning his attitude toward the South. Where others have found him conciliatory, we argue that his position on slavery was calculated to win the nomination, not to propitiate an unavailable audience. That he had made "many similar declarations, and had never recanted any of them"[36] unquestionably contributed to the triumph of availability that was to be his, but his position ultimately pointed to an ideological conflict between North and South. Some Southerners took solace from Lincoln's assurances that slavery would be left alone where it existed, but extremists perceived him as the personification of Black Republicanism, even as the source of the irrepressible conflict doctrine.[37] The latter perceptions were distorted. So are ours, if we blink the realities of political rhetoric, and whatever else the speech might have been, it was certainly an oration designed to meet the immediate problems of a political campaign.

This perspective emphasizes that alternatives sometimes really do exclude and that rhetoric may nurture exclusion. Such a perspective may be uncomfortable for those who want to cast Lincoln as the Great Conciliator, but we are convinced that an accurate reading of the Cooper Union Address demands a frank recognition of the immediate rhetorical motives. Despite the mythology, the man was human, perhaps gloriously so, and it does him no disservice to accept this speech as evidence of his political skill, as evidence that "he was an astute and dextrous operator of the political machine."[38] Nor does this acceptance detract from the speech as literature and as logical exposition. The political artistry and the rhetorical artistry are functions of each other, and an appreciation of this coalescence can only enhance our understanding of the Cooper Union Address. And viewing the speech as a whole, we are quite content to close with a slightly altered evaluation from another context: "The speech is — to put it as crudely as possible — an immortal masterpiece."[39]

## *Notes*

1. J. G. Randall, *Lincoln the President* (New York: Dodd, Mead, 1945), I, 135.
2. Howard Mumford Jones and Ernest E. Leisy, eds., *Major American Writers* (New York: Harcourt, Brace, 1945), p. 681.
3. Benjamin Barondess, *Three Lincoln Masterpieces* (Charleston: Education Foundation of West Virginia, 1954), p. 3.

4. R. Franklin Smith, "A Night at Cooper Union," *Central States Speech Journal* 13 (Autumn 1962), 272.
5. The most influential account of this sort is Carl Sandburg, *The Prairie Years* (New York: Harcourt, Brace, 1927), II, 200–216, but the most complete is Andrew A. Freeman, *Abraham Lincoln Goes to New York* (New York: Coward-McCann, 1960).
6. John G. Nicolay and John Hay, *Abraham Lincoln: A History* (New York: Century, 1917), II, 219–220.
7. Richard Hofstadter, *The American Political Tradition* (New York: Alfred A. Knopf, 1948), p. 364.
8. *Abraham Lincoln: His Speeches and Writings,* ed. Roy P. Basler (Cleveland: World, 1946), p. 32.
9. Allan Nevins, *The Emergence of Lincoln* (New York: Charles Scribner's Sons, 1950), II, 186.
10. Randall, pp. 136–137; Basler, pp. 32–33; Nevins, pp. 186–187; Reinhard H. Luthin, *The Real Abraham Lincoln* (Englewood Cliffs, New Jersey: Prentice-Hall, 1960), p. 210.
11. Randall, p. 136; Barondess, p. 18; Nicholay and Hay, p. 220, Nevins, p. 186; Luthin, pp. 243–244.
12. Freeman treats of the text briefly, pp. 84–88, and although Barondess ranges from preparation to audience reaction, pp. 3–30, Hofstadter's observation applies, n. 7 above. Earl W. Wiley discusses the address in *Four Speeches by Lincoln* (Columbus: Ohio State Univ. Press, 1927), pp. 15–27, but he limits analysis to the first section of the speech, a limitation also applied in his "Abraham Lincoln: His Emergence as the Voice of the People," in *A History and Criticism of American Public Address,* ed. *William N. Brigance* (New York: McGraw-Hill, 1943), II, 859–877. In the same volume, the speech is the basis for comments on delivery in Mildred Freburg Berry, "Abraham Lincoln: His Development in the Skills of the Platform," pp. 828–858.
13. Letter to Lyman Trumbull, April 29, 1860, *The Collected Works of Abraham Lincoln,* ed. Roy P. Basler (New Brunswick, New Jersey: Rutgers Univ. Press, 1955), IV, 45.
14. Letter to William E. Frazer, November 1, 1859, *Collected Works,* III, 491.
15. Richard N. Current, *The Lincoln Nobody Knows* (New York: McGraw-Hill, 1958), p. 199. For an indication of Lincoln's activities see *Collected Works,* III, 384–521.
16. Letter to James A. Briggs, *Collected Works,* III, 494.
17. See Letter to Salmon P. Chase, June 9, 1859, *Collected Works,* III, 384; Letter to Nathan Sargent, June 23, 1859, *Collected Works,* III, 387–388; Letter to Richard M. Corwine, April 6, 1860, *Collected Works,* IV, 36.
18. Paul I. Rosenthal, "The Concept of Ethos and the Structure of Persuasion," *Speech Monographs* 33 (June 1966), 114–126.
19. Rosenthal, p. 120.
20. In 1854, "northern whigs persuaded that their old party was moribund, Democrats weary of planting dominance, and free-soilers eager to exclude slavery from the territories began to draw together to resist the advance of the planting power"; Charles A. Beard and Mary R. Beard, *The Rise of American Civilization* (New York: Macmillan, 1937), II, 22. Cf. Don E. Fehrenbacher, "Lincoln and the Formation of the Republican Party," in *Prelude to Greatness* (Stanford: Stanford Univ. Press, 1962), pp. 19–47.
21. We follow the text in *Complete Works,* ed. John G. Nicolay and John Hay (New York: Francis D. Tandy, 1905), V, 293–328; we include no footnotes

because aside from unimportant exceptions, citations are sequential. This text is more conservative in typography than that edited and published as a campaign document by Charles C. Nott and Cephas Brainerd. The latter appears in *Collected Works*, III, 522–550; 1860, p. 1. Substantive variations in extant see also the *New York Times*, February 28, texts are minuscule, and this consistency deserves comment. Lincoln ignored suggested alterations in the original (Sandburg, II, 210 and 215–216); he proofread the newspaper copy (Freeman, pp. 92–93); pamphlet copies were available by the first of April (*Collected Works*, IV, 38–39); and Lincoln adamantly resisted editorial changes by Nott (*Collected Works*, IV, 58–59). This evidence emphasizes the care with which he constructed the speech, but it also suggests that he anticipated a wider audience from the outset. Publication practices and his own experience told Lincoln that he would reach many who would not hear him speak.

22. General interest in the debates is underlined by the favorable editorial notice appearing in the Brooklyn *Daily Times*, August 26, 1858, an editorial written by one Walt Whitman; Walt Whitman, *I Sit and Look Out*, ed. Emory Holloway and Vernolian Schwartz (New York: Columbia Univ. Press, 1932), p. 96. For letters referring to publication of the debates, see *Collected Works*, III, 341, 343, 372–374, 515, and 516.
23. Letter to Lyman Trumbull, Dec. 11, 1858, *Collected Works*, III, 345.
24. Harry J. Carman and Harold C. Syrett, *A History of the American People* (New York: Alfred A. Knopf, 1952), I, 588. Cf. Fehrenbacher, "The Famous 'Freeport Question,' " in *Prelude to Greatness*, pp. 121–142.
25. Logicians often define *ad hominem* as a fallacy resulting from an attack upon the character of a man rather than the quality of argument. In this essay, however, we use the term as Schopenhauer does in distinguishing between *ad hominem* and *ad rem* as the two basic modes of refutation. He differentiates in this manner: "We may show either that the proposition is not in accordance with the nature of things, *i.e.*, with absolute, objective truth [*ad rem*]; or that it is inconsistent with other statements or admissions of our opponent, *i.e.*, with truth as it appears to him [*ad hominem*]"; Arthur Schopenhauer, "The Art of Controversy," in *The Will to Live: Selected Writings of Arthur Schopenhauer*, ed. Richard Taylor (New York: Anchor Books, 1962), p. 341. See Henry W. Johnstone, Jr., "Philosophy and *Argumentum ad Hominem*," *Journal of Philosophy* 49 (July 1952), 489–498.
26. Lincoln undoubtedly knew that James Wilson, Patrick Henry and Edmund Randolph had discussed the topic (See *Collected Works*, III, 526–527, n. 9.), but he is accurate in asserting that the subject did not come "directly" before the convention.
27. Washington's vote was his signature, as President, on the Act of 1789 which enforced the Ordinance of 1787.
28. Nicolay and Hay, *Abraham Lincoln*, II, 220.
29. See Hofstadter, p. 94; *Collected Works*, III, 396.
30. Randall, I, 136.
31. Nicolay and Hay, *Abraham Lincoln*, II, 220.
32. Nevins, II, 186.
33. *Collected Works*, III, 438–454. Speaking at Cincinnati, September 17, 1859, Lincoln directs so much of his speech across the river "to the Kentuckians" (p. 440) that one listener complained aloud, "Speak to Ohio men, and not to Kentuckians!" (p. 445) Interestingly, Nevins appreciates the *prosopopoeia* in this speech, noting that Lincoln was "ostensibly speaking to Kentuckians," II, 56.

34. The varied interpretations of Washington's warning and their longevity are illustrated in debates, early in 1850, over the purchase of the Farewell Address manuscript for the Library of Congress. Much of the debate is reproduced in William Dawson Johnston, *History of the Library of Congress* (Washington: Government Printing Office, 1904), I, 326–340.
35. The second movement continues the implicit attack upon Seward, and all texts indicate a mimicking of Douglas' "gur-reat pur-rinciple." Buchanan also is a victim here, for he had championed popular sovereignty in his "Third Annual Message," December 19, 1859; *The Works of James Buchanan,* ed. John Bassett More (1908–1911; rpt. New York: Antiquarian Press Ltd., 1960), X, 342. Lincoln's efforts were not lost on a New York *Evening Post* reporter who wrote that "the speaker places the Republican party on the very ground occupied by the framers of our constitution and the fathers of our Republic" and that "in this great controversy the Republicans are the real conservative party." His report is reprinted in the *Chicago Tribune,* 1 Mar. 1860, p. 1.
36. Abraham Lincoln, "First Inaugural Address," in *Collected Works,* IV, 263.
37. Michael Davis, *The Image of Lincoln in the South* (Knoxville: Univ. of Tennessee, 1971), pp. 7–40; traces Southern views from nomination through inauguration. See *Southern Editorials on Secession,* ed. Dwight L. Dumond (1931; rpt. Gloucester, Mass.: Peter-Smith, 1964), pp. 103–105, 112–115, 159–162, *et passim.*
38. David Donald, *Lincoln Reconsidered* (New York: Alfred A. Knopf, 1956), p. 65.
39. The original is Randall Jarrell's comment on a poem. Robert Frost's "Provide Provide," in *Poetry and the Age* (New York: Vintage-Knopf, 1953), p. 41.

# 11

# Critical Reading of Dwight D. Eisenhower's "Atoms for Peace"

## *Atoms for Peace*

DWIGHT D. EISENHOWER

Madame President, Members of the General Assembly: When Secretary General Hammarskjold's invitation to address this General Assembly reached me in Bermuda, I was just beginning a series of conferences with the Prime Ministers and Foreign Ministers of Great Britain and of France. Our subject was some of the problems that beset our world.

During the remainder of the Bermuda Conference, I had constantly in mind that ahead of me lay a great honor. That honor is mine today as I stand here, privileged to address the General Assembly of the United Nations.

At the same time that I appreciate the distinction of addressing you, I have a sense of exhilaration as I look upon this Assembly.

Never before in history has so much hope for so many people been gathered together in a single organization. Your deliberations and decisions during these somber years have already realized part of those hopes.

But the great tests and the great accomplishments still lie ahead. And in the confident expectation of those accomplishments, I would use the office which, for the time being, I hold, to assure you that the Government of the United States will remain steadfast in its support of this body. This we shall do in the conviction that you will provide a great share of the wisdom, the courage, and the faith which can bring to this world lasting peace for all nations, and happiness and well-being for all men.

Clearly, it would not be fitting for me to take this occasion to present to you a unilateral American report on Bermuda. Nevertheless, I assure you that in our deliberations on that lovely island we sought to invoke those same great concepts of universal peace and human dignity which are so cleanly etched in your charter.

Neither would it be a measure of this great opportunity merely to recite, however hopefully, pious platitudes.

I therefore decided that this occasion warranted my saying to you some of the things that have been on the minds and hearts of my legislative and executive associates and on mine for a great many months — thoughts I had originally planned to say primarily to the American people.

I know that the American people share my deep belief that if a danger exists in the world, it is a danger shared by all — and equally, that if hope exists in the mind of one nation, that hope should be shared by all.

Finally, if there is to be advanced any proposal designed to ease even by the smallest measure the tensions of today's world, what more appropriate audience could there be than the members of the General Assembly of the United Nations?

I feel impelled to speak today in a language that in a sense is new — one which I, who have spent so much of my life in the military profession, would have preferred never to use.

The new language is the language of atomic warfare.

The atomic age has moved forward at such a pace that every citizen of the world should have some comprehension, at least in comparative terms, of the extent of this development of the utmost significance to every one of us. Clearly, if the peoples of the world are to conduct an intelligent search for peace, they must be armed with the significant facts of today's existence.

My recital of atomic danger and power is necessarily stated in United States terms, for these are the only incontrovertible facts that I know. I need hardly point out to this Assembly, however, that this subject is global, not merely national in character.

On July 16, 1945, the United States set off the world's first atomic explosion. Since that date in 1945, the United States of America has conducted 42 test explosions.

Atomic bombs today are more than 25 times as powerful as the weapon with which the atomic age dawned, while hydrogen weapons are in the ranges of millions of tons of TNT equivalent.

Today, the United States' stockpile of atomic weapons, which, of course, increases daily, exceeds by many times the total [explosive] equivalent of the total of all bombs and all shells that came from every plane and every gun in every theater of war in all of the years of World War II.

A single air group, whether afloat or land-based, can now deliver to any reachable target a destructive cargo exceeding in power all the bombs that fell on Britain in all of World War II.

In size and variety, the development of atomic weapons has been no less remarkable. The development has been such that atomic weapons have virtually achieved conventional status within our armed services. In the United States, the Army, the Navy, the Air Force, and the Marine Corps are all capable of putting this weapon to military use.

But the dread secret, and the fearful engines of atomic might, are not ours alone.

In the first place, the secret is possessed by our friends and allies, Great Britain and Canada, whose scientific genius made a tremendous contribution to our original discoveries, and the designs of atomic bombs.

The secret is also known by the Soviet Union.

The Soviet Union has informed us that, over recent years, it has devoted extensive resources to atomic weapons. During this period, the Soviet Union has exploded a series of atomic devices, including at least one involving thermonuclear reactions.

If at one time the United States possessed what might have been called a monopoly of atomic power, that monopoly ceased to exist several years ago. Therefore, although our earlier start has permitted us to accumulate what is today a great quantitative advantage, the atomic realities of today comprehend two facts of even greater significance.

First, the knowledge now possessed by several nations will eventually be shared by others — possibly all others.

Second, even a vast superiority in numbers of weapons, and a consequent capability of devastating retaliation, is no preventive, of itself, against the fearful material damage and toll of human lives that would be inflicted by surprise aggression.

The free world, at least dimly aware of these facts, has naturally embarked on a large program of warning and defense systems. That program will be accelerated and expanded.

But let no one think that the expenditure of vast sums for weapons and systems of defense can guarantee absolute safety for the cities and citizens of any nation. The awful arithmetic of the atomic bomb does not permit of any such easy solution. Even against the most powerful defense, an aggressor in possession of the effective minimum number of atomic bombs for a surprise attack could probably place a sufficient number of his bombs on the chosen targets to cause hideous damage.

Should such an atomic attack be launched against the United States, our reactions would be swift and resolute. But for me to say that the defense capabilities of the United States are such that they could inflict terrible losses upon an aggressor — for me to say that the retaliation capabilities of the United States are so great that such an aggressor's land would be laid waste — all this, while fact, is *not* the true expression of the purpose and the hope of the United States.

To pause there would be to confirm the hopeless finality of a belief that two atomic colossi are doomed malevolently to eye each other indefinitely across a trembling world. To stop there would be to accept helplessly the probability of civilization destroyed — the annihilation of the irreplaceable heritage of mankind handed down to us generation from generation — and the condemnation of mankind to begin all over again the age-old struggle upward from savagery toward decency, and right, and justice.

Surely no sane member of the human race could discover victory in such desolation. Could anyone wish his name to be coupled by history with such human degradation and destruction?

Occasional pages of history do record the faces of the "Great Destroyers" but the whole book of history reveals mankind's never-ending quest for peace and mankind's God-given capacity to build.

It is with the book of history, and not with isolated pages, that the United States will ever wish to be identified. My country wants to be constructive, not destructive. It wants agreements, not wars, among nations. It wants itself to live in freedom, and in the confidence that the people of every other nation enjoy equally the right of choosing their own way of life.

So my country's purpose is to help us move out of the dark chamber of horrors into the light, to find a way by which the minds of men, the hopes of men, the souls of men everywhere, can move forward toward peace and happiness and well being.

In this quest, I know that we must not lack patience.

I know that in a world divided, such as ours today, salvation cannot be attained by one dramatic act.

I know that many steps will have to be taken over many months before the world can look at itself one day and truly realize that a new climate of mutually peaceful confidence is abroad in the world.

But I know, above all else, that we must start to take these steps — now.

The United States and its allies, Great Britain and France, have over the past months tried to take some of these steps. Let no one say that we shun the conference table.

On the record has long stood the request of the United States, Great Britain, and France to negotiate with the Soviet Union the problem of a divided Germany.

On that record has long stood the request of the same three nations to negotiate an Austrian Peace Treaty.

On the same record still stands the request of the United Nations to negotiate the problem of Korea.

Most recently, we have received from the Soviet Union what is in effect an expression of willingness to hold a Four Power Meeting. Along with our allies, Great Britain and France, we were pleased to see that this note did not contain the unacceptable pre-conditions previously put forward.

As you already know from our joint Bermuda communique, the United States, Great Britain, and France have agreed promptly to meet with the Soviet Union.

The Government of the United States approaches this conference with hopeful sincerity. We will bend every effort of our mind to the single purpose of emerging from that conference with tangible results toward peace — the only true way of lessening international tension.

We never have, we never will, propose or suggest that the Soviet Union surrender what is rightfully theirs.

We will never say that the peoples of Russia are an enemy with whom we have no desire ever to deal or mingle in friendly and fruitful relationship.

On the contrary, we hope that this coming conference may initiate a relationship with the Soviet Union which will eventually bring about a free intermingling of the peoples of the East and of the West — the one sure, human way of developing the understanding required for confident and peaceful relations.

Instead of the discontent which is now settling upon Eastern Germany, occupied Austria, and the countries of Eastern Europe, we seek a harmonious family of free European nations, with none a threat to the other, and least of all a threat to the peoples of Russia.

Beyond the turmoil and strife and misery of Asia, we seek peaceful opportunity for these people to develop their natural resources and to elevate their lives.

These are not idle words or shallow visions. Behind them lies a story of nations lately come to independence, not as a result of war, but through free grant or peaceful negotiation. There is a record, already written, of assistance gladly given by nations of the West to needy peoples, and to those suffering the temporary effects of famine, drought, and natural disaster.

These are deeds of peace. They speak more loudly than promises or protestations of peaceful intent.

But I do *not* wish to rest either upon the reiteration of past proposals or the restatement of past deeds. The gravity of the time is such that every new avenue of peace, no matter how dimly discernible, should be explored.

There is at least one new avenue of peace which has not yet been well explored — an avenue now laid out by the General Assembly of the United Nations.

In its resolution of November 18th, 1953, this General Assembly suggested — and I quote — "that the Disarmament Commission study the desirability of establishing a sub-committee consisting of representatives of the Powers principally involved, which should seek in private an acceptable solution . . . and report such a solution to the General Assembly and to the Security Council not later than September 1, 1954."

The United States, heeding the suggestion of the General Assembly of the United Nations, is instantly prepared to meet privately with such other countries as may be "principally involved," to seek "an acceptable solution" to the atomic armaments race which overshadows not only the peace, but the very life, of the world.

We shall carry into these private or diplomatic talks a new conception.

The United States would seek more than the mere reduction or elimination of atomic materials for military purposes.

It is not enough to take this weapon out of the hands of the soldiers. It must be put into the hands of those who will know how to strip its military casing and adapt it to the arts of peace.

The United States knows that if the fearful trend of atomic military buildup can be reversed, this greatest of destructive forces can be developed into a great boon, for the benefit of all mankind.

The United States knows that peaceful power from atomic energy is no dream of the future. That capability, already proved, is here — now — today. Who can doubt, if the entire body of the world's scientists and engineers had adequate amounts of fissionable material with which to test and develop their ideas, that this capability would rapidly be transformed into universal, efficient, and economic usage.

To hasten the day when fear of the atom will begin to disappear from the minds of people, and the governments of the East and West, there are certain steps that can be taken now.

I therefore make the following proposal:

The Governments principally involved, to the extent permitted by elementary prudence, to begin now and continue to make joint contributions from their stockpiles of normal uranium and fissionable materials to an International Atomic Energy Agency. We would expect that such an agency would be set up under the aegis of the United Nations.

The ratios of contributions, the procedures and other details would properly be within the scope of the "private conversations" I have referred to earlier.

The United States is prepared to undertake these explorations in good faith. Any partner of the United States acting in the same good faith will find the United States a not unreasonable or ungenerous associate.

Undoubtedly initial and early contributions to this plan would be small in quantity. However, the proposal has the great virtue that it can be undertaken without the irritations and mutual suspicions incident to any attempt to set up a completely acceptable system of world-wide inspection and control.

The Atomic Energy Agency could be made responsible for the impounding, storage, and protection of the contributed fissionable and other materials. The ingenuity of our scientists will provide special safe conditions under which such a bank of fissionable material can be made essentially immune to surprise seizure.

The more important responsibility of this Atomic Energy Agency would be to devise methods whereby this fissionable material would be allocated to serve the peaceful pursuits of mankind. Experts would be mobilized to apply atomic energy to the needs of agriculture, medicine, and other peaceful activities. A special purpose would be to provide abundant electrical energy in the power-starved areas of the world. Thus the contributing powers would be dedicating some of their strength to serve the needs rather than the fears of mankind.

The United States would be more than willing — it would be proud to take up with others "principally involved" the development of plans whereby such peaceful use of atomic energy would be expedited.

Of those "principally involved" the Soviet Union must, of course, be one.

I would be prepared to submit to the Congress of the United States, and with every expectation of approval, any such plan that would:

First — encourage world-wide investigation into the most effective peacetime uses of fissionable material, and with the certainty that they had all the material needed for the conduct of all experiments that were appropriate;

Second — begin to diminish the potential destructive power of the world's atomic stockpiles;

Third — allow all peoples of all nations to see that, in this enlightened age, the great powers of the earth, both of the East and of the West, are interested in human aspirations first, rather than in building up the armaments of war;

Fourth — open up a new channel for peaceful discussion, and initiate at least a new approach to the many difficult problems that must be solved in both private and public conversations, if the world is to shake off the inertia imposed by fear and is to make positive progress toward peace.

Against the dark background of the atomic bomb, the United States does not wish merely to present strength, but also the desire and the hope for peace.

The coming months will be fraught with fateful decisions. In this Assembly; in the capitals and military headquarters of the world; in the hearts of men everywhere, be they governed or governors, may they be the decisions which will lead this world out of fear and into peace.

To the making of these fateful decisions, the United States pledges before you — and therefore before the world — its determination to help solve the fearful atomic dilemma — to devote its entire heart and mind to find the way by which the miraculous inventiveness of man shall not be dedicated to his death, but consecrated to his life.

I again thank the delegates for the great honor they have done me, in inviting me to appear before them, and in listening to me so courteously. Thank you.

## *Eisenhower's "Atoms for Peace" Speech: A Case Study in the Strategic Use of Language*

MARTIN J. MEDHURST

> "Personally, I think this [speech] will be a 'sleeper' as far as this country is concerned — but one of these days when the deserts do bloom, and atomic reactors are turning out electricity where there was no fuel before, and when millions of people are eating who never really ate before . . . the President's December 1953 speech and proposal will be remembered as the starting point of it all."[1]
>
> — C. D. JACKSON, Special Assistant to the President for Psychological Warfare
> February 5, 1955

More than thirty years later the deserts have not bloomed, famine is still a reality, and the nuclear reactor, once the hopeful sign of a better tomorrow, stands as a technological indictment of humanity's inability to see beyond the visions of the moment.

Dwight Eisenhower was not the first president to speak of the peaceful uses of atomic energy, yet it was his "Atoms for Peace" speech, delivered in front of the United Nations' General Assembly on December 8, 1953, that marked the public commencement of a persuasive campaign the dimensions of which stagger the imagination. Planned at the highest levels of government, shrouded in secrecy, aided by the military-industrial complex, and executed over the course of two decades, the campaign to promote the "peaceful" use of the atom was conceived in pragmatism, dedicated in realism, and promoted in the spirit of idealism. At each stage of the campaign rhetorical purposes, some lofty, some base, motivated both words and deeds.

Space does not permit a complete explication of this persuasive effort nor even a perfunctory glance at each of its component parts. That must await some future forum. In this essay the pragmatic atmosphere that prompted Eisenhower to deliver a speech advertised as a step away from the nuclear precipice will be described. At the same time, the realist assumptions and motives that reveal Eisenhower's true purposes for delivering his "Atoms for Peace" speech on December 8, 1953 will be explicated.

The argument has three parts. First, that despite American protestations to the contrary, Eisenhower's "Atoms for Peace" speech was, in fact, a carefully-crafted piece of cold war rhetoric specifically designed to gain a "psychological" victory over the Soviet Union. It was part of an American peace offensive launched, in part, as a response to an ongoing Soviet peace offensive.

Second, that the speech creates one audience on the level of explicit argument, but a much different audience when the implicit arguments are examined. Explicitly, the speech is addressed to the world at large, particularly those non-aligned nations in the midst of industrialization. It is aimed at that amorphous animal called world opinion. Implicitly, it is addressed to the Soviet Union, partly as warning, partly as challenge.

Third, that the speech is intentionally structured to invite the world at large to understand "Atoms for Peace" as a step toward nuclear disarmament. In addition to the internal structure, the persuasive campaign carried on immediately before and after the speech was designed explicitly to portray "Atoms for Peace" as part of the free world's (read America's) commitment to nuclear arms control. That the speech was not, in fact, related to disarmament talks but was, rather, an attempt to gain a psychological, cold war victory will be demonstrated.

## CONCEIVED IN PRAGMATISM

To understand fully how "Atoms for Peace" evolved to the form in which it was delivered, one must return to the opening weeks of the Eisenhower administration, specifically the events of February, March, and April of 1953. Three events are particularly worthy of note.

In February, a top secret report commissioned by President Truman was delivered to the new Secretary of State, John Foster Dulles.

Known internally as the Oppenheimer Report, the document "declared that a renewed search must be made for a way to avert the catastrophe of modern war" (Donovan, 1956, p. 184). Essential to this goal, the report held, was "wider public discussion based upon wider understanding of the meaning of a nuclear holocaust" (Donovan, 1956, p. 184).

As discussion of the policy implications of the Oppenheimer Report ensued, a new factor changed the complexion of American foreign policy: Stalin died. Announced to the world on March 6, 1953, the death of Stalin was viewed as a unique opportunity for advancing the cause of freedom, both in the occupied countries of Europe and within the Soviet Union itself. As historian Louis Halle puts it, the hope was "widespread throughout the West, that the Soviet state, unable to resolve the problem of the succession, would fall into confusion and helplessness upon Stalin's removal from the scene" (Halle, 1967, p. 312). Nowhere was this hope more evident than within Eisenhower's inner circle.

C. D. Jackson, Special Assistant to the President for cold war strategy (also known as psychological warfare), and the man who would later be primarily responsible for the drafting of "Atoms for Peace," viewed the death of Stalin with both elation and alarm. On March 4, 1953, Jackson wrote to General Robert Cutler, head of the National Security Council:

> This morning's developments, both in Moscow and in Washington point up both a great need and a great opportunity. As to the need, it is hardly an exaggeration to say that no agency of this government had in its files anything resembling a plan, or even a sense-making guidance, to cover the circumstances arising out of the fatal illness or death of Stalin. . . . It is both fair and safe to say that, left to itself, the existing machinery will be incapable of assuming the initiative and moving on the first really great opportunity that has been presented to us.
>
> Conversely — and this is the opportunity — if we do not take the initiative and capitalize on the dismay, confusion, fear, and selfish hopes brought about by this opportunity, we will be giving the enemy the time to pull himself together, get his wind back, and present us with a new monolithic structure which we will spend years attempting to analyze. . . .
>
> In other words, shouldn't we do everything possible to overload the enemy at the precise moment when he is least capable of bearing even his normal load. . . . During the present moment of confusion, the chances of the Soviets launching World War III are reduced virtually to zero, and will remain in the low numbers so long as the confusion continues to exist. Our task, therefore, is to perpetuate the confusion as long as possible, and to stave off as long as possible any new crystallization.

> It is not inconceivable that out of such a program might come further opportunities which, skillfully exploited, might advance the real disintegration of the Soviet Empire (Jackson, 1953a).

Thus was set in motion a systematic plan to "exploit" the weakness perceived to accompany a Soviet transfer of power. Within the week plans were being laid, amidst much internal dissension, to take advantage of the historical moment. Against the wishes of John Foster Dulles, Jackson convinced the President to launch an American peace offensive and, with the assistance of Walt Rostow and Emmet Hughes, began to draft a major foreign policy address designed, in Rostow's words, "to hold up a vision of the specific long-range objectives of American diplomacy but to make the negotiations designed to achieve that vision contingent upon a prior Korean settlement" (Rostow, 1982, p. 7).

After "some fourteen drafts" (Rostow, 1982, p. 7) the "Age of Peril" speech was delivered before the American Society of Newspaper Editors on April 16, 1953. It was the opening shot in the psychological warfare advocated by Jackson as a means "to preempt a possible Soviet peace offensive" (Rostow, 1982, p. 4). The speech laid out American objectives: settlement in Korea, peace in Indochina, unification of Germany, an Austrian peace treaty, and, in one line, the peaceful use of atomic energy. The atom for peace, long sought after by scientists and visionaries, had now joined the cold war effort.

Having launched the offensive, Jackson, at Eisenhower's direction, continued to probe for opportunities to exploit the situation. In an effort to line up the American public behind the offensive and to prepare them for the twilight struggle that lay ahead, Jackson and Hughes were charged with producing drafts of what came to be known as Operation Candor — a straightforward report to the American people on the destructive capacity of nuclear weapons.

Both Eisenhower and Jackson agreed with the findings of the Oppenheimer Report: that the public must come to understand the full implications of nuclear war. Moreover, the Soviet peace offensive and public weariness with the Korean War made incorporation of the American audience behind the U.S. effort an absolute necessity lest Americans, in the words of Konrad Adenauer, be tempted "to succumb to the blandishments of a detente which for the time being was nothing but a pipedream" (Adenauer, cited in Rostow, p. 50). It was time to be completely candid with the American public concerning the possibility of mutual destruction, a possibility that now defined the very nature of superpower politics.

Numerous drafts of the Operation Candor speech were produced from late April to early October of 1953. None proved adequate to the task at hand. Furthermore, in the intervening months the situation had changed radically once again. On July 26 a Korean truce had been signed; the war was over. Two weeks later, on August 12, 1953, the Soviet Union tested their first hydrogen bomb. Unbeknownst to the American public, the type of thermonuclear weapon tested by the Soviet Union indicated that they were much closer to the capacity for delivering a hydrogen bomb than anyone imagined.[2] The need for "Candor" was now greater than ever. The public must be prepared for the worst, but there were problems.

On September 2, Jackson wrote to Gordon Arneson at the State Department: "I am afraid that the Candor speech is slowly dying from a severe attack of Committee-itis" (Jackson, 1953b). Though Jackson tried to establish new guidelines for production of the speech, the difficulty of the concepts involved along with a well-publicized leak to *Washington Post* columnist Stewart Alsop (1953, p. 23), resulted in the death of Operation Candor. On September 28, 1953, James Lambie distributed the following memo to the twenty people who were by then involved in the Candor question: "C. D. Jackson asks me to use this outworn method (rather than the more expeditious one of going directly to Stewart Alsop) to make sure you are apprised of the following: Subject Operation, *as a series* of connected and integrated weekly talks is canceled. The President may deliver a single speech of his own in the general area to have been covered by subject series. As of now, however, no final decision has been taken as to such a speech by the President — what, when or whether."[3]

Though no "final decision" had been made, Eisenhower wanted to continue the search for an appropriate speech, though with a different emphasis. Consulting with Jackson, Cutler, and Admiral Lewis L. Strauss, Chairman of the Atomic Energy Commission, Eisenhower proposed, in a very general sort of way, an international pool of fissionable material that could be used strictly for peaceful purposes. It was this idea, first shared with his three top advisors on September 10, that eventually matured into "Atoms for Peace."[4]

The story of the evolution of Project Wheaties, the code name given to the newly-resurrected "Atoms for Peace" speech, is an essay unto itself and must not detain us here. Suffice it to note that starting with the first complete draft on November 3, 1953, "Atoms for Peace" went through eleven major revisions before its presentation on December 8. The last four drafts were completed at the Big Three conference at Bermuda from December 4–7, with the final draft being edited on the flight from Bermuda to New York City on the afternoon of December 8. There is much to be learned from examination of the eleven drafts of the speech, but that, too, is a separate essay. I turn now to the speech delivered by Eisenhower at 4:30 p.m., December 8, 1953, in front of 3500 delegates, guests, and media representatives at the United Nations building in New York City.

## DEDICATED IN REALISM

The address was a masterpiece of "realpolitik," long before the term became fashionable. Every line was included (or excluded) for a purpose, and that purpose was strategic advantage, whether defined in terms of placing the Soviet Union at a psychological disadvantage, or in terms of preparing the American audience for an "age" of peril, or in terms of ingratiating the foreign audience.

From the outset, the public posture of the U.S. was that this was *not* a propaganda speech, but a serious proposal that could, if accepted by the Soviets, lead to a climate more conducive to nuclear disarmament. As Eisenhower himself would later maintain in his memoirs, "if we were successful in making even a start, it was possible that gradually negotiation and cooperation might expand into something broader" (Eisenhower, 1963, p. 254). Possible, yes, but not probable. Indeed, given the relative strengths of each side's nuclear forces, the relative scarcity of mineable uranium within the U.S.S.R., and the diplomatic tradition which held that serious proposals were made through private, not public channels, it seems clear that any public offer would have had a propaganda *effect* by placing the Russians on the spot in front of a world-wide audience. Even if the American offer was sincere, it placed the U.S.S.R. in a position of either accepting the offer (and thereby implicitly testifying to America's long-professed desire for peace) or rejecting the offer (and thereby appearing to the world at large as an aggressor unwilling to explore a plan that, as presented by Eisenhower, would benefit directly the underdeveloped nations as well as the cause of international peace).

The beauty of "Atoms for Peace," as conceived by Jackson and Strauss, its primary authors, was precisely that it would place Russia in an awkward position and allow America to gain a psychological advantage on the stage of world opinion. As Jackson wrote to Eisenhower on October 2, 1953: "It must be of such a nature that its rejection by the Russians, or even prolonged foot-dragging on their part, will make it clear to the people of the world . . . that the moral blame for the armaments race, and possibly war, is clearly on the Russians" (Jackson, 1953c).

*Analysis of the Test.* Eisenhower's speech follows a three-part pattern progressing from the present danger, to past efforts toward reconciliation, to a vision for the future. Each section features an America striving after "peace," a term that occurs twenty-four times in the address.[5]

One might logically expect a deliberative speech structured chronologically to proceed from past to present to future. Why does Eisenhower violate expectations by starting with the present? There are several reasons.

First, the primary purpose of the speech is psychological advantage rather than historical narration. The story is important only insofar as it provides the context for the perceived psychological gains. Four such gains are paramount: to warn the Russians against nuclear attack on the United States; to alert Americans to the potential destructiveness of a nuclear exchange; to position the United States as a peacemaker and friend in the eyes of the developing nations; and to place the Soviet Union in a policy dilemma by issuing to them a public challenge.

Second, had Eisenhower started with the past he would have encountered two disadvantages: he would have been forced to start with a recitation of failure that would have set the wrong tone for the speech by drawing immediate attention to Russian intransigence, thereby establishing an atmosphere of confrontation, precisely the opposite of what needed to be done if the psychological advantage were to be obtained. Further, by elevating the past to the position of primacy, the president would have been forced to bury the present in the middle portion of the speech. This, too, would have been disadvantageous inasmuch as one of the primary purposes of the address is to issue an implicit warning to the Russians who, it was held widely in military circles, would soon possess the requisite number of nuclear weapons to launch a preemptive strike against the United States. Eisenhower wants to feature the warning, not bury it in the midst of an historical narrative.

Finally, by holding the past efforts at reconciliation until the middle portion of the speech, Eisenhower is able dramatically to juxtapose the failures of the past with his visionary plan for the future. The rhetorical disposition adopted adds argumentative force to the atoms-for-peace proposal by highlighting the significant departure from past plans represented by the new proposal for an international pool of fissionable materials dedicated to peaceful purposes. If the past was characterized by suspicions leading to fear, the future is presented as an opportunity leading to hope.

**Atomic Strength of the United States** In the introductory paragraphs the term "hope" or its derivative occurs five times. "Never before in history," claims Eisenhower, "has so much hope for so many people been gathered together in a single organization. Your deliberations and decisions during these somber years have already realized part of those hopes."[6] After paying homage to the organization,

Eisenhower asserts that it would not be "a measure of this great opportunity merely to recite, however hopefully, pious platitudes." He realizes, he says, "that if a danger exists in the world, it is a danger shared by all — and equally, that if hope exists in the mind of one nation, that hope should be shared by all."

Thus, in his opening statement, Eisenhower prepares the audience for a speech about the way out of the atomic dilemma that confronts humanity. At this point it would be easy to slip into a chronological pattern, starting with past efforts to solve the dilemma, the state of present negotiations, and, finally, his new plan for the future. A second alternative might be to review, in summary fashion, the hopes of the past and then to continue without pause into discussions of his plan. Eisenhower chooses a third way.

He begins by speaking of the present. "I feel impelled to speak today in a language that in a sense is new — one which I, who have spent so much of my life in the military profession, would have preferred never to use. That new language is the language of atomic warfare." Thus does Eisenhower launch the first part of the body, a section that might well be labeled "The Nuclear Capability of the United States of America," by confronting the audience with the paradox of a warrior who hates to speak of war, thereby distinguishing the persona of the General from that of the statesman. The General spoke the language of war; the President speaks the language of peace.

Though ostensibly a recitation of the extent to which nuclear weapons have proliferated both in size and number since 1945, the opening section is, in reality, a series of veiled warnings to the Soviet Union. Though ostensibly informative in intent, the opening section is really an exhortation whose central message is that the Soviet Union should reconsider any plans it might have for launching a preemptive strike against the United States.

The entire section is a series of warnings under the guise of a dispassionate report as demonstrated in the following chart:

1. *Explicit Argument:* Today, the United States' stockpile of atomic weapons, which, of course, increases daily, exceeds by many times the explosive equivalent of the total of all bombs and all shells that came from every plane and every gun in every theatre of war in all of the years of World War II.

*Implicit Argument.* Be assured that we are not reducing our weapons program despite reported cutbacks in the defense budget. We are building more nuclear weapons every day and will continue to do so as long as we must.

2. *Explicit Argument.* The development has been such that atomic weapons have virtually achieved conventional status within our armed services. In the United States, the Army, the Navy, the Air Force, and the Marine Corps are all capable of putting this weapon to military use.

   *Implicit Argument.* If you think you can hope to prevail over us merely by knocking out our Air Force bases and missile silos, you are woefully mistaken. We are capable of launching a retaliatory nuclear strike against you with any branch of our services.

3. *Explicit Argument.* Our earlier start has permitted us to accumulate what is today a great quantitative advantage.

   *Implicit Argument.* You may have enough nuclear devices to hurt us, but we have a lot more and can outlast you in any nuclear exchange.

4. *Explicit Argument.* The free world . . . has naturally embarked on a large program of warning and defense systems. That program will be accelerated and expanded.

   *Implicit Argument.* Don't think for a moment that we are letting down our guard. We are prepared both militarily and psychologically.

5. *Explicit Argument.* But for me to say that the defense capabilities of the United States are such that they could inflict terrible losses upon an aggressor — for me to say that the retaliation capabilities of the United States are so great that such an aggressor's land would be laid waste — all this, while fact, is not the true expression of the purpose and the hope of the United States.

   *Implicit Argument.* Think not that the land of Mother Russia will remain inviolate. It will not. We will inflict damage so great that it will make your losses in WW II seem like child's play.

That the movement from explicit to implicit argument was a conscious and intentional strategy is clear from the documentary history. On October 23, 1953, for example, Secretary of State John Foster Dulles sent a "personal and private" memorandum to Eisenhower in which he advises that the speech should "make clear our determination, so long as this danger exists, to take the necessary steps to deter attack, through possession of retaliatory power and the development of continental defense" (Dulles, 1953).

The speech drafts leading up to the December 8 address make it abundantly clear that the writers, principally Jackson and Strauss, are attempting to retain the threat of retaliation while, at the same moment, couching that threat in language that become successively less confrontative. In other words, the rhetoric of the drafts proceeds from bold, outright threats to implied warnings couched in the language of peaceful intentions. By comparing the last "Operation Candor" draft completed on or about October 1, 1953, by presidential speechwriter Emmet Hughes, with the final draft delivered by President Eisenhower on December 8, 1953, the movement from explicit to implicit argument can be clearly observed.

*Candor Draft 10/1/53*

We are today armed with bombs a single *one* of which — with an explosive equivalent of more than 500,000 tons of TNT — exceeds by more than *30 times* the power of the first atomic bombs that fell in 1945. . . . Each *year* sees this mass increase with a power that is many times greater than that of *all* explosives dropped by the aircraft of *all* the Allied nations in World War II.

*Wheaties Draft 12/8/53*

Today, the United States' stockpile of atomic weapons, which, of course, increases daily, exceeds by many times the explosive equivalent of the total of all bombs and all shells that came from every plane and every gun in every theatre of war in all the years of World War II.

*Candor Draft 10/1/53*

Any single *one* of the many air wings of our Strategic Air Command could deliver — in *one* operation — atomic bombs with an explosive equivalent greater than *all* the bombs that fell on Germany through *all* the *years* of World War II.

Any *one* of the aircraft carriers of our Navy could deliver in *one day* atomic bombs exceeding the explosive equivalent of *all* bombs and rockets dropped by Germany upon the United Kingdom through *all* the years of World War II.

We have certain knowledge that we can not only increase greatly the power of our weapons but also perfect their methods of delivery and their tactical use.

These, then, are measures of the fantastic strength we possess.

*Wheaties Draft 12/8/53*

The development has been such that atomic weapons have virtually achieved conventional status within our armed services. In the United States, the Army, the Navy, the Air Force, and the Marine Corps are all capable of putting this weapon to military use.

*Candor Draft 10/1/53*

We possess detailed evidence of the progress, over the past four years, of the Soviet Union's development of atomic and thermonuclear weapons.

*Wheaties Draft 12/8/53*

Our earlier start has permitted us to accumulate what is today a great quantitative advantage.

We know that in this period the Soviet Union has exploded six atomic devices — and quite recently, one involving thermonuclear reaction.

We know, too, how the amassing of these weapons can be speeded by the implacable methods of police state and slave labor.

We know — above all else — this fact: Despite our own swift perfection of new weapons, despite our vast advantage in their numbers — the very nature of these weapons is such that their desperate use against us could inflict terrible damage upon our cities, our industries and our population.

*Candor Draft 10/1/53*

The second decision is to devise for America a defense system unmatched in the world. Such a system — entailing the most developed use of radar, interceptor aircraft, anti-aircraft artillery and guided missiles — is in the making.

The building of this defense will be pressed with uncompromising vigor. . . . Our defenses will be built with vision, care, common sense — and a frank readiness to spend whatever money or energy such a logical program demands.

*Wheaties Draft 12/8/86*

The free world . . . has naturally embarked on a large program of warning and defense systems. The program will be accelerated and expanded.

*Candor Draft 10/1/53*

. . . we declare clearly that if — and wherever — United States forces are involved in repelling aggression, these forces will feel free to use atomic weapons as military advantage dictates.

Any such use of atomic weapons would be strictly governed by a clear order of priority.

(1) They would be used immediately against military forces operating against us or our allies.

*Wheaties Draft 12/8/53*

But for me to say that the defense capabilities of the United State are such that they could inflict terrible losses upon an aggressor — for me to say that the retaliation capabilities of the United States are so great that such an aggressor's land would be laid waste — all this, while fact, is not the true expression of the purpose and the hope of the United States.

The evolution of the speech drafts from early October to early December evidences a shift away from straightforward assertion to implicative argumentation. That the implications are, in most cases, similar or identical to the authorial intentions of the original Candor draft can be seen by comparing the October 1, 1953 draft with the implicit arguments found in the December 8 address.

That the Soviets are likely to have understood the argumentative implications in ways roughly similar to the reconstructions above is a function both of timing and of access. For four months prior to the December 8 address, the American media ran story after story about governmental, military, and scientific concerns about a possible nuclear confrontation. Not only were such concerns easily picked up through environmental cues, but the Soviets were also given advanced warning about the December 8 speech and instructed to pay close attention and to take seriously what the President said.

In a top secret cable sent from Chip Bohlen, U.S. Ambassador to the Soviet Union, to Secretary of State John Foster Dulles, Bohlen apprised the Secretary of his talk with Russian Foreign Minister Vyacheslav Molotov: "The purpose of my visit to him," cabled Bohlen, "was to draw the attention of Soviet Government in advance to great importance which my Government attached to this speech . . . I concluded by saying there was no need to stress to him (Molotov) the immense importance of [the] whole question of atomic weapons and repeated the hope that Soviet Government would receive this suggestion as seriously as it was made" (Bohlen, 1953).

In addition to the special visit of Bohlen to Molotov, the Soviet Union's representative to the United Nations, Andrei Vishinsky, was provided an advance copy of the entire address. Vishinsky, as one reporter noted, "appeared to be the only delegate with a copy of the speech" (James, 1953, p. 3). Thus, through both public and private sources, the Soviets were encouraged to listen closely to "Atoms for Peace."

The dichotomy between the arguments as explicitly stated and those same arguments' implications is matched by the dichotomous audiences created by each argumentative level. The audience created by the explicit argument is the world-at-large, the non-nuclear powers who, as spectators in the deadly game of superpower politics, have a legitimate interest in the state-of-the-standoff as perceived by the U.S. President.

A secondary audience for this explicitly argued content is the American public. Operation Candor was originally planned as a series of addresses to the domestic audience, and Eisenhower explicitly states at the outset of the address that these are "thoughts I had originally planned to say primarily to the American people." Though no longer the primary target audience, the American public will still be informed of the terrible destructive capacity of the U.S. arsenal, and thus Eisenhower is able to accomplish multiple goals simultaneously.

But while the audience for the explicit content is clearly the world at large, the target for the implicitly argued content can be none other than the Soviet Union. Why, in a speech ostensibly devoted to "peace," should Eisenhower spend fully twenty percent of his time issuing veiled warnings to the U.S.S.R.? The reasons are many.

According to C.I.A. estimates the Russians would, within a matter of months, have enough nuclear weapons to launch a preemptive strike against the United States. Knowledgeable sources within the scientific, political, and military establishments believed such an attack to be likely (Herken, 1980, p. 325; Menken, cited in "Briton Warns U.S.," 1953, p. 15; Urey, cited in Strauss, 1962, p. 228). Furthermore, the U.S.S.R. had exploded their first thermonuclear weapon and had immediately followed that test with a series of atomic tests lasting well into September. In the space of ninety days the Soviets had tested as many nuclear weapons as in the previous four years combined. Doubtless the sudden spate of activity could be read as a prelude to an all-out attack.

Hence, Eisenhower conceives his task not only to be the articulation of the atomic pool idea, but also the conveying of a strong warning, implicit though it is, that a "surprise attack" by an "aggressor in possession of the effective minimum number of atomic bombs" would be met with "swift and resolute" action. Though he informs the world of the terrible atomic might of the United States of America, he also exhorts the U.S.S.R. to behave itself or suffer the consequences.

**Western Deeds and Desires** Having given his "report" on the present state of United States atomic strength, Eisenhower then makes a long, almost Churchillian, transition into the second major section of the speech — the past record of the Western Alliance in both word and deed. To stop with the recitation of the atomic dilemma, says Eisenhower, "would be to accept helplessly the probability of civilization destroyed — the annihilation of the irreplaceable heritage of mankind handed down to us generation from generation — and the condemnation of mankind to begin all over again the age-old struggle upward from savagery toward decency, and right, and justice. . . . So my country's purpose is to help us move out of the dark chamber of horrors into the light."

But again, it is not the light of the future to which Eisenhower moves, not to the atoms-for-peace plan. Instead, the President turns to the recent past and a recitation of the actions undertaken by the

United States and her allies in an effort, he claims, to restore peace and justice to the world. While the explicitly argued content again functions as a report to the world, the implications of the report, the "conclusions" to be drawn by the world audience, are that the Soviet Union has been intransigent.

"Let no one say that we shun the conference table," says Eisenhower. "On the record has long stood the request of the United States, Great Britain, and France to negotiate with the Soviet Union the problems of a divided Germany. On that record has long stood the request of the same three nations to negotiate an Austrian Peace Treaty. On the same record still stands the request of the United Nations to negotiate the problems of Korea."

Eisenhower's method is clear. He seeks to establish the willingness of the Western powers to negotiate, and thereby implies the intransigence and bad faith of the U.S.S.R. Moreover, by positioning the Soviets in the role of spoilers in the recent past, he increases the pressure on them to respond favorably to future entreaties, specifically the plan he is about to announce, a plan no peace-loving nation could reasonably refuse.

Eisenhower seeks to leave no route of escape as he concludes the second section by observing: "There is a record, already written, of assistance gladly given by nations of the West to needy peoples, and to those suffering the temporary effects of famine, drought, and natural disaster. These are deeds of peace. They speak more loudly than promises or protestations of peaceful intent." Once again, Eisenhower seeks to back the Russians into a corner. In effect, he is saying to them, as the whole world watches, "put up or shut up." In the final section of the speech he gives them their chance.

**An International Atomic Energy Agency** Eisenhower introduces his atoms-for-peace proposal by quoting a portion of the United Nations resolution passed by the General Assembly only three weeks earlier: "that the Disarmament Commission study the desirability of establishing a sub-committee consisting of representatives of the Powers principally-involved, which should seek in private an acceptable solution. . . . and report on such a solution to the General Assembly and to the Security Council not later than 1 September 1954."

By opening his final section with a quote from the United Nations, itself, Eisenhower accomplishes two goals: first, he establishes a frame of reference with which all delegates are familiar and, ostensibly, with which the vast majority agree; second, he invites the audience to understand his comments within the context of *disarmament.* This fact becomes particularly salient as one seeks to understand precisely what Eisenhower meant by his atoms-for-peace proposal. At the very least, it is clear that the President immediately invites his ostensible audience, the world at large, to believe that what he is about to say has something to do with nuclear disarmament, the subject of both the U.N. resolution and of the first section of the President's own speech.

That such an interpretation could not have been missed by the delegates is assured by the sentence immediately following: "The United States, heeding the suggestion of the General Assembly of the United Nations, is instantly prepared to meet privately with such other countries as may be 'principally involved,' to seek 'an acceptable solution' to the atomic armaments race."

Having committed himself to the exploration of arms control, Eisenhower makes a crucial transition that both shifts the ground from which he originally opened his final section of the speech and commences his challenge to the Soviet Union, a challenge which, whether accepted or rejected by the U.S.S.R., will, it is believed, result in a great psychological victory for the United States: "It is not enough to take this weapon out of the hands of the soldiers. It must be put into the hands of those who will know how to strip its military casing and adapt it to the arts of peace." Thus begins Eisenhower's argument for the development of atomic energy for peaceful purposes.

After proclaiming that "peaceful power from atomic energy is no dream of the future," but rather is "here — now — today," Eisenhower launches into the heart of the atoms-for-peace proposal: "The Governments principally involved, to the extent permitted by elementary prudence, to begin now and continue to make joint contributions from their stockpiles of normal uranium and fissionable materials to an International Atomic Energy." This Agency, said Eisenhower, "could be made responsible for the impounding, storage, and protections of the contributed fissionable and other materials."

"The more important responsibility of this Atomic Energy Agency," he continues, "would be to devise methods whereby this fissionable material would be allocated to serve the peaceful pursuits of mankind. Experts would be mobilized to apply atomic energy to the needs of agriculture, medicine, and other peaceful activities. A special purpose would be to provide abundant electrical energy in the power-starved areas of the world."

The appeal is clearly to those non-nuclear nations represented in the U.N. audience, particularly those to whom power, and agriculture, and medicine are pressing needs. To the world audience of 1953 this would have included the vast majority of member states. The pledge is equally clear: to share of our abundance, in this case our nuclear know-how, with those nations less fortunate. But there is one condition attached.

"The United States would be more than willing," Eisenhower continues, "to take up with others 'principally involved' the development of plans whereby such peaceful use of atomic energy would be expedited. Of those 'principally involved' the Soviet Union must, of course, be one." The proposition could hardly have been put in a more explicit manner. Eisenhower challenges the Soviets to join in an international effort to aid U.S. member nations, and he does so right in front of them so there may be no mistake about his offer. The challenge shifts the burden of proof squarely onto the shoulders of the Soviets. If they really are interested in peace, then here, says Eisenhower, is the perfect chance to demonstrate their commitment.

The International Agency, Eisenhower pledged, would have four tasks:

1. To "encourage world-wide investigation into the most effective peacetime uses of fissionable material";
2. To "begin to diminish the potential destructive power of the world's atomic stockpiles";
3. To "allow all peoples of all nations to see that . . . the great powers of the earth . . . are interested in human aspirations first, rather than in building up the armaments of war";
4. To "open up a new channel for peaceful discussion, and initiate at least a new approach to the many difficult problems that must be solved. . . ."

"Against the dark background of the atomic bomb," he concludes, "the United States does not wish merely to present strength, but also the desire and the hope for peace. . . . To the making of these fateful decisions, the United States pledges before you — and therefore before the world — its determination to help solve the fearful atomic dilemma." The section ends, as it had begun, with allusions to atomic disarmament. Indeed, the implicit message to the assembled delegates is that atoms-for-peace, in addition to helping non-nuclear nations reap the benefits of nuclear energy, is a step toward and a mechanism for converting the means of war into instruments of peace. It is a different approach to the whole disarmament problem and the "awful arithmetic" to which Eisenhower had earlier referred.

The implied content of this final section is directed exclusively toward world opinion. The implications to be drawn by the world-wide audience are roughly as follows:

1. The United States is making a serious offer to share its nuclear materials and expertise with the international community.

2. The United States is doing this because it wants to reduce the risks of war and increase international cooperation.
3. If the "principally-involved" parties all cooperate, then there will be an advance in the quality of life all over the globe.
4. The powers of nuclear energy are near-miraculous and the cures mentioned by Eisenhower are immediately available if only the Soviets will cooperate.

The explicit message directed to the Soviet Union is this: Here's the plan; it will benefit the entire world community whose eyes now rest on you. Will you cooperate? Eisenhower places a challenge squarely before the Soviets and dares them — in front of the whole world — to accept the challenge or suffer the consequences that will be wrought, not by the military might of the United States, but by the psychological weight of world opinion turned sour.

## EXTERNAL REACTION

As Eisenhower finished his speech there was a "burst of applause" (Hamilton, 1953, p. 2) that swelled to a crescendo. Even Soviet representative Andrei Vishinsky joined in the chorus. The next day Eisenhower's proposal was bannered across the nation's leading newspapers, and the effort to decipher precisely what he meant began.

Thomas Hamilton, writing on the front page of the *New York Times,* observed that "implicit in the President's speech was the realization that the United Nations would have to make a new start if the seven-year-old deadlock on international atomic control was ever to be broken" (Hamilton, 1953, p. 1). Hamilton recalled the failure of the Baruch Plan in 1946, and linked Eisenhower's atoms-for-peace proposal to that earlier effort. In Hamilton's opinion the speech clearly was aimed at moving disarmament talks off dead center.

The editorial page of the *Washington Post* also viewed Eisenhower's proposals as precursors to disarmament: "If the nations of the world — meaning Russia and the Western Allies — could cooperate on the diversion of nuclear materials for peaceful purposes, the groundwork might be laid for cooperation on genuine disarmament" ("The Choice," 1953, p. 10). The proposal was viewed as being part of the long-term process of disarmament.

Reaction on Capitol Hill was, if anything, even more infused with apocalyptic visions of peace. Representative James E. Van Zandt (R-PA) claimed that Eisenhower had "sounded the clarion call to all nations to beat the atomic sword of destruction into plowshares by harnessing the power of the atom for peaceful pursuits" ("Ike's Speech Praised," 1953, p. 16). Similar reactions were voiced throughout the corridors of official Washington.

Such reactions, in themselves, should not be surprising in light of the fact that the "correct" interpretation of the speech was carefully orchestrated and planted in the various media organs by none other than C. D. Jackson. It was Jackson who provided advance copies of the speech, then classified top-secret, to Ernest K. Lindley of *Newsweek*, Roscoe Drummond of the *New York Herald Tribune*, and James Shepley of *Time* magazine (McCrum, 1975, pp. 45–46). It was Jackson, who, in his capacity as a member of the Operations Coordinating Board, designed the campaign to "exploit" the speech, a campaign that included use of "leaders of opposition parties," the Voice of America, Radio Free Europe, the C.I.A., and other "non-attributable instrumentalities" (Jackson, 1954). The message, regardless of medium, was the same: "Atoms for Peace" is a serious peace proposal that could lead to control of the atomic armaments race.

Despite Jackson's best efforts, not all opinion leaders bought into the official "line" on the speech. One such group was the leadership of the Canadian government. Reporting from Ottawa, a correspondent for the *New York Times* noted that "as the speech was interpreted here, President Eisenhower's proposal for an international body and a common stockpool of fissionable material was limited to peaceful uses of atomic energy and could not have any decisive effect on the question of the use of atomic weapons in war" ("Canadians Await Details," 1953, p. 3).

Here was the crucial point. Was the atoms-for-peace proposal a serious effort to take the first step toward disarmament or was it not? If it was not intended as a step toward disarmament why was it given in the first place and, why was it placed within the general context of nuclear destruction and within the specific context of the ongoing disarmament debate at the U.N.? Clearly, the structuring of the speech invites the listeners to associate atoms-for-peace with the general disarmament debate.

## INTERNAL DEBATE

If Eisenhower's precise meaning was, despite Jackson's best efforts, a matter of some speculation on the international scene, it was no less obscure within the administration's own inner circles. The debate over what the president meant to say started even before the speech was delivered. As early as mid-October there was fierce disagreement between Jackson and the State Department over the advisability of making any speech at all. As Candor evolved into Wheaties, early in November, the disagreements within the administration began to crystalize.

Jackson chronicled the struggle in his personal log. On November 17, 1953, he wrote: "Meeting in Foster Dulles' office with Lewis Strauss. Unfortunately Bob Bowie invited in. Subject — Wheaties, and UN appearance on December 8. Dulles went into reverse, ably needled by Bowie — he didn't like UN idea; he didn't like Strauss' proposal; he didn't like anything. Bowie kept repeating that this was not the way to do things — quiet, unpublicized negotiations were the only thing that would get anywhere with Ruskies" (Jackson, 1953d).

But quiet diplomacy was anything but what Jackson had in mind. On November 21, 1953, Jackson wrote to Sherman Adams concerning "what we have in mind for December 8," and warning that "if this is *not* properly orchestrated, and these things are dribbled out without organized impact, we will fritter away what is probably the greatest opportunity we have yet had" (Jackson, 1953e). Jackson suggested six specific steps to Adams for insuring proper orchestration. One of these was that "every single one of the Departmental and Agency PR heads should be constantly worked with to see that they keep the news coming out of their departments beamed on a pre-determined frequency" (Jackson, 1953e). Jackson's concern was the psychological victory to be gained and the supposed benefits flowing therefrom. But the State Department had not yet rested its case.

On November 23, 1953, Bob Bowie sent his criticisms of the latest Wheaties draft (draft #4) to Secretary Dulles: "I question whether the proposal on atomic contributions by the United States and the Soviets will have its intended effect. Many people, and probably the Soviets, will treat it as a propaganda tactic rather than a serious proposal if it is made in this way. If serious results were hoped for, many would expect us to attempt private discussions with the Soviets as a beginning" (Bowie, 1953a).

Bowie's reservations came to fruition two days later at a "big meeting in Foster Dulles' office." According to Jackson's log, "red lights started blinking all over the place. Joint Chiefs and Defense have laid their ears back" (Jackson, 1953f). After a one-day Thanksgiving break, the group met again in Dulles' office. The "real problem," as Jackson recorded in his log, "is basic philosophy — are we or are we not prepared to embark on a course which may in fact lead to atomic disarmament? Soldier boys and their civilian governesses say no. Foster Dulles doesn't say yes or no, but says any atomic offer which does not recognize ultimate possibility is a phoney and should not be made. Strauss and I say we won't be out of the trenches by Christmas, or next Christmas or the next one, but let's try to make a start and see what happens. Foster considers this mentally dishonest (he should talk!)" (Jackson, 1953g).

Dulles was not the only one with reservations. His Policy Planning Staff head, Robert Bowie, was also deeply disturbed. As he wrote to Dulles on November 30, 1953: "The only serious point of substance is the one about which we have talked: whether the United

States wishes to achieve full-scale atomic disarmament if that should prove possible. My own view is that we definitely should. But unless this is our view I do not think this speech should be made" (Bowie, 1953b). Bowie's opinion was not heeded. Eisenhower made the speech with no consensus among his inner circle as to precisely what, if anything, the United States would do if confronted with the possibility of disarmament.

## CONCLUSION

The speech, as delivered, reflected the Jackson-Strauss position which held that disarmament, while desirable, was not an immediately realizable goal. The purpose for giving the speech was, therefore, not to establish a framework for talks about control of nuclear weapons, but instead was an effort to position the United States with respect to the peaceful uses of atomic energy and to bid the Soviets in a public forum to adopt that position, thereby gaining a psychological victory whatever the Russian response might be.

Jackson's memo to the Operations Coordinating Board on December 9, the day following the speech, is instructive: "It will be particularly important to impress upon world opinion the sincerity with which the United States seeks international security through the reduction of the arms burden, while at the same time avoiding any premature stimulation of false optimism regarding immediately realizable disarmament, which cannot be fulfilled under present conditions of international tensions" (Jackson, 1953h). From Jackson's point of view there was no doubt that the speech, though clothed in the language of disarmament, was not, itself, a vehicle for such disarmament, at least not at the present time.

That Eisenhower's speech raised the hope of turning weapons into plowshares can hardly be denied. That the majority of those in the inner circle who crafted the speech intended that nothing *more* than hope be offered can also hardly be denied. Though the public "exploitation" of the speech emphasized peace and negotiation, the backroom decision was that the United States would not "be drawn into separate negotiations with the Soviets on the elimination or control of nuclear weapons alone. "For our part," says a summary of a top secret meeting held on January 16, 1954, "we intend to discuss only the peaceful uses of atomic energy" (O.C.B., 1954).

The summary of the January 16, 1954 meeting goes on to note that "Secretary Dulles reiterated that we should try through these discussions to get across to friendly nations the idea that the disagreement over the control of the atomic weapons was not a bilateral difference of opinion between the United States and the U.S.S.R., but rather was a split between the U.S.S.R. and the remainder of the free world" (O.C.B., 1954). If this could be accomplished, if the Soviet Union could be isolated as the foe who refused to cooperate with the rest of the world, then the psychological victory would be won. This was the great, and arguably the primary, purpose for the "Atoms for Peace" speech of December 8, 1953.

By employing both implicit and explicit argumentative techniques, Eisenhower was able to accomplish his goals. He warned the Soviet Union against a preemptive strike; he portrayed the United States as the friend and benefactor of the developing world; and, most importantly, he placed the Soviet Union in a policy dilemma by challenging the U.S.S.R. to accept his atoms-for-peace proposal. Throughout the speech and the subsequent campaign to "exploit" it, the administration portrayed the December 8 speech as a serious offer to negotiate the problems of the nuclear age with any potential adversary. That the speech was, in reality, not such an offer at all testifies to the ease with which human agents can shape language and guide perception in accordance with their own purposes.

Language is not self-explanatory. It is a reflection of the goals, motives, and values of those who choose to use it as an instrument by which to realize their ends. This study demonstrates how a particular group of rhetors used language to address multiple audiences for divergent purposes while, at the same moment, maintaining that the audience was one and the purpose straightforward. Criticism, at this level, is the study of how language is used by humans to channel response, and is, in the case examined, a paradigm both of linguistic deception and strategic posturing at the highest levels of government.

## *Notes*

1. Letter from C. D. Jackson to Merlo Pusey, 5 February, 1955. C. D. Jackson Papers, Box 24, Dwight D. Eisenhower Library.
2. According to Robert A. Devine, "on August 12, 1953, American officials detected the first Soviet hydrogen explosion. . . . What neither Eisenhower nor Strauss revealed, however, was that the Russian device had used dry hydrogen isotopes that did not require unwieldy refrigeration. The Soviets now appeared not only to have caught up with American nuclear technology but to have moved closer than the United States to a deliverable hydrogen bomb." See Devine (1978), *Blowing on the wind: The nuclear test ban debate 1954–1960.* New York: Oxford University Press, pp. 16–17.
3. Memo from James M. Lambie to R. Gordon Arneson, Edmond Gullion, Brig. Gen. P. T. Carroll, Emmet J. Hughes, Abbott Washburn, Roy McNair, William V. Watts, Ralph Clark, Ray Snapp, W. B. McCool, Jack DeChant, George "Pete" Hotchkiss, Edward Lyman, Maj. Gen. A. R. Luedecke, George Wyeth, Lt. Col. Edwin F. Block, William H. Godel, Fred Blachly,

Mrs. Jeanne Singer, William Rogers, 28 September 1953, White House Central Files (WHCF), Box 12, Dwight D. Eisenhower Library.

4. Given the chronology of development of the *idea* for atoms-for-peace, it seems likely that Eisenhower picked up the general concept from a series of articles appearing in the *New York Times* from August 12–14, 1953. The three-part series written by William L. Laurence included the following lines: "The first international conference on atomic energy for industrial power voted unanimously at its closing session today in favor of establishing an international nuclear energy association, open to nuclear scientists of all the nations of the world, including the Soviet Union and other countries behind the Iron Curtain. . . . The purpose of the association would be to promote the peaceful uses of atomic energy through the exchange of knowledge by the various participating countries on subjects not related to military applications." See Laurence (1953, August 14). Atom scientists favor world pool of ideas, *New York Times*, p. 1.
5. The total count of twenty-four includes "peace" and its derivatives "peaceful" and "peacetime."
6. All quotations from Eisenhower's "Atoms for Peace" address are from the text as printed in *Public Papers of the President of the United States, 1953.* Washington, D.C.: Government Printing Office, pp. 813–822.

## *References*

Alsop, S. (1953, September 18). Candor is not enough. *Washington Post*, p. 23.

Bohlen, C. (1953). Unpublished cablegram from Chip Bohlen to J. F. Dulles. John Foster Dulles Papers, Box 1, Dwight D. Eisenhower Library.

Bowie, R. R. (1953a, November 23). Unpublished memo from Robert R. Bowie to Secretary Dulles. John Foster Dulles Papers, Box 1, Dwight D. Eisenhower Library.

Bowie, R. R. (1953b, November 30). Unpublished memo from Robert R. Bowie to Secretary Dulles. John Foster Dulles Papers, Box 1, Dwight D. Eisenhower Library.

Briton warns United States of atomic attack. (1953, August 12). *New York Times*, p. 15.

Canadians await details. (1953, December 9). *New York Times*, p. 3.

Donovan, R. J. (1956). *Eisenhower: The inside story.* New York: Harper and Brothers.

Dulles, J. F. (1953). Unpublished memo from J. F. Dulles to Eisenhower. John Foster Dulles Papers, Box 1, Dwight D. Eisenhower Library.

Eisenhower, D. D. (1963). *Mandate for change.* Garden City: Doubleday.

Halle, L. J. (1967). *The cold war as history.* New York: Harper and Row.

Hamilton, T. J. (1953, December 9). Eisenhower bids Soviets join United States in atomic stockpile for peace. *New York Times*, pp. 1–2.

Herken, G. (1980). *The winning weapon: The atomic bomb in the cold war 1945–1950.* New York: Alfred A. Knopf.

Ike's speech praised generally on 'Hill.' (1953, December 9). *Washington Post,* p. 16.

Jackson, C. D. (1953a, March 4). Unpublished memo from C. D. Jackson to General Robert Cutler. C. D. Jackson Papers, Box 37, Dwight D. Eisenhower Library.

Jackson, C. D. (1953b, September 2). Unpublished memo from C. D. Jackson to Gordon Arneson. White House Central Files, Confidential File, Box 12, Dwight D. Eisenhower Library.

Jackson, C. D. (1953c, October 2). Unpublished memo from C. D. Jackson to the President. C. D. Jackson Papers, Box 24, Dwight D. Eisenhower Library.

Jackson, C. D. (1953d, November 17). Unpublished log entry. C. D. Jackson Papers, Box 56, Dwight D. Eisenhower Library.

Jackson, C. D. (1953e, November 21). Unpublished memo from C. D. Jackson to Sherman Adams. C. D. Jackson Papers, Box 23, Dwight D. Eisenhower Library.

Jackson, C. D. (1953f, November 25). Unpublished log entry. C. D. Jackson Papers, Box 56, Dwight D. Eisenhower Library.

Jackson, C. D. (1953g, November 27). Unpublished log entry. C. D. Jackson Papers, Box 56, Dwight D. Eisenhower Library.

Jackson, C. D. (1953h, December 9). Unpublished memo from C. D. Jackson to members of the Operations Coordinating Board. C. D. Jackson Records, Box 1, Dwight D. Eisenhower Library.

Jackson, C. D. (1954, February 16). Unpublished memo from C. D. Jackson to members of the Operations Coordinating Board. White House Central Files, Confidential File, Box 13, Dwight D. Eisenhower Library.

James, M. (1953, December 9). President's plan stirs doubts in U.N. *New York Times,* p. 3.

McCrum, M. (1975, May 15). Unpublished oral history interview, Dwight D. Eisenhower Library.

Operations Coordinating Board. (1954, January 16). Summary of O. C. B. Meeting. White House Central Files, Confidential File, Box 12, Dwight D. Eisenhower Library.

Rostow, W. W. (1982). *Europe after Stalin: Eisenhower's three decisions of March 11, 1953.* Austin: University of Texas Press.

Strauss, L. L. (1962). *Men and decisions.* Garden City: Doubleday.

The choice on the atom. (1953, December 9). *Washington Post,* p. 10.

# 12

# Critical Reading of Mario Cuomo's "Religious Belief and Public Morality"

## *Religious Belief and Public Morality: A Catholic Governor's Perspective*

MARIO CUOMO

I would like to begin by drawing your attention to the title of this lecture: "Religious Belief and Public Morality: A Catholic Governor's Perspective." I was not invited to speak on "Church and State" generally. Certainly not "Mondale vs. Reagan." The subject assigned is difficult enough. I will try not to do more than I've been asked.

It's not easy to stay contained. Certainly, although everybody talks about a wall of separation between church and state, I've seen religious leaders scale that wall with all the dexterity of olympic athletes. In fact, I've seen so many candidates in churches and synagogues that I think we should change election day from Tuesdays to Saturdays and Sundays.

I am honored by this invitation, but the record shows that I am not the first Governor of New York to appear at an event involving Notre Dame. One of my great predecessors, Al Smith, went to the Army–Notre Dame football game each time it was played in New York.

His fellow Catholics expected Smith to sit with Notre Dame; protocol required him to sit with Army because it was the home team. Protocol prevailed. But not without Smith noting the dual demands on his affections. "I'll take my seat with Army," he said, "but I commend my soul to Notre Dame!"

Today I'm happy to have no such problem. Both my seat and my soul are with Notre Dame. And as long as Father McBrien doesn't invite me back to sit with him at the Notre Dame–St. John's basketball game, I'm confident my loyalties will remain undivided.

In a sense, it's a question of loyalty that Father McBrien has asked me here today to discuss. Specifically, must politics and religion in America divide our loyalties? Does the "separation between church and state" imply separation between religion and politics? Between morality and government? Are these different propositions? Even more specifically, what is the relationship of my Catholicism to my politics? Where does the one end and other begin? Or are the two divided at all? And if they're not, should they be?

Hard questions.

No wonder most of us in public life — at least until recently — preferred to stay away from them, heeding the biblical advice that if "hounded and pursued in one city," we should flee to another.

Now, however, I think that it is too late to flee. The questions are all around us, and answers are coming from every quarter. Some of them have been simplistic, most of them fragmentary, and a few, spoken with a purely political intent, demagogic.

There has been confusion and compounding of confusion, a blurring of the issue, entangling it in personalities and election strategies, instead of clarifying it for Catholics, as well as others.

Today I would like to try to help correct that.

I can offer you no final truths, complete and unchallengeable. But it's possible this one effort will provoke other efforts — both in support and contradiction of my position — that will help all of us understand our differences and perhaps even discover some basic agreement.

In the end, I'm convinced we will all benefit if suspicion is replaced by discussion, innuendo by dialogue; if the emphasis in our debate turns from a search for talismanic criteria and neat but simplistic answers to an honest — more intelligent — attempt at describing the role religion has in our public affairs, and the limits placed on that role.

And if we do it right — if we're not afraid of the truth even when the truth is complex — this debate, by clarification, can bring relief to untold numbers of confused — even anguished — Catholics, as well as to many others who want only to make our already great democracy even stronger than it is.

I believe the recent discussion in my own State has already produced some clearer definition. In early summer, newspaper accounts had created the impression in some quarters that official church spokespeople would ask Catholics to vote for or against specific candidates on the basis of their political position on the abortion issue. I was one of those given that impression. Thanks to the dialogue that ensued over the summer — only partially reported by the media — we learned that the impression was not accurate.

Confusion had presented an opportunity for clarification, and we seized it. Now all of us are saying one thing — in chorus — reiterating the statement of the National Conference of Catholic Bishops that they will not "take positions for or against political candidates" and that their stand on specific issues should not be perceived "as an expression of political partisanship."

Of course the bishops will teach — they must — more and more vigorously and more and more extensively. But they have said they will not use the power of their position, and the great respect it receives from all Catholics, to give an imprimatur to individual politicians or parties.

Not that they couldn't if they wished to — some religious leaders do; some are doing it at this very moment.

Not that it would be a sin if they did — God doesn't insist on political neutrality. But because it is the judgment of the bishops, and most of us Catholic lay people, that it is not wise for prelates and politicians to be tied too closely together.

I think that getting this consensus was an extraordinarily useful achievement.

Now, with some trepidation and after much prayer, I take up your gracious invitation to continue the dialogue in the hope that it will lead to still further clarification.

Let me begin this part of the effort by underscoring the obvious. I do not speak as a theologian; I do not have that competence. I do not speak as a philosopher; to suggest that I could, would be to set a new record for false pride. I don't presume to speak as a "good" person except in the ontological sense of that word. My principal credential is that I serve in a position that forces me to wrestle with the problems you've come here to study and debate.

I am by training a lawyer and by practice a politician. Both professions make me suspect in many quarters, including among some of my own co-religionists. Maybe there's no better illustration of the public perception of how politicians unite their faith and their profession than the story they tell in New York about "Fishhooks" McCarthy, a famous Democratic leader on the lower East Side, and right-hand man to Al Smith.

"Fishhooks," the story goes, was devout. So devout that every morning on his way to Tammany Hall to do his political work, he stopped into St. James Church on Oliver Street in downtown

Manhattan, fell on his knees, and whispered the same simple prayer: "Oh, Lord, give me health and strength. We'll steal the rest."

"Fishhooks" notwithstanding, I speak here as a politician. And also as a Catholic, a lay person baptized and raised in the pre-Vatican II Church, educated in Catholic schools, attached to the Church first by birth, then by choice, now by love. An old-fashioned Catholic who sins, regrets, struggles, worries, gets confused and most of the time feels better after confession.

The Catholic Church is my spiritual home. My heart is there, and my hope.

There is, of course, more to being a Catholic than a sense of spiritual and emotional resonance. Catholicism is a religion of the head as well as the heart, and to be a Catholic is to say "I believe" to the essential core of dogmas that distinguishes our faith.

The acceptance of this faith requires a lifelong struggle to understand it more fully and to live it more truly, to translate truth into experience, to practice as well as to believe.

That's not easy: applying religious belief to everyday life often presents difficult challenges.

It's always been that way. It certainly is today. The America of the late twentieth century is a consumer society, filled with endless distractions, where faith is more often dismissed than challenged, where the ethnic and other loyalties that once fastened us to our religion seem to be weakening.

In addition to all the weaknesses, dilemmas and temptations that impede every pilgrim's progress, the Catholic who holds political office in a pluralistic democracy — who is elected to serve Jews and Muslims, atheists and Protestants, as well as Catholics — bears special responsibility. He or she undertakes to help create conditions under which all can live with a maximum of dignity and with a reasonable degree of freedom; where everyone who chooses may hold beliefs different from specifically Catholic ones — sometimes contradictory to them; where the laws protect people's right to divorce, to use birth control and even to choose abortion.

In fact, Catholic public officials take an oath to preserve the Constitution that guarantees this freedom. And they do so gladly. Not because they love what others do with their freedom, but because they realize that in guaranteeing freedom for all, they guarantee our right to be Catholics: our right to pray, to use the sacraments, to refuse birth control devices, to reject abortion, not to divorce and remarry if we believe it to be wrong.

The Catholic public official lives the political truth most Catholics through most of American history have accepted and insisted on: the truth that to assure our freedom we must allow others the same freedom, even if occasionally it produces conduct by them which we would hold to be sinful.

I protect my right to be a Catholic by preserving your right to believe as a Jew, a Protestant or non-believer, or as anything else you choose.

We know that the price of seeking to force our beliefs on others is that they might some day force theirs on us.

This freedom is the fundamental strength of our unique experiment in government. In the complex interplay of forces and considerations that go into the making of our laws and policies, its preservation must be a pervasive and dominant concern.

But insistence on freedom is easier to accept as a general proposition than in its applications to specific situations. There are other valid general principles firmly embedded in our Constitution, which, operating at the same time, create interesting and occasionally troubling problems. Thus, the same amendment of the Constitution that forbids the establishment of a State Church affirms my legal right to argue that my religious belief would serve well as an article of our universal public morality. I may use the prescribed processes of government — the legislative and executive and judicial processes — to convince my fellow citizens — Jews and Protestants and Buddhists and non-believers — that what I propose is as beneficial for them as I believe it is for me; that it is not just parochial or narrowly sectarian but fulfills a human desire for order, peace, justice, kindness, love, any of the values most of us agree are desirable even apart from their specific religious base or context.

I am free to argue for a governmental policy for a nuclear freeze not just to avoid sin but because I think my democracy should regard it as a desirable goal.

I can, if I wish, argue that the State should not fund the use of contraceptive devices not because the Pope demands it but because I think that the whole community — for the good of the whole community — should not sever sex from an openness to the creation of life.

And surely, I can, if so inclined, demand some kind of law against abortion not because my Bishops say it is wrong but because I think that the whole community, regardless of its religious beliefs, should agree on the importance of protecting life — including life in the womb, which is at the very least potentially human and should not be extinguished casually.

No law prevents us from advocating any of these things: I am free to do so.

So are the Bishops. And so is Reverend Falwell.

In fact, the Constitution guarantees my right to try. And theirs. And his.

But should I? Is it helpful? Is it essential to human dignity? Does it promote harmony and understanding? Or does it divide us so fundamentally that it threatens our ability to function as a pluralistic community?

When should I argue to make my religious value your morality? My rule of conduct your limitation?

What are the rules and policies that should influence the exercise of this right to argue and promote?

I believe I have a salvific mission as a Catholic. Does that mean I am in conscience required to do everything I can as Governor to translate all my religious values into the laws and regulations of the State of New York or the United States? Or be branded a hypocrite if I don't?

As a Catholic, I respect the teaching authority of the bishops.

But must I agree with everything in the bishops' pastoral letter on peace and fight to include it in party platforms?

And will I have to do the same for the forthcoming pastoral on economics even if I am an unrepentant supply sider?

Must I, having heard the Pope renew the Church's ban on birth control devices, veto the funding of contraceptive programs for non-Catholics or dissenting Catholics in my State? I accept the Church's teaching on abortion. Must I insist you do? By law? By denying you Medicaid funding? By a constitutional amendment? If so, which one? Would that be the best way to avoid abortions or to prevent them?

These are only some of the questions for Catholics. People with other religious beliefs face similar problems.

Let me try some answers.

Almost all Americans accept some religious values as a part of our public life. We are a religious people, many of us descended from ancestors who came here expressly to live their religious faith free from coercion or repression. But we are also a people of many religions, with no established church, who hold different beliefs on many matters.

Our public morality, then — the moral standards we maintain for everyone, not just the ones we insist on in our private lives — depends on a consensus view of right and wrong. The values derived from religious belief will not — and should not — be accepted as part of the public morality unless they are shared by the pluralistic community at large, by consensus.

That values happen to be religious values does not deny them acceptability as a part of this consensus. But it does not require their acceptability, either.

The agnostics who joined the civil rights struggle were not deterred because that crusade's values had been nurtured and sustained in black Christian churches. Those on the political left are not perturbed today by the religious basis of the clergy and lay people who join them in the protest against the arms race and hunger and exploitation.

The arguments start when religious values are used to support positions which would impose on other people restrictions they find unacceptable. Some people do object to Catholic demands for an end to abortion, seeing it as a violation of the separation of church and state. And some others, while they have no compunction about invoking the authority of the Catholic bishops in regard to birth control and abortion, might reject out of hand their teaching on war and peace and social policy.

Ultimately, therefore, the question "whether or not we admit religious values into our public affairs" is too broad to yield a single answer. "Yes," we create our public morality through consensus and in this country that consensus reflects to some extent religious values of a great majority of Americans. But "no," all religiously based values don't have an *a priori* place in our public morality. The community must decide if what is being proposed would be better left to private discretion than public policy; whether it restricts freedoms, and if so to what end, to whose benefit; whether it will produce a good or bad result; whether overall it will help the community or merely divide it.

The right answers to these questions can be elusive. Some of the wrong answers, on the other hand, are quite clear. For example, there are those who say there is a simple answer to *all* these questions; they say that by history and practice of our people we were intended to be — and should be — a Christian country in law.

But where would that leave the non-believers? And whose Christianity would be law, yours or mine?

This "Christian nation" argument should concern — even frighten — two groups: non-Christians and thinking Christians.

I believe it does.

I think it's already apparent that a good part of this nation understands — if only instinctively — that anything which seems to suggest that God favors a political party or the establishment of a state church, is wrong and dangerous.

Way down deep the American people are afraid of an entangling relationship between formal religions — or whole bodies of religious belief — and government. Apart from constitutional law and religious doctrine, there is a sense that tells us it's wrong to presume to speak for God or to claim God's sanction of our particular legislation and His rejection of all other positions. Most of us are offended when we see religion being trivialized by its appearance in political throw-away pamphlets.

The American people need no course in philosophy or political science or church history to know that God should not be made into a celestial party chairman.

To most of us, the manipulative invoking of religion to advance a politician or a party is frightening and divisive. The American people will tolerate religious leaders taking positions for or against candidates, although I think the Catholic bishops are right in avoiding that position. But the American people are leery about large religious organizations, powerful churches or synagogue groups engaging in such activities — again, not as a matter of law or doctrine, but because our innate wisdom and democratic instinct teaches us these things are dangerous.

Today there are a number of issues involving life and death that raise questions of public morality. They are also questions of concern to most religions. Pick up a newspaper and you are almost certain to find a bitter controversy over any one of them; Baby Jane Doe, the right to die, artificial insemination, embryos in vitro, abortion, birth control . . . not to mention nuclear war and the shadow it throws across all existence.

Some of these issues touch the most intimate recesses of our lives, our roles as someone's mother or child or husband; some affect women in a unique way. But they are also public questions, for all of us.

Put aside what God expects — assume if you like there is no God — then the greatest thing still left to us is life. Even a radically secular world must struggle with the questions of when life begins, under what circumstances it can be ended, when it must be protected, by what authority; it too must decide what protection to extend to the helpless and the dying, to the aged and the unborn, to life in all its phases.

As a Catholic, I have accepted certain answers as the right ones for myself and my family, and because I have, they have influenced me in special ways, as Matilda's husband, as a father of five children, as a son who stood next to his own father's death bed trying to decide if the tubes and needles no longer served a purpose.

As a Governor, however, I am involved in defining policies that determine *other* people's rights in these same areas of life and death. Abortion is one of these issues, and while it is one issue among many, it is one of the most controversial and affects me in a special way as a Catholic public official.

So let me spend some time considering it.

I should start, I believe, by noting that the Catholic Church's actions with respect to the interplay of religious values and public policy make clear that there is no inflexible moral principle which determines what our *political* conduct should be. For example, on divorce and birth control, without changing its moral teaching, the Church abides the civil law as it now stands, thereby accepting — without making much of a point of it — that in our pluralistic society we are not required to insist that *all* our religious values be the law of the land.

Abortion is treated differently.

Of course there are differences both in degree and quality between abortion and some of the other religious positions the Church takes: abortion is a "matter of life and death," and degree counts. But the differences in approach reveal a truth, I think, that is not well enough perceived by Catholics and therefore still further complicates the process for us. That is, while we always owe our bishops' words respectful attention and careful consideration, the question whether to engage the political system in a struggle to have it adopt certain articles of our belief as part of public morality, is not a matter of doctrine: it is a matter of prudential political judgment.

Recently, Michael Novak put it succinctly: "Religious judgment and political judgment are both needed," he wrote. "But they are not identical."

My church and my conscience require me to believe certain things about divorce, birth control and abortion. My church does not order me — under pain of sin or expulsion — to pursue my salvific mission according to a precisely defined political plan.

As a Catholic I accept the church's teaching authority. While in the past some Catholic theologians may appear to have disagreed on the morality of some abortions (it wasn't, I think, until 1869 that excommunication was attached to all abortions without distinction), and while some theologians still do, I accept the bishops' position that abortion is to be avoided.

As Catholics, my wife and I were enjoined never to use abortion to destroy the life we created, and we never have. We thought Church doctrine was clear on this, and — more than that — both of us felt it in full agreement with what our hearts and our consciences told us. For me life or fetal life in the womb should be protected, even if five of nine Justices of the Supreme Court and my neighbor disagree with me. A fetus is different from an appendix or a set of tonsils. At the very least, even if the argument is made by some scientists or some theologians that in the early stages of fetal development we can't discern human life, the full potential of human life is indisputably there. That — to my less subtle mind — by itself should demand respect, caution, indeed . . . reverence.

But not everyone in our society agrees with me and Matilda.

And those who don't — those who endorse legalized abortions — aren't a ruthless, callous alliance of anti-Christians determined to overthrow our moral standards. In many cases, the proponents of legal abortion are the very people who have worked with Catholics to realize the goals of social justice set out in papal encyclicals: the American Lutheran Church, the Central Conference of American Rabbis, the Presbyterian Church in the United States, B'nai B'rith Women, the Women of the Episcopal Church. These are just a few of the religious organizations that don't share the Church's position on abortion.

Certainly, we should not be forced to mold Catholic morality to conform to disagreement by non-Catholics however sincere or severe their disagreement. Our bishops should be teachers not pollsters. They should not change what we Catholics believe in order to ease our consciences or please our friends or protect the Church from criticism.

But if the breadth, intensity and sincerity of opposition to church teaching shouldn't be allowed to shape our Catholic morality, it can't help but determine our ability — our realistic, political ability — to translate our Catholic morality into civil law, a law not for the believers who don't need it but for the disbelievers who reject it.

And it is here, in our attempt to find a political answer to abortion — an answer beyond our private observance of Catholic morality — that we encounter controversy within and without the Church over how and in what degree to press the case that our morality should be everybody else's, and to what effect.

I repeat, there is no Church teaching that mandates the best political course for making our belief everyone's rule, for spreading this part of our Catholicism. There is neither an encyclical nor a catechism that spells out a political strategy for achieving legislative goals.

And so the Catholic trying to make moral and prudent judgments in the political realm must discern which, if any, of the actions one could take would be best.

This latitude of judgment is not something new in the Church, not a development that has arisen only with the abortion issue. Take, for example, the question of slavery. It has been argued that the failure to endorse a legal ban on abortions is equivalent to refusing to support the cause of abolition before the Civil War. This analogy has been advanced by the bishops of my own state.

But the truth of the matter is, few if any Catholic bishops spoke for abolition in the years before the Civil War. It wasn't, I believe, that the bishops endorsed the idea of some humans owning and exploiting other humans; Pope Gregory XVI, in 1840, had condemned the slave trade. Instead it was a practical political judgment that the bishops made. They weren't hypocrites; they were realists. At the time,

Catholics were a small minority, mostly immigrants, despised by much of the population, often vilified and the object of sporadic violence. In the face of a public controversy that aroused tremendous passions and threatened to break the country apart, the bishops made a pragmatic decision. They believed their opinion would not change people's minds. Moreover they knew that there were southern Catholics, even some priests, who owned slaves. They concluded that under the circumstances arguing for a constitutional amendment against slavery would do more harm than good, so they were silent. As they have been, generally, in recent years, on the question of birth control. And as the Church has been on even more controversial issues in the past, even ones that dealt with life and death.

What is relevant to this discussion is that the bishops were making judgments about translating Catholic teachings into public policy, not about the moral validity of the teachings. In so doing they grappled with the unique political complexities of their time. The decision they made to remain silent on a constitutional amendment to abolish slavery or on the repeal of the Fugitive Slave Law wasn't a mark of their moral indifference: it was a measured attempt to balance moral truths against political realities. Their decision reflected their sense of complexity, not their diffidence. As history reveals, Lincoln behaved with similar discretion.

The parallel I want to draw here is not between or among what we Catholics believe to be moral wrongs. It is in the Catholic response to those wrongs. Church teaching on slavery and abortion is clear. But in the application of those teachings — the exact way we translate them into action, the specific laws we propose, the exact legal sanctions we seek — there was and is no one, clear, absolute route that the Church says, as a matter of doctrine, we must follow.

The bishops' pastoral, "The Challenge of Peace," speaks directly to this point. "We recognize," the bishops wrote, "that the Church's teaching authority does not carry the same force when it deals with technical solutions involving particular means as it does when it speaks of principles or ends. People may agree in abhorring an injustice, for instance, yet sincerely disagree as to what practical approach will achieve justice. Religious groups are entitled as others to their opinion in such cases, but they should not claim that their opinions are the only ones that people of good will may hold."

With regard to abortion, the American bishops have had to weigh Catholic moral teaching against the fact of a pluralistic country where our view is in the minority, acknowledging that what is ideally desirable isn't always feasible, that there can be different political approaches to abortion besides unyielding adherence to an absolute prohibition.

This is in the American-Catholic tradition of political realism. In supporting or opposing specific legislation the Church in this country has never retreated into a moral fundamentalism that will settle for nothing less than total acceptance of its views.

Indeed, the bishops have already confronted the fact that an absolute ban on abortion doesn't have the support necessary to be placed in our Constitution. In 1981, they put aside earlier efforts to describe a law they could accept and get passed, and supported the Hatch Amendment instead.

Some Catholics felt the bishops had gone too far with that action, some not far enough. Such judgments were not a rejection of the bishops' teaching authority: the bishops even disagreed among themselves. Catholics are allowed to disagree on these technical political questions without having to confess.

Respectfully, and after careful consideration of the position and arguments of the bishops, I have concluded that the approach of a constitutional amendment is not the best way for us to seek to deal with abortion.

I believe that legal interdicting of abortion by either the federal government or the individual states is not a plausible possibility and even if it could be obtained, it wouldn't work. Given present attitudes, it would be "Prohibition" revisited, legislating what couldn't be enforced and in the process creating a disrespect for law in general. And as much as I admire the bishops' hope that a constitutional amendment against abortion would be the basis for a full, new bill of rights for mothers and children, I disagree that this would be the result.

I believe that, more likely, a constitutional prohibition would allow people to ignore the causes of many abortions instead of addressing them, much the way the death penalty is used to escape dealing more fundamentally and more rationally with the problem of violent crime.

Other legal options that have been proposed are, in my view, equally ineffective. The Hatch Amendment, by returning the question of abortion to the states, would have given us a checkerboard of permissive and restrictive jurisdictions. In some cases people might have been forced to go elsewhere to have abortions and that might have eased a few consciences but it wouldn't have done what the Church wants to do — it wouldn't have created a deep-seated respect for life. Abortions would have gone on, millions of them.

Nor would a denial of Medicaid funding for abortion achieve our objectives. Given *Row v. Wade*, it would be nothing more than an attempt to do indirectly what the law says cannot be done directly; worse, it would do it in a way that would burden only the already disadvantaged. Removing funding from the Medicaid program would not prevent the rich and middle classes from having abortions. It would not even assure that the disadvantaged wouldn't have them; it would only impose financial burdens on poor women who want abortions.

Apart from that unevenness, there is a more basic question. Medicaid is designed to deal with health and medical needs. But the arguments for the cutoff of Medicaid abortion funds are not related to those needs. They are moral arguments. If we assume health and medical needs exist, our personal view of morality ought not to be considered a relevant basis for discrimination.

We must keep in mind always that we are a nation of laws — when we like those laws, and when we don't.

The Supreme Court has established a woman's constitutional right to abortion. The Congress has decided the federal government should not provide federal funding in the Medicaid program for abortion. That, of course, does not bind states in the allocation of their own state funds. Under the law, the individual states need not follow the federal lead, and in New York I believe we *cannot* follow that lead. The equal protection clause in New York's Constitution has been interpreted by the courts as a standard of fairness that would preclude us from denying only the poor — indirectly, by a cutoff of funds — the practical use of the constitutional right given by *Roe v. Wade.*

In the end, even if after a long and divisive struggle we were able to remove all Medicaid funding for abortion and restore the law to what it was — if we could put most abortions out of our sight, return them to the backrooms where they were performed for so long — I don't believe our responsibility as Catholics would be any closer to being fulfilled than it is now, with abortion guaranteed by the law as a woman's right.

The hard truth is that abortion isn't a failure of government. No agency or department of government forces women to have abortions, but abortion goes on. Catholics, the statistics show, support the right to abortion in equal proportion to the rest of the population. Despite the teaching in our homes and schools and pulpits, despite the sermons and pleadings of parents and priests and prelates, despite all the effort at defining our opposition to the sin of abortion, collectively we Catholics apparently believe — and perhaps act — little differently from those who don't share our commitment.

Are we asking government to make criminal what we believe to be sinful because we ourselves can't stop committing the sin?

The failure here is not Caesar's. This failure is our failure, the failure of the entire people of God.

Nobody has expressed this better than a bishop in my own state, Joseph Sullivan, a man who works with the poor in New York City, is resolutely opposed to abortion and argues, with his fellow bishops, for a change of law. "The major problem the Church has is internal," the Bishop said last month in reference to abortion. "How do we teach? As much as I think we're responsible for advocating public policy issues, our primary responsibility is to teach our own people. We haven't done that. We're asking politicians to do what we haven't done effectively ourselves."

I agree with the Bishop. I think our moral and social mission as Catholics must begin with the wisdom contained in the words "Physician, heal thyself." Unless we Catholics educate ourselves better to the values that define — and can ennoble — our lives, following those teachings better than we do now, unless we set an example that is clear and compelling, then we will never convince this society to change the civil laws to protect what we preach is precious human life.

Better than any law or rule or threat of punishment would be the moving strength of our own good example, demonstrating our lack of hypocrisy, proving the beauty and worth of our instruction.

We must work to find ways to avoid abortions without otherwise violating our faith. We should provide funds and opportunity for young women to bring their child to term, knowing both of them will be taken care of if that is necessary; we should teach our young men better than we do now their responsibilities in creating and caring for human life.

It is this duty of the Church to teach through its practice of love that Pope John Paul II has proclaimed so magnificently to all peoples. "The Church," he wrote in *Redemptor Hominis* (1979), "which has no weapons at her disposal apart from those of the spirit, of the word and of love, cannot renounce her proclamation of 'the word . . . in season and out of season.' For this reason she does not cease to implore . . . everybody in the name of God and in the name of man: Do not kill! Do not prepare destruction and extermination for each other! Think of your brothers and sisters who are suffering hunger and misery! Respect each one's dignity and freedom!"

The weapons of the word and of love are already available to us: we need no statute to provide them.

I am not implying that we should stand by and pretend indifference to whether a woman takes a pregnancy to its conclusion or aborts it. I believe we should in all cases try to teach a respect for life. And I believe with regard to abortion that, despite *Roe v. Wade,* we can, in practical ways. Here, in fact, it seems to me that all of us can agree.

Without lessening their insistence on a woman's right to an abortion, the people who call themselves "pro-choice" can support the development of government programs that present an impoverished mother with the full range of support she needs to bear and raise her children, to have a real choice. Without dropping their campaign to ban abortion, those who gather under the banner of "pro-life" can join in developing and enacting a legislative bill of rights for mothers and children, as the bishops have already proposed.

While we argue over abortion, the United States' infant mortality rate places us sixteenth among the nations of the world. Thousands of infants die each year because of inadequate medical care. Some are born with birth defects that, with proper treatment, could be prevented. Some are stunted in their physical and mental growth because of improper nutrition.

If we want to prove our regard for life in the womb, for the helpless infant — if we care about women having real choices in their lives and not being driven to abortions by a sense of helplessness and despair about the future of their child — then there is work enough for all of us. Lifetimes of it.

In New York, we have put in place a number of programs to begin this work, assisting women in giving birth to healthy babies. This year we doubled Medicaid funding to private-care physicians for prenatal and delivery services.

The state already spends 20 million dollars a year for prenatal care in out-patient clinics and for in-patient hospital care.

One program in particular we believe holds a great deal of promise. It's called "new avenues to dignity," and it seeks to provide a teenage mother with the special service she needs to continue with her education, to train for a job, to become capable of standing on her own, to provide for herself and the child she is bringing into the world.

My dissent, then, from the contention that we can have effective and enforceable legal prohibitions on abortion is by no means an argument for religious quietism, for accepting the world's wrongs because that is our fate as "the poor banished children of Eve."

Let me make another point.

Abortion has a unique significance but not a preemptive significance.

Apart from the question of the efficacy of using legal weapons to make people stop having abortions, we know our Christian responsibility doesn't end with any one law or amendment. That it doesn't end with abortion. Because it involves life and death, abortion will always be a central concern of Catholics. But so will nuclear weapons. And hunger and homelessness and joblessness, all the forces diminishing human life and threatening to destroy it. The "seamless garment" that Cardinal Bernardin has spoken of is a challenge to all Catholics in public office, conservatives as well as liberals.

We cannot justify our aspiration to goodness simply on the basis of the vigor of our demand for an elusive and questionable civil law declaring what we already know, that abortion is wrong.

Approval or rejection of legal restrictions on abortion should not be the exclusive litmus test of Catholic loyalty. We should understand that whether abortion is outlawed or not, our work has barely begun: the work of creating a society where the right to life doesn't end at the moment of birth; where an infant isn't helped into a world that doesn't care if it's fed properly, housed decently, educated adequately; where the blind or retarded child isn't condemned to exist rather than empowered to live.

The bishops stated this duty clearly in 1974, in their statement to the Senate Sub-Committee considering a proposed amendment to restrict abortions. They maintained such an amendment could not be seen as an end in itself. "We do not see a constitutional amendment as the final product of our commitment or of our legislative activity," they said. "It is instead the constitutional base on which to provide support and assistance to pregnant women and their unborn children. This would include nutritional, prenatal, child birth and postnatal care for the mother, and also nutritional and pediatric care for the child through the first year of life. . . . We believe that all of these should be available as a matter of right to all pregnant women and their children."

The bishops reaffirmed that view in 1976, in 1980, and again this year when the United States Catholic Committee asked Catholics to judge candidates on a wide range of issues — on abortion, yes; but also on food policy, the arms race, human rights, eduction, social justice and military expenditures.

The bishops have been consistently "pro-life" in the full meaning of that term, and I respect them for that.

The problems created by the matter of abortion are complex and confounding. Nothing is clearer to me than my inadequacy to find compelling solutions to all of their moral, legal and social implications. I — and many others like me — are eager for enlightenment, eager to learn new and better ways to manifest respect for the deep reverence for life that is our religion and our instinct. I hope that this public attempt to describe the problems as I understand them will give impetus to the dialogue in the Catholic community and beyond, a dialogue which could show me a better wisdom than I've been able to find so far.

It would be tragic if we let that dialogue become a prolonged, divisive argument that destroys or impairs our ability to practice any part of the morality given us in the Sermon on the Mount, to touch, heal and affirm the human life that surrounds us.

We Catholic citizens of the richest, most powerful nation that has ever existed are like the steward made responsible over a great household: from those to whom so much has been given, much shall be required. It is worth repeating that ours is not a faith that encourages its believers to stand apart from the world, seeking their salvation alone, separate from the salvation of those around them.

We speak of ourselves as a body. We come together in worship as companions, in the ancient sense of that word, those who break bread together, and who are obliged by the commitment we share to help one another, everywhere, in all we do, and in the process, to help the whole human family. We see our mission to be "the completion of the work of creation."

This is difficult work today. It presents us with many hard choices.

The Catholic Church has come of age in America. The ghetto walls are gone, our religion no longer a badge of irredeemable foreignness. This new-found status is both an opportunity and a temptation. If we choose, we can give in to the temptation to become more and more assimilated into a larger, blander culture, abandoning the practice of the specific values that made us different, worshipping whatever gods the marketplace has to sell while we seek to rationalize our own laxity by urging the political system to legislate on others a morality we no longer practice ourselves.

Or we can remember where we come from, the journey of two millennia, clinging to our personal faith, to its insistence on constancy and service and on hope. We can live and practice the morality Christ gave us, maintaining His truth in this world, struggling to embody His love, practicing it especially where that love is most needed, among the poor and the weak and the dispossessed. Not just by trying to make laws for others to live by, but by living the laws already written for us by God, in our hearts and in our minds.

We can be fully Catholic; proudly, totally at ease with ourselves, a people in the world, transforming it, a light to this nation. Appealing to the best in our people not the worst. Persuading not coercing.

Leading people to truth by love. And still, all the while, respecting and enjoying our unique pluralistic democracy. And we can do it even as politicians.

## *Cuomo at Notre Dame: Rhetoric Without Religion*

CALVIN L. TROUP

Etiquette makes conversation about religion and politics difficult if not taboo in American society. But an American politician who speaks publically about *both* religion *and* politics in the same speech defies not only etiquette, but conventional political wisdom. Practicing politicians rarely entertain the risk.

New York Governor Mario Cuomo accepts this risk in his address, "Religious Belief and Public Morality: A Catholic Governor's Perspective." On September 13, 1984, in the wake of his sudden rise to prominence as the keynote speaker at the 1984 Democratic National Convention, Cuomo delivered the speech at Notre Dame University (Henry, 1988, pp. 105, 117). In the Notre Dame speech, Cuomo defends his complex position as a Roman Catholic and national leader of the Democratic party.[1] The discourse displays Cuomo's rhetorical agility in negotiating a situation marked by contradiction, paradox, and ambivalence between personal religious convictions and public policy.

The Notre Dame speech also registers Cuomo as a contemporary voice in the American debate over how religion and politics interact in a pluralistic, democratic society. From before the American revolution, the issue of separation of church and state has produced an ongoing battle between the power of religion to promote public virtue and the counteracting resistance to any form of establishment (Wood, 1969, pp. 427–429). Among a cacophony of voices speaking on church/state relations in American society, Cuomo's is conspicuous by its association with two other politicians of national prominence who, like Cuomo, felt compelled to address the relationship between their political and religious professions as American Catholics: Alfred E. Smith and John F. Kennedy.[2]

Cuomo's address must be heard within this historical stream of American Catholic politicians. The following review will present, in sharper relief, the very different rhetorical problem facing Cuomo. In this context the Notre Dame speech reveals and contributes to the shape of Church-State relations in America. When state policy and religious principles coincide, how does one who stands at the center of that conjunction evoke a response that is fitting for the occasion? In what follows, I will examine Cuomo's response to this rhetorical challenge. I will argue that, with respect to the nature and style of religious rhetoric that relates to public issues, his response promotes a chilling environment for religious rhetoric in public contexts — one that silences rhetoric before it begins.

**Al Smith and JFK: Political Predecessors**

Cuomo invokes the memory of Al Smith early in the Notre Dame speech, noting that Smith's divided loyalties at Army-Notre Dame football games required him — as Governor of New York — to sit with Army but to retort, "commend my soul to Notre Dame!" (Andrews and Zarefsky, 1992, p. 329). In his second term as governor of New York, Smith was the 1928 Democratic nominee for President, the first viable candidate for that office who belonged to the Roman Catholic Church (Fuchs, 1967, p. 66; White, 1961, p. 131). His presidential campaign drew staunch opposition from a broad spectrum of protestants who were concerned that the Catholic church contradicted American constitutional principles and threatened the separation of church and state (Barrett, 1964, p. 259; McClerrin, 1967, pp. 104–105).

Despite Smith's protestations that Americanism and Catholicism were compatible and that no conflict existed between the church and public office, opponents insisted that a Catholic president would serve under the direct influence of the Catholic hierarchy and alleged that Smith had already shown favoritism to Catholics as a governor (Fuchs, 1967, p. 66; McClerrin, 1967, p. 109). Finally, in September, 1928, at Oklahoma City, Smith devoted an entire campaign speech to the issue. He proclaimed that "absolute separation of State and Church is part of the fundamental basis of our Constitution. I believe in that separation and all that it implies" (McClerrin, 1967, p. 105). Any Democratic candidate would likely have lost the 1928 election to incumbent Herbert Hoover (Fuchs, 1967, p. 68). Nevertheless, the 1928 election led to the widespread assumption that Catholicism and the U.S. presidency were mutually exclusive (Fuchs, 1967, pp. 152–153; Windt, 1988, p. 246).

The notion that no Catholic could serve as U.S. President persisted for 32 years, until challenged directly by John F. Kennedy. The Kennedy campaign was first tested on the religious issue in the West Virginia primary (Windt, 1988, p. 246). However, organized resistance to Kennedy's candidacy escalated during the general election campaign (Barrett, 1964, p. 260; Fuchs, 1967, pp. 176–177; McClerrin, 1967, p. 106).

Protestant groups opposed the Kennedy nomination even before the Democratic national convention was over (White, 1961, p. 269). Sermons and pamphleteering surpassed the volume targeted at

Smith's candidacy, with groups representing protestant constituencies as diverse as the National Council of Churches and the National Association of Evangelicals once again questioning whether the nation ought to elect a Catholic to the presidency (McClerrin, 1967, p. 105).

The "religious question" was as singular as the label suggests. Protestants were unified against the prospect of the Roman Catholic Church hierarchy — particularly the Pope — employing religious authority to control a Catholic president's public policies (Barrett, 1964, p. 260; McClerrin, 1967, p. 109). In the view of the protestants who raised the question, the Catholic church did not believe either by doctrine or practice in the separation of church and state (Barrett, 1964, p. 260; McClerrin, 1967, p. 106). They eyed Kennedy as a candidate with divided loyalties and were suspicious about his ability to sustain the separation. Speaking of church-state separation as a central tenet of the American covenant, John M. Murphy (1989) indicates the root of such protestant suspicions:

> The election of a Catholic threatened the covenant in terms both of a Catholic's ability to articulate the national faith, as Presidents are expected to do, and of JFK's willingness to abide by the rules of the covenant. (pp. 268–269)

The homogeneity of the concern coalesced into an organized group called The National Conference of Citizens for Religious Freedom. The organization, comprised of protestant ministers and editors of protestant periodicals, included preachers like Norman Vincent Peale and magazines like *Christian Century, Christian Heritage,* and *Christianity Today* (Fuchs, 1967, pp. 177, 178, 182; Murphy, 1989, p. 268; White, 1961, p. 259). This national protestant coalition along with grassroots reports gathered by the campaign prompted Kennedy to accept the invitation of the Greater Houston Ministerial Association to address the "religious question" on September 12, 1960 (White, 1961, p. 260).[3]

Like Al Smith, speaking two months before the presidential election as the Democratic Party's candidate, Kennedy boldly pledged allegiance to separation of church and state:

> I believe in an America where the separation of church and state is absolute — where no Catholic prelate would tell the President (should he be a Catholic) how to act and no Protestant minister would tell his parishioners for whom to vote. (1961, p. 391)

Unlike Al Smith, Kennedy went on to win the presidency. The direct effect of his Houston speech on the outcome of the election is difficult to gauge. The address had a limited immediate effect on the editorial positions of protestant periodicals, winning the endorsement of only a few of the more liberal journals already supporting Kennedy and tempering commentary among those still harboring misgivings (Fuchs, 1967, p. 182). But Kennedy's Houston message contributed to an election which ultimately settled the "religious question" for protestants (Murphy, 1989, p. 277). The Kennedy Administration proved that the Democrats, not the Vatican, controlled the White House.

### Notre Dame in 1984: The Conflict Between State Policy and Religious Principle

In summary form, Cuomo's Notre Dame address might seem to share much in common with Smith's Oklahoma City address and Kennedy's Houston Speech (Wills, 1990, p. 308). Although Cuomo was not on the Democratic presidential ticket, his keynote address at the convention made him as much a national spokesperson for the party as Walter Mondale or Geraldine Ferraro. Notre Dame's invitation came in response to the questioning of his position on the separation of church and state by church leaders at a critical time in the presidential campaign — early September.

However, Smith and Kennedy were speaking hypothetically about church/state separation. Cuomo had to address direct opposition from the religious community in response to an existing policy agenda and legislation enacted under his leadership. Smith and Kennedy were responding to protestant leaders. Kennedy had received support for his position from bishops and other Catholic clergy (Fuchs, 1967, 180; Murphy, 1989, 273). Catholic candidates' allegiance to the state was challenged on the basis of their devotion to the church. Cuomo's allegiance to the church was being challenged on the basis of his devotion to the state. Cuomo's fiercest critics were Catholic officials who were making the very sort of political pronouncements that Kennedy's Catholic supporters had asserted would never be made in America (Fuchs, 1967, p. 184).[4]

The seeds of the conflict prompting the Notre Dame address were sown some ten years earlier, when Cuomo reversed his political stance on the legality of abortion. Consistent with the church's reaction to Roe v. Wade, Cuomo had opposed the expansion of access to abortion. Cuomo's biographer, Robert S. McElvaine, reports that in his 1974 campaign for lieutenant governor,

> Cuomo stated that "had he been a member of the Legislature he would have voted against the 1970 law that relaxed abortion curbs in the state." Such liberal friends as Janie Eisenberg argued with Cuomo for years

> before convincing him that abortion and homosexuality, while clearly moral issues, were matters of *private* morality that ought not to be dictated by the government. Eventually Cuomo concluded that this was the case and that the Church and its adherents should "teach by example rather than through legislation." (1988, p. 91)

Cuomo's reversal on abortion, coupled with other political circumstances, brought him to the podium at Notre Dame advocating a policy that defied his personal moral conviction and his church's doctrine. While paradoxical, Cuomo's position was common and perhaps even more conservative than the position held by most Roman Catholics at the time (Wills, 1990, p. 310).[5] Bruce Babbitt, former governor of Arizona, in his 1988 Democratic primary campaign appealed to "the Cuomo position" articulated at Notre Dame — demonstrating the utility of Cuomo's argument for other Catholic politicians seeking to satisfy both conscience and constituency on the abortion issue (Wills, 1990, p. 307).

The Notre Dame speech was not the first occasion on which Cuomo had voiced his revised position on abortion policy *vis-à-vis* church doctrine. In his 1982 New York gubernatorial campaign against Lewis Lehrman, Cuomo faced the issue directly. Lehrman attacked Cuomo on abortion and other issues, invoking the moral agenda of the religious right (Cuomo, 1984, pp. 327, 337).

Lehrman's attacks failed politically, but the public rhetoric of the religious right kept Cuomo's attention. He spoke on "The Stewardship of Political Power" at St. John the Divine Episcopal Church in New York City on November 27, 1983 (Cuomo, 1984, p. 462). Outlining his position on politics and religion, the governor rehearsed many of the themes that would appear less than a year later at Notre Dame.

Between the address at St. John the Divine and the Notre Dame speech came the Democratic National Convention keynote and national prominence. But while the Reagan campaign was scurrying to respond to Cuomo's convention speech, national attention became focused on New York City and Archbishop John O'Connor.

In June of 1984, before Cuomo's keynote address, O'Connor questioned how a faithful Roman Catholic could vote for a political candidate who supported pro-choice policies. O'Connor's remarks thrust Cuomo into the complex, actual situation that Kennedy's Houston speech foreshadowed. About a month later — and after the keynote — Cuomo reacted publicly to O'Connor. He charged that the Archbishop's statement prohibited Roman Catholics from voting for specific candidates. O'Connor backed down, claiming only to teach the doctrines of the church and allowing individuals to apply the teachings in the political arena (Byrnes and Segers, 1992, pp. 141–142; 151).

A *Time* magazine story highlighted the debate, reporting that Bishop James W. Malone, head of the U.S. Catholic Conference, had released a statement supporting O'Connor's position. The *Time* story linked the vice-presidential campaign of Geraldine Ferraro and the debate between Cuomo and O'Connor ("Pulpit Politics," 1984, p. 26). The O'Connor-Ferraro connection became public in early September, when O'Connor — referring to a letter from a Roman Catholic pro-choice organization signed by Ferraro — objected to Ferraro's claim that Roman Catholic teaching was not "monolithic" on abortion. The interchange between Ferraro and O'Connor occurred September 9–12, 1984 in the *New York Times*. Ferraro finally agreed that the teaching of the church was indeed monolithic, but that many Roman Catholics disagreed with the teaching of the church on this point (Byrnes and Segers, 1992, pp. 141, 151). Cuomo spoke at Notre Dame the next day.

Cuomo's address was forged through five weeks of work and 17 drafts. Though reviewed by his speechwriter, the governor composed the address himself, defying his speechwriter's advice on key issues. He opted for a 45-minute speech rather than the recommended 20 minute limit and constructed more complex intellectual arguments rather than resorting to political boilerplate (McElvaine, 1988, pp. 351–352). Almost ten years later he would say of the Notre Dame address, "It is the piece of work that took more of me than any other. . . . I labored over it for weeks" (Cuomo, 1993, p. 32).

Therefore, while Kennedy had settled the question of whether Catholicism could be accepted as a proper denominational affiliation for a U.S. President, Cuomo was forced to address a deeper religious question — one that has never been settled in America: What is the proper relationship between Church and State, such that neither unduly infringes on the rights of the other?

### Cuomo's Vision in Text and Context

As suggested earlier, this question creates a distinct rhetorical problem. How does one effect a rapprochement of the conflicting currents while protecting against the religious establishment of public policy and simultaneously promoting public virtue? This is the challenge Cuomo faced. In his response, he invites listeners to participate in a vision of public consciousness with distinct coordinates for appropriate rhetorical action, including when arguments based on religious thought are appropriate in the public policy forum.

The "method" I employ to consider Cuomo's response falls within the scope of textual studies, an approach best characterized as a broadly-conceived set of critical assumptions rather than a carefully defined methodology (Gaonkar, 1989, p. 255). Edwin Black articulates the most prominent of these assumptions, arguing that rhetorical critics can and should consider oratorical transactions — Cuomo's address in this case — as worthy of rhetorical inquiry in their own right. Such practical criticism works from "the non-theoretic or nominalistic or emic viewpoint, which approaches a rhetorical transaction in what is hoped to be its own terms, without conscious expectations drawn from any sources other than the rhetorical transaction itself" (1980, pp. 331–332).

Instead of applying a general theory deductively to a text as an exemplary case, the critic attends to the internal dynamics of the text and how it interacts with its context — a more inductive approach. As Gaonkar (1989) has noted, in textual studies like this one, "critical interest focuses on particular texts rather than on the discovery and organization of abstract theoretical principles" (p. 267)

In other words, this study informs no particular theory of rhetoric. I foreground the text and address it critically, proceeding on the assumption that an oratorical text will yield its "own essential form of disclosure" (Black, 1980, p. 332). The non-theoretical approach to a text does not commit the critic to criticism for its own sake. "Rather, such understanding would acquire intellectual respectability only as it moved toward or issued in general truths about human experience" (Black, 1980, pp. 332–334). Neither does this approach proceed on the basis that the critic can or should maintain a naive or objectivist viewpoint toward the text. As Black notes, such an approach is not the sum total of the critical enterprise, but only a phase which precedes evaluation, serving as "an avenue into a fair and full" critical judgment (1980, p. 334). Therefore the critical task incorporates both interpretive and evaluative aspects.

*The Function of the Wall and Decorum.* Declaring the difficulty of staying within the subject defined for him, Cuomo's *ingratio* — the introductory appeal to establish good will between speaker and audience — provides coordinates for understanding not only the propositional content of the Notre Dame address, but the stylistic and structural moves which engage Cuomo's listeners. In this case, the *ingratio* launches a full-blown discussion of church and state and marks an early division that elevates civic order through the use of spatial metaphors. "It's not easy to say contained," Cuomo states as he engages in a defense which relies upon the entire field of American history to examine this particular moment in the continuing dialectic of church-state relations (Andrews and Zarefsky, 1992, p. 329).[6]

Responding to the challenge of Catholic church officials and political activists of various religious stripes, Cuomo invites listeners to adopt a version of America's political ancestry grounded in Thomas

Jefferson's mythical "wall of separation" between church and state. He invokes the wall in the opening lines of the address, "I've seen religious leaders scale that wall with all the dexterity of olympic athletes" (p. 329). Cuomo envisions enrobed prelates and collared clerics climbing an impervious wall.

Consistent with the wall metaphor, and by contrast to the religionists, Cuomo resurrects the image of Governor Al Smith, who sits on the appropriate, civic side of the wall for the Army-Notre Dame game. When faced with even this humorous and nostalgic case of divided loyalties, the governor did what good governors do, and "protocol prevailed" (Andrews and Zarefsky, 1992, p. 329).

With the primacy of protocol established, Cuomo visits the complexity of the questions arising on the issue of the relation between religion and politics in America. The questions are unavoidable and Cuomo finds most answers unsatisfactory: "Some of them have been simplistic, most of them fragmentary, and a few spoken with purely political intent, demagogic" (p. 329).

Speaking from above the confusion, Cuomo suggests an approach that resonates with a Ciceronean ideal for civil discourse. First, there will be no final truths, but a hope for discovery of "some basic agreement" (p. 329). Through antithesis, Cuomo offers dialogue, discussion and reason as an alternative to the suspicion, innuendo, and naive simplicity he assigns to other perspectives. The antidote of civil discourse will ultimately lead to truth that will relieve the confusion of Catholics and others — not final truth, but finally, truth (p. 329). The truth being sought, though undetermined in content, Cuomo settles structurally before the discussion begins. He indicates that the application of greater intelligence will yield a description of "the role religion has in our public affairs, and the limits placed on that role" (p. 329).

Through the Notre Dame speech's account of how the conflict was resolved, Cuomo interprets O'Connor and Malone's statements as an inappropriate application of church doctrine and authority in the political arena. Listeners are urged to embrace a separation which judges church voices in the public forum as a violation against decorum, not law:

> But they [the bishops] have said they will not use the power of their position, and the great respect it receives from all Catholics, to give an imprimatur to individual politicians or parties.
>
> Not that they couldn't do it if they wished to — some religious leaders do; some are doing it at this very moment.
>
> Not that it would be a sin if they did — God doesn't insist on political neutrality. But because it is the judgment of the bishops, and most of us

> Catholic lay people, that it is not wise for prelates and politicians to be tied too closely together.
>
> I think that getting this consensus was an extraordinarily useful achievement. (p. 330)

From the bishops' clarification Cuomo turns to his personal credentials as a politician and Roman Catholic. "The Catholic Church is my spiritual home," Cuomo says (p. 330). This not only affirms his religious faith, the language also situates that faith exclusively in the private sphere (McElvaine, 1988, pp. 61–98). Cuomo judges even his own spiritual devotion as more acceptable by being in its proper place, that is, in submission to political pluralism and democratic freedom.

> Catholic public officials take an oath to preserve the Constitution that guarantees this freedom [of religion]. . . . Because they realize that in guaranteeing freedom for all, they guarantee our right to be Catholics: our right to pray, to use the sacraments, to refuse birth control devices, to reject abortion, not to divorce and remarry if we believe it to be wrong.
>
> I protect my right to be a Catholic by preserving your right to believe as a Jew, a Protestant or non-believer, or as anything else you choose.
>
> We know that the price of seeking to force our beliefs on others is that they might some day force theirs on us.
>
> This freedom is the fundamental strength of our unique experiment in government. In the complex interplay of forces and considerations that go into the making of our laws and policies, its preservation must be a pervasive and dominant concern. (p. 330)

The officeholder's task is to "create conditions under which" people who may "hold beliefs different from specifically Catholic ones" are guaranteed Constitutional freedoms (p. 330). In this way, Cuomo divides personal, private, religious convictions from corporate, public, political commitments. The division also subordinates the institution and practice of the spiritual home to the political state, and makes religion dependent on the state.

Freedom of religion becomes the warrant which makes the protection from religious coercion a prime mission of government. The question of the legitimacy of religion's voice within the political realm comes into focus as Cuomo discusses how these two *ought* to relate. He reiterates that the ideal pluralism envisioned in the discourse is not statutory, but volitional:

> The same amendment of the Constitution that forbids the establishment of a State Church affirms my legal right to argue that my religious belief would serve well as an article of our universal public morality. (p. 331)

Cuomo sets up a foil, listing several hypothetical cases in which one might argue from Catholic religious convictions in terms of the common good, and then calls such rhetorical approaches into question (p. 331). He introduces moral guidelines for the deployment of religious arguments in the public forum, but negates the same guidelines. The negation never approaches statutory prohibition. Rather, Cuomo appeals exclusively to decorum, a sense of public discretion.

Arguments overtly based on religious values can, by law, be made. But Cuomo casts doubt on the practice with a volley of rhetorical queries:

> But should I? Is it helpful? Is it essential to human dignity? Does it promote harmony and understanding? Or does it divide us so fundamentally that it threatens our ability to function as a pluralistic community? (p. 331)

Cuomo's progression presents religious rhetoric in the public forum as a common sense threat to pluralism. To reinforce the conclusion that religious views must be subordinate to democratic pluralism, he offers an open question immediately after the yes/no series: "When should I argue to make my religious value your morality?" (p. 331).

In answer, another series of rhetorical questions weaves its way through the text, exploring the "oughts" of bringing arguments informed by religious doctrine into such a pluralistic political arena. All of these questions, occurring through eight brief paragraphs, refute positions assigned to those who would employ religious arguments in a pluralistic democracy (p. 331). Through the process of questioning, the wall of separation is reinforced and would-be climbers are instructed not to scale the wall for the sake of public protocol. The discourse marshalls form and substance convincingly to judge religious arguments as legal but illegitimate in the formation of public policy. Spatial metaphors create a place outside the wall of public affairs into which Cuomo's arguments deposit religious arguments as exclusively private, personal considerations.

*Consensus and the use of Religious Arguments.* With the wall intact and protocol preserved, Cuomo now introduces the condition by which the legitimacy of rhetoric from religious sources may be judged: consensus. Consensus serves as the standard of public entry for religious arguments. Recalling that Cuomo's ultimate question was, "When should I *argue* to make my religious value your morality?" [italics added]. Cuomo begins to answer this question by defining public morality.

> Our public morality, then — the moral standards we maintain for everyone, not just the ones we insist on in our private lives — depends on a consensus view of right and wrong. The values derived from religious belief will not — and should not — be accepted as part of the public morality unless they are shared by the pluralistic community at large, by consensus. (p. 331)

By defining public morality this way, Cuomo does not prohibit all religious discourse. So far, he only makes the salient point that public policy should not be made by religious fiat; that consensus should be the basis upon which religious values are accepted. He proceeds to an example of when religious values are welcome in public discourse:

> The agnostics who joined the civil rights struggle were not deterred because that crusade's values had been nurtured and sustained in black Christian churches. Those on the political left are not perturbed today by the religious basis of the clergy and lay people who join them in the protest against the arms race and hunger and exploitation. (p. 331)

Such examples accentuate Cuomo's move from public consensus as the standard for acceptance of religious values into public morality to consensus as a prerequisite for whether or not rhetoric informed by religious values is acceptable. He confirms the shift by declaring that religious voices from outside of the public consensus are unwelcome:

> The arguments start when religious values are used to support positions which would impose on other people restrictions they find unacceptable. (pp. 331–332)

Religious arguments belong in the public sphere only when they correspond with a popular consensus that precedes their introduction into the public debate. As he explains:

> "Yes," we create our public morality through consensus and in this country that consensus reflects to some extent religious values of a great majority of Americans. But "no," all religiously based values don't have an *a priori* place in our public morality. (p. 332)

The passage executes a crucial transposition for Cuomo. First, he points out that arguments should not be accepted into public morality by virtue of their religious sources, and that religious voices should be regarded as a few among many on issues of public morality. From the assumption that an American consensus on public morality includes certain religious common denominators, the text implies strongly that those who argue from explicit religious grounds automatically assume that such arguments "have an *a priori* place in our public morality."

Taken in isolation, the passage seems to suggest less, perhaps only that public morality obviously does not include every religious scruple practiced by Americans. In its context, however, these two sentences provide a warrant that serves to deny legitimacy to any religious argument that challenges existing policy or popular morality. Such arguments, and any merit they might contain, become overshadowed by their religious source.

Initially, Cuomo invokes the stereotype of religious fundamentalism as a reason for suppressing personal, religiously-grounded arguments that bear on public policy. Cuomo's "fundamentalist" is one who claims that a religious consensus already exists within the American public — a Christian consensus (p. 332).

> The right answer to these questions can be elusive. Some of the wrong answers, on the other hand, are quite clear. For example, there are those who say there is a simple answer to *all* these questions; they say that by history and practice of our people we were intended to be — and should be — a Christian country in law.
>
> But where would that leave non-believers? And whose Christianity would be law, yours or mine? (p. 332)

Cuomo responds to the fundamentalist stereotype by cultivating fear of religious fanaticism, a traditional worry in America at least since the deists of the 18th century (Bellah, Madsen, Sullivan, Swidler, & Tipton, 1985, p. 221). But the appeal to the stereotype supposedly produces a deeply rational fear, not a phobia. Cuomo further instructs listeners about exactly who should fear Christian fundamentalists: "non-Christians and thinking Christians" (p. 332). Only irrational fanatics would voice arguments which challenge status quo public morality from a religious perspective.

The discourse proceeds from the fundamentalist stereotype to enlist resistance against any religious argument in a political context as a "natural" response. Thinking Americans understand, "if only instinctively," that "the establishment of a state church, is wrong and dangerous" (p. 332). The introduction of establishment invokes a broader web of fear-inducing commonplaces:

> Way down deep the American people are afraid of an entangling relationship between formal religions — or whole bodies of religious belief — and government. (p. 332)

Furthermore, "The American people" know that God is non-partisan, find invocation of religion for political purposes "frightening and divisive," and are "leery about large religious organizations, powerful churches or synagogue groups engaging" in political activities. Cuomo reminds us that these concerns run far deeper than the variabilities of public opinion, "our innate wisdom and democratic instinct teaches us these things are dangerous" (p. 332).

By alluding to mainstream religions, the text makes an almost imperceptible shift from most Americans fearing "Christian nation" proponents to being leery of all major religious organizations voicing political arguments. Listeners are also subtly asked to equate political arguments by religious groups as a prima facie violation of the spirit of the establishment clause in the Constitution. This places all religious Americans in a position to censor their own religious convictions with Cuomo for the sake of democratic pluralism. Censorship is necessary, not because all religious convictions are fanatical, but because religious arguments threaten pluralism.

The Notre Dame speech studiously avoids an unqualified possibility for responsible rhetorical engagement in the public sphere for religious argument. By contrast, the text offers many negative characterizations of religion in public as trivialized or manipulative. When bishops retract their political statements or choose not to speak — even though they could — they are praised. When religious activists protest alongside people of different faiths or no faith, they are accepted because of consensual goals, not out of respect for the religious grounds of their arguments (p. 332).

*Abortion Policy: Politics Separate from Religion.* In the larger context of the speech, abortion — the catalyst driving the dispute between Cuomo and O'Connor — serves as a case study supporting Cuomo's logic on separation and consensus. He maintains an adversarial relationship between organized religion — whether "fundamentalist" or mainstream — and pluralism. But separation does not mean that religious people should not participate in the public forum.

Cuomo repeatedly insists that public judgment without reference to religious doctrine is legitimate for Roman Catholics operating in the political arena. Based on the progression of earlier arguments this would seem to follow without saying.

However, the construction of appropriate political behavior for religious adherents gains intensity and becomes more sharply paradoxical when understood in the context of Cuomo's deep personal faith, prior pro-life position, encounters with the religious right, and the movement of this discourse toward a national policy challenge to the American Roman Catholic Church. Thus situated, Cuomo appears to be bound to advocate the rhetoric of political judgment and discourage religious rhetoric in the public arena. These are the grounds upon which he can maintain his "personally opposed, but . . ." stance on abortion.

Discussing abortion policy, Cuomo states with numbing redundancy that no official church position exists for translating doctrine into a fixed policy agenda (p. 333). In the midst of a particular discussion of abortion, the repetition of these claims invites listeners to observe the fabled "wall of separation" in a particular way, one that promotes a marked dichotomy between religious and political praxis. Cuomo argues that political strategies should only be based on political judgment in the pluralistic context, and that religion should not contribute to the debate. The church maintains custody of religious truth, but such truth should not contribute to the development of political policy (p. 334).

Cuomo then launches a critique of Republican policy initiatives on abortion, faults the church for the problems of abortion, and reviews the programs in the state of New York that directly relate to the abortion issue (pp. 334–337). Concluding, Cuomo asserts that his position on abortion does not call for religious quietism, after which he proceeds to reinforce the pattern established through the discourse. He refers to the importance of "personal faith" and recounts that faith should be practiced "not just by trying to make laws for others to live by, but by living the laws already written for us by God, in our hearts and in our minds" (p. 337). Finally, he holds out the hope that Catholics, by persuasion, not coercion, can transform the world, "all the while, respecting and enjoying our unique pluralistic democracy" (p. 337).

### An Evaluation

Unlike many political speeches, this text overtly addresses the permissibility of public speech, what should and should not be said in public. No politician wants to be targeted by voting directives from church officials to their parishioners. Such activities seem to compromise the mission of the church as much as the sanctity of democratic pluralism. But Cuomo's Notre Dame speech should not be read merely as a response to Archbishop O'Connor. Likewise, Cuomo's call for people who consider themselves religious to consistently live "the laws already written for us by God, in our hearts and in our minds" should be heeded and hypocrisy deplored (p. 337). But the Notre Dame address serves as more than a platform for platitudes. A close look at the interaction between text and context broadens the scope of the address to the extent that the Cuomo–O'Connor interchange becomes a catalyst for Cuomo to construct his own version of religion and democratic pluralism in which he prescribes certain protocols for rhetorical conduct.

The rhetoric that Cuomo promotes in this speech strikes me as problematic — despite the engaging appeal of the Notre Dame address. My concerns begin with the invocation of decorum which follows the division and compartmentalization of religion and politics. Cuomo's construct resembles what Richard John Neuhaus (1984), himself a leader in both the civil rights and antiwar movements and an outspoken critic of the religious right, has termed "The Naked Public Square," which he claims is "the result of political doctrine and practice that would exclude religion and religiously grounded values from the conduct of public business" (p. vii).[7] The forum becomes denuded "when religious transcendence is excluded, when the public square has been swept clean of divisive sectarianisms" (Neuhaus, 1984, pp. 8–9). To conclude that such loyalties cannot, in fact, be so neatly divided violates protocol — an unforgiveable sin against the decorum that holds democratic pluralism together.

Consistent with accepting the religion/politics dichotomy, Cuomo invites listeners to embrace a number of tensions. One of them, identified by Gary Wills (1990), "is that Cuomo claims to believe the church's teaching on abortion, but *acts* as if he does not" (p. 312). The discourse relentlessly moves listeners toward adopting this paradox in broader terms, urging them to check their religious rhetoric at the door to the public square — a practical prohibition of religious rhetoric in public policy discourse. To practice this intentional dualism is promoted as a positive good.

But the rigid distinction Cuomo advocates between religion and public affairs conflicts with how people experience these two aspects of life. As Martin E. Marty (1993) has noted in his critique of spatial metaphors to define the relation between religion and public affairs, such appeals are particularly useful in legal arguments, but they stifle productive interpersonal and intrapersonal conversation. He suggests that, "those who too rigidly make the distinction between private and public affairs in religion do justice only to codified technical knowledge and overlook the practical ways citizens individually and collectively do their living" (pp. 121–123).

Therefore, to the question of when arguments from religious values should contribute to public policy debate, Cuomo answers *never,* unless a public moral consensus already exists. In practice, people — by their own volition — should censor their religious arguments in deference to status quo public morality and policy until the debate is over. Religious voices are relegated to cheerleading status, effectively prohibited from contributing to new instances of public consensus in Cuomo's version of public discourse. If rhetoric plays the central role in building public consensus that we believe it does, then religion can contribute nothing of value to public discourse. Without prior political consensus, religious rhetoric is inappropriate; if a consensus exists the rhetoric is unnecessary.

Cuomo fears that religious arguments must bring divisiveness that would threaten to destroy democratic pluralism. Initially, the text is littered with religious voices, including the bishops', fundamentalists', and Cuomo's own voice. Cuomo introduces circumstances in which religious arguments potentially have a place in political rhetoric, and then systematically rules out each one. The exclusivity of political pluralism and religion constrain him to advise that statements of bishops and officials from other religions necessarily jeopardize the smooth functioning of pluralistic democracy. On contested issues of public morality, those who argue publically from religious grounds are consistently presented as irrational, fanatical, insincere, and coercive.

Ironically, Cuomo's own examples of appropriate religious rhetoric suggest quite the opposite. For instance, Cuomo displays civil rights activism and arguments by African-American Christians as appropriate, even when explicitly religious, because of a supposed preexisting public consensus on the issue. However, African-American Christians spoke and marched at the dawn of the civil rights movement, and their explicit religious rhetoric was being voiced publically long before anything like a public consensus emerged.

Movements like abolitionism, civil rights, and the anti-war movement of the 1960s all threatened to divide and destroy democratic pluralism as we have known it. And in every case, religious people voiced religious values publically long *before* public consensus was achieved and *before* new instances of public morality were accepted. In these cases, the religious rhetoric was deployed for the sake of democracy, not as a threat. A democracy that would not embrace these changes was considered by their advocates to be a sham democracy.

Cuomo suggests one other exception to silence for the sake of democratic pluralism. He says that his opposition to legal prohibitions on abortion "is by no means an argument for religious quietism" (p. 336). However, by the time he raises the point, religious activism cannot be construed as anything but a private sector activity; perhaps exemplary, but with no public *voice* in the policy debate — which coincides with the recommended religious response to abortion. Cuomo advocates an American pluralist public forum in which religious rhetoric can play no legitimate role in building new instances of consensus.

The imperative for the conscientious suppression of religious arguments from public rhetoric is validated and reinforced by the Notre Dame speech's image of democratic pluralism as the protector of religion. The same force that guards private religions would prefer that adherents of religions which call for direct political engagement would compromise their religious commitments for the sake of pluralism. Religious organizations which advocate their religious values as relevant to public policy debate cannot be trusted to value a pluralistic state within Cuomo's vision of American democracy.

Therefore, in public discourse, religious rhetoric constitutes a special case. As promised, Governor Cuomo defines the proper limits to religion in public affairs. While Kennedy told protestants that if he were elected president he would not be taking orders from the Vatican, Cuomo was telling Vatican representatives, fellow Catholics, and protestants that he would not, and neither should they, argue from personal religious convictions for public policy changes.

The understanding Cuomo reached with O'Connor, about not telling people how to vote, created a lull in which the Notre Dame speech was delivered. However, events since the Notre Dame address suggest its enduring relevance. In one instance involving Cuomo personally, a coalition of anti-abortion groups petitioned Pope John Paul II in 1991 asking him to excommunicate Cuomo, Senator Edward Kennedy, and 25 other American lawmakers who support abortion rights ("Abortion Foes," 1991, p. 7; Steinfels, 1991, p. 3). A Roman Catholic priest in Riverside, California, warned his parishioners before the 1992 elections that to vote for Bill Clinton or any other prochoice candidate would be a mortal sin (Wilkinson, 1992, p. 3). Most recently, in the summer of 1994 the National Conference of Catholic Bishops threatened to fight any government health care plan that would cover abortions while the Vatican was preparing its opposition to any abortion initiative that might emerge during the U.N. Population Conference in Cairo, Egypt (Hasson, 1994, p. 10; Povich, 1994, p. 4; Usdansky, 1994, p. 7).

These events should come as no surprise in light of the Notre Dame speech, for Cuomo's discourse is predisposed — both in style and substance — to advance the polarization between policymakers engaged in public debate and religious leaders who interact with the public and public affairs. The text offers listeners a world in which religious voices ought not to speak their consciences in public, in which a basic rhetorical activity — building new instances of public consensus is denied by decorum, and in which violations of these protocols brand religious voices as irrational purveyors of coercion, not persuasion.

The Notre Dame speech ignores the possibility that religious pluralism could exist in our public forum, just as ideological pluralism does. Polarities are maintained, instead of risking a moderate position where religious rhetoric could flourish in the midst of a robust public, pluralistic discourse. Such a position might recognize the holistic character of values and knowledge, argue forcefully without forcing beliefs, and maintain — consistent with public legal codes — that policies be established by public consensus.

The Notre Dame address early claims a preference for persuasion over coercion. In a recently published collection of his speeches, Cuomo's (1993) own analysis of Notre Dame judges it to be a contribution in this vein. He says, "I've been told it helped turn the discussion [of the role of religious belief in the public forum, focused specifically on abortion and Catholics] toward a more constructive phase. The truth is, since 1984, the discussion has been more reasonable, and whatever part in that development this speech had, the change relieves and gratifies me" (p. 32). Other currents in Cuomo's discourse ring true as well: no one church or religion controlling public policy, practical decorum, the warning against the tendency of politics to divert the church and its leaders from their highest priorities, and a call to religious integrity. Thus, Cuomo invites us to participate in a discursive framework — both complex and in many ways appealing — called democratic pluralism.

However, in other ways the version of democratic pluralism listeners are invited to adopt appears to be unlivable rhetorically. Instead of encouraging a responsible religious rhetoric — a plurality of religious voices seeking to contribute to new instances of public consensus — Cuomo fashions a "wall" between church and state that conflicts with citizens' practical experience of the interaction of religion and public affairs. Cuomo's wall becomes a ceiling, subordinating religious discourse to the interests of democratic pluralism to the extent that when public morality and religious values conflict, democratic pluralism is always supposed to take precedence. Religious rhetoric that would renegotiate that public morality presumably violates the orthodoxy of democratic pluralism at its very core. Therefore, religiously-minded Americans — clergy and laity — ought to conscientiously absent their religious thoughts, convictions, and voices from public discourse.

Cuomo presents an appealing rhetoric, because it correctly identifies the practical dilemma people face in church/state issues, but the distinction between private religious conviction and appropriate public rhetoric on moral policy is too absolute. It assumes an antagonism that splits otherwise integrated loyalties and encourages people to tolerate an internally adversarial posture. In the process, the vision presented in the Notre Dame speech ultimately compromises pluralism and impoverishes the rhetoric of the public forum it claims to protect. This public forum struggles to answer to the name "pluralist" by judging religious rhetoric as only violating and never contributing to the American experiment. From its elevated position, the same public forum excels at teaching religion its proper rhetorical role. In the end, American citizens are gently exhorted to hold sincere religious beliefs, but to do so without taking public action — especially rhetorical action.

## *Notes*

1. The Reagan Campaign was revising its itineraries to recover Reagan Democrats it feared were lost in the wake of Cuomo's Democratic Convention keynote address — hailed by the entire political spectrum, including Senator Barry Goldwater (Henry, 1988, pp. 105, 117).
2. For a full discussion of contemporary relations between church and state see Bellah, et al. (1984), Noll (1990), Wills (1990), and Wuthnow (1988).
3. White reports that Kennedy developed the Houston speech with aide Ted Sorensen, who commented prior to the speech that, "We can win or lose the election right there in Houston on Monday night" (1961, p. 260). On the other hand, Fuchs says that the campaign had data which suggested that anti-Catholic opposition had already reached its zenith of electoral effect, and that Kennedy decided to speak about the religious issue based on the hypothesis that "continued discussion might gain votes" (1967, p. 179).
4. In October of 1960, during Kennedy's election campaign, the bishops of Puerto Rico forbade their parishioners from voting for the Popular Democratic Party of Governor Munoz Marin (McClerrin, 1967, p. 107). In a pastoral letter circulated on the island and supported by Vatican news releases the bishops stated that anyone who did cast a vote for the Popular Democrats would be guilty of a "sin of disobedience" (Fuchs, 1967, p. 184). Kennedy chose not to address the issue in a speech, fearing that the voters would recognize Puerto Rico as American soil and that the connection would doom his candidacy (Fuchs, 1967, p. 185).
5. Hans Lotstra maintains that American Catholics at the time held many differences from the "church's declared stand," without becoming dissenters. Instead they were arguing from Catholic principles, and even in their dissent were not advocating major changes from the doctrinal position of the church (Lotstra, 1986, pp. 275–276).
6. All subsequent quotations from the speech are from the Andrews and Zarefsky text and are noted by page numbers only. The text has been anthologized twice (Andrews and Zarefsky, 1992, pp. 329–337; Jung and Shannon, 1988, pp. 202–216) and was more recently published by Cuomo himself in a collection of his speeches (1993, pp. 32–51). Excerpts were published in the *New York Times* the day after the speech ("Excerpts," 1984, p. A21). Jung and Shannon acknowledge Cuomo as a source of their text (1988, p. 328). The Andrews and Zarefsky text is identical to Jung and Shannon, except for a few instances of comma placement and paragraph breaks. Likewise, Cuomo's published version matches Andrews and Zarefsky quite precisely, although Cuomo seems to have edited out ". . . with me and Matilda" (cf. Andrews and Zarefsky, 1992, p. 333; Cuomo, 1993, p. 42).
7. Neuhaus's book was published in 1984; it was written prior to the Notre Dame speech.

## *References*

"Abortion foes urge excommunication of Kennedy, Cuomo." (1991, November 23). *The Boston Globe*, p. 7.

Andrews, J. R., & Zarefsky, D. (1992). *Contemporary American voices: Significant speeches in American history.* New York: Longman.

Barrett, H. (1964). John F. Kennedy before the Greater Houston Ministerial Association. *Central States Speech Journal, 15,* 259–266.

Bellah, R. N., Madsen, R., Sullivan, W. M., Swidler, A., & Tipton, S. M. (1984). *Habits of the heart.* New York: Harper and Row.

Black, E. (1980). A note on theory and practice in rhetorical criticism. *Western Journal of Speech Communications, 44,* 331–336.

Byrnes, T. A., & Segers, M. C. (1992). *The Catholic church and the politics of abortion.* Boulder: Westview Press.

Cuomo, M. (1984). *Diaries of Mario M. Cuomo: The campaign for governor.* New York: Random House.

Cuomo, M. (1993). *More than words: The speeches of Mario Cuomo.* New York: St. Martin's Press.

"Following Are Excerpts from the Text of an Address by Governor Cuomo Last Night at the University of Notre Dame . . ." (1984, September 14). *The New York Times*, p. A21.

Fuchs, L. H. (1967). *John F. Kennedy and American Catholicism.* New York: Meredith Press.

Gaonkar, D. P. (1989). Epilogue and the oratorical text: the enigma of arrival. In M. C. Leff and F. J. Kauffeld. (Eds.). *Texts in context: Critical dialogues on significant episodes in American political rhetoric* (pp. 255–275). Davis, CA: Hermagoras.

Hasson, Judi. (1994, July 14). Abortion: Health debate divider. *USA Today*, p. A10.

Henry, D. (1988). The rhetorical dynamics of Mario Cuomo's 1984 keynote address: Situation, speaker, metaphor. *Southern Speech Communication Journal, 53,* 105–120.

Jung, P. B., & Shannon, T. A. (1988). *Abortion and Catholicism: The American debate.* New York: Crossroad.

Lotstra, H. (1985). *Abortion, the Catholic debate in America.* New York: Irvington.

Marty, M. E. (1993). Religion: A private affair, in public affairs. *Religion and American culture, 3*(2), 115–127.

McClerrin, B. F. (1967). Southern Baptists and the religious issue during the presidential campaigns of 1928 and 1960. *Central States Speech Journal, 18,* 104–112.

McElvaine, R. S. (1988). *Mario Cuomo: A biography.* New York: Scribner's.

Murphy, J. M. (1989). Comic strategies and the American covenant. *Communication Studies, 40,* 266–279.

Neuhaus, R. J. (1984). *The naked public square.* Grand Rapids: Eerdmans.

Noll, M. (Ed.) (1990). *Religion and American politics from the colonial period to the 1980s.* New York: Oxford University Press.

Povich, E. S. (1994, July 13). Bishops enter health battle with a warning on abortion. *The New York Times,* p. A1.

"Pulpit politics: Religion enters the campaign." (1984, August 20). *Time,* p. 26.

Steinfels, P. (1991, November 24). Pope called unlikely to oust officials on abortion. *The New York Times,* p. 31.

Udansky, M. L. (1994, July 18). Catholic leaders balk at birth control, abortion. *USA Today,* p. A7.

White, T. H. (1961). *The making of the president: 1960.* New York: Atheneum.

Wilkinson, T. (1992, September 18). Voting for Clinton is sin, priest says. *The Los Angeles Times,* A3.

Wills, G. (1990). *Under God: Religion and American politics.* New York: Simon and Schuster.

Windt, T. O., Jr. (1988). John Fitzgerald Kennedy. In B. K. Duffy and H. R. Ryan (Eds). *American orators of the twentieth century* (pp. 245–253). New York: Greenwood.

Wood, G. S. (1969). *The creation of the American republic, 1776–1787.* New York: W. W. Norton.

Wuthnow, R. (1988). *Restructuring of American religion, society and faith since World War II.* Princeton, N.J.: Princeton University Press.

# 13

# Critical Reading of John Dickinson's "Letter from a Farmer in Pennsylvania"

## *The Pastoral Voice in John Dickinson's First Letter from a Farmer in Pennsylvania*

STEPHEN H. BROWNE

### The Political Uses of Pastoral: Rhetorical Dynamics in John Dickinson's First *Letter from a Farmer in Pennsylvania*

Among the traditions of western letters, few have endured with such appeal as pastoralism, perhaps because the tensions that prompt pastoral impulses endure: often our gaze turns beyond the inroads of urban strife and back to a simpler, more virtuous time and place. From the age of Theocritus, this need to reclaim the pastoral virtues has emerged in various forms from the ode to the utopian novel. It continues to live, as one scholar writes, "by a capacity to move out of its old haunts in the Arcadian pastures and to inhabit the ordinary country landscapes of the modern world, daily contracted by the encroachments of civilization and as a consequence daily more precious as a projection of our desires for simplicity."[1]

Although pastoralism has stimulated substantial literary scholarship, its use as a resource for public controversy and rhetorical expression has been neglected by critics and historians of public address. This essay examines as a significant instance of pastoral John Dickinson's first *Letter from a Farmer in Pennsylvania.* Close analysis of its textual dynamics reveals that pastoral configurations of time create a model of rhetorical judgment. As the primary characteristic of the first letter, it helps frame and direct how the following are to be interpreted. My reading of this text seeks to demonstrate how this model emerges from pastoral and to establish its relationship to rhetorical practice generally.[2]

How does the *Letter,* the richest and best-known of the series function rhetorically as pastoral? Why was pastoral especially suitable for Dickinson's audience? To answer these questions I will first probe the textual complexities which characterize the *Letter.* I will argue that, by assuming the pastoral voice, Dickinson redirects his audience's perception of time from the immediate world to an artistically created past, in which certain values and abiding principles of civic life are celebrated. This shift of attention allows Dickinson to suggest that citizens can take proper action when they suspend immediate concerns and willingly relocate their judgment in another realm of deliberation. Finally, I will argue that Dickinson's pastoral voice was especially appealing to an audience uncertain of its future and still fearful of political dissolution.

As a genre, pastoral represents a range of conventional meanings and appeals extensive enough to incorporate diverse expressions.[3] Pastoral is, clearly, a formal pattern of allusions which draw on identifiable *topoi.* According to Abrahams, pastoral is "any work which represents a withdrawal from ordinary life to a place apart, close to the elemental rhythms of nature, where a person achieves a news perspective on life in the complex social world."[4] More specifically, pastoral promotes a certain kind of attitude, a posture which exhibits the ideals of a Golden Age for present purposes. Thus, the "great characteristic of pastoral poetry," Peter Marinelli writes, "is that it is written when an ideal or at least more innocent world is felt to be lost, but not so wholly as to destroy the memory of it or to make some imaginative intercourse between present reality and past perfections impossible."[5]

Pastoral, moreover, entails a reconfiguration of time and space, which takes the present and relocates author, text, and audience in a different realm. By abandoning the confusion of the near world, pastoral presents a world of clearer, simpler meanings. As a rhetorical strategy, however, pastoral must address current issues by redefining the terms of public action and rhetorical judgment. Dickinson, I hope to demonstrate, skillfully uses pastoral appeals in this way to urge action on his contemporary scene.

### The Letter in Context

Dickinson, who was closely associated with the Quaker conservatives and was from a very wealthy family, had an active political life before the Revolution.[6] He was, in turn, Speaker of the Delaware Assembly (1760), representative in the Pennsylvania Assembly (1762–5), delegate to the Stamp Act Congress in 1765, President (Governor) of Delaware in 1781, and delegate to the Constitutional Convention. Labelled the "penman of the Revolution," Dickinson, in addition to the *Letters,* authored the *Resolutions of the Stamp Act Congress* (1764), *Late Regulations Respecting the British Colonies in America* (1765–66), drafted the *Articles of Confederation,* and later published the letters of "Fabius" in 1788. Although some considered him a founding father, the "Glorious Farmer" refused to sign the Declaration of Independence, a costly decision. Dickinson was, as H. Trevor Colburn writes, "one of America's most distinguished and perplexing conservatives, a political personality replete with challenge and apparent paradox."[7]

If Dickinson's political status was uneven, the significance of the *Letters* has never been doubted. Written during the winter of 1766–7 in response to British imperial policy, they targeted specifically the Quartering Act of 1765, the Restraining Act of the following year, and the Townshend Duties of June, 1767.[8] The twelve *Letters* comprise what Berhard Knollenberg describes as a "kind of colonial Bill of Rights."[9] They articulated and summarized colonial grievances, although the issues and positions were not especially novel. Their appeal lay not in the originality of their arguments, but in their expression. Stephen Lucas suggests that their impact "was due to the manner in which they articulated the most elemental yet often conflicting political fears and aspirations of the colonists."[10]

While the series unquestionably benefitted from promotional tactics, they were popular enough to go quickly into seven editions in pamphlet form and were distributed widely in Paris and London. The Farmer's *Letters,* Carl Kaestle notes, "appeared in 19 of the 23 English language newspapers published in the colonies in early 1768," and although the "combined circulation of these newspapers is impossible to determine with accuracy . . . an estimate of 15,000 is probably conservative, and several people may have read each newspaper." Kaestle concludes that "the *Farmer's Letters* reached more people than any previous published writing and remained unequalled in popular fame until Paine's *Common Sense.*"[11] To date, however, there has not been a corresponding interest in the *Letters'* specific strategies of inducement, and summary restatements of arguments have displaced extensive analysis of their imagery, allusions, structure, and modes of implication.[12]

Written in the form of a public letter, Dickinson's first essay exploits that eighteenth-century convention to create a particular relationship between author and reader.[13] The *Letter's* personal mode of address is ideally suited to its rhetorical ends, allowing Dickinson to accommodate the *Letter's* form to its pastoral appeal. A public letter is neither speech nor treatise; it functions between the volatile demands of immediate action and the serene remove of the contemplative world. Thus, the epistolary mode of address advances the ideological character of its argument. The essay is short — only eleven paragraphs long — and it is pointed. At its most general level of organization, the *Letter* begins with introductory remarks on the author's station in life, where Dickinson is concerned to establish authorial voice and enhance his *ethos.* The author then moves to a more explicit discussion of why he is obliged to write the *Letter* and presents his argument against British imperial policy. Dickinson concludes the *Letter* by offering a guarded call to action. The *Letter's* overt structure, is, therefore, conventional, but to understand its rhetorical ingenuity, we must track its internal dynamics. A copy of the *Letter* at the end of this essay will facilitate such close study.

**Letter from a Farmer in Pennsylvania: An Analysis of the Text**

*Introduction* Dickinson's tract begins with the familiar effort to establish credibility and to identify the terms of dispute. The farmer introduces himself before arguing against recent imperial measures. But a closer scrutiny of the early passage reveals its inventive ingenuity. Delaying his confrontation until paragraph seven, the author engages the reader not with the conflict, but with attributes of his own character. Hence the first line: "I am a farmer, settled, after a variety of fortunes, near the banks of the river Delaware, in the province of Pennsylvania." This simple, direct sentence syntactically mirrors the pastoral virtue of the Farmer. Significantly the author is a farmer, not, by implication, a merchant; he is settled, not a transient malcontent; he has enjoyed a "variety of fortunes," and, thus, can claim the fruits of experience and reflection, resting now "near the banks of the river Delaware," far from the crowds of Boston and New York. In the following sentences, first person pronouns (ten in three sentences) precede a simple statement of circumstances. But these lines do not simply convey concrete details; rather, each fact has a moral counterpart. He is a farmer, but liberally educated; once busy, now contemplative, thus happy; a small planter, but well served; prosperous, but prudent; at ease, but never idle. In other words, the humbleness of the Farmer's circumstances constitutes his *ethos* and authority. He is rural but not crude, placid but not languid. These brief statements establish his virtue from which he can proceed to offer his argument.

While the opening paragraph couples circumstance with virtue, the second more directly authorizes the Farmer's claim to his reader's belief by moving from what the author is to what the author does, from character to character-in-action. "Being generally master of my time," the Farmer begins, "I spend a good deal of it in a library, which I think the most valuable part of my small estate." Moreover, the Farmer continues, "being acquainted with two or three gentlemen of abilities and learning, who honor me with their friendship, I have acquired, I believe, a greater knowledge in history, and the laws and constitution of my country, than is generally attained by men of my class, many of them not being so fortunate as I have been in the opportunities of getting information."

These brief comments locate the site of deliberation and signal the author's commitment to the quiet pursuit of knowledge and informed judgment. Retiring to his library, the author has freely chosen the *vita contemplativa,* a world and perspective removed from the hectic, distorted scenes of city life. But this removal from urban life does not disable him, rather it offers him an opportunity for greater insight into the affairs of his community. Thus, paragraph two sustains the process of accumulating credentials, deepens the concrete and simple appeal of the Farmer's persona, and hints at Dickinson's conservative rationale for public action. Together, these lines focus on the Farmer as a temperate, intelligent man, and in so doing draw on pastoral virtues as the basis of his *ethos.*

In paragraph three, the Farmer takes a slightly different direction. "From my infancy I was taught to love humanity and liberty," the Farmer begins, and "enquiry and experience have since confirmed my reverence for the lesson then given me by convincing me more fully of these truths and excellence." By association, the Christian values of truth and humanity are related to the republican virtues of liberty and excellence, and Dickinson produces a much deeper motivation for action. The next statements continue this synhesis:

> Benevolence toward mankind excites wishes for their welfare, and such wishes endear the means of fulfilling them. These can be found in liberty only, and therefore her sacred cause ought to be espoused by every man, on every occasion to the utmost of his power. . . . Perhaps he may 'touch some wheel', that will have been an effect greater than he could reasonably expect.

Were it not for the dominating presence of the Farmer's character, paragraph three would seem quite anomalous. Slightly longer, more complex syntactically, it sustains an introductory function, but its tone and content shift. Here the first explicit statements of principle appear; but while these set this portion somewhat apart from the preceding paragraphs, the section remains consistent with the terms of the *Letter* so far. In effect, the paragraph rationalizes the ensuing argument; it aligns the proper relationship between character and principle which defines the *Letter* generally. In other words, principles remain fixed according to the terms of character: they can then act as premises from which the Farmer will argue his case.

In a different way from the earlier paragraphs, this section confirms the Farmer's capacity for sound judgment. Continuing to stress the rewards of informed and dispassionate opinion, the author justifies his appeal to action with sacred and secular motives. Here the emphasis on principled action in the affairs of the community mirrors earlier descriptions of contemplative virtue. Within the logic of Dickinson's *Letter,* these realms are portrayed, not as incompatible, as *vita contemplativa* vs. *vita activa,* but as correlates to a fully justified will to power.

*Argument* Having established his *ethos* through affirmation of pastoral virtue, Dickinson moves into his argument by delineating the situation which compels him to act. The author begins by effacing himself:

> Conscious of my own defects, I have waited some time, in expectation of seeing the subject treated by persons much better qualified for the task; but being therein disappointed, and apprehensive that longer delays will be injurious, I venture at length to request the attention of the public, praying, that these lines may be read with the same zeal for the happiness of British America with which they were wrote.

The author is moved to act, he does not incite; he appears concerned for the general welfare, but he is not "interested" since he has nothing to gain personally from the consent of his readership. Paragraph five elaborates on this image by stressing Parliament's threat to suspend New York's Assembly: "With a good deal of surprise I have observed, that little notice has been taken of an act of parliament, as injurious in its principle to the liberties of these colonies, as the Stamp-Act was: I mean the act for suspending the legislation of New-York." From his position, the Farmer is able to see what others apparently cannot, hence the "surprise." The variations on this act of perception — "enquiry," "appears to me," "I have observed," "perceive" — underscore the Farmer's privileged insight.

Working from the model of pastoral judgment implicit in the introduction, the four paragraphs making up the *Letter's* body become exercises in careful reason. The process of inference is wholly consistent with what we would expect of the Farmer; as the paragraphs progress, the reader sees not only previously unperceived threats, but an example of how to apprehend them.

Paragraph six functions as a brief *narratio,* or review of the events leading up to Parliament's challenge to colonial liberties. The New York Assembly, in complying only in part to British demands for support, signalled its resistance to the spirit and letter of imperial law. Immediately following this rather cursory review, the author reflects at greater length upon the action of the Assembly. "In my opinion," the Farmer writes, "they acted imprudently, considering all circumstances, in not complying as far as would have given satisfaction, as several colonies did." His assessment of their judgment opens the way for the following critical passage. "But my dislike of their conduct in that instance," the Farmer concludes, "has not blinded me so much, that I cannot plainly perceive, that they have been punished in a manner pernicious to American freedom, and justly alarming to all the colonies." Implicitly and skillfully, Dickinson contrasts his insight, made possible by his pastoral remove, to others' blindness, produced by their too close involvement in the details.

This short and simple review of circumstances aligns the facts according to the perspective of the author. The relatively slight provocation by the Assembly contrasts sharply with the greater folly of British law. This contrast, in turn, orders the following attack on the reasoning behind such law. These paragraphs, in short, represent a study in contrasts of political inclination and judgment itself.

"If the British Parliament," the Farmer reasons, "has a legal authority to issue an order, the we shall furnish a single article for the troops here, and to compel obedience to that order," then, he concludes, "they have the same right to issue an order for us to supply those troops with arms, cloths, and every necessary . . . in short, to lay any burthens they please upon us." By framing his objection in the form of a hypothetical syllogism, the author is able to speculate on the consequences of British policy. As the paragraph develops, those consequences become increasingly odious; the hypothetical syllogism moves into a *reductio ad absurdum.* The recurrent use of questions emphasizes his incredulity at this extreme state of affairs. "What is this," the Farmer asks, "but taxing us at a certain sum, and leaving to us only the manner of raising it? How is this made more tolerable than the Stamp Act?"

In much the same fashion, paragraphs eight and nine use forceful reasoning about the deliberations of Parliament to the extent of British depredations. Together these paragraphs pursue a common theme: the decision to suspend New York's legislature is a dangerous precedent for the destruction of colonial liberties. Significantly, the author analysis issues in diverse ways, relentlessly exposing through reason the irrationality and injustice of the British. These three paragraphs reveal the Farmer's insight and power of inference. Moving forcefully to a condemnation of the coercive measures, they create the force of logical necessity as the questions continue. The final lines from paragraph nine summarize the earlier points and conclude this section of the *Letter* climactically:

> In fact, if the people of New-York cannot be legally taxed but by their own representatives, they cannot be legally deprived of the privilege of taxation. If they may be legally deprived in such a case, of the privilege of legislation, why may they not, with equal reason, be deprived of every other privilege? Or why may not every colony be treated in the same manner, when any of them shall dare to deny their assent to any impositions, that shall be directed? Or what signifies the repeal of the Stamp-Act, if these colonies are to lose their other privileges, by not tamely surrendering that of taxation?

Having established this point, in paragraph ten the author extends his analysis to embrace a variety of issues and concerns. The *Letter* expands quite literally at this point: the paragraph is the longest in the text. More importantly, as the pace quickens and his intensity builds, the Farmer dramatizes the conflict. He perceives: "It is a parliamentary assertion of the supreme authority of the British legislature over these colonies, in the point of taxation, and is intended to COMPEL New-York into a submission of that authority and impending doom, whoever seriously considers the matter, must perceive that a dreadful stroke is aimed at the liberty of these colonies." These observations require a call to action; the cause of one is the cause of all. While these sentiments are not usually associated with pastoral, the author has prepared for these appeals through the *ethos* which his pastoral situation has provided. Out of context, they appear incendiary; but within context, they are the inevitable conclusions of the pastoral Farmer's rigorous arguments, the product of his "quiet contemplation." Had the Farmer not so carefully established his pastoral *ethos* in the introductory section, his arguments here would have seemed more radical and unacceptable.

*Conclusion to the Letter* The final paragraph returns quickly to the more contemplative stance of the *Letter's* opening. Here, more than elsewhere, the ambivalence of Dickinson's conservatism is clear. Following the climactic lines of the penultimate paragraph, the following passage is quite significant: "I am by no means fond of inflammatory measures; I detest them. I should be sorry that anything should be done, which might justly displease our sovereign, or our mother country." Balanced against this caution is an equally compelling obligation to act; "But a firm, modest exertion of a free spirit, should never be wanting on public occasions." For the author, conservatism does not commit a citizen to quiescence; on the contrary, it obliges the colonists to undertake the revolutionary act of return. The concluding line of the *Letter* affirms not only this principle, but the requirements of community for its successful employment. The first person pronouns of the introduction give way to the collective "our" and "we." "It appears to me," the Farmer advises, "that it would have been sufficient for the assembly, to have ordered our agents to represent to the King's ministers, their sense of the suspending act, and to pray for its repeal. Thus we should have born our testimony against it," he concludes, "and might therefore reasonably expect that, on a like occasion, we might receive the same assistance from the other colonies." In one sense, the Senecan maxim at the end captures the essential appeal of Dickinson's *Letter: "Concordia res parve crescunt"*: Small things grow great by concord.

### The Rhetorical Functions of Pastoral

How can the *Letter* be usefully and accurately described as pastoral? First, it manifestly draws on pastoral *topoi,* including the steady Farmer, who tends his fecund land and is resolute in his allegiance to common values, to strengthen the arguments which follow in the text. The *Letter,* moreover, exploits pastoral conventions by invoking a model of judgment implicit in pastoral; and in making it explicit, the text promotes that model as a means of inducement.[14] Accordingly, the rhetorical effect of the *Letter* is a function of its pastoral appeal: the colonists would be moved not by its aesthetic pleasantries, but because its pastoral values of sound judgment, restrained action, and civic accountability were compelling for a distressed but essentially conservative public. Dickinson, finally, could count on a public sympathetic to his values and situation — his pastoralism — because his prospective readers were members of a community conscious of its own pastoral impulses. The text functions rhetorically to induce consent because of the pastoral values it contains.

In addition to its textual ingenuity, the *Letter* reveals an interaction between the conventions of pastoral and public action. Embodied in the rhetorical form of the *Letter,* this relationship is clearest in the nature and display of judgment. The Farmer's judgment is distinctively pastoral because it endorses values inherent in the genre, but to an unusual rhetorical end. Taking advantage of his condition, the Farmer blends the divergent demands of his private happiness and his public obligation. Reshaped for rhetorical ends, pastoral is most appealing when the public world is too much with us. But as Dickinson understood and as this reading of the *Letter* suggests, pastoral promises to remake the world by returning it to a better time and place. This function is the source of its deep conservatism; this was its appeal to the pre-revolutionary world of British America.

The inherently conservative character of pastoral appeal makes it significant as a resource for rhetorical practice generally. It seems especially prominent, perhaps most appropriate, in times of intense political activity. Pastoral, moreover, works precisely because it simultaneously requires distance but mandates action. Far from being paradoxical, this trait represents pastoral's great rhetorical strength. Dickinson's appropriation is efficacious because it avoids both the immediacy of an oration and the privacy of meditation. The *Letter* in its pastoral mode negotiates a return to a putatively better world, a time when citizens acted with deliberate and reasoned will. Thus, part of its rhetorical force can be attributed to its play "between present reality and past perfection." In pastoral, the will to return does not entail escape; rather pastoral encourages constructive activity. As Marinelli observes, "the chief stress is upon the exercise of virtue in the active life, in the restoration or renewal of a fallen society, and though contemplation is a necessary precondition, it is only through activity that mankind can cleanse his surroundings."[15] Pastoral does not offer the sanguine rustic as an ideal; rather, it esteems an ideally situated actor, who is perspicacious and has an unusual opportunity for calm, wise judgment.

This conservative appeal helps us to understand why a pastoral letter was such an appropriate resource for Dickinson at that particular time and place. Two features of the text's context are worth considering at this point. At the time of the *Letter's* publication, the colonies were not yet committed to rebellion. Indeed, no colonist of any public stature was openly declaring for revolt when Dickinson composed his tracts. For as long as they thought possible, colonists sought to reconcile and confirm relations with England, in short, to return to more halcyon days. Thus the pastoral's appeal was to a people by nature and habit conservative; it expresses a mode of deliberation and a sensibility in keeping with colonial aspirations. At the same time, it allows the author to advocate public action without appearing strident or, indeed, revolutionary. A second, more general but closely related consideration enters at this point: this pastoral sensibility has its source in the origins and growth of colonial life. A people whose very founding embraced the Adamic ideals associated with pastoral, whose "errand into the wilderness" nurtured deep commitments to the virtues of pastoral life, would probably be receptive to pastoral appeals.[16]

Pastoral, in short, commands the rhetorical virtues of propriety: it is a timed invocation to a people habituated to its appeal. At its very founding, Marx writes, "the idea that the American continent may become the site of a new golden age could be taken seriously in politics" and ever since we have read "descriptions of the New World as a kind of Virgilian pasture — a land depicted as if it might become the scene, at long last, of a truly successful 'pursuit of happiness',"[17] To the extent that the *Letter* addresses a collective inclination to view particular political issues in these terms, it can be said to induce in its readers habits of response appropriate to pastoral. This perspective is one key to understanding the text: it functions rhetorically through its inventional appropriation of pastoral *and* by encouraging its audience to read it *as* pastoral. Together, author and audience collaborate in a fusion of style and substance.

### Theoretical Implications

As a rhetorical form, pastoral invokes a cluster of values, most prominently the agrarian virtues of steady perspective and prudence. When these values and their constituents are exploited as inventive resources, they function in at least two ways. First, they draw upon the force of literary convention to give voice to rhetorical expression.[18] Second, these values help define a standard of judgment which the author would have the audience assume. Pastoral provides a vocabulary not only for promoting specific claims, but also for promoting the deliberative processes through which those claims can be established. By design, pastoral draws attention to itself: the author says at once "this is what we should do," and "this is how I arrived at that decision." This claim to exemplary judgment links pastoral with rhetorical judgment and merits more complete description.

An essential tension exists within pastoral, a confrontation of impulses which becomes especially evident in rhetorical practice. The tension involves the conflict between private and public rationales for action. By convention, pastoral demands its own marginality; its voice can be heard only at a distance and emerges from the quiet haunts of the study, village, and farm. The virtues that ground pastoral are nurtured untrodden by the ways of city and crowd. Hence, the traditional site of pastoral: a geographic region defined by the moral requisites of distance, reflection, and disinterest. In part, pastoral may be understood by what it poses as counterparts: urbanity, artifice, ambition, and imprudence, the secular sins of the *vita activa*. These are the familiar commonplaces of pastoral convention and may in occur in a variety of literary strains. But when they serve rhetorical ends, pastoral *topoi* become something more than a conceit. Marx writes that "the story of its emergence illustrates the turning of an essentially literary device to ideological or (using the word in its extended sense) political uses."[19] But if pastoral, seemingly a private sensibility, can serve persuasive ends, how does it serve public ends?

If patently rhetorical texts evince pastoral functions, then the expansion of its scope seems warranted. Dickinson's *Letter* not only makes this possible, but deepens the analysis by illustrating how the convergence of two traditions results in a concept of rhetorical judgment. Specifically, the *Letter* appropriates from pastoral a complex of values and authorial voice, which in turn create a compelling aesthetic appeal. At the same time, the public and practical character of the *Letter* promotes principles of responsibility, reasoning from experience, and commitment to civic action. Dickinson's tract draws upon the private to become public, assumes a provisionally contemplative stance as a basis for action, and stresses distance to secure sympathy. Its persuasive appeal is located precisely in this tension, where the character of the Farmer resides, detached enough to command perspective, not so detached that he cannot advance deliberative ends. The result is to display a principle of judgment fundamental to the meaning of the *Letter.*

Rhetorical judgment, as distinguished from certain expressions of aesthetic or moral judgment, finds its authorizing source in public knowledge; it occupies a space between the particular and the general; it occurs in the diverse conditions of human community. Ronald Beiner, who has carefully explored such a conception of judgment, provides a theoretical insight into Dickinson's achievement. Such judgment, Beiner writes, "must embrace the standpoints of both the spectator and the actor: it calls for both distance and experience, and its consequence is both dignity and wisdom."[20] For readers of Dickinson's *Letter,* the Farmer must have embodied just such a mixture of "distance and experience," and thus "both dignity and wisdom."

### Letter from a Farmer in Pennsylvania

[1] I am a Farmer, settled, after a variety of fortunes, near the banks of the river Delaware, in the province of Pennsylvania. I received a liberal education, and have been engaged in the busy scenes of life; but am now convinced, that a man may be as happy without bustle, as with it. My farm is small; my servants are few, and good; I have a little money as interest; I wish for no more; my employment in my own affairs is easy; and with a contented grateful mind, undisturbed by

worldly hopes or fears, relating to myself, I am completing the number of days allotted to me by divine goodness.

[2] Being generally master of my time, I spend a good deal of it in a library, which I think the most valuable part of my small estate; and being acquainted with two or three gentlemen of abilities and learning, who honour me with their friendship, I have acquired, I believe, a greater knowledge in history, and the laws and constitution of my country, than is generally attained by men of my class, many of them not being so fortunate as I have been in the opportunities of getting information.

[3] From my infancy I was taught to love *humanity* and *liberty.* Enquiry and experience have since confirmed my reverence for the lessons then given me, by convincing me more fully of their truth and excellence. Benevolence towards mankind, excites wishes for their welfare, and such wishes endear the means of fulfilling them. *These* can be found in liberty only, and therefore her sacred cause ought to be espoused by every man, on every occasion, to the utmost of his power. As a charitable, but poor person does not withhold his *mite,* because he cannot relieve *all* the distresses of the miserable, so should not any honest man suppress his sentiments concerning freedom, however small their influence is likely to be. Perhaps he "may touch some wheel," that will have an effect greater than he could reasonably expect.

[4] These being my sentiments, I am encouraged to offer to you, my countrymen, my thoughts on some later transactions, that appear to me to be of the utmost importance to you. Conscious of my own defects, I have waited some time, in expectation of seeing the subject treated by persons much better qualified for the task; but being therein disappointed, and apprehensive that longer delays will be injurious, I venture at length to request the attention of the public, praying, that these lines may be *read* with the same zeal for the happiness of British America with which they were *wrote.*

[5] With a good deal of surprise I have observed, that little notice has been taken of an act of parliament, as injurious in its principle to the liberties of these colonies, as the Stamp-Act was: I mean the act of suspending the legislation of New York.

[6] The assembly of that government complied with a former act of parliament, requiring certain provisions to be made for the troops in America, in every particular, I think, except the articles of salt, pepper and vinegar. In my opinion they acted imprudently, considering all circumstances, in not complying so far as would have given satisfaction, as several colonies did: But my dislike of their conduct in that instance, has not blinded me so much, that I cannot plainly perceive, that they have been punished in a manner pernicious to American freedom, and justly alarming to all the colonies.

[7] If the British parliament has a legal authority to issue an order, that we shall funish a single article for the troops here, and to compel

obedience to *that* order, they have the same right to issue an order for us to supply those troops with arms, cloths, and every necessary; and to compel obedience to *that* order also; in short, to lay *any burthens* they please upon us. What is this but *taxing* us at a *certain sum,* and leaving us only the *manner* of raising it. How is the mode more tolerable than the Stamp Act? Would that act have appeared more pleasing to Americans, if being ordered thereby to raise the sum total of the taxes, the mighty privilege had been left to them, of saying how much should be paid for an instrument of writing on paper, and how much for another on parchment?

[8] An act of parliament, commanding us to do a certain thing, if it has any validity, is a *tax* upon us for the expence that accrues in complying with it; and for this reason, I believe, every colony on the continent, that chose to give a mark of their respect for Great-Britain, in complying with the act relating to the troops, cautiously avoided the mention of that act, lest their conduct should be attributed to its supposed obligation.

[9] The matter being thus stated, the assembly of New-York either had, or had not, a right to refuse submission to that act. If they had, and I imagine no American will say they had not, then the parliament had *no right* to compel them to execute it. If they had not *that right,* they had *no right* to punish them for not executing it; and therefore *no right* to suspend their legislation, which is a punishment. In fact, if the people of New-York cannot be legally taxed but by their own representatives, they cannot be legally deprived of the privilege of legislation, only for insisting on that exclusive privilege of taxation. If they may be legally deprived in such a case, of the privilege of legislation, why may they not, with equal reason, be deprived of every other privilege? Or why may not every colony be treated in the same manner, when any of them shall dare to deny their assent to any impositions, that shall be directed? Or what signifies the repeal of the Stamp-Act, if these colonies are to lose their *other* privileges, by not tamely surrendering *that* of taxation?

[10] There is one consideration arising from their suspension, which is not generally attended to, but shews its importance very clearly. It was not *necessary* that this suspension should be caused by an act of parliament. The crown might have restrained the governor of New-York, even from calling the assembly together, but its prerogative in the royal governments. This step, I suppose, would have been taken, if the conduct of the assembly of New-York had been regarded as an act of disobedience *to the crown alone;* but it is regarded as an act of "disobedience to the authority of the BRITISH LEGISLATURE." This gives the suspension of consequence vastly more affecting. It is a parliamentary assertion of the *supreme authority* of the British legislature over these colonies, in *the point of taxation,* and is tended to COMPEL New-York into a submission to that authority. It seems therefore to me as much a violation of the liberty of the people of that province, and consequently of all these colonies, as if the parliament had sent a number of

regiments to be quartered upon them till they should comply. For it is evident, that the suspension is meant as a *compulsion;* and the *method* of compelling is totally indifferent. It is indeed probable, that the sight of red coats, and the hearing of drums, would have been most alarming; because people are generally more influenced by their eyes and ears, than by their reason. But whoever seriously considers the matter, must perceive that a dreadful stroke is aimed at the liberty of these colonies. I say, of these colonies; for the cause of *one* is the cause of *all.* If the parliament may lawfully deprive New-York of any of *her* rights, it may deprive any, or all the other colonies of *their* rights; and nothing can possibly so much encourage such attempts, as a mutual inattention to the interests of each other. *To divide, and thus to destroy,* is the first political maxim in attacking those, who are powerful by their union. He certainly is not a wise man, who folds his arms, and reposes himself at home, viewing, with unconcern, the flames that have invaded his neighbour's house, without using any endeavours to extinguish them. When Mr. *Hampden's* ship money cause, for *Three Shillings* and *Four-pence,* was tried, all the people of England, with anxious expectations, interested themselves in the important decision; and when the slightest point, touching the freedom of *one* colony, is agitated, earnestly wish, that *all the rest* may, with equal ardour, support their sister. Very much may be said on this subject; but I hope, more at present is unnecessary.

[11] With concern I have observed, that *two* assemblies of this province have sat and adjourned, without taking any notice of this act. It may perhaps be asked, that would have been proper for them to do? I am by no means fond of inflammatory measures; I detest them. I should be sorry that any thing should be done, which might justly displease our sovereign, or our mother country: But a firm, modest exertion of a free spirit, should never be wanting on public occasions. It appears to me, that it would have been sufficient for the assembly, to have ordered our agents to represent to the King's ministers, their sense of the suspending act, and to pray for its repeal. Thus we should have borne our testimony against it; and might therefore reasonably expect that, on a like occasion, we might receive the same assistance from the other colonies.

*Concordia res parvae crescunt.*

Small things grow great by concord.

## Notes

1. Peter V. Marinelli, *Pastoral* (London: Methuen, 1973), 3.
2. Full title: *Letters From a Farmer in Pennsylvania to the Inhabitants of the British Colonies.* All references are to the reprinted version found in Merrill

Jensen, Ed., *Tracts of the American Revolution, 1763–1776* (Indianapolis: Bobbs-Merrill, 1976), 128–133. Citations are sequential.

3. Background and critical studies of pastoral include Frank Kermode, *English Pastoral Poetry From the Beginning to Marvell* (London: Hanrap, 1952); J. E. Congleton, *Theories of Pastoral Poetry in England, 1684–1798* (Gainseville: University of Florida Press, 1952), esp. 3–12; 75–96; 157–294; William Empson's classic *Some Versions of Pastoral* (Norfolk, Conn: New Directions, rpt. 1960); John F. A. Heath-Stubbs, *The Pastoral* (London: Oxford University Press, 1969); Thomas G. Rosenmeyer, *The Green Cabinet: Theocritus and the European Pastoral Lyric* (Berkeley: University of California Press, 1969); Harold E. Toliver, *Pastoral Forms and Attitudes* (Berkeley: University of California Press, 1971); and Renato Poggioloi, *The Oaten Flute: Essays on Pastoral Poetry and the Pastoral Ideas* (Cambridge: Harvard University Press, 1975).
4. M. H. Abrahms, *A Glossary of Literary Terms* (New York: Holt, Rinehart, & Winston, 1988), 128.
5. Marinelli, 9.
6. For more extensive biography and political background, see Robert A. Richards, *The Life and Character of John Dickinson* (Wilmington: Historical Society of Delaware, 1901); David Jacobson, *John Dickinson and the Revolution in Pennsylvania, 1764–1776* (Berkeley and Los Angeles: University of California Press, 1965); Milton Flower, *John Dickinson, Conservative Revolutionary* (Charlottesville: University of Virginia Press, 1983); and Sandra S. Hynes, "The Political Rhetoric of John Dickinson, 1764–1776," Ph.D. dissertation, University of Massachusetts, 1982.
7. "John Dickinson, Historical Revolutionary," *Pennsylvania Magazine of History and Biography* 88 (1959): 271.
8. The remaining letters dealt with: distinctions between taxation and revenue; constitutional methods of reform; attacks on the distinction between internal and external taxation; questions of who should determine tax rates and sources; observations on anti-Americanism in England; appeals for unity; and subsidiary issues. See Jacobson, 43–69; and Stephen E. Lucas, *Portents of Rebellion: Rhetoric and Revolution in Philadelphia, 1765–1776* (Philadelphia: Temple University Press, 1976), 63–73.
9. Bernhard Knollenberg, *Growth of the American Revolution, 1766–1775* (New York: Free Press, 1975), 53.
10. Lucas, 70.
11. Carl F. Kaestle, "The Public Reaction to John Dickinson's Farmer's Letters," *American Antiquarian Society Proceedings* 78 (1969): 329–359.
12. An exception in Pierre Marambaud, "Dickinson's Letters From a Farmer in Pennsylvania: Ideology, Imagery, and Rhetoric," *Early American Literature* 12 (1977): 63–72.
13. This relationship is discussed at greater length in Stephen H. Browne, "Edmund Burke's Letter to a Noble Lord: A Textual Study in Political Philosophy and Rhetorical Action," *Communication Monographs* 55 (1988): 215–229.
14. See Ronald Beiner, *Political Judgment* (Chicago: University of Chicago Press, 1983), 83–101.
15. Beiner, 109.
16. See James Macher, "The Urban Idyll of the New Republic: Moral Geography and the Mythic Heroes of Franklin's Autobiography," *Pennsylvania Magazine of History and Biography* 110 (1986): 220; Frank Shuffleton, "Philo-

sophical Solitude and the Pastoral Politics of William Livingston," *Early America Literature* 17 (1982): 52; and Lewis P. Simpson, *The Dispossessed Garden: Pastoral and History in Southern Literature* (Athens: University of Georgia Press, 1975) for more extensive treatments of pastoral influences in early American culture.

17. Leo Marx, *The Machine in the Garden: Technology and the Pastoral Ideal in America* (New York: Oxford University Press, 1964), 74.
18. The appropriation of literary voice for political ends is discussed in Stephen H. Browne, "The Gothic Voice in Eighteenth-Century Oratory," *Communication Quarterly* 36 (1988): 227–236.
19. Marx, 73.
20. Beiner, 109.

# Bibliographies

## Select Bibliography of Recent Critical Studies

*The following bibliography is not exhaustive; it is meant to provide a sample of critical studies published over the last decade or so that illustrates a variety of critical purposes, approaches, and objects for study that are open to the rhetorical critic.*


Adams, John Charles. "Linguistic Values and Religious Experiences: An Analysis of Clothing Metaphors in Alexander Richardson's Ramist-Puritan Lectures on Speech, 'Speech is a garment to cloath our reason,' " *Quarterly Journal of Speech* 76 (1990): 58–68.

Andrews, James R. "The Rhetorical Shaping of National Interest: Morality and Contextual Potency in John Bright's Parliamentary Speech Against Recognition of the Confederacy," *Quarterly Journal of Speech* 79 (1993): 40–60.

Ball, Moya Ann. *Vietnam-on-the-Potomac.* New York: Praeger, 1992.

Bass, Jeff. "The Appeal to Efficiency as Narrative Closure: Lyndon Johnson and the Dominican Crisis, 1965," *Southern Speech Communication Journal* 50 (1985): 103–120.

Benson, Thomas, ed. *Landmark Essays on Rhetorical Criticism.* Davis, CA: Hermagoras, 1993.

Benson, Thomas W., ed. *American Rhetoric: Context and Criticism.* Carbondale, IL: Southern Illinois University Press, 1989.

Benson, Thomas W., ed. *Rhetoric and Political Culture in Nineteenth-Century America.* Lansing, MI: Michigan State University Press, 1997.

Birdsell, David S. "Ronald Reagan on Lebanon and Grenada: Flexibility and Interpretation in the Application of Kenneth Burke's Pentad," *Quarterly Journal of Speech* 73 (1987): 267–279.

Black, Edwin. *Rhetorical Questions: Studies of Public Discourse.* Chicago: University of Chicago Press, 1992.

Bormann, Ernest G. *The Force of Fantasy: Restoring the American Dream.* Carbondale, IL: Southern Illinois University Press, 1985.

Bowers, John Waite, Donovan J. Ochs, and Richard J. Jensen. *The Rhetoric of Agitation and Control.* Prospect Heights, IL: Waveland Press, 1993.

Brown, Stephen H. "Generic Transformation and Political Action: A Textual Interpretation of Edmund Burke's Letter to William Elliot, Esq." *Communication Quarterly* 30 (1990): 54–63.

Browne, Stephen H. "Edmund Burke's *Letter to a Noble Lord:* A Textual Study in Political Philosophy and Rhetorical Action," *Communication Monographs* 55 (1988): 215–229.

Browne, Stephen H. *Edmund Burke and the Discourse of Virtue.* Tuscaloosa: University of Alabama Press, 1993.

Brummet, Barry. *Rhetorical Dimensions of Popular Culture.* Tuscaloosa: University of Alabama Press, 1991.

Burgehardt, Carl R. "Discovering Rhetorical Imprints: La Follette, 'Iago,' and the Melodramatic Scenario," *Quarterly Journal of Speech* 71 (1985): 441–456.

Campbell, Karlyn Kohrs, *Man Cannot Speak for Her: A Critical Study of Early Feminist Rhetoric.* New York: Praeger, 1989.

Campbell, Karlyn Kohrs, and Kathleen Hall Jamieson. *Deeds Done in Words: Presidential Rhetoric and the Genres of Governance.* Chicago: University of Chicago Press, 1990.

Carlson, A. Cheree. "Creative Casuistry and Feminist Consciousness: A Rhetoric of Moral Reform," *Quarterly Journal of Speech* 78 (1992): 16–32.

Carlson, A. Cheree. "Narrative as the Philosopher's Stone: How Russell H. Conwell Changed Lead into Diamonds," *Western Journal of Speech Communication* 53 (1989), 342–355.

Carlson, A. Cheree. "Defining Womanhood: Lucretia Coffin Mott and the Transformation of Femininity," *Western Journal of Communication* 58 (Spring 1994): 85–97.

Carlson, A. Cheree. "John Quincy Adams' 'Amistad Address': Eloquence in a Generic Hybrid," *Western Journal of Speech Communication* 49 (1985): 14–26.

Carlson, A. Cheree. "The Role of Character in Public Moral Argument: Henry Ward Beecher and the Brooklyn Scandal," *Quarterly Journal of Speech* 77 (1991): 38–52.

Carpenter, Ronald H. "America's Tragic Metaphor: Our Twentieth Century Combatants as Frontiersmen," *Quarterly Journal of Speech* 76 (1990): 1–22.

Condit, Celeste Michelle. *Decoding Abortion Rhetoric: Communicating Social Change.* Urbana, IL: University of Illinois Press, 1990.

Corcoran, Farrel. "The Bear in the Back Yard: Myth, Ideology, and Victimage Ritual in Soviet Funerals," *Communication Monographs* 50 (December 1983): 305–320.

Daughton, Suzanne M. "Women's Issues, Women's Place: Gender-Related Problems in Presidential Campaigns," *Communication Quarterly* 42 (Spring 1994): 106–119.

Daughton, Suzanne M. "Metaphorical Transcendence: Images of the Holy War in Franklin Roosevelt's First Inaugural," *Quarterly Journal of Speech* 79 (1993): 427–446.

DiMare, Leslie. "Functionalizing Conflict: Jessie Jackson's Rhetorical Strategy at the 1984 Democratic Convention," *Western Journal of Speech Communication* 51 (1987): 218–226.

Dow, Bonnie J., and Mari Boor Tonn. " 'Feminine Style' and Political Judgment in the Rhetoric of Ann Richards," *Quarterly Journal of Speech* 79 (1993): 286–302.

Griffin, Cindy L. "Rhetoricizing Alienation: Mary Wollstonecraft and the Rhetorical Construction of Women's Oppression," *Quarterly Journal of Speech* 80 (1994): 293–312.

Hahn, Dan F., and Anne Morland. "A Burkean Analysis of Lincoln's Second Inaugural Address," *Presidential Studies Quarterly* 9 (1979): 376–389.

Hart, Roderick P. *The Sound of Leadership: Presidential Communication in the Modern Age.* Chicago: University of Chicago Press, 1987.

Hogan, J. Michael. *The Panama Canal in American Politics.* Carbondale, IL: U of Southern Illinois Press, 1986.

Hogan, J. Michael. *The Nuclear Freeze Campaign: Rhetoric and Foreign Policy in the Telepolitical Age.* East Lansing: Michigan State University Press, 1994.

Jablonski, Carol J. "Rhetoric, Paradox, and the Movement for Women's Ordination in the Roman Catholic Church," *Quarterly Journal of Speech* 74 (1988): 164–183.

Jamieson, Kathleen Hall. *Dirty Politics.* New York: Oxford University Press, 1992.

Jamieson, Kathleen Hall. *Packaging the Presidency: A History and Criticism of Presidential Campaign Advertising.* New York: Oxford University Press, 1984.

Jamieson, Kathleen Hall. *Eloquence in an Electronic Age.* New York: Oxford University Press, 1988.

Japp, Phyllis M. "Esther or Isaiah? The Abolitionist-Feminist Rhetoric of Angelina Grimke," *Quarterly Journal of Speech* 41 (1985): 335–348.

Jasinski, James. "The Feminization of Liberty, Domesticated Virtue, and the Reconstruction of Power and Authority in Early American Political Discourse," *Quarterly Journal of Speech* 79 (1993): 146–164.

Jensen, Richard J., and Cara J. Abeyta. "The Minority in the Middle: Asian-American Dissent in the 1960s and 1970s," *Western Journal of Speech Communication* 51 (1987): 402–416.

Johannesen, Richard L. "Ronald Reagan's Economic Jeremiad," *Central States Speech Journal* 37 (1986): 79–89.

Jorgensen-Earp, Cheryl R. "The Lady, the Whore, and the Spinster: The Rhetorical Use of Victorian Images of Women," *Western Journal of Speech Communication* 54 (1990): 82–98.

King, Robert L. "Transforming Scandal into Tragedy: A Rhetoric of Political Apology," *Quarterly Journal of Speech* 71 (1985): 289–301.

Lee, Ronald, and James R. Andrews. "Rhetorical-Ideological Transformation in History: The Case of Eugene Debs," *Quarterly Journal of Speech* 77 (February 1991): 20–37.

Lee, Ronald. "The New Populist Campaign for Economic Democracy: A Rhetorical Exploration." *Quarterly Journal of Speech* 72 (1986): 274–289.

Lee, Sang-Chul, and Karlyn Kohrs Campbell. "Korean President Roh Tae-Woo's 1988 Inaugural Address: Campaigning for Investiture," *Quarterly Journal of Speech* 80 (February 1994): 37–52.

Leff, Michael, and Andrew Sachs. "Words the Most Like Things: Iconicity and the Rhetorical Text," *Western Journal of Speech Communication* 54 (1990): 252–273.

Leff, Michael C., and Fred J. Kauffeld, eds. *Text in Context: Critical Dialogues on Significant Episodes in American Political Rhetoric.* Davis, CA: Hermagoras Press, 1989.

Lessi, Thomas M. "Science and the Sacred Cosmos: The Ideological Rhetoric of Carl Sagan," *Quarterly Journal of Speech* 71 (1985): 175–187.

Lewis, William F. "Telling America's Story: Narrative Form and the Reagan Presidency," *Quarterly Journal of Speech* 73 (1987): 280–302.

Logue, Calvin M., and Howard Dorgan, eds. *A New Diversity in Contemporary Southern Rhetoric.* Baton Rouge: Louisiana State University Press, 1987.

Lucas, Stephen E. "Genre Criticism and Historical Context: The Case of George Washington's First Inaugural Address," *Southern Speech Communication Journal* 51 (1986): 354–370.

Manoff, Robert Carl. "Modes of War and Modes of Social Address: The Text of SDI," *Journal of Communication* 39 (1989): 59–84.

Medhurst, Martin J., ed. *Landmark Essays in American Public Address.* Davis, CA: Hermagoras Press, 1993.

Medhurst, Martin J. "Truman's Rhetorical Reticence, 1945–1947: An Interpretative Essay," *Quarterly Journal of Speech* 74 (1988): 52–70.

Medhurst, Martin J., ed. *Eisenhower's War of Words: Rhetoric and Leadership.* East Lansing: Michigan State University Press, 1993.

Medhurst, Martin J. "Postponing the Social Agenda: Reagan's Strategy and Tactics," *Western Journal of Speech Communication* 48 (1984): 262–276.

Mister, Steven M. "Reagan's Challenger Tribute: Combining Generic Constraints and Situational Demands," *Central States Speech Journal* 37 (1986): 158–165.

Mohrmann, G. P. "Place and Space: Calhoun's Fatal Security," *Western Journal of Speech Communication* 51 (1987): 143–158.

Moore, Mark P. "Reagan's Quest for Freedom in the 1987 State of the Union Address," *Western Journal of Speech Communication* 53 (1989): 52–65.

Oliver, Robert T. *Public Speaking in the Reshaping of Great Britain.* Newark, DE: University of Delaware Press, 1987.

Oliver, Robert T. *The Influence of Rhetoric in the Shaping of Great Britain.* Newark, DE: University of Delaware Press, 1986.

Olson, Gregory A. *Mansfield and Vietnam: A Study in Rhetorical Adaptation.* East Lansing: Michigan State University Press, 1995.

Olson, Lester C. *Emblems of American Community in the Revolutionary Era.* Washington, DC: Smithsonian Institution Press, 1991.

Osborn, Michael. "The Abuses of Argument," *Southern Communication Journal* 49 (1983): 1–11.

Peterson, Carla L. *'Doers of the Word': African-American Women Speakers and Writers in the North (1830–1880).* New York: Oxford University Press, 1995.

Philipsen, Gerry. "Mayor Daley's Council Speech: A Cultural Analysis," *Quarterly Journal of Speech* 72 (1986): 247–260.

Ritter, Kurt W. "Drama and Legal Rhetoric: The Perjury Trials of Alger Hiss," *Western Journal of Speech Communication* 49 (1985): 83–102.

Rosteck, Thomas. "Narrative in Martin Luther King's 'I've Been to the Mountaintop,' " *Southern Communication Journal* 58 (1992): 22–32.

Rushing, Janice Hocker. "Ronald Reagan's 'Star Wars' Address: Mythic Containment of Technical Reasoning," *Quarterly Journal of Speech* 72 (1986): 415–433.

Rushing, Janice Hocker. "Evolution of 'The New Frontier' in *Alien* and *Aliens*: Patriarchal Cooptation of the Feminine Archetype," *Quarterly Journal of Speech* 75 (1989): 1–24.

Ryan, Halford Ross, ed. *American Rhetoric from Roosevelt to Reagan.* Prospect Heights: Waveland Press, 1983.

Ryan, Halford R., ed. *The Inaugural Addresses of Twentieth-Century American Presidents.* New York: Praeger, 1993.

Schiappa, Edward. "The Rhetoric of Nukespeak," *Communication Monographs* 56 (1989): 253–272.

Short, C. Brant. *Ronald Reagan and the Public Lands.* College Station: Texas A&M University Press, 1989.

Short, C. Brant. "Comic Book Apologia: The 'Paranoid' Rhetoric of Congressman George Hansen," *Western Journal of Speech Communication* 51 (1987): 189–203.

Slagell, Army. "Anatomy of a Masterpiece: A Close Textual Analysis of Abraham Lincoln's Second Inaugural Address," *Communication Studies* 42 (1991): 155–171.

Smith, Craig Allen. "Mister Reagan's Neighborhood: Rhetoric and National Unity," *Southern Speech Communication Journal* 52 (1987): 219–239.

Smith, Craig R. "Daniel Webster's July 17th Address: A Mediating Influence in the 1850 Compromise," *Quarterly Journal of Speech* 71 (1985): 349–361.

Smith, Craig R. "Ronald Reagan's Attempt to Build a National Majority," *Central States Speech Journal* 30 (1979): 98–102.

Smith, Craig Allen, and Kathy B. Smith. "Presidential Values and Public Priorities: Recurrent Patterns in Addresses to the Nation, 1963–1984," *Presidential Studies Quarterly,* 15 (1985): 743–753.

Soloman, Martha. "Ideology as Rhetorical Constraint: The Anarchist Agitation of 'Red Emma' Goldman," *Quarterly Journal of Speech* 74 (1988): 184–200.

Soloman, Martha. *Emma Goldman.* Boston: Twayne Publishers, 1987.

Turner, Kathleen J. *Lyndon Johnson's Dual War: Vietnam and the Press.* Chicago: University of Chicago Press, 1985.

Windt, Theodore Otto Jr. *Presidents and Protesters: Political Rhetoric in the 1960s.* University, AL: University of Alabama Press, 1990.

Zagacki, Kenneth S. "The Rhetoric of American Decline: Paul Kennedy, Conservatives, and the Solvency Debate," *Western Journal of Communication* 56 (1992): 372–393.

Zarefsky, David. *President Johnson's War on Poverty.* Tuscaloosa: University of Alabama Press, 1986.

Zarefsky, David. *Lincoln, Douglas, and Slavery: In the Crucible of Public Debate.* Chicago: University of Chicago Press, 1990.

# Select Bibliography of Works on the Nature of and Approaches to Rhetorical Criticism

*The following bibliography samples from a large body of work on the theory and practice of rhetorical criticism written over the past half-century.*


Andrews, James R. *A Choice of Worlds: The Practice and Criticism of Public Discourse.* New York: Harper & Row, 1973.

Auer, Jeffery, ed. *Antislavery and Disunion, 1858–1861: Studies in the Rhetoric of Compromise and Conflict.* New York: Harper & Row, 1963.

Baskerville, Barnet. *The People's Voice: The Orator in American Society.* Lexington: University of Kentucky Press, 1979.

Baskerville, Barnet. "Must We All Be 'Rhetorical Critics'?" *Quarterly Journal of Speech* 63 (1977): 107–116.

Benson, Thomas, ed. *Landmark Essays on Rhetorical Criticism.* Davis, CA: Hermagoras Press, 1993.

Bitzer, Lloyd F. "The Rhetorical Situation," *Philosophy and Rhetoric* 1 (1968): 1–14.

Black, Edwin. *Rhetorical Criticism: A Study in Method.* New York: Macmillian, 1965; rpt. Madison, Wisconsin: University of Wisconsin Press, 1978.

Booth, Wayne C. *The Rhetoric of Fiction.* Chicago: University of Chicago Press, 1961.

Bormann, Ernest G. "Fantasy and Rhetorical Vision: The Rhetorical Criticism of Social Reality," *Quarterly Journal of Speech* 58 (1972): 396–407.

Bostdorff, Denise. *The Presidency and the Rhetoric of Foreign Crisis.* Columbia: University of South Carolina Press, 1995.

Braden, Waldo W., ed. *Oratory in the Old South.* Baton Rouge: Louisiana State University Press, 1970.

Brigance, William Norwood, ed. *History and Criticism of American Public Address.* 2 vols. New York: McGraw-Hill, 1943.

Brock, Bernard L., Robert L. Scott, and James W. Chesebro, eds. *Methods of Rhetorical Criticism: A Twentieth Century Perspective.* 3rd ed. Detroit, MI: Wayne State University Press, 1989.

Brockriede, Wayne. "Rhetorical Criticism as Argument," *Quarterly Journal of Speech* 60 (1974): 165–174.

Bryant, Donald C. *Rhetorical Dimensions on Criticism.* Baton Rouge: Louisiana State University Press, 1973.

Burgchardt, Carl R. *Readings in Rhetorical Criticism.* State College, PA: Strata Publishing, 1995.

Campbell, Karlyn Kohrs. "Criticism: Ephemeral and Enduring," *Speech Teacher* 23 (1974): 9–14.

Campbell, Karlyn Kohrs, and Kathleen Hall Jamieson, eds. *Form and Genre: Shaping Rhetorical Action.* Falls Church: Speech Communication Association, 1978.

Carpenter, Ronald H. *History as Rhetoric: Style, Narrative and Persuasion.* Columbia: University of South Carolina Press, 1995.

Condit, Celeste Michelle. "Crafting Virtue: The Rhetorical Construction of Public Morality," *Quarterly Journal of Speech* 73 (1987): 79–97.

Conrad, Charles. "Phases, Pentads, and Dramatistic Critical Process," *Central States Speech Journal* 35 (1984): 94–104.

Corbett, Edward P. J., ed. *Rhetorical Analysis of Literary Works.* New York and London: Oxford University Press, 1969.

Croft, Albert J. "The Functions of Rhetorical Criticism," *Quarterly Journal of Speech* 42 (1956): 283–291.

Farrell, Thomas B. "Narrative in Natural Discourse: On Conversation and Rhetoric." *Journal of Communication* 35 (1985): 109–127.

Farrell, Thomas B. "Rhetorical Resemblance: Paradoxes of Practical Art," *Quarterly Journal of Speech* 72 (1986) 1–19.

Fisher, Walter R. *Human Communication as Narration: Toward a Philosophy of Reason, Value, and Action.* Columbia: University of South Carolina Press, 1987.

Foss, Sonja K. "Rhetorical Criticism as the Asking of Questions," *Communication Education* 38 (1989): 191–196.

Foss, Sonja K., ed. *Rhetorical Criticism: Exploration and Practice.* Prospect Heights, IL: Waveland, 1989.

Goldzwig, Steven, and George N. Dionisopoulos. *"In a Perilous Hour:" The Public Address of John F. Kennedy.* New York: Preager, 1995.

Gregg, Richard B. "A Phenomenologically Oriented Approach to Rhetorical Criticism," *Communication Studies* 17 (1966): 83–90.

Gregg, Richard B. "The Criticism of Symbolic Inducement: A Critical-Theoretical Connection." In *Speech Communication in the 20th Century,* Thomas W. Benson, ed. Carbondale: Southern Illinois University Press, 1985: 41–62.

Griffin, Leland M. "The Rhetoric of Historical Movements," *Quarterly Journal of Speech* 38 (1952): 184–188.

Hariman, Robert. *Political Style: The Artistry of Power.* Chicago: University of Chicago Press, 1995.

Hart, Roderick P. *Verbal Style and the Presidency: A Computer-Based Analysis.* Orlando FL: Academic Press, 1984.

Hart, Roderick P. *Modern Rhetorical Criticism.* Glenview, IL: Scott Foresman/Little, Brown, 1990.

Iltis, Robert S., and Stephen H. Browne. "Tradition and Resurgence in Public Address Studies." In *Speech Communication: Essays to Commemorate the 75th Anniversary of The Speech Communication Association,* Gerald M. Phillips and Julia T. Woods, eds. Carbondale: Southern Illinois University Press, 1990: 81–93.

Kauffman, James L. *Selling Outer Space: Kennedy, the Media, and Funding for Project Apollo, 1961–1963.* Tuscaloosa: University of Alabama Press, 1995.

Klumpp, James E., and Thomas A. Hollihan. "Rhetorical Criticism as Moral Action," *Quarterly Journal of Speech* 75 (1989): 84–97.

Lee, Ronald. "Moralizing and Ideologizing: An Analysis of Political Illocutions," *Western Journal of Speech Communication* 52 (1988): 291–307.

Leff, Michael C. "Things Made by Words: Reflections on Textual Criticism," *Quarterly Journal of Speech* 78 (1992): 223–231.

Leff, Michael C., ed. "Rhetorical Criticism: The State of the Art," *Western Speech* 44 (1980). This symposium contains the following essays: G. P. Mohrmann, "Elegy in a Critical Graveyard"; Suzanne Volmar Riches, and Malcolm O. Sillars, "The Status of Movement Criticism"; Walter R. Fisher, "Genre: Concepts and Applications in Rhetorical Criticism"; Thomas B. Farrel, "Critical Models in the Analysis of Discourse"; Bruce E. Gronbeck, "Dramaturgical Theory and Criticism: The State of the Art (or Science?)"; Edwin Black, "A Note on Theory and Practice in Rhetorical Criticism"; Michael C. Leff, "Interpretation and the Art of the Rhetorical Critic."

Lucas, Stephen E. *Portents of Rebellion: Rhetoric and Revolution in Philadelphia, 1765–1776.* Philadelphia: Temple University Press, 1976.

McGee, Michael Calvin. "In Search of the 'The People': A Rhetorical Alternative," *Quarterly Journal of Speech* 61 (1975): 141–154.

Medhurst, Martin, ed. *Landmark Essays in American Public Address.* Davis, CA: Hermagoras Press, (1993).

Moore, Mark P. "The Rhetoric of Ideology: Confronting a Critical Dilemma," *Southern Speech Communication Journal* 54 (1988): 74–92.

Murphy, Richard. "The Speech as Literary Genre," *Quarterly Journal of Speech* 44 (1958): 117–127.

Nichols, Marie Hochmuth. *Rhetoric and Criticism.* Baton Rouge: Louisiana State University Press, 1963.

Nichols, Marie Hochmuth. *History and Criticism of American Public Address.* Vol. 3. London: Longmans, Green, 1955.

Nothstine, William, Carole Blair, and Gary Copeland, eds. *Critical Questions: Invention Creativity, and the Criticism of Discourse and Media.* New York: St. Martin's Press, 1994.

Osborn, Michael, and Douglas Ehninger. "The Metaphor in Public Address," *Speech Monographs* 29 (1962): 223–234.

Osborn, Michael. "Archetypal Metaphor in Rhetoric: The Light-Dark Family," *Quarterly Journal of Speech* 53 (1967): 115–126.

Ritter, Kurt, and James R. Andrews. *The American Ideology.* Falls Church VA: Speech Communication Association, 1978.

Rosenfeld, Lawrence W. "The Anatomy of Critical Discourse," *Speech Monographs* 35 (1968): 50–69.

Sillars, Malcolm O. *Messages, Meanings, and Culture: Approaches to Communication Criticism.* New York: Harper/Collins, 1991.

Simons, Herbert W., ed. *The Rhetorical Turn: Invention and Persuasion in the Conduct of Inquiry.* Chicago: University of Chicago Press, 1990.

Simons, Herbert W., and Aram A. Aghazarian, eds. *Form, Genre, and the Study of Political Discourse.* Columbia: University of South Carolina Press, 1986, numerous essays, pp. 203–277.

Thonssen, Lester A., Craig Baird, and Waldo W. Braden. *Speech Criticism.* 2nd ed. Malabar, FL: Krieger, 1981.

Wander, Philip, and Steve Jenkins. "Rhetoric, Society, and the Critical Response," *Quarterly Journal of Speech* 58 (1972): 441–450.

Wander, Philip. "The Rhetoric of American Foreign Policy," *Quarterly Journal of Speech* 70 (1984): 339–361.

Wander, Philip. "The Third Persona: An Ideological Turn in Rhetorical Theory," *Communication Studies* 35 (1984): 197–216.

White, Eugene, ed. *Rhetoric in Transition: Studies in the Nature and Uses of Rhetoric.* University Park: Pennsylvania University Press, 1980.

White, Eugene E. *The Context of Human Discourse: A Configurational Criticism of Rhetoric.* Columbia, SC: South Carolina University Press, 1992.

Wrage, Ernest J. "Public Address: A Study in Social and Intellectual History," *Quarterly Journal of Speech* 33 (1947): 451–457.

# Index

# Acknowledgments

Permission to reprint the following materials is hereby gratefully acknowledged:

**Chapter 7:** Robert P. Newman, "Under the Veneer: Nixon's Vietnam Speech of November 3, 1969," *Quarterly Journal of Speech* 56: 168–178. Reprinted by permission of the Speech Communication Association.
Hermann G. Stelzner, " The Quest Story and Nixon's November 3, 1969 Address," *Quarterly Journal of Speech* 57: 163–172. Reprinted by permission of the Speech Communication Association.
Karlyn Kohrs Campbell, "An Exercise in the Rhetoric of Mythical America," *Critiques of Contemporary Rhetoric* (Belmont, CA: Wadsworth, 1972), pp. 50–57. Reprinted by permission of the publisher.
Forbes Hill, "Conventional Wisdom-Traditional Form: The President's Message of November 3, 1969," *Quarterly Journal of Speech* 68: 373–386. Reprinted with permission of the Speech Communication Association.
Karlyn Kohrs Campbell, "The Forum: 'Conventional Wisdom-Traditional Form': A Rejoinder" and Forbes I. Hill, "Reply to Professor Campbell," *Quarterly Journal of Speech* 58:451–460. Reprinted by permission of the Speech Communication Association.

**Chapter 8:** Paula Wilson, "The Rhythm of Rhetoric: Jesse Jackson at the 1988 Democratic National Convention," *Southern Communication Journal* 61: 253–264. Reprinted by permission of the Southern States Communication Association.
Patricia A. Sullivan, "Signification and African-American Rhetoric: A Case Study of Jesse Jackson's 'Common Ground and Common Sense' Speech," *Communication Quarterly* 43: 167–181. Reprinted by permission of the Eastern Communication Association.

**Chapter 9:** Elizabeth Cady Stanton, "Solitude of Self," from Karlyn Kohrs Campbell, *Man Cannot Speak for Her,* v. 2. Copyright 1989 by Karlyn Kohrs Campbell. Reproduced with permission of Greenwood Publishing Group, Inc., Westport, CT.
Karlyn Kohrs Campbell, "Stanton's 'Solitude of Self': A Rationale for Feminism," *Quarterly Journal of Speech* 67: 304–312. Reprinted by permission of the Speech Communication Association.

**Chapter 10:** Michael C. Leff and Gerald P. Mohrmann, "Lincoln at Cooper Union: A Rhetorical Analysis of the Text," *Quarterly Journal of Speech* 60: 346–358. Reprinted by permission of the Speech Communication Association.

**Chapter 11:** Martin J. Medhurst, "Eisenhower's 'Atoms for Peace' Speech: A Case Study in the Strategic Use of Language," *Communication Monographs* 54: 204–220. Reprinted by permission of the Speech Communication Association.

**Chapter 12:** Mario Cuomo, "Religious Belief and Public Morality: A Catholic Governor's Perspective." Reprinted by permission of Mario Cuomo.
Calvin L. Troup, "Cuomo at Notre Dame: Rhetoric Without Religion," *Communication Quarterly* 43: 167–181. Reprinted by permission of the Eastern Communication Association.

**Chapter 13:** Stephen H. Browne, "The Pastoral Voice in John Dickinson's First Letter from a Farmer in Pennsylvania," *Quarterly Journal of Speech* 76: 46–57. Reprinted by permission of the Speech Communication Association.